TANGLED MEMORIES

The Vietnam War, the AIDS Epidemic, and the Politics of Remembering

MARITA STURKEN

UNIVERSITY OF CALIFORNIA PRESS

BERKELEY   LOS ANGELES   LONDON

An earlier version of Chapter 2 was published as "The Wall, the Screen, and the Image: The Vietnam Veterans Memorial," *Representations* 35 (Summer 1991): 118–42; and an earlier version of Chapter 6 was published as "Conversations with the Dead: Bearing Witness in the AIDS Memorial Quilt," *Socialist Review* (October/November 1992): 65–93.

Figure 1 is reproduced by permission from the LMH Company. ©1967 LMH Co., © renewed 1992 LMH Co., c/o James Lorin Silverberg Esquire, Washington, D.C., (202) 332-7978.

University of California Press
Berkeley and Los Angeles, California

University of California Press, Ltd.
London, England

Library of Congress Cataloging-in-Publication Data
Sturken, Marita, 1957–
    Tangled memories : the Vietnam War, the AIDS epidemic, and the politics of remembering / Marita Sturken.
        p.   cm.
    Includes bibliographic references and index
        ISBN 0–520–08653–8 (alk. paper).—ISBN 0–520–20620–7 (pbk. : alk. paper)
        1. Memory—Political aspects—United States.   2. Political culture—United States—History—20th century.   3. Vietnamese Conflict, 1961–1975—Influence.   4. AIDS (Disease)—United States.   5. Persian Gulf War, 1991—Influence.   6. Popular culture—United States—History—20th century.   7. Television and history—United States.   8. Motion pictures and history. I. Title.
E169.12.S849   1997
    306.2′0973—dc 20   96–12609

Printed in the United States of America

9   8   7   6   5   4   3   2   1

The paper used in this publication meets the minimum requirements of American National Standards for Information Sciences—Permanence of Paper for Printed Library Materials, ANSI Z39.48-1984.

In memory of
Karyn Gladstone
1944–1995

Contents

Acknowledgments

In writing this book I was supported and encouraged by many people. They have all, in their own ways, contributed to my understanding of culture, memory, and loss.

I am deeply grateful to my parents, who have provided unfailing enthusiasm. My father, Robert Sturken, has been a consistent supporter without whom the process would have been much more arduous. It is a tribute to him as well. My mother, Marie Sturken, has always offered an example of creativity and productivity through her own work. My sister Barbara has provided steady encouragement and seasoned advice. I am also grateful to Carl Sturken, Cheryl-Anne Sturken, and Bill Peterson.

Those who have read and provided helpful criticisms on this book in manuscript form have been essential to its thinking and rethinking. I am particularly indebted to Lauren Berlant, whose insights and careful reading compelled and challenged me in new ways. Colleagues at the University of California, Santa Cruz, the University of California, San Diego, and the University of Southern California have been important influences at various stages. I am grateful to Hayden White for his fine-tuned advice, to Donna Haraway for her intellectual integrity, and to Vivian Sobchack for her skillful readings; and, for their support, to many colleagues, including Ron Balderrama, Geoffrey Batchen, Megan Boler, Elena Creef, Satish Deshpande, Walter Fisher, Mary John, Vicki Kirby, Nathalie Magnan, Vicente Raphael, and Lisa Yoneyama. I owe thanks to Lisa Cartwright for her helpful advice on chapter 7, and to David Sloane, who read many chapters under deadline duress and who has helped me to understand better the process of history. Vicente Diaz was the first critical reader of this book, and I am indebted to many of his insights.

To those friends who have been reliable and relied upon throughout this process, I offer my deepest thanks, in particular to Ann Chisholm, Marcy Darnovsky, Giovanna Di Chiro, Hartley Ferguson, Valerie Hartouni, Joanna Hefferen, Maria LaPlace, Joanne Ross, Lynn Spigel, Douglas Thomas, and Patty Wild. For the wide net of support from others, I am grateful: Bill Bridgers, Jim Campbell, John Epstein, Lucinda Furlong, John Giancola, JoAnn Hanley, Louis Hock, Jytte Jensen, Elizabeth and Bernard Laulhé, Nancy Legge, Chip Lord, Al Macchioni, Barbara Osborn, Roger and Jennifer Pinkham, Robert Riley, Arthur Silverman, Elizabeth Sisco, Robin Smith, Ella Taylor, Arthur Tsuchiya, and Debra Weier.

I would like to thank Duery Felton Jr. of the Vietnam Veterans Memorial archive and Cleve Jones, Anthony Turney, the late David Lemos, and Michelle Cinq Mars of the NAMES Project for their time and research assistance. The American Association of University Women provided crucial, well-timed, and deeply rewarding support for this work at an early stage of its development. At the University of California Press, this book has been shepherded through its development with skill and unfailing support. I am particularly grateful to Naomi Schneider for her enthusiasm, her faith in the final product, and her expert advice, and to William Murphy for keeping it on track. Larry Borowsky streamlined my often long-winded prose with impressive subtlety, and Erika Büky was a skilled reader and editor.

Finally, I dedicate this book to the memory of Karyn Gladstone, who was my friend, therapist, and mentor. Karyn taught me crucial lessons in understanding the creative process and ways of being in and observing the world. She was an important teacher and colleague who read every chapter and considered every line and who challenged me to make this a meaningful work. Her untimely death as I was finishing this book was a profound loss for the many people whose lives she enriched. It is my hope that it offers a fitting tribute to the integrity and uniqueness with which she lived her life.

Introduction

Memory forms the fabric of human life, affecting everything from the ability to perform simple, everyday tasks to the recognition of the self. Memory establishes life's continuity; it gives meaning to the present, as each moment is constituted by the past. As the means by which we remember who we are, memory provides the very core of identity.

What does it mean for a *culture* to remember? The collective remembering of a specific culture can often appear similar to the memory of an individual—it provides cultural identity and gives a sense of the importance of the past. Yet the process of cultural memory is bound up in complex political stakes and meanings. It both defines a culture and is the means by which its divisions and conflicting agendas are revealed. To define a memory as cultural is, in effect, to enter into a debate about what that memory means. This process does not efface the individual but rather involves the interaction of individuals in the creation of cultural meaning. Cultural memory is a field of cultural negotiation through which different stories vie for a place in history.

This book is about how cultural memory operates in the United States in the 1980s and 1990s. It examines cultural memory's role in producing concepts of the "nation" and of an "American people" and explores how individuals interact with cultural products.[1] Cultural memory is produced in the United States in various forms, including memorials, public art, popular culture, literature, commodities, and activism. It is generated in the context of a debate over who defines

1

cultural memory, what counts as cultural memory, and, indeed, what cultural memory means.

As a study in cultural memory, this book focuses on two primary events: the American participation in the Vietnam War from 1959 to 1975 and the AIDS epidemic, which emerged in the United States in the early 1980s. These are both events of trauma in which many lives have been lost and attempts to find meaning have been fraught with grief. They have resulted in tremendous social upheaval and have disrupted definitions of family, gender, morality, and the nation. As a result, they have produced very rich kinds of memories and memory debates.

American political culture is often portrayed as one of amnesia, and the media seem complicit in the public's apparent ease in forgetting important political facts and events. However, this definition of American culture is highly superficial, relying on evidence of memory in traditional forms and narratives. It is the central premise of this book that American culture is not amnesiac but rather replete with memory, that cultural memory is a central aspect of how American culture functions and how the nation is defined. The "culture of amnesia" actually involves the generation of memory in new forms, a process often misinterpreted as forgetting. Indeed, memory and forgetting are co-constitutive processes; each is essential to the other's existence.

A desire for memory has often made it appear fragile and threatened when it is actually fluid and changing. The instability of memory is not specific to postmodern times, and it does not offer evidence of the past's insignificance; however, it is what makes memory both political and subject to debate. The changeability of memory raises important concerns about how the past can be verified, understood, and given meaning. Yet it is important not to allow discussions of memory to bog down in questions of reliability. Memory is crucial to the understanding of a culture precisely because it indicates collective desires, needs, and self-definitions. We need to ask not whether a memory is true but rather what its telling reveals about how the past affects the present.

I define cultural memory specifically through its distinction from both personal memory and history. It is a field of contested meanings in which Americans interact with cultural elements to produce concepts of the nation, particularly in events of trauma, where both the structures and the fractures of a culture are exposed. Examining cultural memory thus provides insight into how American culture functions, how oppositional politics engages with nationalism, and how cultural arenas such as art, popular culture, activism, and consumer culture intersect.

Cultural Memory

I use the term "cultural memory" to define memory that is shared outside the avenues of formal historical discourse yet is entangled with cultural products and imbued with cultural meaning. Hence, the AIDS Memorial Quilt—a collection of quilt panels, each bearing the name of someone who has died of AIDS—is both a device through which personal memories are shared and an object seen by its makers to have cultural meaning. Employing the term "cultural memory" thus allows me to examine how, for instance, popular culture has produced memories of the Vietnam War and how these film and television images have moved between cultural memory and history. The self-consciousness with which notions of culture are attached to these objects of memory leads me to use the term "cultural" rather than "collective."

I therefore want to distinguish between cultural memory, personal memory, and official historical discourse. I am not concerned in this book with memories insofar as they remain individual. Yet when personal memories of public events are shared, their meaning changes. When individual possessions are left at the Vietnam Veterans Memorial in Washington, D.C., they become a part of cultural memory. When they are then placed in a government archive, they acquire both aesthetic and historical meaning. However, the very nature of these objects, in particular their often cryptic quality, prevents them from fitting neatly into traditional narratives of historical discourse.

Definitions of cultural memory beg the question of what constitutes personal memory. Does some kind of purely individual memory exist? All contemporary theories of personal memory are influenced by the work of Sigmund Freud, specifically his contention that the memories of all experiences are stored in the unconscious.[2] Though one cannot automatically access all of one's memories, in Freud's view they remain present within. Indeed, Freud believed that many psychosomatic illnesses and physical symptoms result from the reassertion of repressed childhood memories. This hypothesis depends on the concept that memories accumulate and are often inarticulable. Many of Freud's assertions about repression of memories and their inevitable if unintelligible accumulation have been the subject of serious disagreement. In recent years the concept of repression has been the focus of a particularly volatile debate over recovered memories of incest and abuse. However, Freud's work is an important source for thinking about memory's changeability—in effect, its unreliability. Freud examined the rescripting of memories in "secondary revision," the relationship of memory and fantasy, and the role of screen memories in blocking out other memories. Indeed, he provided twentieth-century debates about memory with compelling images of both the fragility and the endurance of memory.

Many theorists consider the idea of shared or collective memory antithetical to that of personal memory. Maurice Halbwachs, one of the most influential philosophers of collective memory, believed, in opposition to Freud, that all personal memory was socially produced. Halbwachs wrote that individuals often recall and rescript their memories through the recollections of others.[3] Unlike Freud, who envisioned a vast reservoir of memory in the unconscious, Halbwachs saw individual memory as fragmentary and incomplete, something guided by the script that collective memory provides. His work has been highly influential in destabilizing the definitions of individual and collective remembrance.

Cultural memory can be distinct from history yet, I would argue, is essential in its construction. It is unwise to generalize about the practice of history-making; the profession of history encompasses a broad array of methodologies, many of which are critical of traditional historiography. History can be thought of as a narrative that has in some way been sanctioned or valorized by institutional frameworks or publishing enterprises. One cannot say that history comprises a single narrative; many histories are constantly under debate and in conflict with each other. However, each of the events discussed in this book can be said to have a history. The history of the Vietnam War, for instance, consists of conflicting narratives, but there are particular elements within those stories that remain uncontested, such as the war's divisive effect on the United States.

Moreover, history-making adheres to specific codes about the nature of shared reality and the communicability of experience. History has often been seen as standing in opposition to memory. Indeed, writes Pierre Nora, "History is perpetually suspicious of memory, and its true mission is to suppress and destroy it."[4] However, Nora's concept of memory is highly nostalgic. I would posit cultural memory and history as *entangled* rather than oppositional. Indeed, there is so much traffic across the borders of cultural memory and history that in many cases it may be futile to maintain a distinction between them. Yet there are times when those distinctions are important in understanding political intent, when memories are asserted specifically outside of or in response to historical narratives.

Traditional history has a paradoxical relationship to the body of the individual who has lived through a given event—the Vietnam veteran, the Gulf War veteran, or the person with AIDS. The survivors of recent political events often disrupt the closure of a particular history; indeed, history operates more efficiently when its agents are dead. Yet the survivors of historical events are often figures of cultural authority and values.

This book examines the process of history-making as it relates to cultural memory—insofar as memory objects and narratives move from the realm of cultural memory to that of history and back. In analyzing the process of history-making, I will draw on the work of many historians for whom the materials of history reside in archives, textual remains, and oral histories. However, I am primarily concerned with questions of the popularization of history, specifically how histories are told through popular culture, the media, public images, and public memorials—how cultural memory engages with historical narrative in this public sphere.

Personal memory, cultural memory, and history do not exist within neatly defined boundaries. Rather, memories and memory objects can move from one realm to another, shifting meaning and context. Thus, personal memories can sometimes be subsumed into history, and elements of cultural memory can exist in concert with historical narratives. For instance, survivors of traumatic historical events often relate that as time goes on, they have difficulty distinguishing their personal memories from those of popular culture. For many World War II veterans, Hollywood World War II movies have subsumed their individual memories into a general script. Because of these kinds of boundary crossings in what is remembered, true distinctions between personal memory, cultural memory, and history cannot be made.

I am indebted in many of the formulations of this book to the works of Michel Foucault, whose philosophical writings on knowledge, power, and the modern state reveal both the constructive process of histories and the voices from archives and unlegitimated sources that tangle with history's stories. Foucault termed these "subjugated knowledges," knowledges "that have been disqualified as inadequate to their task or insufficiently elaborated: naive knowledges, located low down on the hierarchy, beneath the required level of cognition or scientificity."[5] Foucault was interested in the "low-ranking knowledge" of the psychiatric patient or the nurse, for instance, rather than that of the medical institution. I take him to be speaking ironically in using the term "naive"; indeed, it seems that he felt these kinds of unrecognized knowledges were crucial to understanding the past. He also spoke of "popular memory" as a form of collective knowledge for those who don't have access to publishing houses or movie studios. Memory was a political force for Foucault: "Since memory is actually a very important factor in struggle (really, in fact, struggles develop in a kind of conscious moving forward of history), if one controls people's memory, one controls their dynamism."[6]

It is with respect to this issue, the political nature of memory, that I want to both build on Foucault's work and distinguish this project from his. Foucault was highly influential in provoking historians to rethink the process of history-making. His formulation of subjugated knowledges made explicit the political nature of what gets to count as knowledge of the past. In this book I attempt to apply these understandings to recent events in American history and to examine the political nature of memory as it has been produced and shared in these contexts. Making an AIDS Quilt panel for someone who has died of AIDS may be a personal act of remembrance; it is also a political act.

However, I would like to distinguish the concept of cultural memory from the romanticization of popular memory implicit in Foucault's definition. Indeed, most of his work interweaves complex questions of resistance and conformity. Cultural memory may often constitute opposition, but it is not automatically the scene of cultural resistance. As I have noted, cultural memory is often entangled with history, scripted through the layered meanings in mass culture, and itself highly contested and conflictual. Although cultural memory unquestionably is produced at the Vietnam Veterans Memorial in Washington, D.C., its forms are highly varied, ranging from reclamation of concepts of sacrifice and honor to profound opposition to the codes of war. There is nothing politically prescribed in cultural memory.

Memory and Forgetting

This book is based on the premise that memory is a narrative rather than a replica of an experience that can be retrieved and relived. It is thus an inquiry into how cultural memories are constructed as they are recollected and memory as a form of interpretation. The degree to which memories are "faithful" to original experiences is difficult to ascertain. What we remember is highly selective, and how we retrieve it says as much about desire and denial as it does about remembrance.

All memories are "created" in tandem with forgetting; to remember everything would amount to being overwhelmed by memory.[7] Forgetting is a necessary component in the construction of memory. Yet the forgetting of the past in a culture is often highly organized and strategic. Milan Kundera has said: "Forgetting is a form of death ever present within life. . . . But forgetting is also the great problem of politics. When a big power wants to deprive a small country of its national consciousness it uses the method of *organized forgetting*. . . . A nation which loses awareness of its past gradually loses its self."[8] Though Kundera speaks of the "organized forgetting" propagated, for instance, by an occupying state, cultures can also participate in a "strategic" forgetting of painful events that may be too dangerous to keep in active memory. At the same time, all cultural memory and all history are forged in a context in which details, voices, and impressions of the past are forgotten. The writing of a historical narrative necessarily involves the elimination of certain elements. Hence, the narrative of the Vietnam War as told in the United States foregrounds the painful experience of the American Vietnam veteran in such a way that the Vietnamese people, both civilians and veterans, are forgotten. This effacement is in part the result of the narrative process—the political reinscription into American history of the disruptive story of a war lost. A desire for coherence and continuity produces forgetting. Hayden White has written that the "value attached to narrativity in the representation of real events arises out of a desire to have real events display the coherence, integrity, fullness, and closure of an image of life that is and can only be imaginary. The notion that sequences of real events possess the formal attributes of the stories we tell about imaginary events could only have its origin in wishes, daydreams, reveries."[9] The desire for narrative closure thus forces upon historical events the limits of narrative form and enables forgetting.

Freud's work has been particularly significant in problematizing the concept of forgetting. He was primarily interested not in why memories were retained but in what they were hiding. He was struck, for instance, by the phenomenon of infantile amnesia—that we remember nothing from our infancy—and by the fact that childhood memories are so often of exceptionally ordinary and "indifferent" material. The idea that these memories may actually have displaced more charged and emotional memories led him to the concept of a "screen memory"—that is, one that substitutes for other memories that are too painful or disturbing to retrieve.[10] In Freud's formulation, forgetting is an *active* process of repression, one that demands vigilance and is designed to protect the subject from anxiety, fear, jealousy, and other difficult emotions. The concept of a screen memory is particularly useful in thinking about how a culture remembers. Cultural memory is produced through representation—in contemporary culture, often through photographic images, cinema, and television. These mnemonic aids are also screens, actively blocking out other memories that are more difficult to represent.

The question of memory's accuracy hovers around the issue of forgetting. Does it matter whether we remember "correctly"? Certainly it does. Yet memory is notoriously unverifiable. Even a photographic image is subject to interpretation about what it actually proves. The original experiences of memory are irretrievable; we can only "know" them through memory remains—images, objects, texts, stories. Saying that memory is changeable does not imply that it is only constructed through the agendas of the present. Rather, it shifts the discussion of memory, in particular cultural memory, away from questions of truth and toward questions of political intent. I do not know how many of the stories in this book about the Vietnam War and AIDS are actually true. I am concerned rather with the impact they have once they are told. What memories tell us, more than anything, is the stakes held by individuals and institutions in attributing meaning to the past.[11]

Technologies of Memory

Cultural memory is produced through objects, images, and representations. These are technologies of memory, not vessels of memory in which memory passively resides so much as objects through which memories are shared, produced, and given meaning.

Memory is articulated through processes of representation. Andreas Huyssen writes:

Re-presentation always comes after, even though some media will try to provide us with the delusion of pure presence. Rather than leading us to some authentic origin or giving us verifiable access to the real, memory, even and especially in its belatedness, is itself based on representation. The past is not simply there in memory, but it must be articulated to become memory. The fissure that opens up between experiencing an event and remembering it in representation is unavoidable. Rather than lamenting or ignoring it, this split should be understood as a powerful stimulant for cultural and artistic creativity.[12]

It is the tension between the representation of memory and the experience of an event, Huyssen argues, that inspires artistic engagement with a notion of the past.

The cultural memory of the events I discuss in this book—the Vietnam War, the AIDS epidemic, the Kennedy assassination, the

Challenger explosion, the police beating of Rodney King, the Persian
Gulf War—has been produced through a range of cultural products—public art, memorials, docudramas, television images, photographs, advertisements, yellow ribbons, red ribbons, alternative media, activist art, even bodies themselves. These are *technologies* of
memory in that they embody and generate memory and are thus
implicated in the power dynamics of memory's production. Foucault
wrote about "technologies of the self, which permit individuals to
effect by their own means or with the help of others a certain number
of operations on their own bodies and souls, thoughts, conduct, and
way of being, so as to transform themselves in order to attain a certain
state of happiness, purity, wisdom, perfection, or immortality."[13] In
Foucault's formulation, technologies are social practices that are inevitably implicated in power dynamics. They are also practices that people enact upon themselves. In this sense, the embodiment of memory
(and its perceived location in objects that act as substitutes for the
body) is an active process with which subjects engage in relation to
social institutions and practices.

The memorial is perhaps the most traditional kind of memory object or technology. Both the Vietnam War and the AIDS epidemic
have generated memorials, albeit unusual ones. The design of the
Vietnam Veterans Memorial has been the subject of intense public
debate and participation; the AIDS Memorial Quilt is an unusual
refiguring of the traditional family quilt. These two innovative memorials have emerged at a period of time when modernism had pronounced the form dead. They share a memory culture with memorials of the Holocaust and with several innovative museums—including
the United States Holocaust Memorial Museum, which opened in
1993—that attempt to present artifacts of the past in the context of
memory's complexities.[14]

Through the sharing of memory at the Vietnam Veterans Memorial and within the AIDS Quilt, individuals participate in giving
meaning to the past. Although the quilt travels, it can be said to
embody within it a location, or site, of memory; indeed, it is often
perceived as the place where survivors can find and speak to the
AIDS dead. At the same time, the Vietnam Veterans Memorial has
come to symbolize the location of American memory of the war in
the nation's capital. Both attest to the fact that memory is often per-

ceived to be located in specific places or objects. As Pierre Nora writes, "Memory attaches itself to sites, whereas history attaches itself to events."[15]

Although the memorial and the quilt provide evidence of the continued importance of place in cultural memory, it can also be said that the camera image constitutes a significant technology of memory in contemporary American culture. Camera images, whether photographs, films, or television footage, whether documentary, docudrama, or fiction, are central to the interpretation of the past. Photographs are often perceived to embody memory, and cinematic representations of the past have the capacity to entangle with personal and cultural memory. Just as memory is often thought of as an image, it is also produced by and through images.

Roland Barthes once wrote that the photograph had, in fact, replaced the monument: "Earlier societies managed so that memory, the substitute for life, was eternal and that at least the thing which spoke Death should itself be immortal: this was the Monument. But by making the (mortal) Photograph into the general and somehow natural witness of 'what has been,' modern society has renounced the Monument."[16] Barthes's statement reveals a nostalgia for the so-called tenacity of earlier forms of memory; he wrote it before the resurgence of memorial culture in the 1980s. Memorials such as the Vietnam Veterans Memorial and the AIDS Quilt demonstrate that the monument/memorial has not been replaced by so much as it has demanded the presence of the image. People often leave photographs at the memorial and incorporate them into the quilt panels. The image, it would seen, remains the most compelling of memory objects.

It is evidence of the complexity of American culture in the late twentieth century that memory is produced not only through memorials and images but also through commodities. Marxist theorists such as Theodor Adorno alleged that the "hollowed out" objects of commodity culture could be imbued with any meaning.[17] He and others defined the emergence of commodity culture as a kind of cultural forgetting. However, from the perspective of the 1990s, the dismissal of commodities as sources of cultural meaning no longer seems a viable option. We live in a society in which commercialization and marketing tactics are so pervasive, in which the boundaries of art, commodity, and remembrance are so easily traversed, and in which merchandise is so often grassroots-produced that it no longer makes sense, if it ever did, to dismiss commodities as empty artifacts. These trends are particularly evident in the context of the AIDS epidemic, in which nonprofit service organizations raise money to support people with AIDS by marketing red ribbons, T-shirts, books, buttons, posters, coffee mugs, and other objects. These commodities inevitably tend to reduce AIDS to a slogan or a package, but they are nonetheless part of a broader context of AIDS education and its politics of representation.

Finally, I take the term "technology of memory" to mean not only memorials, objects, and images but the body itself. Throughout history, the body has been perceived as a receptacle of memory, from the memory of bodily movement, such as walking, to the memory of past events in physical scars, to the memory of one's genetic history in every cell. In the final chapter of this book, I discuss how biomedical discourse defines the immune system as a system of memory, remembering, for instance, the viruses it has previously encountered.

The presence of bodies is essential to the production of cultural memory. Survivors, be they Vietnam veterans, people with AIDS, or others who have lived through traumatic public events, testify through the very presence of their bodies to the materiality of memory. The body of a disabled veteran standing at the memorial speaks volumes about the war's cost. The empty clothing sewn into the AIDS Quilt speaks loudly of the absence of the bodies of the AIDS dead. Survivors stand at the juncture of cultural memory and history, their bodies offering evidence of the multiplicity of memory stories. However, the discourse of survivors is not strictly one of resistance. Although the body of a wounded veteran at the memorial may testify to the war's cost, his presence may also be intended to reinforce the precise codes of honor and sacrifice in war that resulted in his injury.

Cultural Memory and the Nation

The debates over what counts as cultural memory are also debates about who gets to participate in creating national meaning. When people participate in the production of cultural memory at sites such as the Vietnam Veterans Memorial, they do so both in opposition to and in concert with a concept of the nation. Cultural memory can thus be seen to work in tension with what Lauren Berlant has termed the "national symbolic." She writes that the national symbolic "transforms individuals into subjects of a collectively held history. Its traditional icons, its metaphors, its heroes, its rituals, and its narratives provide an alphabet for a collective consciousness or national subjectivity. . . . This pseudo-generic condition not only affects profoundly the citizen's subjective experience of her/his political rights, but also of civil life, private life, the life of the body itself."[18] The national symbolic is the capacity of a sense of nationalism to affect one's subjectivity pervasively.

Cultural memory is a means through which definitions of the nation and "Americanness" are simultaneously established, questioned, and refigured. For instance, when the AIDS Quilt is displayed on the Mall in Washington, D.C., it both resists and demands inclusion in the nation. Laid out in the most symbolic national place of the United States, the quilt form evokes a sense of Americana, yet it also represents those who have been symbolically excluded from America—drug users, blacks, Latinos, gay men. The Washington Mall is the site of a particularly circumscribed narrative of nationalism in its white monuments, yet it is also the primary location of national protest. Thus, the Vietnam Veterans Memorial gains a particular meaning from its location on the Mall; it is a place where artifacts of both patriotism and protest are left.[19]

Cultural memory reveals the demand for a less monolithic, more inclusive image of America. For this reason, it has often intersected with contemporary battles over identity politics and political correctness. Questions of who is sanctioned to speak of particular memories are often raised, and issues of difference and exclusion from the "imagined community" of the nation come to the fore.

Concepts of America vary a great deal and are used with different intents by many different people. Yet I think it important to take note of those moments when people perceive themselves to be participants in the nation. One of the ways in which this happens is through the media. When Americans watch events of "national" importance—the Persian Gulf War, the Anita Hill/Clarence Thomas hearings, the explosion of the Challenger—on television, they perceive themselves to be part of a national audience regardless of their individual political views or cultural background. Citizenship can thus be enacted through live television.

In the same way, participation in sites of cultural memory also involves the perception of the nation as an audience. When the makers of the AIDS Quilt go to Washington, D.C., they see themselves as communicating to the nation. When people leave personal artifacts at the Vietnam Veterans Memorial, they often see themselves as speaking to the dead before the nation. These forms of participation are contingent on the idea that the nation is listening.

The Vietnam War
and the AIDS Epidemic

The Vietnam War and the AIDS epidemic are the two events in the late twentieth century through which the concept of the nation has most powerfully been called into question. Although this book touches on several other incidents of national importance, such as the Kennedy assassination, the Challenger explosion, the Rodney King beating, and the Persian Gulf War, it focuses on the Vietnam War and AIDS precisely because these are the two distinguishing markers of what America means at this particular moment in history. Both have seriously disrupted previously held popular beliefs about the United States, and both have irrevocably altered the country's image in a global context. Although AIDS may be cured and its meaning will change, such developments likely would not affect the AIDS narrative as it has been scripted so far—the virus that both exposed divisions and created new communities in American society. John Erni writes: "The power of the AIDS narrative resides in its relative independence of the material events of AIDS. A drug or vaccine which kills the virus can hardly kill the stories that are told about and around it. Once, a friend remarked about a different crisis with a strangely familiar parallel: 'It is unthinkable of a world without AIDS, just as it is unthinkable of an America without a Vietnam.' "[20] Both the Vietnam War and the AIDS epidemic have profoundly affected the experience of nationality. America is inconceivable without them.

How the Vietnam War and the AIDS epidemic have been remembered and commemorated is indicative of their respective moments in history. The Vietnam War marks the beginning of the end of the Cold War. It follows on the historic upheaval of the civil rights movement and intersects with the rise of the feminist movement. It has refigured the image not only of American technology and global power but also of American manhood and its relation to the feminine. It has irrevocably altered the image of the American veteran. The AIDS epidemic emerged in the United States at a moment when the gay and lesbian movement was at a new height, when understandings of marginalism and identity politics were acute, and when the religious right began gaining political power and waging a culture war around morality and art.

The production of cultural memory around these two events is thus historically situated and specific, and important generational differences exist regarding their impact. My generation witnessed the Vietnam War from a temporal distance, too young to have been directly affected yet old enough to be fascinated with it and to partake of the nostalgia for the intensity of its time. The year the war ended for the United States I was eighteen, caught between what is now called the "Vietnam Generation" and the generation born during the war. The images of the Vietnam War were everywhere when I was growing up, but the war itself was at a comfortable remove.

I am also part of the generation for whom the AIDS epidemic is a primary crisis, an event that has shaped notions of loss, helplessness, empowerment, morality, and responsibility. AIDS is very present for my generation and for the generation born during the Vietnam War; indeed, it defines in many ways our self-image, be it one of activism, condemnation, defiance, social responsibility, or anger at previous generations. For this generation, the Vietnam War is irrevocably tied to AIDS. AIDS activists compare the epidemic to the war and liken AIDS activism to antiwar activism. These two events are also allied through the fact that Vietnam veterans were among the first to die of AIDS and that many young people died in Vietnam and many more continue to die of AIDS.

It is because these are traumas that they have been so prominent in producing cultural memory. Friedrich Nietzsche once wrote that the oldest and most enduring psychology on earth was that of mnemotechnics: "[I]f something is to stay in the memory it must be burned in: only that which never ceases to *hurt* stays in the memory."[21] Nietzsche's statement evokes the enactment of trauma within and upon the body. That cultural memory has been prominently produced in these contexts of pain testifies to memory's importance as a healing device and a tool for redemption—and to the body's importance to memory. However, discourses of healing produce varied meanings and can often be employed as forms of forgetting and depoliticization. Attempts to rescript the Vietnam War have been as much about healing, with its bodily metaphors, as they have been about smoothing over the disruptions of the war's narratives. At the same time, the desire to memorialize the AIDS epidemic while it is still occurring reveals the need to find healing amid death.

Ironically, both the Vietnam veteran and the person with AIDS have become appealing figures. In the memorializing of the war, many people (such as the actors and directors of Hollywood films about the Vietnam War) have proclaimed themselves to have veteran status, and the once-maligned Vietnam veterans have been rewritten as repositories of special wisdom. Similarly, in the "second wave" of the AIDS epidemic, certain gay men have expressed a desire to become HIV-positive in order to gain what they perceive as a sense of purpose in life. Hence, the memorialization of both these events has also romanticized them. Inevitably, finding the "good" in these events has entailed a desire to find meaning in the suffering they have produced.

Postmodern Memory:
Recollection and Reenactment

I situate the Vietnam War and the AIDS epidemic in the context of postmodern culture not only because they have disrupted previously held truths but also because they force a rethinking of the process of memory itself. Both the Vietnam War and the AIDS epidemic can be said to disrupt master narratives, those of American imperialism, technology, science, and masculinity.

The postmodern condition has often been theorized as a context in which all sense of history is lost, amnesia reigns, and the past is vandalized by the pastiche forms of the present. In this book I argue that postmodernism's relationship to the past is not ahistorical or amnesiac. Although memory's relationship to original experience is difficult if not impossible to verify, this does not make memory any less crucial. Linda Hutcheon writes: "What postmodernism does, as its very name suggests, is confront and contest any modernist discarding or recuperating of the past in the name of the future. It suggests no search for transcendent, timeless meaning but rather a re-evaluation of, and a dialogue with the past in light of the present. . . . It does not deny the *existence* of the past; it does question whether we can ever *know* that past other than through its textualized remains."[22] Cultural memory is produced and resides in new forms. Indeed, it can often be disguised as forgetting.

Discussions of memory in the context of modernism and postmodernism have often referred to a memory crisis. Many theorists have lamented memory's demise by proclaiming that collective memory used to be—before modernism and modern technology—a simple and defining script. Much of current writing about memory reiterates this notion that once, back in the village, before writing, cities, and computers, collective memory was stable and pure, passed by word of mouth.[23] This troubling cultural cliché helps to fuel proclamations of cultural amnesia. Throughout history, the most prominent characterization of memory has been the idea that it is in crisis. Memory has been seen to be threatened by technology since ancient times. Indeed, Plato saw the development of writing itself as a threat to individual memory.[24]

Rather than steep concepts of memory in a nostalgic longing for its wholeness, I would like to consider how its role as a changeable script is crucial to its cultural function. Indeed, memory often takes the form not of recollection but of cultural reenactment that serves important needs for catharsis and healing.[25] In the films about the Vietnam War, in the actions of Vietnam veterans at the memorial, and in the artistic works about AIDS, reenactment is crucial in providing a means to confront loss and transform it into healing. It is precisely the instability of memory that allows for renewal and redemption without letting the tension of the past in the present fade away.

Chapter One

Camera Images
and National Meanings

> I remember that month of January in Tokyo, or rather I
> remember the images that I filmed of the month of Janu-
> ary in Tokyo. They have substituted themselves for my
> memory. They *are* my memory.
>
> Chris Marker, *Sans Soleil*

Memory is often embodied in objects—memorials, texts, talismans, images. Though one could argue that such artifacts operate to prompt remembrance, they are often perceived actually to contain memory within them or indeed to be synonymous with memory. No object is more equated with memory than the camera image, in particular the photograph. Memory appears to reside within the photographic image, to tell its story in response to our gaze.

Since its invention, the photograph has been associated with memory and loss. An early emphasis on portrait photography demonstrated the desire to fix an identity in the image, to have the image live after the individual's death.[1] Hence, the photograph evokes both a trace of life and the prospect of death. Roland Barthes famously wrote, "Ultimately, what I am seeking in the photograph taken of me . . . is Death: Death is the *eidos* of that Photograph."[2] In its arrest of time, the photograph appears to hold memory in place and to offer a means to retrieve an experience of the past.

Yet memory does not reside in a photograph, or in any camera image, so much as it is produced by it. The camera image is a technology of memory, a mechanism through which one can construct the past and situate it in the present. Images have the capacity to create, interfere with, and trouble the memories we hold as individuals and as a nation. They can lend shape to histories and personal stories, often providing the material evidence on which claims of truth are based, yet they also possess the capacity to capture the unattainable.

However, the relationship of the camera image to memory and history is one of contradiction. On one hand, photographed, filmed, and videotaped images can embody and create memories; on the other hand, they have the capacity, through the power of their presence, to obliterate them. Some Vietnam veterans say they have forgotten where some of their memories came from—their own experience, documentary photographs, or Hollywood movies. The AIDS Quilt, as a means of forgetting the gaunt figures of people who have died of AIDS, often presents images of them as healthy and robust individuals. For every image memory produced, something is forgotten.

I would like to examine the role of the image in producing both memory and amnesia, both cultural memory and history. Camera images, still and moving, provide important evidence of the past and help define its cultural meaning. They offer incomplete but often compelling versions of the past that often eclipse more in-depth historical texts. They are also a primary mechanism through which individuals participate in the nation. Indeed, national stories are often mediated through specific camera images. This chapter addresses the role of camera images in the production of cultural memory and history through three well-known images: the Zapruder film of John F. Kennedy's assassination, the television image of the Challenger explosion, and the home video image of the Rodney King beating.

Remembering the Image

When Chris Marker says the images he filmed *"are* my memory," he is invoking the common conception of the photographic image as a receptacle of memory, the place where memory resides. What does it mean to say that an image, which remains caught in time, is the equivalent of memory? One of the most fundamental characteristics of camera images is their apparent fixing of an event at a single moment. Yet it is precisely this quality of the camera image that distinguishes it from memory. For, unlike photographs or film images, memories do not remain static through time—they are reshaped and reconfigured, they fade and are rescripted. Though an image may fix an event temporally, the meaning of that image is constantly subject to contextual shifts.

A photograph provides evidence of continuity, reassuring in its "proof" that an event took place or a person existed. Though it is commonly understood that photographs can be easily manipulated, this knowledge has had little effect on the conviction that the camera image provides evidence of the real.[3] One seemingly cannot deny that the camera has "seen" its subject, that "it has been there." One looks through the image to the "reality" it represents, forgetting, in essence, the camera's mediating presence. Thus, the camera image testifies to that which has been.

In Ridley Scott's 1982 science fiction film *Blade Runner*, replicants (cyborgs with four-year life spans) are given photographs depicting childhoods they never had. The photographs provide evidence of their humanness, prove the existence of mothers and fathers and childhood homes, record birthdays celebrated. These photographs establish "fake" memories for the replicants, their designer Tyrell explains, to compensate for their emotional inexperience. Yet the images do not simply render the replicants more docile and emotionally stable; they provide the replicants with evidence of their subjectivity. As Kaja Silverman notes, the fake memories of the photographs are constitutive—they construct the replicants as the subjects they appear to be, subjects with childhoods.[4]

The emphasis on photographs as providers of memory in *Blade Runner* has been discussed at length, precisely because of the anxiety it provokes concerning the veracity of memories and the role of camera images in their construction. The photographs in *Blade Runner* raise the fundamental question of whether one can ever judge a memory to be "fake" or "real" and what role the camera image plays in creating that uncertainty. How can one know, for instance, that all memories derived from photographs are not as "fake" as the replicants'?

In a certain sense, all camera images can be seen as "screen memories." Freud defined screen memories as memories that function to hide, or screen out, more difficult memories the subject wants to keep at bay.[5] Similarly, an image can substitute for a memory. The distinction between the image and the memory, between the screen and the real, becomes imperceptible. There is no "original" memory to be retrieved; it has already been rewritten and transformed. Freud noted that all memories from childhood may be screen memories:

It may indeed be questioned whether we have any memories at all *from* our childhood: memories *relating to* our childhood may be all we possess. Our childhood memories show us our earliest years not as they were but as they appeared at the later periods when memories were aroused. In these periods of arousal, the childhood memories did not, as people are accustomed to say, *emerge;* they were *formed* at that time. And a number of motives, with no concern for historical accuracy, had a part in forming them, as well as in the selection of the memories themselves.[6]

This distinction between the formation, rather than emergence, of memories is crucial. Does the photographic image allow the memory to come forth, or does it actually create the memory?

This critical question applies not only to personal memories of childhood but also to collective and national memories induced by camera images. Freud not only suggests that memories are often formed or scripted at a later time but also elucidates the relationship between memory and fantasy. He defines memory as the object of desire, formed in "periods of arousal" to create a tangle of memory and fantasy within the individual. In analogous fashion, fantasy becomes central to the stories told in the larger narrative of the nation.

The image plays a central role in shaping the desire for cultural memory, specifically the need to share personal experiences. Indeed, the camera image blurs the boundary between cultural memory and history. Well-known images frequently become part of our personal recollections, personal (and "amateur") images often move into public arenas, and Hollywood docudramas can rewrite once personal recollections of "national" events.

At the same time, camera images are evidence of history and can themselves become the historical. Indeed, history is often described in image metaphors. The writings of Walter Benjamin are perhaps the most influential in representing history as an image.[7] In a famous passage in his "Theses on the Philosophy of History," Benjamin wrote:

The true picture of the past flits by. The past can be seized only as an image which flashes up at the instant when it can be recognized and is never seen again. . . . To articulate the past historically does not mean to recognize it "the way it really was" . . . It means to seize hold of a memory as it flashes up at a moment of danger.[8]

For Benjamin, history is the image of a fleeting moment. The historical image announces absence, loss, irretrievability. Like a screen memory, it offers itself as a substitute.

The image Benjamin writes about in "Theses on the Philosophy of History" is an instant image, conjured up in a flash. It is the image of history arrested, a moment of historical rupture when everything stops and is irrevocably altered. This is history as the photographic image, history standing still.[9] Still and moving images shape memory and history in fundamentally different ways. The still image carries a particular power, in its arrested time, to evoke the what-has-been; it seems to have an aura of finality. Stillness is precisely what allows the photograph to be, in Eduardo Cadava's phrase, "the uncanny tomb of our memory."[10] The photograph achieves its moment of certitude in its evidence of death, its capacity to conjure the presence of the absent one.[11]

Yet the historical image is not only represented in still photographs. It is also constructed in the realm of cinematic and television narrative, as both drama and docudrama. The Hollywood docudrama is a central element in the construction of national meaning. The films of World War II, for instance, retain a powerful cultural currency; they provide popular narratives of the war that supersede and overshadow documentary images and written texts. Similarly, as I will discuss in Chapter 3, the history of the Vietnam War is being "written" not only by historians but also through Hollywood narrative films produced for popular audiences. These films are ascribed historical accuracy by the media and reenact famous documentary images of the war. They represent the history of the war, in particular to a generation too young to have seen it represented contemporaneously on television.

The historical television image would seem at first to evoke not a fixed history but, in its immediacy and continuity, a kind of history in the making. The essence of the television image is transmission. It is relentlessly in the present, immediate, simultaneous, and continuous. Hence, television is defined by its capacity to monitor (in the form of surveillance cameras) and to be monitored, to transmit images regardless of whether anyone is watching. The primary elements of television's historicization are repetition, reenactment, and docudrama.

The blurring of boundaries between the image of history and history as an image, between the still and moving image, between document and reenactment, between memory and fantasy, and between cultural memory and history is evident in the construction of national memory. Camera images—photographic, cinematic, televisual, documentary, and docudrama—play a vital role in the development of national meaning by creating a sense of shared participation and experience in the nation. It was the collective viewing of television images of the Gulf War, for instance, that made possible a "national experience" of the war. Similarly, the television image of the Challenger space shuttle exploding prompts a shared cultural memory of that event. Though the still photographic image is crucial to memory, and memory and history are often evoked by flashes of images, it could also be argued that memory most often takes the form of cultural reenactment, the retelling of the past in order to create narratives of closure and to promote processes of healing.

It does not follow, however, that the collective experience of watching "national" events on television leaves all viewers with similar and singular interpretations. Rather, in watching national television events, viewers engage with, whether in agreement or resistance, a concept of nationhood and national meaning. Benedict Anderson has written of the "imagined community" of the modern nation as being crucial to its coherence:

[The nation] is an imagined political community—and imagined as both inherently limited and sovereign. It is *imagined* because the members of even the smallest nation will never know most of their fellow-members, meet them, or even hear of them, yet in the minds of each lives the image of their communion. . . . [The nation] is imagined as a *community*, because, regardless of the actual inequality and exploitation that may prevail in each, the nation is always conceived as a deep, horizontal comradeship. Ultimately, it is this fraternity that makes it possible, over the past two centuries, for so many millions of people, not so much to kill, as willingly to die for such limited imaginings.[12]

Anderson points to the tombs of the unknown soldiers as emblems of the modern culture of nationalism precisely because they are either empty or filled with unidentified bodies; the bodies they contain (either literally or symbolically) are defined solely by their national status. These tombs do not mark individuals, as do the Vietnam Veterans Memorial and the AIDS Quilt. They are, in Anderson's words, "saturated with ghostly national imaginings." Similarly, when one views a "national" text such as a Hollywood docudrama or television coverage of an event of intense public scrutiny, one participates as part of an imagined audience specifically coded as American.

National events are often traumatic ones; we remember where we were when they happened. The assassinations of John F. Kennedy, Martin Luther King, Jr., and Robert Kennedy, and the Challenger explosion, stand out as some of these moments of shock, experienced not as part of the continual flow of history but as ruptures in it. (Earlier events such as the bombing of Pearl Harbor and the death of President Roosevelt, primarily experienced via radio, also produced a collective national witnessing.)

Psychologists Roger Brown and James Kulik call these kinds of memories "flashbulb memories" that "suggest surprise, an indiscriminate illumination, and brevity."[13] They find a correlation between the fixed memories of national events and traumatic personal events and suggest that surprise, extraordinariness (seeing an authority figure cry, for instance), and consequentiality (the effect of the event on their lives) are central aspects of this memory retention. These vivid memories evoke photographic ("flashbulb") moments in which history appears to stand still. Yet research on flashbulb memories has shown that, however vivid they may be, they often bear little resemblance to the initial experience.

Increasingly, Americans participate in the witnessing of history through camera images; "where we were" when it happened was in front of the television screen. Indeed, recent psychological research shows that people often misremember the moment when they first heard of a national catastrophe by reimagining themselves in front of a television set.[14] This particular mechanism of remember-ing, whereby we imagine our bodies in a spatial location, is also a means by which we situate our bodies in the nation. Photography, film, and television thus help define citizenship in twentieth-century America. The experience of watching "national" events, from the Kennedy assassination to the first moon walk, enables Americans, regardless of the vast differences among them, to situate themselves as members of a national culture. This experience is an essential com-ponent in generating the sense that a national culture, a "people," persists.

The Zapruder Film: From Still to Reenactment

When an image coincides with traumatic events of historical rupture, it plays a central role in the construction of national meaning. Abra-ham Zapruder's film of President Kennedy's assassination in 1963 (Figure 1) is perhaps the most famous piece of documentary film in American history. It is both a still and moving image icon: because the moving image was restricted from public view, for twelve years it was seen in public only as a series of stills. The Zapruder film repre-sents history as a succession of individual frames sliding forward in slow motion, offering only fragments of clues to what happened. It is a secret image, hidden from view, imbued with a kind of sacred status, as if it holds within it an essential clue to the meaning of this event. Never before had a piece of film been so dissected (in this case, as a surrogate for Kennedy's absent corpse) in the belief that it contained the truth—a truth existing somewhere between the frames.

In the Zapruder film, the limousine carrying the president, Jacque-line Kennedy, Texas governor John Connally, and his wife, Nellie, drives past the camera in a matter of seconds. Briefly obstructed by a stand of trees, Kennedy reemerges into the frame the moment after he is shot for the first time; the camera then witnesses the impact of the fatal shot and follows the car swiftly to the right as it speeds away. Jacqueline Kennedy, clad in a pink suit and pillbox hat, first cradles her husband's head, then crawls backward onto the trunk of the car,

Figure 1. Still from the Zapruder film.

presumably to aid a Secret Service agent running toward it. The original Super-8 film presents a grainy color image, its detail blurred by motion—an image that hides as much as it reveals.

The Zapruder film has its own history, and its cultural status has changed several times. It was shot on a home movie camera by Abraham Zapruder as he watched Kennedy ride by. Although an amateur, Zapruder, who ran a dress factory in Dallas, was a skilled cameraman. Richard Stolley, who purchased the film from Zapruder for Time-Life, has stated:

He thought the gunshot was a backfire, then through the viewfinder saw Kennedy slump and realized he had been wounded. "If I'd had any sense I would have dropped to the ground," he said, "because my first impression was that the shots were coming from behind me." Instead, he froze, screaming, "They killed him, they killed him," and kept his camera trained on the limousine and the bloody chaos inside until it went through the underpass.[15]

Zapruder sold the film to Time-Life for $150,000, which published still images from it the following week in *Life* magazine, without mention of Zapruder. By presenting "exclusive" photos, as if one of its photographers had been present, *Life* erased the film's amateur status. The footage was then locked away by Time-Life, which permitted only select viewers to see it (among them Dan Rather, whose success in journalism owed much to his proximity to this event). Some assassination historians contend that frames were reversed when they were printed in the Warren Report and that the captions and order for the frames published in *Life* were misleading.[16]

The Zapruder film thus has a different meaning as still images than as a moving image. The power of the film image lies precisely in its sequence of frames that appear to tell a story, a horrible story, with temporal precision. When *Life* publisher C. D. Jackson saw the film, he is reported to have been so disturbed that he had Time-Life acquire the motion-picture rights to it; although *Life* only needed print rights, Jackson wanted to suppress what the *moving* image showed.[17] Certainly, the sequence is much more palatable as a succession of still images. Indeed, its public release as a moving image in 1975 resulted in calls for another investigation. The relentless scrutiny of the image in both government analysis and public discourse has concentrated on precisely what its movement means: Did Kennedy's head fall backward or forward? From which direction was the bullet fired? This image retains power not only as the documentation of a national tragedy but also as evidence of the crucial role of the camera. The iconic power of these few film frames derives from what they demonstrate about the camera's technical ability to capture a crucial moment, to tell the story unseen by the "naked" eye.

The Zapruder film thus changed over time from an amateur home movie to a copyrighted news image to a piece of legal and historical evidence to "evidence" of a conspiracy. This filmed image, so central to the American historical consciousness, so inseparable from the event itself, has played a particular role in symbolizing Kennedy's life and what is scripted in retrospect as America's loss of national innocence. The instant captured in this film is historicized as the moment when the country changed, when it went from being a nation of promise, good intentions, and youthful optimism to one of cynicism, violence, and pessimism. This historical narrative not only promotes a simplistic nostalgia about the America of the 1950s and the "Camelot" years of the Kennedy administration but also prevents healing from taking place. As Michael Rogin writes:

The widespread feeling that America began to fall apart after Kennedy was killed prolongs national mourning. . . . The unresolved assassination, combined with Kennedy's complicity with the forces suspected of doing him in, has blocked a national mourning of the president he actually was, encouraging the regression from what [Melanie] Klein calls the depressive position, where loss can be acknowledged and overcome, to idealization, splitting, and paranoia.[18]

The trope of America's losing its innocence at a precise moment is a well-worn one, a concept reiterated with Pearl Harbor, the Vietnam War, the Watergate scandal, the 1995 Oklahoma City bombing, and other events. The "regression" noted by Rogin is inextricable from the idea that the moment of the assassination, the instant captured by Zapruder, changed everything. In a certain sense, it is not possible to imagine the event in the absence of the Zapruder images. The film has become the event.

That the assassination, whether photographed or not, would be an ongoing subject of debate is incontrovertible. The existence of the film opened the door for scientific inquiry, but the sequence clearly has defied such analysis. The image withholds its truth, clouds its evidence, and tells us, finally, nothing. Science cannot fix the meaning of the Zapruder film precisely because the narrative of national and emotional loss outweighs empirical investigation. We cannot have, perhaps ultimately do not want to have, a definitive answer to why and how it happened—the answer is potentially overwhelming. Hence, fantasies about what happened are as important in national meaning as any residue of the "truth."[19]

The Zapruder film, imbued as it is with fantasy and nostalgia, has also been rescripted in retrospect. For subsequent generations, it has become so synonymous with the assassination that some think it was seen live on television. In 1975 the film was first shown on television by assassination researcher Robert Groden and television journalist Geraldo Rivera. Inspired by the image, Ant Farm and T. R. Uthco, two media art collectives in San Francisco, went to Dallas to reenact the film for a videotape called *The Eternal Frame* (1976; see Figure 2).[20] In what they saw as an attempt to get at the "truth" (which was the image) and, secondarily, as an exercise in bad taste, they drove repeatedly through Dealey Plaza, with various members of the group

Figure 2. *The Eternal Frame,* by Ant Farm and T. R. Uthco. Photo by Diane Andrews Hall, 1975.

(one in drag as Jackie) replaying the famous scene. The event they were reenacting, however, was not the assassination so much as the taking of the Zapruder film itself. Just as the image had been rerun again and again, the artists drove through the plaza again and again. Ant Farm and T. R. Uthco reiterate the primacy of the image by having artist Doug Hall, as the "artist-president" Kennedy, state in a speech:

Like all presidents in recent years, I am in reality nothing more than another image on your television sets. . . . I am in reality only another link in that chain of pictures which makes up the sum total of information accessible to us all as Americans. Like my elected predecessors, the content of the image I present is no different than the image itself. Because I must function only as an image, I have chosen in my career to begin with the end and to be born in a sense even as I was dying.

Uncanny in its presaging of the image politics of the 1980s and 1990s, *The Eternal Frame* is an attempt to produce a compelling simulacrum of the event. The "frame"—which is, by implication, eternally rerun—is primary here.

Yet in striving for macabre humor, these artists did not anticipate the power of mimetic interpretation and reenactment. Dealey Plaza is a popular tourist destination; people make pilgrimages and now visit the museum on the sixth floor of the book depository building, the point from which Lee Harvey Oswald is said to have fired the fatal shots. Rather than stand in horror, the tourists who witnessed the artists' performance wept, reminisced, and took photographs, apparently under the impression that this was an officially sanctioned event. For them, the reenactment was a conduit to participation, a cathartic reliving of where they had been. They made comments such as: "I saw all of it on television after it happened"; "It looks so real now"; "I'm glad we were here. . . . It was a beautiful enactment." Rescripting the film like the artists, they found pleasure in re-experiencing this moment of trauma—one could even say that, despite its intent to the contrary, the parody had a healing effect.

The reenactment of *The Eternal Frame* had a small audience, and it has since been usurped by Oliver Stone's controversial film *JFK* (1991), which incorporated the Zapruder film itself. This docudrama contends, among other things, that the Zapruder film is a crucial piece of evidence that the conspirators who killed Kennedy had not counted on, thus accounting for its suppression. *JFK* focuses on the real-life efforts of Jim Garrison, a Louisiana district attorney (played by Kevin Costner), during the late 1960s to bring someone, anyone, to trial for participation in the alleged assassination plot. Eventually Garrison tried Clay Shaw, a New Orleans businessman, on charges of conspiracy but failed to win a conviction.

Mixing documentary footage and reenactment, fact and fictionalization, *JFK* attempts to establish the existence of a wide conspiracy by debunking many of the facts of the case against Oswald. The film centers on a group of shady figures in New Orleans with connections to Oswald, the anti-Castro movement, and an underground homosexual community. The focus of the film, however, is Garrison and his fervent belief that the truth of the assassination can be found through the American legal system. Stone invented "consolidated" characters and fictional scenes that he contended were "close to the truth," and he spent much of the ensuing debate about the film defending his facts and research.

The opening sequence of *JFK* has Kennedy arriving in Dallas and culminates with the motorcade moving through the streets. Intercutting historical footage with reenacted scenes of the crowd, the film builds to the moment of the shot but defers its image. As the shots ring out, the screen goes black, and viewers see its aftermath—a flock of birds flying to the sky and fleeting glimpses of the limousine speeding away. It is not until much later, during the climactic courtroom scene, that the Zapruder film is shown—in a new, improved, close-up version. The Shaw trial, which took place in 1969, was the first public screening of the Zapruder film. Thus, *JFK* reenacts both the withholding of the Zapruder film and its charged emergence as an historical image; the audience waits for the image, the moment of impact, again.

The official reason for the suppression of the Zapruder film was to protect the Kennedy family and, as *Life*'s publisher concluded, to protect the American public from the disturbing moving image. In *JFK*, Garrison is portrayed as neglecting his family in his obsession with the assassination; it is specifically during the screening of the Zapruder film that he is seen reuniting with his wife and son as they sit and watch. The Zapruder film, of course, depicts the demise of the First Family, and *JFK* attempts to reinscribe the image of the American family shattered by tragedy. This convention of the film is underscored by its insistent indictment of homosexuals, for which it has been criticized by Rogin and others.

Much of the controversy surrounding *JFK* concerned Oliver Stone's audacity at playing the historian. Yet in their criticism of Stone media critics overlooked the power of his role as docudrama-maker. The meanings of the Zapruder film continue to shift each time it is reenacted, and mimesis becomes history. Indeed, the impressionistic style of Stone's film, with its mix of fact, fiction, and docudrama, is precisely what makes it a memory text. Like memory, the film combines fantasy with fragments of facts. The Zapruder film has the capacity to replace personal memories of the Kennedy assassination, to *become* those memories; *JFK* has the capacity to replace the Zapruder film. All subsequent depictions of the Zapruder film are irrevocably altered by its inscription in *JFK*. Like the films of

World War II, Stone's docudrama may operate twenty years from now to encapsulate the story of the assassination at the expense of its documentary image.

In its transformation from still image to moving image to reenactment, the Zapruder film reveals the phenomenological relationship of the image to history and the role of the docudrama as a site of history-making. Reenactment as a historical strategy long preceded the television and film docudrama through the tradition of historical theater and fiction. However, the mass-media context of film and television docudrama amplifies the effects of cultural reenactment. Part of what makes the mimesis of reenactment cathartic is the anticipation of the event we know is coming. Our bodies wait for the moment of the shot.

The Challenger Explosion:
Voyeuristic History

Although the Zapruder film is mythologized as a live television image, it filtered into the national consciousness slowly, through still images. The live images of history in the 1960s were the shooting of Oswald and the first steps on the moon, images produced by the rare live television camera. Television news images in the field were almost exclusively shot on film, and hence subject to delay, until the late 1970s. The television image of the 1986 Challenger disaster marked a turning point in the visual recording of American history, a transition from film to television. In contrast to the Zapruder film, a secret image that was restricted from the public eye in its original form, the television images of the Challenger explosion were unanticipated, unedited, and broadcast live (see Figure 3). These images were unyielding and distant yet relentless and voyeuristic. The blurry image of the cloud of smoke of the exploded space shuttle was emphatically a video image, an image of surveillance; viewers also watched Christa McAuliffe's parents and students, live, at the moment they realized that their daughter and teacher had just been blown up.[21]

The capacity of television technology to transmit images instantly via satellite implicates spectators in new ways. With the Challenger explosion, Americans were witness to a high-tech space-exploration spectacle gone awry, a tragedy with roots in the Cold War space race.

Figure 3. Challenger explosion. AP/Wide World Photos.

The image of the explosion was endlessly repeated, the repetition itself forming a kind of reenactment. Voyeuristically watching the parents and students of Christa McAuliffe, Americans were pre-scripted to share their pride and enthusiasm over the fact that an "ordinary" teacher could experience space flight via U.S. technology. The mission was even timed to allow President Reagan to interview McAuliffe in space during his State of the Union address. As a public relations event, a nationalistic project intended to promote U.S. technology and give the average American a personal stake in the space program, the Challenger failed spectacularly.

In this context, the McAuliffes' moment of realization became a shared national event. They were primary actors in the construction of an American myth about the family's sacrificing for the nation and mourning the loss of a child. In an essay on remembering Christa McAuliffe, Constance Penley notes that McAuliffe was chosen not because of her talents (there were many more qualified candidates) but, in essence, because of her ordinariness—and she knew it.[22] She was to be emphatically normal in space. Ironically, her story has almost completely overshadowed those of the other astronauts who died in the explosion. Her story also dominates the television movie that was inevitably made about the disaster, *Challenger*, which aired in 1989 and which begins, eerily, with McAuliffe (played by Karen Allen) rehearsing what was to be her message from space. Christa McAuliffe's narrative, designed to make Americans identify with her as an ordinary, non-astronaut space traveler, thus backfired, instead causing viewers to imagine their own deaths in space. Yet the image of McAuliffe's naiveté and patriotic earnestness, chronicled in her biography, "*I Touch the Future . . . ,*" and in the *Challenger* movie, has to a certain extent restored NASA as the Kennedy-inspired symbol of optimistic promise for the future.

Both the Zapruder film and the television image of the Challenger disaster allow us to witness, yet they are central in the American historical imagination in part because they defer the meaning of what is witnessed. The Zapruder film does not tell us who fired the fatal shots and why, and the Challenger image does not reveal what happened to the astronauts. NASA has since acknowledged, for instance, that the capsule of the Challenger continued to climb for twenty-five seconds after the explosion and then descended for three minutes to the water—and that the astronauts died not in the explosion but at the moment of impact with the water. NASA has also acknowledged the existence of audiotapes of the final moments after the explosion, which it has, despite several lawsuits by media organizations, managed to keep secret. According to *Time,* the tapes reveal that pilot Michael Smith can be heard saying "uh-oh" and that among the last words heard is one astronaut saying to another, "Give me your hand."[23]

Moreover, a purported transcript of the tape, supposedly from McAuliffe's personal recorder, appeared on a private computer bulletin board.[24] This transcript supposedly documents someone yelling, "What happened? What happened? Oh God, no, no." Other voices say, "Turn on your airpack! Turn on your air!" and yell in desperation, and the transcript ends with a voice saying the Lord's Prayer. Haunting and disturbing but completely unverifiable, this transcript nevertheless speaks of a desire to know what the image defers and of the fantasy of bearing witness. The question *How did they react to imminent death?* becomes *How would I react in the face of death?* This desire and the fantasies it produces are components of cultural memory. In the world of computer bulletin boards, where information moves from one system to another, from private space to public space, cultural memory is shared, pushing at official history and the ongoing promotion of the space program as a civilian and scientific enterprise rather than a military one.

Does the American public have a right to this information? Penley argues that empirical evidence facilitates mourning. However difficult those details, we need to know them for mourning and closure. She notes that people continue to bring in from Florida beaches artifacts that they claim are refuse from the Challenger, although NASA says it has recovered all possible parts. These acts—the collection of objects, the construction of a fantasy of death—are rituals of mourning.

For those who remember where they were when Kennedy was assassinated, the Challenger disaster may seem less significant. But for those who were in school at the time, many of them watching the launch live as part of the promotion of the teacher-in-space program, it was a defining event. Studies have examined the trauma felt by these children, who generally remembered years later where they were when they saw or heard about it and who often identified McAuliffe with their own teachers. Some fantasized about themselves exploding or about the obliteration of their teachers (in both fear and wish fulfillment).[25] Christa McAuliffe's death is not only a public story but the subject of nightmares, sick jokes, and fantasies.

The memory of "where we were" when the Challenger exploded is, like all memories, a fluid memory of rescripting, reenactment, and imagination. Psychologists Ulric Neisser and Nicole Harsch interviewed a group of students the day after the explosion about their "flashbulb" memories of where they were when they heard of the accident and what their reaction had been; they then reinterviewed the subjects several years later. Not only did many of the students misremember entirely or in part where they had been but, when shown their initial recollections, they were still unable to remember them. Significantly, the study seemed to demonstrate not only that the "original" memories had disappeared but that students who had heard of the explosion in a variety of contexts later remembered that they first heard of it while watching television.[26] The insistent television image was thus highly instrumental in rewriting the memory script. As Neisser and Harsch state, "The hours of later television watching may have been more strongly rehearsed, more unique, more compatible with a social script than the actual occasions of first contact."[27]

By remembering themselves as watching the Challenger explosion on television, these students situate themselves within a "national" experience of the event, sharing the shock of its spectacular and tragic failure with a national audience. Ironically, though, the image that allows the public to feel as though it participated in the event does not aid us in mourning. Rather, we invest it with a truth it cannot reveal. It is the reenactment, the replaying, the fantasizing of the story that allow the mourning process to proceed and the event to acquire meaning. The Challenger explosion is rescripted as a loss of innocence—America once again conceived of as a naive nation, one that believes unfailingly in its technology and feels betrayed—that is recovered through a figure of ordinariness. Through Christa McAuliffe the national trauma of the Challenger explosion can be smoothed over and subsumed into a narrative of patriotic sacrifice.[28]

Figure 4. From videotape of Rodney King beating. AP/Wide World Photos.

The Rodney King Video:
The Problem of Reenactment

Whereas the Zapruder film and the image of the Challenger explosion depict nationally traumatic events that would have had historical significance even without their respective images, the videotape of the Rodney King beating is an image that in itself created history (see Figure 4). It is also an image of the 1990s, during which the boundary between domestic and public space is increasingly being blurred as amateur videotapes move effortlessly into the public realm of popular entertainment, news, and history. This brutal beating of a black man by white police officers, captured on a home video camera, came to represent all race relations in the 1990s. This was not a "flash" of history or a moment when people registered "where we were." Rather, it was an image of the endless repetition of history, an "ordinary" image that became history.

In some ways George Holliday's videotape of the Rodney King beating is the Zapruder film of the 1990s, although its meaning retains a different kind of urgency. Whereas the Zapruder film symbolizes a moment of national loss that prompted a nostalgic mourning, the King video signifies the relentless violence of the present. Whereas Abraham Zapruder's film was an exception as an amateur film that changed cultural status, Holliday's videotape was made at a time when video cameras are everywhere; indeed, in the riots that ensued in Los Angeles after the acquittal of the officers who beat King, home video cameras proliferated as much as news cameras.

Like the Zapruder film, the King video changed meaning when it became a series of still images. The defense attorneys deconstructed the sequence and effectively neutralized its violence by presenting it frame by frame. Like the still images of the Kennedy assassination in *Life* magazine, the stills of the King video reduced events to isolated gestures; blows became hands raised in anticipation, frozen postures without dynamic violence. These images made it possible to rescript King as a threatening and resisting figure and to refigure the beating as a reasonable attempt to restrain a dangerous suspect. Kimberle Crenshaw and Gary Peller write:

The eighty-one-second video was, in short, broken into scores of individual still pictures, each of which was then subject to endless reinterpretation. Then, since no single picture taken by itself could constitute excessive force, taken together, the video tape as a whole said something different—not incredibly clear evidence of racist police brutality, but instead ambiguous slices of time in a tense moment that Rodney King had created for the police.[29]

In both the Zapruder film and the King video, the rupturing of persistence of vision, which allows viewers to fill in the gaps between frames in a moving image, changed the meaning. In the Zapruder film, the space between the still images rendered Kennedy's body movements and the direction of the shots ambiguous; in the King video, it rescripted Rodney King as the agent of his interaction with the police rather than the object of brutal and unreasonable force. What had been popularly seen as incontrovertible evidence of excessive police force when the videotape was first released became, in the course of the first trial, an ambiguous document that was used instead to prove that the police were vulnerable to and threatened by King—an image of Rodney King "in complete control" of the situation, in the words of one juror. This ambiguity undermined assumptions about the nature of the documentary image. If this image was not evidence, then did visual evidence exist?[30]

Rodney King's reluctance to become a public figure, his every move under public scrutiny, is well known. Why, then, did the King video become a national image rather than merely a local one? At what moment did Rodney King's story become part of the nation's story? Not at the moment when the police beat him up—that incident was appallingly ordinary. Nor was it at the moment when George Holliday's camera was focused upon the incident—community organizations in Los Angeles had been distributing cameras and gathering footage of the Los Angeles Police Department's excessive violence for years, but the media had never before been interested. Rodney King's story became the nation's story when news organizations across the country deemed it newsworthy—perhaps at the moment when the mystique about video vigilantes coincided with concern over urban violence. The awkwardness with which King has become a celebrity is precisely attributable to the clash of this image's narrative with nationalistic themes. This is an image of rupture, and Rodney King can't be an American hero.

The Rodney King video shifted status during the Los Angeles riots, when a helicopter news crew videotaped the brutal beating of a white truck driver by four black men. From then on, the King video became one half of two images that defined a national issue: America at war over race. The amateur, low-to-the-ground image taken by George Holliday was replaced by the slick, omniscient view from the helicopter. This image does not show the heroic actions taken by four black strangers who left their home to help Reginald Denny escape and saved his life. The participation of television is crucial here; it was only after they saw him being beaten on TV that these people came to help Denny. Another reluctant public figure, Denny awoke in the hospital without memory of the incident and confused to find Jesse Jackson and Arsenio Hall waiting to see him.

This evolution of the image from a videotape to a series of still images to one of two symmetrical images is crucial in its national meaning. The anger that propelled the Los Angeles riots, an anger at the jury's interpretation of an image everyone had seen, was compellingly and gruesomely enacted in the reverse image of the four young black men beating Reginald Denny as he lay defenseless in the street. This image provided a collective relief in its symmetry with the King video—it somehow balanced the scales, somehow mitigated the troubling image, loaded with historical references, of a black man being beaten by whites. For many, the image of Denny's beating served retroactively to justify the brutal force evident in the King video.

The meaning of the image of Rodney King's beating thus continues to shift, yet it will likely not be subject to the type of reenactment the Zapruder film underwent. There will probably be no television movie of the Los Angeles riots. The television series *L.A. Law* reenacted the uprising by having one of the lawyers lose his memory after being pulled from his car and beaten. This story of the innocent white victim, in the wrong neighborhood at the wrong time, may be as close as television will get. Do the hyperdocumented, ultratelevised L.A. riots defy the docudrama form because the formulas of mimetic interpretation can't fit the story of four heroic young black people racing from their home to save a white man's life? Though docudrama reenactments of major disasters such as earthquakes and hurricanes are standard television fare, the L.A. riots remain too difficult, too dangerous, for television movie formulas.

However, reenactment is a central aspect of the narrative of the L.A. riots. In the trial of the men involved in the Denny beating, several witnesses—including Denny—testified to events of which they had no memory.[31] Instead, with the prodding of lawyers, they narrated their experience for the jury while watching videotapes of what their experience had been. That the video image became the memory was not new, but what was remarkable was that the court gave it legal and experiential sanction. To this day, the videotape is Reginald Denny's only memory of his ordeal.

In addition, the King video gained a new meaning when placed in a contemporary docudrama, Spike Lee's *Malcolm X* (1992). Inserted into the opening credit sequence of the film, the King video represents the entire history of violence against American blacks and, as Malcolm X's voice-over states, the ways in which blacks are still outsiders in America. The videotape is no longer Rodney King's story

but rather is the story of all disenfranchised black men. It is replayed
not as a particular moment in history but as the emblem of an ongoing history, one that appears not to be changing but to be replaying
constantly, repeating again and again.

The videotape of the beating of Rodney King and its counterpart
image of the beating of Reginald Denny thus emerge as particular
kinds of screen memories that provide evidence of memories that
were never acquired, that never "existed." Irrevocably tied together,
these images constitute elements of the cultural memory of the upheaval in Los Angeles, a strange symmetry in the national "experience" of the event.

The relentlessness of television thus operates in tension with the
creation of nationally experienced events as moments when we register "where we were." This is no longer the shock of history described
by Walter Benjamin, a flash, an arrested moment, a rupture. Rather,
the history evoked by the Rodney King video is an endlessly replayed
loop.

Yet it is precisely the illusion of continuous flow that is most problematic about televised "history." Television audiences never saw
Rodney King's car chase or the desperate rescue of Reginald Denny.
They saw snippets of violence with endless commentary, a partial
picture with the illusion of completeness.

Reenactment and National Meaning

Thus, historical images are reduced either to still images or to reenactments. When Freud wrote about secondary revision, the process
by which a subject revises and narrativizes a dream or memory in
order to give it coherence, he was referring to the way in which memories are continuously rewritten and transformed over time until they
may bear little resemblance to the initial experience.[32] Renarrativiza-
tion is essential in memory; indeed, it is its defining quality. Photographs and images from television and film build on the traditions of
lithography, historical drama, and the historical novel in retelling the
past, but the cultural value of the camera image as evidence of the
real shifts this reenactment into new territory of verisimilitude. The
reenactments in docudramas can thus be seen not simply as history

and memory's reinscription but rather as indicators of the fluid realm of memory itself. Docudramas smooth over historical ruptures, yet, ironically, it is often through reenactment that healing takes place—a healing that necessitates forgetting.

Participation in the nation thus often takes the form of watching or taking part in reenactments. Many historical ceremonies involve the reenactment of battles, with participants sporting historical costumes. On the anniversary of D-Day, World War II veterans parachuted into France to reenact their war experience, reliving what was perhaps the most meaningful moment of their lives. Members of the Veterans Vigil of Honor camp out at the Vietnam Veterans Memorial as if to guard it, replaying the codes of war. In the making of Hollywood war films, directors and actors do "battle" on location. Films such as *Platoon* (1986) reenact famous documentary photographs of the Vietnam War. In television movies, recent events, such as the FBI's standoff with Branch Davidians in Waco, Texas, and the O. J. Simpson freeway chase, are reenacted almost before they are over.

Reenactment is a cathartic means for people to find closure in an event. It is not clear whether this sense of healing involves an erasure and smoothing over of difficult material or a constant rescripting that, like memory, enables an active engagement with the past. Memories and histories are often entangled, conflictual, and co-constitutive. In the context of postmodernity, the slippage between real and fiction, between invention and recovery, is marked.

Yet there also is tension between individual processes of mourning and the simple closure offered by Hollywood docudramas, between the individual memory of traumatic events and their remembrance as national stories. Each carries different cultural meanings and implications. Though an individual may find closure in reenacting an experience, the reenactment of national events through the apparatus of popular culture offers venues for forgetting. The political implications of each are quite different. It is in examining the traffic of cultural events across the porous boundaries of personal memory, cultural memory, and history that the stakes of reenactment can be understood.

Chapter Two

The Wall and the
Screen Memory

The Vietnam Veterans Memorial

The forms remembrance takes indicate the status of memory within a given culture. In acts of public commemoration, the shifting discourses of history, personal memory, and cultural memory converge. Public commemoration is a form of history-making, yet it can also be a contested form of remembrance in which cultural memories slide through and into each other, creating a narrative tangle. With the Vietnam War, public commemoration is inextricably tied to the question of how war is brought to closure in American society. How does a society commemorate a war whose central narrative is one of division and dissent, a war whose history is still formative and highly contested? The Vietnam War, with its lack of a singular, historical narrative defining a clear-cut purpose and outcome, has led to a unique form of commemoration.

Questions of public remembrance of the Vietnam War can be examined through the concept of the screen. A screen is a surface that is projected upon; it is also an object that hides something from view, that shelters or protects. The Vietnam Veterans Memorial in Washington, D.C., both shields and is projected upon; the black walls of the memorial act as screens for innumerable projections of memory and history—of the United States' participation in the Vietnam War and of the experiences of Vietnam veterans since the war.

A singular, sanctioned history of the Vietnam War has not yet coalesced, in part because of the disruption of the standard narratives of American imperialism, technology, and masculinity that the war's loss represented. The history of the Vietnam War is still being composed from many conflicting histories, yet two particular elements within the often opposing narratives are uncontested—the divisive effect of the war on American society and the marginalization of Vietnam veterans. In this chapter I analyze how narratives of the war have been constructed out of and within the cultural memory of the Vietnam Veterans Memorial. I examine how the walls of the memorial act to eclipse—to screen out—personal and collective memories of the Vietnam War in the design of history and how the textures of cultural memory are nevertheless woven throughout, perhaps over and under, these screens.

The 1980s and 1990s have witnessed a repackaging of the 1960s and the Vietnam War—a phenomenon steeped in the language of nostalgia, healing, and forgiveness. Within this rescripting of history, the Vietnam Veterans Memorial has become a central icon in the process of healing, of confronting difficult past experiences. When it was constructed in 1982, the memorial was the center of a debate over how wars should be remembered and who should be remembered (those who died, those who participated in it, those who engineered it, those who opposed it). The memorial has received an extraordinary amount of attention: it has been the subject of innumerable coffee-table books, several exhibitions, and a television movie, among other things. Virtually all texts written today concerning Vietnam veterans make reference to it. It has played a significant role in the rehistoricization of the Vietnam War.

The Status of a Memorial

Although now administered by the National Park Service of the federal government, the impetus for the creation of the Vietnam Veterans Memorial came from a group of Vietnam veterans who raised the funds and negotiated for a site on the Washington Mall. Situated on the grassy slope of the Constitutional Gardens near the Lincoln Memorial, the Vietnam Veterans Memorial, which was designed by Maya Lin, consists of a V shape of two walls of black granite set into the earth at an angle of 125 degrees. Together, the walls extend almost five hundred feet, with a maximum height of approximately ten feet at the central hinge. These walls are inscribed with the names of the 58,196 men and women who died in the war, listed chronologically by date of death, with opening and closing inscriptions. The listing of names begins on the right-hand side of the hinge and continues to the end of the right wall; it then begins again at the far end of the left wall and ends at the center again. Thus, the name of the first American soldier killed in Vietnam, in 1959, is on a panel adjacent to that containing the name of the last killed there, in 1975.[1] The framing dates of 1959 and 1975 are the only dates listed on the wall; the names are listed alphabetically within each "casualty day," although those dates are not noted. Each name is preceded by a diamond shape; names of the approximately 1,300 MIAs (those missing in action) are preceded by a small cross, which, in the event that the remains of that person are identified, is changed to a diamond. If an MIA should return alive, this symbol would be changed to a circle (but, as one volunteer at the memorial told me, "We don't have any circles yet"). Eight of the names on the wall represent women who died in the war. Since 1984 the memorial has been accompanied by a figurative sculpture of three soldiers, which faces the memorial from a group of trees south of the wall. In 1993 a statue commemorating the women who served in Vietnam was added three hundred feet from the wall.

The memorial functions in opposition to the codes of remembrance evidenced on the Washington Mall. Virtually all the national memorials and monuments in Washington are made of white stone and designed to be visible from a distance. In contrast, the Vietnam Veterans Memorial cuts into the sloping earth: it is not visible until one is almost upon it; if approached from behind, it seems to disappear into the landscape (see Figure 5). Although the polished black granite walls of the memorial reflect the Washington Monument and face the Lincoln Memorial, they are not visible from the base of either structure. The black stone creates a reflective surface, one that echoes the reflecting pool of the Lincoln Memorial and allows viewers to participate in the memorial; seeing their own image reflected in the names, they are implicated in the listing of the dead. The

Figure 5. Vietnam Veterans Memorial, by Maya Lin. Photo by the author.

etched surface of the memorial has a tactile quality, and viewers are compelled to touch the names and make rubbings of them.

Its status as a memorial, rather than a monument, situates the Vietnam Veterans Memorial within a particular code of remembrance. Monuments and memorials can often be used as interangeable forms, but there are distinctions in intent between them. Arthur Danto writes:

We erect monuments so that we shall always remember, and build memorials so that we shall never forget. Thus we have the Washington Monument but the Lincoln Memorial. Monuments commemorate the memorable and embody the myths of beginnings. Memorials ritualize remembrance and mark the reality of ends. . . . The memorial is a special precinct, extruded from life, a segregated enclave where we honor the dead. With monuments we honor ourselves.[2]

Monuments are not generally built to commemorate defeats; the defeated dead are remembered in memorials. Whereas a monument most often signifies victory, a memorial refers to the life or lives sacrificed for a particular set of values. Whatever triumph a memorial may refer to, its depiction of victory is always tempered by a fore-grounding of the lives lost.

Memorials are, according to Charles Griswold, "a species of peda-gogy" that "seeks to instruct posterity about the past and, in so doing, necessarily reaches a decision about what is worth recovering."[3] The Lincoln Memorial, for example, is a funereal structure that gains its force from its implicit reference to Lincoln's untimely death. It em-bodies the man and his philosophy, with his words inscribed on its walls. The Washington Monument, by contrast, operates purely as a symbol, making no reference beyond its name to the mythic political figure. This distinction between the two outlines one of the funda-mental differences between memorials and monuments: Memorials tend to emphasize specific texts or lists of the dead, whereas monu-ments offer less explanation; a memorial seems to demand the nam-ing of those lost, whereas monuments are usually anonymous. Danto states, "The paradox of the Vietnam Veterans Memorial in Washing-ton is that the men and women killed and missing would not have been memorialized had we won the war and erected a monument instead."[4]

The traditional Western monument glorifies not only its subject but the history of classical architecture as well. The obelisk of the Washington Monument, which was erected between 1848 and 1885, has its roots in Roman architecture; long before Napoleon pilfered them from Egypt to take to Paris, obelisks carried connotations of the imperial trophy. The Lincoln Memorial, which was built in 1922, is modeled on the classic Greek temple, specifically referring to the Parthenon. The Vietnam Veterans Memorial, however, makes no di-rect reference to the history of classical art or architecture.[5] It does not chart a lineage from the accomplishments of past civilizations.

Yet the Vietnam Veterans Memorial is unmistakably representative of a particular period in Western art. In the uproar that accompanied its construction, it became the focus of a debate about the role of modernism in public sculpture. Just one month prior to the dedica-tion of the memorial in November 1982, Tom Wolfe wrote a vitriolic attack on its design in the *Washington Post:*

What she [designer Maya Lin] had designed was a perfect piece of sculp-tural orthodoxy for the early 1980s. The style of sculpture the mullahs [of modernism] today regard as most pure (most non-bourgeois) is minimal sculpture. The perfect minimal sculpture is an elemental, even banal, form comprised solely of straight lines and flat planes. . . . As for the veterans, they, like the city fathers of Hartford, will now have a chance to bang their heads with the heels of their hands and make imaginary snowballs and look at their wall. Far from lifting the accusing finger from those who fought in Vietnam—it will be the big forefinger's final perverse prank. A tribute to Jane Fonda![6]

Wolfe and other critics of modernism compared the memorial to two infamously unpopular government-funded public sculptures: Carl Andre's *Stone Field Piece* (1980) in Hartford, Connecticut, and Richard Serra's *Tilted Arc* (1981) in downtown Manhattan. Andre's work, which consists of thirty-six large boulders positioned on a lawn near Hartford's city hall, is widely regarded with derision by residents as a symbol of the misguided judgments of their government.[7] Serra's now notorious *Tilted Arc*, an oppressive, leaning slab of Cor-Ten steel that bisected the equally inhospitable Federal Plaza, inspired several years of intense debate and was dismantled in March 1989 after workers in the Federal Building petitioned to have it removed.[8] In the media, these two works came to symbolize the alienating effect of modern sculpture on the viewing public and people's questioning of the mechanisms by which tax-funded sculpture is imposed upon them. The debates surrounding both works centered on whom the "public" of public sculpture comprises and what responsibilities artists have to the communities in which their public art will reside.

Before it was built, the memorial was seen by many veterans and critics of modernism as yet another work of abstract form that the public would find difficult to interpret. Frederick Hart, the sculptor who was chosen to design the realist statue that accompanies the memorial, stated (somewhat condescendingly, one could argue) that figurative art was the only artistic style that was truly public. Sarcastically employing adjectives of modernism, Hart wrote:

The simple, bold, flat, unequivocal truth is that modernism has failed in its utopianist dream of creating a new and universal language. . . . The figure is a necessary element if public art is in any sense to be truly public. The simple fact is that the philosophical arrogance rooted in the concept of "Art for Art's Sake" has led to continuously diminishing levels of substance and meaning in art. Art is now nothing more than a cult, held to the bosom of smug elitists who dictate what is, and is not, fit for public consumption.[9]

Yet in situating the Vietnam Veterans Memorial purely within the context of modernism, Wolfe, Hart, and their fellow critics ignore fundamental aspects of this work, an omission that, it might be added, the sketches of the design may have aided. The memorial is not simply a flat, black, abstract wall; it is a wall inscribed with names. When members of the "public" visit this memorial, they do not go to contemplate long walls cut into the earth but to see and touch the names of those whose lives were lost in this war. Hence, to call this a modernist work is to overemphasize its physical design and to negate its commemorative purpose.

Modernist sculpture has been defined by a kind of sitelessness.[10] Yet the Vietnam Veterans Memorial is a site-specific work that establishes its position within the symbolic history embodied in the national monuments on and around the Washington Mall. Pointing from its axis to both the Washington Monument and Lincoln Memorial, the Vietnam Veterans Memorial references, absorbs, and reflects these classical forms. Its black walls mirror not only the faces of its viewers and passing clouds but also the obelisk of the Washington Monument, thus forming a kind of pastiche of monuments. The memorial's relationship to the earth shifts between context and decontextualization, between an effacement and an embracement of the earth; approached from above, it appears to cut into the earth; from below, it seems to rise from it. The site-specificity of the Vietnam Veterans Memorial is crucial to its position as both subversive of and continuous with the nationalist discourse of the Mall.[11]

It is as a war memorial that the Vietnam Veterans Memorial most distinguishes itself from modernist sculpture. As the first national war memorial built in the United States since those commemorating World War II, it makes a statement on war that diverges sharply from the declarations of prior war memorials. The Vietnam Veterans Memorial Fund (VVMF), which organized the construction of the memorial, stipulated only two things—that it contain the names of all of those who died or are missing in action and that it be apolitical and harmonious with the site. The veterans' initial instructions stated: "The memorial will make no political statement regarding the war or its conduct. It will transcend those issues. The hope is that the creation of the memorial will begin a healing process."[12] Implicit within these guidelines was the desire that the memorial offer some kind of closure to the debates on the war. Yet, with these stipulations, the veterans set the stage for the dramatic disparity between the message of this memorial and that of its antecedents. The stipulation that the work not espouse a political stand in regard to the war—a stipulation that, in the ensuing controversy, would appear naive—ensured that the memorial would not glorify war.

The traditional war memorial achieves its status by enacting closure on a specific conflict. This closure contains the war within particular master narratives either of victory or of the bitter price of victory, a theme dominant in the "never again" texts of World War I memorials. In declaring the end of a conflict, this closure can by its very nature serve to sanctify future wars by offering a complete narrative with cause and effect intact. In rejecting the architectural lineage of monuments and the aesthetic codes of previous war memorials, the Vietnam Veterans Memorial refuses to sanction the closure and implied tradition of those structures. It can be said both to condemn and to justify future memorials.

The Black Gash of Shame

Before the memorial was built, its design came under attack not only because of its modernist aesthetics but, more significant, because it violated unspoken taboos about the remembrance of wars. When it was first unveiled, the design was condemned by certain veterans and others as a highly political statement about the shame of an unvictorious war. The memorial was termed the "black gash of shame and sorrow," a "degrading ditch," a "tombstone," a "slap in the face," and a "wailing wall for draft dodgers and New Lefters of the future." These dissenters included a certain faction of veterans and members of the "New Right" ranging from conservative activist Phyllis Schlafly to future presidential candidate Ross Perot, who had contributed the money for the design contest. Many of these critics saw the memorial as a monument to defeat, one that spoke more directly to a nation's guilt than to the honor of the war dead and the veterans. Veteran Tom Carhart, who had been active in the VVMF, was among many who objected to the fact that the jury had not included any veterans and saw the memorial as insulting the Vietnam veterans: "The proposed design is defended on artistic grounds, but the issue is not one of art: If Americans allow that black trench to be dug, future generations will understand clearly what America thought of its Vietnam veterans."[13]

Such criticism showed how the memorial was being "read" by its opponents, and their readings compellingly reveal codes of remembrance of war memorials. Many saw its black walls as evoking shame, sorrow, and dishonor and perceived its refusal to rise above the earth as indicative of defeat. Thus, a racially coded reading of the color black as shameful was combined with a reading of a feminized earth as connoting a lack of power. The argument against the black stone was terminated by Gen. George Price, who is black, when he said at a meeting concerning the memorial: "Black is not the color of shame. I am tired of hearing it called such by you. Color meant nothing on the battlefields of Korea and Vietnam. We are all equal in combat. Color should mean nothing now."[14]

Precisely because of its deviation from traditional commemorative codes—white stone rising above the earth—the design was read as a political statement. In a defensive attempt to counter aesthetic arguments, an editorial in the *National Review* stated:

Our objection to this Orwellian glop does not issue from any philistine objection to new conceptions in art. It is based upon the clear political message of this design. The design says that the Vietnam War should be memorialized in black, not the white marble of Washington. The mode of listing the names makes them individual deaths, not deaths in a cause: they might as well have been traffic accidents. The invisibility of the monument at ground level symbolizes the "unmentionability" of the war—which war, as we say, is not in fact mentioned on the monument itself. Finally, the V-shaped plan of the black retaining wall immortalizes the antiwar signal, the V protest made with the fingers.[15]

This analysis of the memorial's symbolism, indeed a perceptive reading, points to several crucial aspects of the memorial: Its listing of names does emphasize individual deaths rather than the singular death of a body of men and women; the relationship of the memorial to the earth does refuse to evoke heroism and victory. Yet these conservative readings of the memorial, though they may have been accurate in interpreting the design, did not anticipate the public response to the inscription of names.

The angry reactions to the memorial design go beyond the accusation of elite pretensions of abstraction—the uncontroversial Washington Monument itself is the epitome of abstraction. Rather, I believe the memorial's primary (and unspoken) subversion of the codes of war remembrance is its antiphallic presence. By "antiphallic" I do not mean to imply that the memorial is somehow a passive or "feminine" form but rather that it opposes the code through which vertical monuments symbolize power and honor. The memorial does not stand erect above the landscape; it is continuous with the earth. It is contemplative rather than declarative. The V shape of the memorial has been interpreted by various commentators as standing for Vietnam, victim, victory, veteran, violate, and valor. Yet one also finds a disconcerting subtext in this debate in which the memorial is seen as implicitly evoking castration. The V of the two black granite walls, it seems, is read as a female V. The "gash" is not only a wound, it is slang for the female genitals. The memorial contains all the elements that have been associated psychoanalytically with the specter of woman—it embraces the earth; it is the abyss; it is death.

Some critics overtly called for a phallic memorial. James Webb, a member of the VVMF's sponsoring committee, wrote:

Watching then the white phallus that is the Washington Monument piercing the air like a bayonet, you feel uplifted. You are supposed to feel uplifted. That is the intention of the designers. That is the political message. And then when you peer off into the woods at this black slash of earth to your left, this sad, dreary mass tomb, nihilistically commemorating death, you are hit with that message also. That is the debate. That is the tragedy of this memorial for those who served.[16]

To its critics, this antiphallus symbolized the open wound of this country's castration in an unsuccessful war, a war that "emasculated" the United States. The "healing" of this wound would therefore require a memorial that revived the narrative of the United States as a technologically superior military power and rehabilitated the masculinity of the American soldier.

The person who designed this controversial, antiphallic memorial

was unlikely to reiterate traditional codes of war remembrance. At
the time her anonymously submitted design was chosen by a group
of eight art experts, Maya Ying Lin was a twenty-one-year-old under-
graduate at Yale University. She had produced the design as a project
for a funerary architecture course. She was not only young and uncre-
dentialed but also Chinese-American and female. Initially, the veterans of the VVMF were pleased by this turn of events; they assumed
the selection would only show how open and impartial their design
contest had been.[17] However, the selection of someone with "marginal" cultural status as the primary interpreter of a controversial war
inevitably complicated matters. Eventually Maya Lin was defined, in
particular by the media, not as American but as "other." This definition not only shaped how she was perceived by the media and some
of the veterans but also raised the question of whether or not her
otherness had informed the design itself. Architecture critic Michael
Sorkin wrote:

Perhaps it was Maya Lin's "otherness" that enabled her to create such a
moving work. Perhaps only an outsider could have designed an environment
so successful in answering the need for recognition by a group of people—
the Vietnam vets—who are plagued by a sense of "otherness" forced on
them by a country that has spent ten years pretending not to see them.
Women have been invisible a lot longer than that. Maya Lin has been able
to make a memorial that doesn't insult the memory of the war by compro-
mising the fact of its difference.[18]

To Sorkin, Lin's marginal status as a Chinese-American woman gave
her insight into the marginalization experienced by Vietnam veterans,
an analogy that noticeably erased the differences in race and age that
existed between them.

When Lin's identity became known, there was a tendency in the
press to characterize her design as passive, as having both a female
and an Asian aesthetic. There is little doubt that in its refusal to
glorify war, it is an implicitly pacifist work and, by extension, a political work. It is also emphatically antiheroic. Yet as much as it is contemplative and continuous with the earth, it can also be seen as a
violent work that cuts into the earth. Lin has said: "I wanted to work
with the land and not dominate it. I had an impulse to cut open the
earth . . . an initial violence that in time would heal. The grass would

grow back, but the cut would remain, a pure, flat surface, like a geode when you cut into it and polish the edge."[19] The black walls cannot connote a healing wound without also signifying the violence that created the wound, cutting into the earth and splitting it open.

Trouble began almost immediately between Maya Lin and the veterans. "The fund has always seen me as a female—as a child," she has said. "I went in there when I first won and their attitude was— O.K. you did a good job, but now we're going to hire some big boys— boys—to take care of it."[20] Lin was situated outside the veterans' discourse because she was a woman and an Asian-American and because of her approach to the project. She had made a decision deliberately not to inform herself about the war's political history to avoid being influenced by debates about the war. According to veteran Jan Scruggs, who was the primary figure in getting the memorial built: "She never asked, 'What was combat like?' or 'Who were your friends whose names we're putting on the wall?' And the vets, in turn, never once explained to her what words like 'courage,' 'sacrifice,' and 'devotion to duty' really meant."[21]

Lin's ethnicity doubly displaced her in the public debate. She took exception to the characterization of the memorial design as having an "Asian aesthetic"; she grew up in Athens, Ohio, worked at McDonald's as a teenager, and considers herself an average Midwesterner who has little sense of ethnic identity. Yet her Asian-American identity was read as particularly ironic, given her role in defining the discourse of remembrance of a war fought in Indochina (even if, with the volatile and complex politics between China and Vietnam, this conflation of ethnic identities is a particularly American one). In the debate, Lin's status as an American disappeared, and she became simply "Asian." In a *60 Minutes* broadcast at the time of the controversy, Morley Safer asked, "Was it the design that provoked such controversy or the designer, who was a student, a woman, an American, a Chinese-American?" Lin responded, "I think it is, for some, very difficult for them. I mean they sort of lump us all together, for one thing. There is a term used . . . it's called a gook."

However, Lin emphasized her position as a outsider by consistently referring to "the integrity of my design," whereas the veterans were primarily concerned with its ability to offer emotional comfort

to themselves and the families of the dead, either in terms of forgiveness or honor. The initial disagreements on design between the veterans and Lin, which ultimately led to several compromises (the veterans agreed to the chronological listing—with indexes at the site to
facilitate location—and Lin agreed to the addition of opening and
closing inscriptions), were not about aesthetics but about to whom
the memorial belongs.

In the larger political arena, these discourses of aesthetics and
commemoration were also at play. Several well-placed funders of the
memorial, including Ross Perot, were unhappy with the design, and
Secretary of the Interior James Watt withheld its permit.[22] It became
clear to the veterans of the VVMF that they had either to compromise or to postpone the construction of the memorial (which was to
be ready by November 1982, in time for Veterans Day). Consequently, a plan was devised to erect a statue and flag close to the
walls of the memorial; realist sculptor Frederick Hart was chosen to
design it. Hart was paid $330,000, whereas Maya Lin received just
$20,000 for her design from the same fund.[23] Originally, the veterans
intended to place the flag and statue at the apex of the walls, a plan
that so insulted Maya Lin that she hired a law firm to help her oppose
it. Finally it was decided to place the statue in a grove of trees that
stands apart from the memorial.

Erected in 1984, Hart's bronze sculpture consists of three soldiers—one black, one Hispanic, and one white—standing and looking in the general direction of the memorial (Figure 6).[24] It is eight
feet tall, looming over visitors. The soldiers' military garb is realistically rendered, with guns slung over their shoulders and ammunition
around their waists, and their expressions are somewhat bewildered
and puzzled. Hart, one of the most vociferous critics of modernism
in the debates over the memorial, said at the time: "My position is
humanist, not militarist. I'm not trying to say there was anything good
or bad about the war. I researched for three years—read everything.
I became close friends with many vets, drank with them in bars. Lin's
piece is a serene exercise in contemporary art done in a vacuum with
no knowledge of its subject. It's nihilistic—that's its appeal."[25]

Hart bases his credentials on a kind of "knowledge" strictly within
the male domain—drinking with the veterans in a bar—and unavail-

Figure 6. Statue by Frederick Hart. Photo by the author.

able to Maya Lin, whom he on another occasion referred to as "a mere student." She described the addition of his statue as "drawing mustaches on other people's portraits."[26] Hart characterizes Lin as having designed her work with no "knowledge" and no "research," as a woman who works with feeling and intuition rather than expertise. He ultimately defines realism as not only a male privilege but also an aesthetic necessity in remembering war.

In Hart's sculpture, the veterans and the dead are subsumed into a singular narrative. It thus follows the tradition of the Marine Corps War Memorial that depicts the raising of the U.S. flag at Iwo Jima, a work that has attained an iconic status as *the* realist war memorial and a symbol of the United States's ability to raise its flag on foreign soil.[27] Hart's statue presents a symbolic image of men in war, yet one that deviates in certain ways, with its soldier's puzzled faces, from the master narrative of the male soldier as heroic figure. Ironically, the conflict over Lin's design forestalled any potential debate over the atypical expressions of Hart's soldiers.

The battle over what kind of aesthetic style best represents the

Vietnam War was, quite obviously, a battle over the discourse of the war itself. In striving for an "apolitical" design, the veterans of the VVMF had attempted to separate the memorial, itself a contested narrative, from the contested narratives of the war, ultimately an impossible task. The memorial could not be a neutral site precisely because of the divisive effects of the Vietnam War. Later, Maya Lin noted the strange appropriateness of the two memorials: "In a funny sense the compromise brings the memorial closer to the truth. What is also memorialized is that people still cannot resolve that war, nor can they separate issues, the politics, from it."[28]

However, after Lin's memorial had actually been constructed, the debate about aesthetics and remembrance surrounding its design simply disappeared. The controversy was eclipsed by a national discussion on remembrance and healing. The experience of viewing Lin's work was so powerful for the general public that criticism of its design vanished.

The Names

There is little doubt that the memorial's power is due to the 58,196 names inscribed on its walls in a form that engages visitors (see Figure 7). The design of the memorial draws spectators inward and down toward its center, so that one has the sensation both of descending below the ground and the Washington Mall and of being pulled inward toward the walls. Hence, the design creates spaces in which the names surround visitors and invite them to touch and to see themselves within the listings.[29]

These names, by virtue of their multiplicity, situate the Vietnam Veterans Memorial within the multiple strands of cultural memory. The memorial does not validate the collective over the value of the individual. In response to the memorial, visitors commonly think of the widening circle of pain emanating from each name, imagining for each the grieving parents, sisters, brothers, girlfriends, wives, husbands, friends, and children—imagining, in effect, the multitude of people who were directly affected by the war.

This listing of names creates an expanse of cultural memory, one that could be seen as alternately subverting, rescripting, and contrib-

Figure 7. Names on the Vietnam Veterans Memorial. Photo by the author.

uting to the history of the Vietnam War as it is being written. The histories these names evoke and the responses they generate are necessarily multiple and replete with complex personal stakes. These narratives concern the effect of the war on the Americans who survived it and whose lives were irrevocably altered by it. The listing of names is steeped in the irony of the war—an irony afforded by retrospect, of lives lost for no discernible reason.[30] All accounts of the war are tinged with the knowledge that this country did not accept its memory and that the veterans were stigmatized by the nation's defeat.

Although these names are now marked within an official history, that history cannot contain the ever-widening circles that expand outward from each. The names on the walls of the memorial constitute a chant; they were read out loud at the dedication ceremony and at the tenth anniversary as a roll call of the dead.[31] They are etched into stone. The men and women who died in the war thus achieve a historical presence through their absence. These names are listed without elaboration, with no place or date of death, no rank, no place of origin. The lack of military rank allows the names to transcend a military context and to represent the names of a society. It has often been noted that these names display the diversity of America: Fredes Mendez-Ortiz, Stephen Boryszewski, Bobby Joe Yewell, Leroy Wright. Veteran William Broyles, Jr., writes:

These are names which reach deep into the heart of America, each testimony to a family's decision, sometime in the past, to wrench itself from home and culture to test our country's promise of new opportunities and a better life. They are names drawn from the farthest corners of the world and then, in this generation, sent to another distant corner in a war America has done its best to forget.[32]

Broyles is not atypical in portraying the diversity of names as indicative of America as the promised land (what of those who came here not by choice, for instance?) or in positioning the United States at the center, from which these places of cultural origins and foreign wars are seen as "distant corners." His reading of the ethnicity of the names on the walls does not consider the imbalances of that diversity—that this war was fought by a disproportionately high number of blacks and Hispanics, that the soldiers predominantly came from working- and middle-class backgrounds. Proper names in our culture have complex legal and patriarchal implications, identifying individuals specifically as members of society. On this memorial, these names are coded as American—not as Asian, black, or white. The ethnic derivations of these names are subsumed into a narrative of the American melting pot—into which, ironically, Maya Lin, as an agent of commemoration, will not fit.

The names act as surrogates for the bodies of the Vietnam War dead. It is now a ritual at the memorial for visitors to make rubbings of the names to take away with them, to hold with them the name marked in history. These names thus take on significant symbolic value as representations of the absent one. Yet what exactly do they evoke? Clearly they mark the dead irrevocably as a part of the history of the United States's involvement in the Vietnam War; but what sense of the individual can a name in stone portray? Judith Butler asks: "But do names really 'open' us to an intersubjective ground, or are they simply so many ruins which designate a history irrevocably lost? Do these names really signify for us the fullness of the lives that were lost, or are they so many tokens of what we cannot know, enigmas, inscrutable and silent?"[33] The name evokes both everything and nothing as a marker of the absent one. This may be why, with both the AIDS Quilt and the Vietnam Veterans Memorial, visitors have felt compelled to add photographs, letters, and other memorabilia in attempts to fill the names with individual significance.

It is crucial to their effect that the names are listed not alphabetically but in chronological order. This was Lin's original intent, so that the wall would read "like an epic Greek poem" and "return the vets to the time frame of the war." The veterans were originally opposed to this idea; because they conceived the memorial specifically in terms of the needs of the veterans and family members who would visit it; they were worried that people would be unable to locate a name and simply leave in frustration. They changed their opinion, however, when they examined the Defense Department listing of casualties. Listed alphabetically, the names presented not individuals but cultural entities. There were over six hundred people named Smith, sixteen named James Jones. Read alphabetically, the names became anonymous, not individuals but statistics.

Read chronologically, however, the names on the Vietnam Veterans Memorial create a narrative framework; they chart the story of the conflict. By walking along the wall, one figuratively walks through the history of the war. As the number of names listed alphabetically within a casualty day swells, the escalation of the fighting is conveyed. In addition, the fact that visitors must look up a name in the index and then find it on the wall places them in an active role; Lin and others have referred to it as a "journey." For veterans, the chronological listing provides a spatial reference for their experience of the war, a kind of memory map. They can see in certain clumps of names the scene of a particular ambush, the casualties of a doomed night patrol, or the night they were wounded.

This is not a linear narrative framework. Rather, the names form a loop, beginning as they do at the central hinge of the memorial and circling back to the center. This refusal of linearity is appropriate to a conflict that has had no narrative closure. The hinge between the two walls thus becomes a pivotal space, the narrow interval between the end of one war and the beginning of another; it connotes a temporary peace within the cycle of war.

The question of who is named and not named on the wall is crucial to the intersection of cultural memory and history in the memorial. Veterans of the VVMF intended the memorial as a tribute not only to those who died but also to those who survived the war, hence the opening and closing inscriptions that read, in part: "In honor of the men and women of the Armed Forces who served in the Vietnam War. The names of those who gave their lives and of those who remain missing are inscribed in the order they were taken from us." There is little doubt that the memorial has become a powerful symbol for all Vietnam veterans, yet only the names of the war dead and the MIAs are inscribed on the wall, and thus within history. The distinction between the named and unnamed will determine how this memorial constructs the history of the Vietnam War after the generation of Vietnam veterans has died.

One could also argue that the listing of names limits the narrative of the memorial because of who remains unnamed. In the nationalist context of the Washington Mall, the Vietnamese become unmentionable; they are conspicuously absent in their roles as collaborators, victims, enemies, or simply the people on whose land and over whom (supposedly) this war was fought. Those whose lives were irrevocably altered or who were killed because of their opposition to the war are also absent from the discourse surrounding the memorial, except insofar as antiwar protesters are referred to by the more conservative participants in the debate as the people who would not let the war be won.

As a practical matter, the inscription of names on the memorial has posed many taxonomic problems. Though the VVMF spent months cross-checking and verifying statistics, errors have occurred. There are at least fourteen and possibly as many as thirty-eight men who are still alive whose names are inscribed in the wall.[34] More than two hundred names have been added to the memorial since it was first built (the initial number inscribed on the walls was 57,939), names that were held up previously for "technicalities" (such as, for example, a dispute over whether or not someone was killed within the "presidentially designated" war zone).[35] Such problems signify the war's lack of closure. The impossibility of managing 58,196 sets of statistics, of knowing every detail (who died, when, and where) in a war in which human remains were often unidentifiable, has prevented any kind of closure. It has been barely noted in the media, for instance, that the Tomb of the Unknown Soldier for the Vietnam War, which was approved by Congress in 1974, was left empty and uninscribed until 1984, when some publicity drew attention to the situation.[36] The reason for this delay, according to the Army, was the absence of any unidentifiable remains (although the Army did have unidentified remains in its possession). Technology's ability to decipher the individual identity of a body and hence to achieve a kind of closure is thus at stake here.

Names will continue to be added to the Vietnam Veterans Memorial; there is no definitive limit to the addition of names. It has been noted that the names of veterans who have died since the war from causes stemming from it are not included on the memorial—veterans who committed suicide, for instance, or who died from complications from their exposure to Agent Orange.[37] Are they not casualties of the war? The battles still being fought by the veterans foreclose a simple narrative of the Vietnam War.

Yet the memorial, like all memorials, is essentially a "forgetful monument," to use James Young's term. He writes, "A nation's monuments efface as much history from memory as they inscribe in it."[38] Framed within the nationalist context of the Washington Mall, the Vietnam Veterans Memorial must necessarily "forget" the Vietnamese and cast the Vietnam veterans as the primary victims of the war.[39]

The Vietnam Veteran:
The Perennial Soldier

Experience has fallen in value. . . . Was it not noticeable at the end of the [First World] war that men returned from the battle-field grown silent—not richer but poorer in communicable experience? What ten years later was poured out in the flood of war books was anything but experience that goes mouth to mouth.

*And there was nothing remarkable about that. For never has
experience been contradicted more thoroughly than strategic experience by tactical warfare, economic experience by inflation,
bodily experience by mechanical warfare, moral experience by
those in power. A generation that had gone to school on a horse-
drawn streetcar now stood under the open sky in a countryside
in which nothing remained unchanged but the clouds, and beneath these clouds, in a field of force of destructive torrents and
explosions, was the tiny, fragile, human body.*

Walter Benjamin
"The Storyteller"

The incommunicability of experience described in Walter Benjamin's
famous essay, "The Storyteller," is the result of a discontinuous, fragmented experience, the experience of modern warfare. Similarly, the
incommunicability of the experience of the Vietnam veterans has
been a primary narrative of Vietnam War representation. This silence
has been depicted as a consequence of an inconceivable kind of war,
one that fit no prior images of war, one that the American public
would refuse to believe. The importance of the Vietnam Veterans
Memorial lies in its communicability, which in effect has mollified
the incommunicability of the veterans' experience.

Though the Vietnam Veterans Memorial most obviously pays tribute to the memory of those who died during the war, it is a central
icon for the veterans. It has been noted that the memorial has given
them a place—one that recognizes their identities, a place at which
to congregate and from which to speak. The Veterans Vigil of Honor
maintains a twenty-four-hour watch at the memorial for the MIAs.
Vietnam veterans haunt the memorial, often coming at night after
the crowds have dispersed. It is a place where veterans can speak to
their dead friends, a place of contemplation, a place that specifically
marks their identities.[40] Two veterans have shot themselves at the
site; a Washington, D.C., police officer who killed himself there in
1984 was called "the first casualty of the wall."[41] After one suicide
attempt, the wife of a veteran stated: "If my husband has something
on his mind to sort out . . . he'll go to the Wall. He doesn't care if it's
2:00 A.M., raining, and below zero. All the guys are like that. There

is something about the Wall. It's like a magnet."[42] Many veterans regard the wall as a site where they visit their memories. Several Veterans Administration hospitals bring patients with post-traumatic stress disorder on regular visits to the memorial.[43] Hence, the memorial is as much about survival as it is about mourning the dead.

The construction of an identity for the veterans has become the most conspicuous and persistent narrative of the memorial. The central theme of this narrative is the veterans' initial marginalization, before the memorial's construction generated discussion about them. The "welcome home" parades for the Vietnam veterans all took place after the construction of the memorial, and the huge celebration for the returning Iran hostages in January 1981 marked a turning point in popular recognition of the "nonhomecoming" of the Vietnam veterans.[44]

The treatment of the veterans can be only partially explained by the uniqueness of the Vietnam War. In his well-known essay, "What Did You Do in the Class War, Daddy?" James Fallows points to the stark class division affecting American military service, a division that began with the Vietnam War.[45] Thus, the treatment of the veterans was also a direct result of who the veterans were—not the white middle-class men who had graduate school deferments but working-class whites, blacks, Latinos, Guamanians, and Native Americans. The initial shock and acquiescence with which Vietnam veterans initially accepted their postwar treatment was a direct result of their lack of privilege.[46] In the World War II paradigm, the veterans return home to a prospering country, are greeted by a ticker-tape parade and a V-Day celebration, and find jobs waiting for them. That this mythical story omits many things—such as the discriminatory treatment of black veterans, the significant (and unacknowledged) amount of post-traumatic stress disorder among World War II veterans, and the displacement of women from factory jobs to provide employment for returning soldiers—does not lessen the influence it has had upon subsequent experiences of war.[47]

The Vietnam veterans did not arrive home en masse for a celebration. Some of the most difficult stories of the veterans' experiences concern their mistreatment upon their return. Soldiers were sent to

Vietnam on one-year tours of duty. A direct consequence of this policy was that the vets returned separately, often with no transportation or support services awaiting them. Many vets have recounted how they were greeted at the airport by strangers who stared in anger and even spat at them. These incidents serve as icons for the extended alienation and mistreatment felt by the veterans. So many stories surfaced after the memorial's dedication about soldiers rejoicing at finding friends they thought were dead that one has to wonder why they were all so isolated upon their return.[48]

Many veterans ended up in underfunded and poorly staffed Veterans Administration hospitals. They were expected to put their war experiences behind them and to assimilate quickly back into society. That many were unable to do so exacerbated their marginalization—they were labeled social misfits and stereotyped as potentially dangerous men liable to erupt violently at any moment. Veteran George Swiers writes:

The message sent from national leadership and embraced by the public was clear: Vietnam veterans were malcontents, liars, wackos, losers. . . . Hollywood, ever bizarre in its efforts to mirror life, discovered a marketable villain. *Kojak, Ironside,* and the friendly folks at *Hawaii Five-O* confronted crazed, heroin-addicted veterans with the regularity and enthusiasm [with which] Saturday morning heroes once dispensed with godless red savages. No grade-B melodrama was complete without its standard vet—a psychotic, axe-wielding rapist every bit as insulting as another one-time creature of Hollywood's imagination, the shiftless, lazy, and wide-eyed black.[49]

The scapegoating of the veteran as a psychopath absolved the American public of complicity and allowed the narrative of American military power to stand. Implied within these conflicting narratives is the question of whether or not the veterans are to be perceived as victims of or complicit with the war. Peter Marin writes, "Vets are in an ambiguous situation—they were the agents and the victims of a particular kind of violence. That is the source of a pain that almost no one else can understand."[50] Ironically, their stigma has resulted in many Vietnam veterans' assumption of hybrid roles; they are both, yet neither, soldiers and civilians.

Although the marginalization of the Vietnam veterans has been acknowledged in the current discourse of healing and forgiveness about the war, within the veterans' community another group has struggled against an imposed silence: the women veterans. Eight women military nurses were killed in Vietnam and are memorialized on the wall. It is estimated that 11,500 women, half of whom were civilians and many of whom were nurses, served in Vietnam and that 265,000 women served in the military during the Vietnam War. The experience of the women who served in Vietnam was equally affected by the difference of the war from previous U.S. wars: an unusually large proportion of them, three-quarters, were exposed to hostile fire. Upon their return, they not only were subject to post-traumatic stress but also were excluded from the male veteran community. Lynda Van Devanter recounts that she was not allowed to participate in a veterans' protest march because the male veterans thought "Nixon and the network news reporters might think we're swelling the ranks with non-vets."[51] Many women have revealed that they kept their war experience a secret, not telling even their husbands about their time in Vietnam.

These women veterans were thus doubly displaced, unable to speak as veterans or as women. As a result, several women veterans began raising funds for their own memorial, and in November 1993 the Vietnam Women's Memorial was dedicated near the Vietnam Veterans Memorial (see Figure 8). The statue, which was designed by Glenna Goodacre, depicts three uniformed women with a wounded soldier. Initially the women's memorial was turned down by the Commission of Fine Arts; in rejecting the proposal, J. Carter Brown, director of the National Gallery of Art and chair of the commission, stated that Hart's three men were "symbolic of human kind and everyone who served" and that the addition of a women's statue would "open the doors to others seeking added representation for their ethnic group or military specialty," adding that the National Park Service had even heard from Scout Dog associations.[52] The women of the Vietnam Women's Memorial Project (VWMP) were insulted by the implication: "How could any intelligent human being consider comparing those brave women to dogs?"[53]

The two women who direct the VWMP, Diane Carlson Evans and Donna Marie Boulay, say it is Hart's depiction of three men that makes the absence of women so visible and that they would not have

Figure 8. Diane Carlson Evans and other women veterans at the dedication ceremony for the Vietnam Women's Memorial by Glen Goodacre. Photo by Greg Gibson. AP/Wide World Photos.

initiated the project had Lin's memorial stood alone. Says Evans, "The wall in itself was enough, but when they added the men it became necessary to add women to complete the memorial."[54] Hence, the singular narrative of Hart's realist depiction is one of inclusion and exclusion. Much has been written about the ethnicity of the three men in the statue: one is obviously black, but the one intended as Hispanic is somewhat ambiguous, leading some observers to speculate that he is Jewish. (In fact, Hart used a Hispanic model.) Yet the women's memorial raises the question of what makes a memorial complete and whether all memorials are not, in some sense, incomplete.[55]

One could argue that the widespread public discourse of healing around the original memorial led women veterans to speak of their memorial as the beginning rather than the culmination of a healing process. At the time, Evans said, "The journey for most of us still isn't over. Many are just beginning their healing. But this is our place to start."[56] Yet the radical message of commemorating women in war is undercut by the conventionality of the statue itself. A contemporary version of the *Pietà*, the statue presents one woman nurse heroically holding the body of a wounded soldier, one searching the sky for help, and one looking forlornly at the ground.[57] Benjamin Forgery, who called the women's memorial "one monument too many" in the *Washington Post*, has criticized it for cluttering up the landscape with ineffectual sculpture:

In spirit and pose the sculptor ambitiously invokes Michelangelo's "Pietà," the great Vatican marble of a grieving Mary holding the crucified body of Jesus. But the ambition is sabotaged by the subject and the artist's limited talent—compared with Michelangelo's Christ figure, this GI is as stiff as a board. The result is more like an awkward still from a "M°A°S°H" episode. ... This sincere, blatheringly sentimental sculpture clearly satisfies the women vets' need to have their service and sacrifices recognized more dramatically than by the eight names among the wall's thousands.[58]

The decision to build the women's memorial was not about aesthetics (except insofar as it reaffirms the representational aesthetic of Hart's statue) but about recognition and inclusion. However, by reinscribing the archetypal image of woman as caretaker, one that foregrounds the male veteran's body, the memorial reiterates the main obstacle to healing that women veterans face. Before several women Vietnam veterans drew attention to post-traumatic stress disorder in women, the only option many of them had in trying to deal with their memories was to go to support groups of male veterans— where, inevitably, they wound up taking care of the men. Writes Laura Palmer, "After all, these women had *degrees* in putting the needs of others before their own. 'I would sit there and triage the group,' a former nurse says."[59] Furthermore, the experience of these women differed from the men in the relentlessness of their contact with death. In an unusual statement at the ground-breaking ceremony for the women's memorial, Chairman of the Joint Chiefs of Staff Gen. Colin Powell said: "I realized for the first time that for male soldiers, the war came in intermittent flashes of terror, occasional death, moments of pain; but for the women who were there, for the women who helped before the battle and for the nurses in particular, the terror, the death and the pain were unrelenting, a constant terrible weight that had to be stoically carried."[60]

The difficulty of adequately and appropriately memorializing the women veterans falls within the larger issue of masculine identity in the Vietnam War. The traditionally male enclave of soldiers in battle by its very nature excludes women (with the front defined as the place where women are not). Women are perceived as unstable and threatening to the male bonds of combat, hence they cannot partake of the codes of that shared experience. In addition, the Vietnam veterans have a particularly complex set of codes, one that ironically has been strengthened by their marginalization. The Vietnam War is depicted as an event in which American masculinity was irretrievably damaged, and the rehabilitation of the Vietnam veteran is thus also a reinscription of American masculinity. The pain and suffering the veterans experienced since the war continue to be defined as masculine, whereas the inclusion of women into that discourse of remorse and anger is regarded as a dilution of its intensity and a threat to the rehabilitation of that masculinity.

The Vietnam veteran has thus become an emblem of the American male's crisis of masculinity, which was prompted in part by the feminist movement. Susan Jeffords writes: "The male Vietnam veteran—primarily the white male—was used as an emblem for a fallen and emasculated American male, one who had been falsely scorned by society and unjustly victimized by his own government. . . . No longer the oppressor, men came to be seen, primarily through the imagery of the Vietnam veteran, as themselves oppressed."[61]

The memorial's primary narrative is not about the veterans' war experience but rather about their mistreatment since the war. This narrative takes the form of a combat story, in which the enemy has been transposed from the North Vietnamese and the Vietcong to the antiwar movement, the callous American people, the Veterans Administration, and the government. The story of the struggle to build the memorial also takes on this combat form. In his book *To Heal a Nation* (which was later made into a television movie), veteran Jan Scruggs, who conceived the memorial and was the main force behind its being built, equates the battle to have the memorial built with the battles of Vietnam itself: "Some 58,000 GIs were, in death, what they had been in life: pawns of Washington politics."[62]

To Heal a Nation constitutes the memorial's origin story. Scruggs vows to build a memorial when, after seeing the film *The Deer Hunter* (1978) and sitting up late with a bottle of whiskey, he realizes that he cannot remember the names of the friends whose deaths fill his flashbacks. Scruggs is the lone fighter for much of this story; initially many veterans deem the idea of a memorial ludicrous, given that they do not even have adequate support services. In this combat tale, the enemies range from senators reluctant to approve the land to Secretary of Interior James Watt (who halted the project until the Hart statue was approved) and Ross Perot. The heroes include Senators Charles Mathias and John Warner, Scruggs, and several other hardworking veterans. In Scruggs's story, "grunts"—those who experienced the "real" war of combat—battle the establishment and win. It is highlighted with dramatic moments—a woman engraving the name of her brother in stone, the solidarity felt by the vets on the dedication day, veterans being reunited at the wall, and a re-enactment of combat when, on the eve of the dedication, someone threatens to blow up the memorial: "The Fund called local police, the U.S. Park Police, and the FBI. Many were Vietnam veterans who expressed a special interest in providing protection. Furthermore, as word of the threat spread, groups of ex-Green Berets volunteered to stand 24-hour-a-day guard duty. The names on the wall would not be alone."[63]

This depiction of the memorial as a continuous battleground is echoed in the activities of the Veterans Vigil for Honor, which still keeps watch at the memorial. Harry Haines writes:

Members of the Vigil dress in camouflage uniforms, jungle boots, combat helmets, and "boonie" hats. They maintain a large army tent near the Memorial where they store Coleman lanterns, flags, petitions and other supplies. At night, an anonymous and mysterious figure dressed in camouflage and a cowboy hat steps out from a tree line near the Memorial and plays taps. For these veterans and many others like them, The Wall is more than a sacred depository of memory; The Wall *is* Vietnam.[64]

As a form of reenactment, this conflation of the memorial and the war is a ritual of healing, although one that appears to be stuck in its ongoing replay, its resistance to moving beyond narratives of the war.[65] For the Veterans Vigil, only the war can provide meaning. In refighting that war every day, they are also reinscribing narratives of heroism and sacrifice.

But for others there is a powerful kind of closure at the memorial. The one story for which the memorial appears to offer resolution is that of the shame felt by veterans for having fought in an unpopular war, a story that is their primary battle with history.

The Healing Wound

The "healing wound" metaphor that has prevailed in descriptions of the Vietnam Veterans Memorial is a bodily metaphor. It evokes many different bodies—the bodies of the Vietnam War dead, the bodies of the veterans, and the body of the American public. This wound is seen to heal through the process of remembering and commemorating the war. To dismember is to fragment a body and its memory; to remember is to make a body complete.

Where are the bodies of the memorial? The chronology of names represents bodies destroyed and inscribed permanently with the identity of war dead. Families seek out names as they would visit a grave, as the receptacle of the body; indeed, the names act as surrogates for the bodies. Many people imagine that the bodies of the dead lie behind the walls, where Lin envisioned them.[66] The status of these bodies has been transformed by the context of technological warfare. Some families of the war dead claim they did not receive the correct remains—that the remains weighed too much, for instance.[67] In addition, the unpublicized controversy over the Tomb of the Unknown Soldier was a dispute over the status of bodily remains. The belief that technology has rendered all remains identifiable ironically conflicted with the destructive capacity of modern warfare; some men's remains amounted to less than 30 percent of their bodies. This destructive power, which dates from World War I, renders the status of the bodies of the war dead highly problematic. Many of the most horrific descriptions of combat in Vietnam deal with the total annihilation of whole bodies. In *Dispatches*, Michael Herr wrote:

Far up the road that skirted the TOC was a dump where they burned the gear and uniforms that nobody needed anymore. . . . A jeep pulled up to the dump and a Marine jumped out carrying a bunched-up fatigue jacket held out away from him. He looked very serious and scared. Some guy in his company, some guy he didn't even know, had been blown away right next to him, all over him. He held the fatigues up and I believed him. "I guess you couldn't wash them, could you?" I said. He really looked like he was going to cry as he threw them into the dump. "Man," he said, "you could take and scrub them fatigues for a million years, and it would never happen."[68]

In war, the "tiny, fragile, human body" becomes subject to dismemberment, relegated to the "dump," to a kind of antimemory. The absence of these bodies—obliterated, interred—is both eclipsed and invoked by the names on the memorial's walls. Yet the bodies of the living Vietnam veterans have not been erased of memory. As the bodies of survivors, they have complicated the history of the war. Indeed, history operates more efficiently when its agents are no longer alive. These veteran bodies, dressed in fatigues, scarred and disabled, contaminated by toxins, refuse to let certain narratives of completion stand. Memories of war have been deeply encoded in these bodies, marked literally and figuratively in their flesh—one of the most tragic aftermaths of the war is the widespread genetic deformity caused by Agent Orange among veterans' children and the Vietnamese.

The bodies of the surviving veterans resist the closure of history and provide a perceptible site for a continual remembering of the war's effects. In *The Body in Pain,* Elaine Scarry describes how the war wounded serve as vehicles for memorialization. She notes that "injuries memorialize without specifying winner or loser" and have "no relation to the contested issues." The act of injuring, according to Scarry, has two functions: as "the activity by means of which a winner and a loser are arrived at" and as a means of providing "a record of its own activity."[69] The wound functions as a testament to the act of injuring. Thus, the body of the veteran itself is a tangible record, a kind of war memorial.

The veterans' healing process requires an individual and collective closure on certain narratives of the war. But when that healing process is ascribed to a nation (as in the title of Scruggs's book, *To Heal a Nation*), the effect is to erase the individual bodies involved; the wounds of individuals become subsumed into the nation's healing. Similarly, Scarry writes, the traditional perception of an army as a single body tends to negate the body of the individual soldier:

We respond to the injury as an imaginary wound in an imaginary body, despite the fact that that imaginary body is itself made up of thousands of real human bodies, and thus composed of actual (hence woundable) human tissue. . . . A colossal severed artery, if anything, works to deflect attention away from rather than call attention to what almost certainly lies only a very short distance behind the surface of that image, a terrifying number of bodies with actually severed arteries.[70]

Yet the body Scarry describes is the wounded body of the conventional army—the army of fronts, rears, flanks, and arteries. In the Vietnam War the army was not, from the beginning, a whole body but rather a body of confused signals, infiltrated bases, mistaken identities, fragging (the killing of incompetent or unpopular officers by their own troops), and a confusion of allies and enemy. In this already fragmented body, remembering (restoring the wholeness of the body) is highly problematic. What happens when the body to be restored is the nation? Does healing mean a foreclosing or an expansion of the discourse of the war? Is it a coming to terms or a desire to put the war behind us? The healing process of the veterans has been couched in terms of atonement and asking forgiveness; when applied to the nation, this process connotes not remembrance but forgetting, an erasure of problematic events in order to smooth the transition of difficult narratives into the present.

The Memorial as Shrine

The Vietnam Veterans Memorial has been the subject of an extraordinary outpouring of emotion since it was built. More than 150,000 people attended its dedication ceremony, and some days as many as 20,000 people walk by its walls. It is the most heavily visited site on the Washington Mall, with an estimated total of 22 to 30 million visitors.[71] The memorial has taken on all of the trappings of a religious shrine; it has been compared to Lourdes and the Wailing Wall in Jerusalem. People bring personal artifacts to leave at the wall as offerings, and coffee-table photography books document and interpret these experiences as a collective recovery from the war. The wall has also spawned the design of at least 150 other memorials, including the Korean War Veterans Memorial, which was dedicated in July

1995. That sculpture, a group of nineteen gray, larger-than-life figures walking across a field, stands on the opposite side of the reflecting pool from the Vietnam memorial.[72]

The rush to embrace the memorial as a cultural symbol reveals
not only the relief of telling a history that has been taboo but also a
desire to reinscribe that history. The black granite walls of the memorial act as a screen for myriad cultural projections; it is easily appropriated for a variety of interpretations of the war and of the experience of those who died in it. To the veterans, the memorial makes
amends for their treatment since the war; to the families and friends
of those who died, it officially recognizes their sorrow and validates a
grief that was not previously sanctioned; to others, it is either a profound antiwar statement or an opportunity to recast the narrative of
the war in terms of honor and sacrifice.

The memorial's popularity must thus be seen within the context of
a very active scripting and rescripting of the war and as an integral
component in the recently emerged Vietnam War nostalgia industry.
This sentiment is not confined to those who wish to return to the
intensity of wartime; it is also felt by the news media, which long to
recapture their moment of moral power—the Vietnam War made
very good television. Michael Clark writes:

Vietnam was recollected by the cultural apparatus that had constituted our
memory of the war all along . . . [it] summoned a cast of thousands to the
streets of New York, and edited out information that was out of step. It
healed over the wounds that had refused to close for ten years with a balm
of nostalgia, and transformed guilt and doubt into duty and pride. And with
a triumphant flourish it offered us the spectacle of its most successful creation, the veterans who will fight the next war.[73]

As the healing process is transformed into spectacle and commodity,
a complex industry of nostalgia has grown. The veterans are not simply actors in this nostalgia; some are actively involved in orchestrating
it. Numerous magazines that reexamine and recount Vietnam War
experiences have emerged; the merchandising of Frederick Hart's
statue (posters, T-shirts, a Franklin Mint miniature, and a plastic
model kit) generates about $50,000 a year, half of which goes to
the VVMF and half to Hart;[74] and travel agencies market tours to

Indochina for veterans. In the hawkish *Vietnam* magazine, advertisements display a variety of war-related products: the Vietnam War Commemorative Combat Shotgun, the Vietnam Veterans Trivia Game, Vietnam War medallions, posters, T-shirts, and calendars. Needless to say, the Vietnam War is also now big business in both television drama and Hollywood movies.

As a kind of "history without guilt," according to Michael Kammen, nostalgia is not a singular activity pursued by former participants. Nostalgia about the Vietnam War takes many forms. Those who fought and experienced the war—the veterans, the war reporters, the support staff—look back on the highly charged experience of combat, the intensified relationships they formed, and the feeling of purpose that many of them, however ironically, felt (this latter response is most notable in the accounts of women nurses). The media have become nostalgic for their own moment of purposefulness in covering and exposing the "real" stories of the war, which the military and political establishment attempted to hide. Finally, those who were too young to experience the Vietnam War or the antiwar movement are fascinated by this particular time. As I will discuss in chapter 3, this generation has flocked to see films about the war, their concepts of it shaped by *Apocalypse Now* (1979) and *Platoon* (1986).[75] This nostalgia represents a desire to experience war.

Though the design of Maya Lin's memorial does not lend itself to marketable reproductions, the work has functioned as a catalyst for much of this nostalgia.[76] The Vietnam Veterans Memorial is the subject of no fewer than twelve books, many of them photography collections that focus on the interaction of visitors with the names.[77] The memorial has tapped into a reservoir of need to express in public the pain of this war, a desire to transfer private memories into a collective experience. Many personal artifacts have been left at the memorial: photographs, letters, poems, teddy bears, dog tags, combat boots and helmets, MIA/POW bracelets, clothes, medals of honor, headbands, beer cans, plaques, crosses, playing cards (see Figure 9).[78] At this site the objects are transposed from personal to cultural artifacts, items bearing witness to pain suffered.

Thus, a very rich and vibrant dialogue of deliberate, if sometimes very private, remembrance takes place at the memorial. Of the ap-

Figure 9. Artifacts at the Vietnam Veterans Memorial. Photo by the author.

proximately 40,000 objects left at the wall, the vast majority have been left anonymously. Relinquished before the wall, the letters tell many stories:

—Dear Michael: Your name is here but you are not. I made a rubbing of it, thinking that if I rubbed hard enough I would rub your name off the wall and you would come back to me. I miss you so.

—We did what we could but it was not enough because I found you here. You are not just a name on this wall. You are alive. You are blood on my hands. You are screams in my ears. You are eyes in my soul. I told you you'd be all right, but I lied, and please forgive me. I see your face in my son, I can't bear the thought. You told me about your wife, your kids, your girl, your mother. And then you died. Your pain is mine. I'll never forget your face. I can't. You are still alive.

—Dear Sir, For twenty-two years I have carried your picture in my wallet. I was only eighteen years old that day that we faced one another on that trail in Chu Lai, Vietnam. Why you didn't take my life I'll never know. You stared at me for so long, armed with your AK-47, and yet you did not fire. Forgive me for taking your life, I was reacting just the way I was trained, to kill V.C. . . .[79]

The memorial is perceived by visitors as a site where they can speak to the dead (where, by implication, the dead are present) and to a particular audience—seen variously as the American public and the community of veterans. It is because of this process that the wall is termed by many a "living memorial." It is the only site in the Washington, D.C., area that appears to be conducive to this kind of artifact ritual.[80]

Many of these letters are addressed not to visitors but to the dead. They are messages for the dead that are intended to be shared as cultural memory. Often they reflect on the lives the dead were unable to live: one offers symbols of traditional life passages, such as a wedding bouquet, baby shoes, Christmas tree ornaments, and champagne glasses to "celebrate your 25th wedding anniversary"; another is placed in a gold frame with the sonogram image of a prospective grandchild. The voices of the Vietnam War dead are also heard through their own words, as many families leave copies of letters written by GIs, letters tinged with irony because they represent lives cut short.

For many, leaving artifacts at the memorial is an act of catharsis, a release of long-held objects to memory. A well-worn watch, for instance, was accompanied by a note explaining that it was being left for a friend who was always asking what time it was and who died wearing it. A Vietcong wedding ring was accompanied by a note reading, "I have carried this ring for 18 years and it's time for me to lay it down. This boy is not my enemy any longer." Other objects include a can of C-rations, a "short stick" (on which GIs would mark how much longer they were "in country"), a rifle marked with eighteen notches (possibly signifying either kills or months spent in country), Vietnamese sandals, and a grenade pin, each imbued with memory and carried for many years. For those who left these objects, the memorial represents a final destination and a relinquishing of their memory.

The artifacts left at the memorial are talismans of redemption, guilt, loss, and anger. Many offer apologies to the war dead, and many are addressed to "those who died for us." Some appear to be ironically humorous—a shot of whiskey or a TV set—whereas others display deep-set anger (a "Hanoi Jane Urinal Sticker"). A few are simply startling: someone left a Harley-Davidson motorcycle. The dominant tone, though, is one of asking forgiveness for the suffering, the loss, for having lived.

The National Park Service, which is now in charge of maintaining the memorial, operates an archive of the materials left there.[81] Originally the Park Service classified these objects as "lost and found." Later, Park Service officials realized the artifacts had been left intentionally and began to save them. The objects thus moved from the cultural status of being "lost" (without category) to being historical artifacts. They have now even turned into artistic artifacts; the manager of the archive writes:

These are no longer objects at the Wall, they are communications, icons possessing a substructure of underpinning emotion. They are the products of culture, in all its complexities. They are the products of individual selection. With each object we are in the presence of a work of art of individual contemplation. The thing itself does not overwhelm our attention since these are objects that are common and expendable. At the Wall they have become unique and irreplaceable, and, yes, mysterious.[82]

Labeled "mysterious" and thus coded as original works of art, these objects are given value and authorship. Some of the people who left them have since been traced. To write *Shrapnel in the Heart*, Laura Palmer sought out and eventually interviewed the authors of various letters (although some declined), and several television shows concerning the memorial have attempted to assign authorship to the artifacts.[83] The attempt to tie these objects and letters to their creators reveals again the shifting realms of personal and cultural memory. Assigned authorship and placed in a historical archive, the objects are pulled from cultural memory, a realm in which they are meant to be shared and to participate in the memories of others.

That the majority of objects are left anonymously testifies to the memorial's power as a site of cultural remembrance. Initially, many of the items left at the memorial indicated a certain spontaneity: letters scribbled on hotel stationery, for instance. Now more letters are computer printed, and some are personally addressed to Duery Felton, Jr., curator of the collection. It would seem that people now leave things at the memorial precisely because they know that they will be preserved and thus attain the status of historical artifacts. This cataloguing affects the capacity of visitors at the memorial to experience the artifacts. Many of them are placed in plastic bags by volunteers, which makes people reluctant to touch them, and they are all removed at the end of the day they are left.

The memorial has become not only the primary site of remembrance for the Vietnam War but also a site where people pay homage to current conflicts and charged public events. Artifacts concerning the abortion debate, the AIDS epidemic, gay rights, and the Persian Gulf War have been left at the memorial. Hence, the memorial's collection inscribes a history not only of the American participation in the Vietnam War but also of national issues and events since the war. It is testimony to the memorial's malleability as an icon that both prowar and antiwar artifacts were left there during the Persian Gulf War.

The ritual of leaving something behind can be seen as an active participation in the accrual of many histories; the archiving of these artifacts also subsumes these artifacts within history. Michel Foucault has written:

The archive is first the law of what can be said, the system that governs the appearance of statements as unique events. But the archive is also that which determines that all these things said do not accumulate endlessly in an amorphous mass . . . they are grouped together in distinct figures, composed together in accordance of specific regularities . . . it is that which . . . defines at the outset *the system of enunciability.* [84]

The traditional archive serves a narrative function, prescribing the limits of history and defining what will and will not be preserved. The archive determines what will speak for history. However, the archive of the Vietnam Veterans Memorial is less restrictive than many archives. It contains all artifacts left at the memorial that have been personalized in some way (flowers are not saved, and flags are only saved if they have writing on them).[85] Objects are collected daily and marked with the date and location. The criteria of inclusion in the archive are thus decided by the public, whose leaving of artifacts increasingly reflects a conscious participation in history-making.

Because the collection of artifacts has received significant attention, including a book, *Offerings at the Wall,* Felton has been concerned with increasing public access to it. In 1992 an exhibition of artifacts opened at the Smithsonian Museum of American History. Though it was only intended to remain on display for six months, the public response was so huge that the show has been extended indefinitely. Since that time several other exhibits have been held throughout the country, and the collection is being photographed and assembled on CD-ROM. However, public exhibition and publication of the artifacts raise issues of copyright and ownership. To whom do the artifacts actually belong? Felton has created standards to protect the privacy of the living (he will not exhibit objects that display the name and address of a living person). He also feels issues of religious belief must be observed. For this reason, he invited several Native American shamans to conduct a blessing ceremony at the archive before the artifacts were placed on exhibit.[86]

One of the most compelling features of the Vietnam Veterans Memorial collection is its anonymity, mystery, and ambiguity. Felton, himself a combat veteran, has established a network of veterans throughout the country who help him to identify obscure insignia and the meanings of some objects. Through this network, a very specific history is being compiled, one informed by the particular codes of the participants of the war. According to Felton, those who have left artifacts range from those who want to tell only him the story behind it, to those who don't want to talk about it all, to those who seek press attention. However, it appears that the stories behind a substantial number of artifacts may never be known and that the telling of these stories to history was never the purpose of their being placed at the memorial. Though couched within an official history and held by a government institution, these letters and offerings to the dead will continue to assert individual narratives, strands of cultural memory, that disrupt historical narratives. They resist history precisely through their obscurity, their refusal to yield specific meanings.

The Construction of a History

The politics of memory of the Vietnam Veterans Memorial shifts continuously in a tension of ownership and narrative complexity. Who is actually being allowed to speak for the experience of the war? Has the Vietnam Veterans Memorial facilitated the emergence of the voices of veterans and their families and friends in opposition to the voices of the media and the government? Healing can be an individual process or a national or cultural process; the politics of each is quite different.

The walls of the Vietnam Veterans Memorial act as a screen for many projections about the history of the Vietnam War and its aftermath. Beyond its foregrounding of individual names and the condemnation of war implicit in that listing, the memorial does not endorse any of the contested versions of the Vietnam War. It has nevertheless catalyzed a rewriting of the history of that war, primarily because its emphasis on the veterans and war dead has allowed the themes of heroism, sacrifice, and honor to resurface.

Although this closure of the veterans' period of estrangement seems not only just but also long overdue, its implications can become insidious when transferred into mainstream discourse about the memorial. When, for instance, *Newsweek* printed a story in 1982 entitled, "Honoring Vietnam Veterans—At Last," the desire not only to rectify but also to forget the mistreatment of the veterans was obvious. Much of the current embrace of the memorial amounts to historical revisionism. The period between the end of the war and the positioning of the memorial as a national wailing wall has been more than long enough for memories and culpability to fade. Ironically, the memorial allows for an erasure of many of the specifics of history. It is rarely noted that the discussion surrounding the memorial never mentions the Vietnamese people. This is not a memorial to their loss; they cannot even be mentioned in the context of the Mall. Nor does the memorial itself allow for their mention; though it allows for an outpouring of grief, it does not speak to the intricate reasons why the lives represented by the inscribed names were lost in vain.

Thus, remembering is in itself a form of forgetting. Does the remembrance of the battles fought by the veterans in Vietnam and at home necessarily screen out any acknowledgment of the war's effect on the Vietnamese? In its listing of U.S. war dead, and in the context of the Mall, the memorial establishes Americans, rather than Vietnamese, as the primary victims of the war. For instance, questions about the 1,300 American MIAs are raised at the memorial, yet in that space no mention can be made of the 300,000 Vietnamese MIAs. Does the process of commemoration necessitate choosing sides?[87]

Artist Chris Burden created a sculpture in 1991, *The Other Vietnam Memorial,* in reaction to the memorial's nonacknowledgment of the Vietnamese. Burden's piece consists of large copper leaves, twelve by eight feet, arranged as a kind of circular standing book, on which are engraved 3 million Vietnamese names to commemorate the 3 million Vietnamese who died in the war. He says: "Even though I feel sorry for the individuals named on [the Vietnam Veterans Memorial], I was repulsed by the idea. I couldn't help but think that we were celebrating our dead, who were aggressors, basically, and wonder where were the Vietnamese names?"[88] Burden's listing is not unproblematic; he was unable to get an actual listing of the dead, so he took 4,000 names and repeated them over and over again. Despite its awkward generic naming, however, Burden's sculpture exposes a fundamental limit of commemoration within nationalism. Why must a national memorial reenact conflict by showing only one side of the conflict? What is the memory produced by a national memorial?

The memorial's placement on the Washington Mall inscribes it within a nationalist discourse, restricting the discourse of memory it can provide. Its presence indicates both the limitations and the complexity of that nationalist discourse. Lauren Berlant writes:

When Americans make the pilgrimage to Washington they are trying to grasp the nation in its totality. Yet the totality of the nation in its capital city is a jumble of historical modalities, a transitional space between local and national cultures, private and public property, archaic and living artifacts. . . . It is a place of national *mediation,* where a variety of nationally inflected media come into visible and sometimes incommensurate contact.[89]

The memorial asserts itself into this "jumble of historical modalities," both a resistant and compliant artifact. It serves not as a singular statement but as a site of mediation, a site of conflicting voices and opposing agendas. This multiplicity of meanings renders the memorial central to Berlant's definition of the complexity of public space in Washington.

However, commemoration is ultimately a process of legitimation and the memorial lies at the center of a struggle between narratives. It has spawned two very different kinds of remembrance: one a retrenched historical narrative that attempts to rewrite the Vietnam War in a way that reinscribes U.S. imperialism and the masculinity of the American soldier, the other a textured and complex remembrance that allows the Americans affected by this war—the veterans, their families, and the families and friends of the war dead—to speak of loss, pain, and futility.[90] The memorial thus stands in a precarious space between these opposing interpretations of the war.

Chapter Three

Reenactment and the Making of History

The Vietnam War as Docudrama

History and cultural memory converge in very particular ways in the form of the docudrama. As a melding of historical fact and dramatic form, the docudrama is in essence a mimetic interpretation of the past. In the cultural reenactment of the original drama, coherence and narrative structure emerge, and fragments of memory are made whole.

The cinematic docudrama exerts significant influence in the construction of national meaning in the United States. For much of the American public, docudramas are a primary source of historical information. They afford a means through which uncomfortable histories of traumatic events can be smoothed over, retold, and ascribed new meanings. Like a memorial, the docudrama offers closure, a process that can subsume cultural memory and personal memory into history.

The history of the Vietnam War is being written from multiple perspectives and in multiple media. Historians have examined issues raised by the war, the artifacts it produced, and the memories of the Vietnam veterans from a variety of viewpoints. In addition, the history of the war is packaged in television documentaries, anniversary specials, and even CD-ROMs. Within this complex array of histories, I would like to examine the role of movie docudramas precisely because of their capacity to create popular interpretations of the war. Although they are necessarily less complete and less accurate than historical texts, they have greater cultural significance because they reach mass audiences and younger people who may have little prior knowledge of the war.

Whereas documentary photographic and film images of the Vietnam War carry particular national meanings, contemporary Hollywood films play a primary role in telling the story of the war. These popular films have come to represent the "authentic" story of the war. They have eclipsed the documentary images of the war; indeed, many deliberately reenact iconic documentary images. In these films the politics of gender and race surrounding the war are represented and rescripted; the myths about the war are established, questioned, and replaced with new myths; and the primary representation of the Vietnam veteran is constructed. Veteran William Adams writes:

When *Platoon* was first released, a number of people asked me, "Was the war really like that?" I never found an answer, in part because, no matter how graphic and realistic, a movie is after all a movie, and war is only like itself. But I also failed to find an answer because what "really" happened is now so thoroughly mixed up in my mind with what has been said about what happened that the pure experience is no longer there. This is odd, even painful, in some ways. But it is also testimony to the way our memories work. The Vietnam War is no longer a definite event so much as it is a collective and mobile script in which we continue to scrawl, erase, rewrite our conflicting and changing view of ourselves.[1]

The narratives of popular films weave themselves into the experiences and memories of those who took part in the war and those who remember viewing news coverage of it. They become part of cultural memory. At the Vietnam Veterans Memorial, for instance, people often crowd around to take rubbings of one particular name—Arthur John Rambo.[2] The fiction of the Rambo films is thus inseparable from the memory expressed at the memorial. For the generations born since the war, these films provide an "experience" of what it was like. Hence, claims to the authenticity and realism of these films reflect a desire to construct through them a particular set of historical narratives: the brutal experience of the Americans in Vietnam, the futility of the war, the victimization of the "grunt" soldiers, and the Vietnam veteran as a figure of wisdom and truth.

The question of representability has haunted depictions of the

Vietnam War in popular culture. As a war of highly contested narratives, it has often been analyzed as unrepresentable, the veterans' experience as incommunicable. This concept borrows from the legacy of the Holocaust, which has often been termed unrepresentable, and dominates all representations of the war. Miriam Cooke writes, "Vietnam resolutely refuses representation, yet this refusal is insistently represented."[3] Hence, critical discussions of the war have tended to reiterate the idea of its unrepresentability even as they interpret its endless representation.[4]

This quality of unrepresentable representation also accounts for the immense popularity of Michael Herr's *Dispatches*, the most critically lauded book about the war. It is written in a fragmented, fast-talking, cinematic style, filled with images edited together in a rapid-paced and sharp-witted montage. In 1978 Herr wrote: "In any other war, they would have made movies about us too, *Dateline: Hell!*, *Dispatch From Dong Ha*. . . . But Vietnam is awkward, everyone knows how awkward, and if people don't even want to hear about it, you know they're not going to pay money to sit there in the dark and have it brought up. . . . So we have all been compelled to make our own movies, as many movies as there are correspondents, and this one is mine."[5] Herr not only positions himself as a filmmaker (he was later to co-author the scripts for Francis Ford Coppola's film *Apocalypse Now* [1979] and Stanley Kubrick's *Full Metal Jacket* [1987]) but throughout his book places himself in the role of the ground soldier. The mythic status of his book can be attributed to its depiction of the incommunicability of the experience of the war.

What is unrepresentable about the American experience in the Vietnam War? Clearly, docudramas of World War II presented only the thinnest representations of actual combat, and the same limits of cinematic representation apply equally to the subject of Vietnam. But does the essential problem of representability lie in the combat experience itself or rather in the Vietnam War's resistance to standard narratives of technology, masculinity, and U.S. nationalism? It could be argued that what *was* representable was the conflict, the tension, the chaos, but that within the context of the American entertainment industry these images were simply too unpalatable, too shocking, too disruptive.

David James has divided the mainstream films made about the Vietnam War into four groups:[6] films that were made during the war and up until the late 1970s, of which there are very few and of which the most famous is *The Green Berets* (John Wayne and Ray Kellogg, 1968); films from the late 1970s, including *Coming Home* (Hal Ashby, 1978), *Who'll Stop the Rain* (Karel Reisz, 1978), *Go Tell the Spartans* (Ted Post, 1978), *The Boys in Company C* (Sidney Furie, 1978), *The Deer Hunter* (Michael Cimino, 1978), and *Apocalypse Now* (Francis Ford Coppola, 1979), which could be called the first wave of Vietnam films; films made in the early 1980s (the era of revisionist history launched by the Reagan administration) that depict MIAs as icons of the veterans' victimization and feature vengeful veterans refighting the war, including *First Blood* (Ted Kotcheff, 1982), *Uncommon Valor* (Ted Kotcheff, 1983), *Missing in Action* (Joseph Zito, 1984), *Missing in Action 2—The Beginning* (Lance Hool, 1985), *Rambo: First Blood, Part II* (George Cosmatos, 1985), and *Rambo III* (Peter MacDonald, 1988); and the fourth phase, films made in the late 1980s and 1990s and concerned primarily with questions of realism, including *Platoon* (Oliver Stone, 1986), *Full Metal Jacket* (Stanley Kubrick, 1987), *Hamburger Hill* (John Irvin, 1987), *Casualties of War* (Brian DePalma, 1989), *84 Charlie MoPic* (Patrick Duncan, 1989), *Born on the Fourth of July* (Oliver Stone, 1989), and *Heaven and Earth* (Oliver Stone, 1993). This final group of films represents the work of several Vietnam veterans and major directors; it has often been characterized as representing America's finally coming to terms with the war.[7]

As narrative films depicting a highly charged event in U.S. history, Vietnam War docudramas often have two conflicting intentions—to represent the war realistically and to examine its larger meanings through metaphoric interpretation. The films in the late 1970s subordinated codes of realism in order to depict the war metaphorically and find its larger meaning. Michael Cimino's *The Deer Hunter* hinged on several blatant inaccuracies, the most famous of which involved American POWs being held in water cages and forced to play Russian roulette. Francis Coppola's *Apocalypse Now* depicted a marine surfing at a nearby beach during a napalm attack, a scene that reflected the film's mixed intentions: to provide an image of the "real" war (many of its scenes came from the recollections of scriptwriter

John Milius's veteran friends) and, as an interpretation of Joseph Conrad's *Heart of Darkness*, to tell a larger story about the limitations of men in war. The MIA revenge films that followed were more blatant rewritings of history, with Americans refighting the war and rescuing the MIAs, thereby redeeming the forgotten veterans. The most recent Vietnam War films were in many ways a reaction against the inaccuracy of the earlier films. Produced after the construction of the Vietnam Veterans Memorial, they constitute part of the rewriting of the war's narrative generated by the memorial and the accompanying process of healing and memory. These films are also more self-conscious about their role as historical works.

In this chapter I will examine the relationship between the documentary image and its reenactment, from the iconic image documents of the war to narrative films that address the war through codes of realism. These films are sites of cultural reenactment both in their production and their exhibition. Their retelling of the war smooths over the ruptures of history, simplifying its narrative and providing a site for healing and redemption. As elements of mass culture, they operate in tension with cultural memory. These films can subsume personal and cultural memory, but they also work to rescript it as, in William Adams's words, a "collective and mobile script in which we continue to scrawl, erase, rewrite our conflicting and changing view of ourselves." Like the Vietnam Veterans Memorial, these films tell the story of the Vietnam veteran's struggle for closure.

Image Documents of History

The many images generated by the Vietnam War made possible a collective witnessing of the war by Americans. The Vietnam War has been unanimously described as a "television war," fought not only among sentient bodies in Southeast Asia but also in images and body counts before Congress and the American public. The impact of the image war is still debated, in particular whether television and newspaper coverage sensitized the public to the war's horrors or simply reduced the carnage to a series of banal moments in the everyday flow of current events.

However, the popular interpretation of the documentary images of the Vietnam War is quite clear: they are regarded as essential to the American public's eventual turning against the war. In retrospect, they blur together into clumps of iconic images. Today, when a television news program wants to recap the Vietnam War in a few minutes, it invariably resorts to a now familiar catalogue of images: the view from above as American bombs fall endlessly on forested landscapes, the pleading faces of Vietnamese villagers, American soldiers laden with equipment walking through burned-out villages, GIs running away from the rotating blades of a helicopter. The recording of these documentary images on film rather than videotape is crucial to how they have achieved historical status. They have the sharp-edged, gritty quality of film images; as they have aged, their grainy black-and-white and faded color have enhanced their historicity.

However, the most iconic image documents that have emerged from the Vietnam War are not television film images but black-and-white photographs: the 1972 photograph by Huynh Cong (Nick) Ut of a young girl, Kim Phuc, naked and running down a road toward the camera and away from a napalm explosion, her body burned and her face astonished, filled with pain and disbelief (Figure 10); the 1968 photograph by Eddie Adams of Brig. Gen. Nguyen Ngoc Loan, chief of the South Vietnamese National Police, shooting a Vietcong suspect in the head at point-blank range (Figure 11); and the 1968 images by Ronald Haeberle of the My Lai massacre victims, huddled together in fear moments before being shot, and lying dead in a pile on a country road (Figure 12).[8]

Both the Adams and Ut photographs also exist as film images, yet they are much more famous and widely seen as photographic images, for several reasons. The film image of the Vietcong suspect being shot and falling to the ground with blood flowing from his head is extremely difficult to watch; moreover, the still image derives much of its power from the suspect's expression of terror at the instant he is shot. The film image of the napalm strike is more confusing than the still and does not capture the expression on the face of Kim Phuc as clearly. Most significant, photographic images in general have a greater capacity than moving images to achieve iconic status. Still images are widely distributed in books and other publications, so people are more likely to own copies of them; moreover, they possess an ability to connote completeness and to evoke the past.

Figure 10. Accidental napalm strike on Trang Bang Village, 1972. Photo by Huynh
Cong (Nick) Ut. AP/Wide World Photos.

Figure 11. General Nguyen Ngoc Loan shooting Vietcong suspect, 1968. Photo by
Eddie Adams. AP/Wide World Photos.

Figure 12. My Lai, 1968. Photo by Ronald Haeberle, *Life* magazine.
© Time, Inc.

The Vietnam War generated innumerable photographic images, including the personal snapshots taken by American soldiers, many of which have appeared at the Vietnam Veterans Memorial. Douglas Kahn writes, "There are shoe boxes stuck in attics and closets all across America right now filled with what really went on in Vietnam." Kahn argues that the images of the most painful memories of the Vietnam War are not public images:

There was one vet, in fact, who was in a psychiatric hospital, although he had never been to Vietnam itself; he had been a photo and film archivist at the Department of Defense. He once told another vet, "You may have participated in this or that atrocity, but I saw them all. And it drove me crazy." I grew up in a military town where, during high school in the late 1960s, I saw numerous snapshots of necromutilations, of Vietcong beheaded with their cocks coming out of their mouths, brought back by older brothers of students. These were secretly passed from one person to the next in the same manner as pornographic playing cards and other taboo photos.[9]

Each of these countless images, public and private, is a kind of talisman. Why, then, do the photographs of Kim Phuc, General Loan, and the My Lai massacre possess the capacity to conjure the entire war? It is not incidental that they are all images of sheer brutality that involve depictions of the Vietnamese as victims. The expression of disbelief on Kim Phuc's face is emblematic of Americans' disbelief at "what we did." Because Phuc is a young, innocent victim burned by American napalm (the image documents an accidental strike on Trang Bang village in 1972), the image is a serious indictment of the United States's methods of conducting war. As a young, female, naked figure, Kim Phuc represents the victimized, feminized country of Vietnam.

Adams's picture of the shooting of the Vietcong suspect became famous for its depiction of the indiscriminate brutality of the war; it subsequently was credited with having changed the course of history. Much of the image's initial power lay in its emergence at the height of the Tet offensive in 1968, a time when both the war and the antiwar movement escalated. In fact, an earlier photograph of a similar killing had been rejected by the press.[10] The man killed by Loan had been captured by South Vietnamese troops and marched down the street toward the general, who waved away the soldiers and shot him before the press.[11] Hence, as initially interpreted this photograph depicted a man shot without trial when mounting activity made the war's futility increasingly apparent. Today, however, it is a simpler image, an image of Vietnamese killing Vietnamese. Its simplicity is crucial—the war depicted in this photograph is man against man, not the complex war of bombs, defoliation, and unseen enemies. Its iconic power further derives from its demonstration of the camera's ability to capture the moment of death.

The photographs of the My Lai massacre are iconic because they depict terror and American atrocities in intimate detail. Haeberle's account of this incident is well known for its apparent detachment: "Guys were about to shoot these people. I yelled 'Hold it' and I shot my pictures. M16s opened up and from the corner of my eye I saw bodies falling but I did not turn to look."[12] His photographs were only released a year and a half later when the killings came to light. Like both the Ut and Adams photographs, the My Lai images acquired iconic status by shocking the American public and creating widespread disillusionment over the U.S. role in the war.

Although the history of the Vietnam War is often told in brief film clips, these still photographs retain the capacity to symbolize the war in its entirety—the Vietnamese as victims of American force, the brutality and arbitrariness of the war's violence. As still images they arrest the past, yet their meaning continues to shift. For instance, Dutch filmmaker Manus van de Kemp tracked down Kim Phuc twenty years after her photograph was taken and updated her wartime image with her present image.[13] Like the assignment of authorship to the artifacts at the Vietnam Veterans Memorial, the desire to name and realize the "real" Kim Phuc reveals a shift in the image from a national symbol to a personal story of survival. Kim Phuc's image has currency in American cultural memory, reemerging often as an icon in art about the war.[14]

These image icons of the Vietnam War are emblems of rupture, unyielding in their stillness, demanding narration. They offer not closure but a sense of the war's horror. Rather, closure is offered in the form of Hollywood narratives and docudramas. These films constitute the dominant representation of the U.S. experience of the war. Despite their role as fictional narratives, these films rescript the war and subsume documentary images. Indeed, many deliberately restage documentary images, blurring the boundaries between the reenactment and the original event.

The Cinema of War, the War of Cinema

The first narrative films to influence the representation of the Vietnam War were the Hollywood films of World War II, films that tell a powerful narrative of patriotism, good versus evil, and masculine prowess. These films essentially determined how the generation of soldiers who fought in the Vietnam War imagined warfare. A dominant theme in Vietnam War films and literature is how soldiers and correspondents went off to Vietnam with images of World War II movies in their heads. In a famous passage from *Dispatches*, whose cinematic style can be said to have influenced a generation of films about the war, Michael Herr writes:

I keep thinking about all the kids who got wiped out by seventeen years of war movies before coming to Vietnam to get wiped out for good. You don't know what a media freak is until you've seen the way a few of these grunts would run around during a fight when they knew that there was a television crew nearby; they were actually making war movies in their heads, doing little guts-and-glory Leatherneck tap dances under fire, getting their pimples shot off for the networks. They were insane, but the war hadn't done that to them. Most combat troops stopped thinking of the war as an adventure after their first few firefights, but there were always the ones who couldn't let that go, these few who were up there doing numbers for the camera. . . . The first few times that I got fired at or saw combat deaths, nothing really happened, all the responses got locked in my head. It was the same familiar violence, only moved over to another medium; some kind of jungle play with giant helicopters and fantastic special effects, actors lying out there in canvas body bags waiting for the scene to end so they could get up and walk it off. But that was some scene (you found out), there was no cutting it.[15]

This is merely the best known of innumerable depictions of Americans in Vietnam who were haunted by their images of World War II. This contrast between Vietnam and Hollywood war movies is represented not simply as difficult for American soldiers to negotiate but as hurting their chances for survival. Veterans reiterate this theme constantly:

—I'll never forget Audie Murphy in *To Hell and Back.* At the end he jumps on top of a flaming tank that's just about to explode and grabs the machine gun blasting it into the German lines. He was so brave I had chills running down my back, wishing it were me up there. There were gasoline flames roaring around his legs, but he just kept firing that machine gun. It was the greatest war movie I ever saw in my life.[16]

—I lost my footing and slipped into a ditch, went under the water and came up and out, screaming, "This ain't a war movie! This ain't a John Wayne movie!" I started to laugh, and all the guys in the column started laughing, too, because they also got it. Vietnam wasn't a war movie. It took me six months in Vietnam to wake up and turn all the World War II movies off in my mind. They could no longer help me deflect reality, black out the pain and anger or justify me as the good American who had come to rescue the Vietnamese by killing Vietnamese. Why? Because they were really propaganda films.[17]

—I hate this movie.[18]

—Honest, it was such a swell war, they should have made it into a movie.[19]

The anger in these passages is an anger not only at the war myths of the previous generation—the lies of fathers, so to speak—but also at the very form of representation. A veteran who places a bumper sticker on his car that reads, "Vietnam Was a War Not a Movie," is also reacting to the popular sentiment that viewing a Vietnam War movie can provide a legitimate experience of the war.

Popular films not only significantly shape historical narratives but also provide a catharsis for viewers and, ultimately, for the nation. Reenactment is a form of reexperiencing; within the codes of realism, viewers are allowed to feel that they, too, have undergone the trauma of the war by experiencing its cinematic representation. Categories of experience become confused; the directors and actors of these films claim to have experienced the war on the battleground of film-making. Veteran Henry Allen writes:

Then the movies started coming out, such as "Apocalypse Now," "Coming Home," and "The Deer Hunter." People said I should go see them. They wanted to know what I thought. I'd tell them. "But it's such a good movie," they'd say. "How isn't it like Vietnam?" I'd try to explain that it was just a movie, it was colored light moving around on a screen. It wasn't that these folks couldn't tell the difference between a war and a movie; they didn't want to. . . . In their way, I think, they wanted to be veterans, too.[20]

In their entanglement of cultural memory and history, Vietnam War films produce a catharsis for veterans, filmmakers, and the American public; yet the politics and status of that catharsis differ for each. Debates about these films reveal the widespread desire to acquire aspects of "veteranness"—the catharsis of survival, the right to be angry, and what many perceive to be the wisdom gained from difficult experience.

The positioning of viewership as a kind of veteranness results directly from the particular codes of realism applied in Vietnam War films. In the last wave of these films, the stakes of establishing realism and authenticity are high, especially when the filmmaker himself is a veteran. For instance, when it was first released, Oliver Stone's *Platoon* was lauded as "the first real Vietnam film." More than any previous work in this genre, *Platoon* was praised for its ability to make spectators feel they were there, in the jungle, waiting for the ambush, feeling, seeing, smelling combat:

—It is more than a movie; it's like being in Vietnam. *Platoon* makes you feel you've been there and never want to go back.[21]

—More than any other film, *Platoon* gives the sense—all five senses—of fighting in Viet Nam. You can wilt from the claustrophobic heat of this Rosseauvian jungle; feel the sting of the leeches as they snack on Chris' flesh; hear all at once the chorus of insects, an enemy's approaching footsteps on the green carpet and Chris' heartbeat on night patrol.[22]

—Indeed, the film's greatest strength lies in its social realism—its feeling of verisimilitude for the discomfort, ants, heat, and mud—of the jungle and the brush: the fatigue of patrols, the boredom and sense of release of base camp, the terror of ambushes, and the chaos and cacophony of night firefights.[23]

—The other Hollywood Viet Nam films have been a rape of history. But *Platoon* is historically and politically accurate. It understands something that the architects of the war never did: how the foliage, the thickness of the jungle, negated U.S. technological superiority. You can see how the forest sucks in American soldiers; they just disappear. I think the film will become a classic. Thirty years from now, people will think of the Viet Nam War as *Platoon*.[24]

Stone promoted the film's heavily autobiographical nature, and *Platoon*'s marketing campaign highlighted these connections, featuring posters with a wartime photograph of Stone and other GIs. These claims to authenticity were also fueled by the way in which the film was produced. Not only had Stone spent years "at war" with Hollywood trying to get the script produced, but he also hired a former Marine captain, Dale Dye, to put the actors through an intensive training session in the Philippine jungle where the film was shot, forcing them to haul sixty-pound packs and eat C-rations. The actors reacted as if this exercise made them veterans; said Tom Berenger, "We didn't even have to act. We were there."[25] Hollywood heartily embraced the film, congratulating itself on its newfound interest in depicting the war from the perspective of its participants.

Several American filmmakers have suggested that their struggle to produce a Vietnam War film was somehow akin to the actual

war. Coppola's *Apocalypse Now*, for instance, became notorious well
before its release because of its huge budget and the director's
long battles with his investors, the Philippine jungle, and the weather
(newspaper headlines about the production quipped, "Apocalypse
When?" and "Apocalypse Forever"). Coppola stated at the Cannes
Film Festival in 1979: "My film is not a movie. My film is not about
Vietnam. It *is* Vietnam. It's what it was really like. It was crazy. And
the way we made it was very much like the way Americans were in
Vietnam. We were in the jungle, there were too many of us, we had
access to too much money, too much equipment, and little by little
we went insane." [26] Clearly, this statement equates the experience
of producing a film about the war with the experience of the war itself. Initially, Coppola and directors George Lucas and John Milius
wanted to shoot the film in 1969 in Vietnam—to produce the war's
simulacrum in the middle of the war—but no studio was interested.

In *Hearts of Darkness: A Filmmaker's Apocalypse*, the documentary film about the making of *Apocalypse Now*, Coppola struggles
with mounting problems and a desperate feeling that his film is a
"$20 million mistake." The Philippine government, which owns the
helicopters Coppola is using, often commandeers them at crucial moments in the filming for use in a real-life campaign against rebels in
the nearby hills. Martin Sheen, who plays the lead role of Captain
Willard—the assassin sent upriver to "terminate" an American captain who has apparently gone insane—has a heart attack during the
filming, and monsoons delay filming for months. Hence, the jungle
hinders the technology of cinema, just as it neutralized U.S. military
technology in the war. In declaring himself a virtual veteran ("My
film is not a movie. It *is* Vietnam."), Coppola proclaims his own (and
his cast's and crew's) cathartic transformation through the experience
of war and equates the Philippine jungle with Vietnam. Films such
as Brian DePalma's *Casualties of War* and Stone's *Platoon* reiterated
this theme of the replication of the war in the filmmaking process,
with the directors doing battle with "exotic" landscapes—the Philip-
pines, Thailand, Mexico—which are viewed as interchangeable with
Vietnam.

What does it mean to say, as David Halberstam does, that "people
will think of *Platoon* as Vietnam," or, as Spielberg says, that "it's more

than a movie; it's like being in Vietnam"? Perhaps more important, why does the spectator *want* the experience of being in Vietnam, and what notion of experience is in operation here? The statement, "We didn't have to act; we were there," implies that artifice has been overcome, that reenactment is documentary, and that reenactment has cultural authority. This is a notion of experience as the primary basis of truth. Joan Scott writes: "When evidence offered is the evidence of 'experience,' the claim for referentiality is further buttressed— what could be truer, after all, than a subject's own account of what he or she has lived through?"[27] The viewer of the Vietnam War film thus lays claim to having had an authentic experience of the war. Lurking behind this characterization is a nostalgia for the war. Just as the Vietnam Veterans Memorial prompted a complex nostalgia for the intense experiences of the war while providing a space to mourn its loss, a Hollywood docudrama such as *Platoon,* despite its implicit critique of the war's futility and cruelty, is seen to depict through its spectacle the "real" experience of war, through which one acquires the truth.

That *Platoon* could provide this "experience" was contingent on its following certain codes of cinematic realism—portraying the details of a patrol, the boredom, the confusion of combat, the presence of the jungle. Heightened "naturalized" sound of the jungle at night, rapidly edited combat scenes, and on-location shooting gave it at moments the feel of a documentary. Yet it is also a highly stylized film with dramatically staged scenes and a prominent soundtrack of classical music.

In self-consciously presenting itself as a historical document, *Platoon* establishes its ideology as naturalized. The film tells the story of a platoon through the eyes of a young arrival, Chris Taylor (played by Charlie Sheen), who is Stone's stand-in, and his experiences of night patrols, search-and-destroy missions, and escalated battles. The film follows the indoctrination of Taylor from an opening shot in which he and other "cherries," or new arrivals, are born, in effect, from a cargo plane (even as it is refilled with body bags) through his transformation into a cynical, wiser soldier. Taylor arrives looking fresh-faced and eager and exchanges glances with a hardened and beaten soldier, his future self. Like Stone, he is a middle-class enlistee, in Vietnam because he wants to be "anonymous," and learns quickly that the only goal is to survive a one-year stint. In his platoon there is a rivalry between two sergeants, both of whom are "lifers"—Barnes (played by Tom Berenger), the hardened and calculating fighting machine, the soldier who won't die, without morals or scruples, a man honed by the insanity of war (it is evidence of the overdetermined style of the film that Barnes has a deep, disfiguring scar on his cheek); and Elias (played by Willem Dafoe), compassionate and idealistic, who is losing his faith in the war yet retains a moral standard about what kinds of behavior are unacceptable even in combat, a guerrilla fighter who is daring and skilled, a natural warrior. Predictably, Taylor is taken under Elias's wing, and reveres him. When Barnes and some of the men brutally kill several villagers in a scene obviously intended to evoke both the My Lai massacre and the Adams photograph of Loan's killing of the Vietcong suspect, Elias arrives in time to stop his rival from murdering a young girl. In *Platoon,* Chris Taylor is the witness to this struggle of good and evil, the person through whom it is enacted, and the Vietnamese are the bodies on which this conflict takes place.

Platoon is a morality tale in which the battles between good and evil in the platoon are presented as a microcosm of the Vietnam War, the American male psyche, and the collective psyche of the country. Ironically, in his desire to make a film that can be emblematic of the Vietnam War, Oliver Stone dehistoricizes it so that it becomes all wars. The film's story of a young man's loss of innocence, rite of passage, and transformation through combat into a seasoned and more knowing veteran is a hackneyed narrative that transcends this war. In its focus on the American soldier as the ideological center of the war, *Platoon* effaces many aspects of the war, including the ideological apparatus that brought this country to Southeast Asia.

Whereas *Platoon* ascribes to conventions of Hollywood cinema, Patrick Duncan's *84 Charlie MoPic* is an independently produced film that applies a more rigorous and literal agenda of realism in its pseudodocumentary style. Duncan, who is also a veteran, chose to avoid the device of a central protagonist by foregrounding the camera's role in defining the war. The entire film is told from the viewpoint of a cameraman who has been sent with a "green" lieutenant to document a squad on patrol in order to help instruct GIs about tactics in the bush. Duncan foregrounds the role of the camera image in perceptions of the war—to remind us that the war was mediated through, influenced by, and is now remembered through photographic and film images. With no well-known actors or rock-and-roll soundtrack, the film uses stark codes of cinematic realism: black-and-white images shot on 16mm film, ambient sound, slow pacing, and handheld camera. Duncan has stated, "I didn't need Michael Herr. I respect him, but his is once more the point of view of an educated observer, someone who can put himself outside the conflict to understand it. I was in it, I felt it from the inside, and I express it from within. . . . I think a lot of people prefer Herr's approach because it gives you enough distance not to feel the horrible disaster of dying at the hands of an unseen enemy. Nobody knows *how* they die, much less why."[28] By choosing not to attempt to tell *the* story of the war, Duncan's film avoids the morality tale of *Platoon*. Yet, the style of *84 Charlie MoPic* does ascribe to another agenda of realism, the belief that the documentary camera can show us something as if we are really there.

The Grunt War: Innocents in the Jungle

In most Vietnam War representations, the "real" war is portrayed as the war of the ground soldier, the "grunt." Most Vietnam War films center on an innocent protagonist who, either by circumstance or through misguided naiveté, is drawn into the war and irrevocably altered by it. In *Platoon*, this role is fulfilled by Taylor. The ads for *Platoon* stated, "The first casualty of war is innocence," and it is clear that the innocence lost is that of Taylor and other Americans. In *Born on the Fourth of July* Ron Kovic (played by Tom Cruise), is raised on Long Island in an ideological context of Catholic anticommunism; in *Casualties of War* Eriksson (played by Michael J. Fox) refuses to participate in a rape; and in *Full Metal Jacket* Joker (played by Matthew Modine) is given an assignment as a military reporter that allows him to play the observer. These characters all enter the war naively. Their transformations are offered as a means for viewers to mourn and feel redemption for the war, to experience vicariously the loss and pain of the war in order to exorcise its troubling memory. The public can feel that, like these protagonists, America was innocent in the beginning; we did not know what we were getting into; we had good intentions.

Pat Aufderheide refers to these films as "noble grunt" films that depict the "real" war as the war of the ground soldier and ignore the high-tech air war. The grunts, who have no control over the policies or the military tactics of the war, are established in these films as its primary victims. Aufderheide writes: "Vietnam, in these movies, becomes a Calvary of the powerless—not just for the grunts, but also for the viewers. The American moviegoer—a citizen-consumer who, like the soldier in Vietnam, is far from decision-making yet still accountable for its consequences—can find much to empathize with here. The moviegoer, too, is plagued with a nagging sense of guilt and suffused with a dull anger for carrying that burden."[29] This transference of the anger of the veteran to the American public often took the form of scapegoating that veteran for the bitter memories he or she represented.

Yet the grunt in these films is posed as a figure of the "real" American, the spirit of American men that was destroyed in the war. Taylor's thoughts are presented in *Platoon* as letters to his grandmother. He writes:

Well here I am—anonymous all right, with guys nobody really cares about—they come from the end of the line, most of 'em, small towns you never heard of—Pulaski, Tennessee, Brandon, Mississippi, Pork Bend, Utah, Wampum, Pennsylvania. Two years' high school's about it, maybe if they're lucky a job waiting for 'em back in a factory, but most of 'em got nothing, they're poor, they're the unwanted of our society, yet they're fighting for our society and our freedom and what we call America, they're the bottom of the barrel—and they know it, maybe that's why they call themselves 'grunts' cause a 'grunt' can take it, can take anything. They're the backbone of this country, grandma, the best I've ever seen, the heart and soul—I've found it finally, way down here in the mud.

Here the grunts are situated not only as hard-working icons of American freedom but as the means by which middle- and upper-class individuals can find their true selves. The working class, which, without the privilege of graduate school deferments, bore the brunt of the war, is thus portrayed as more genuinely American, both in its initial naiveté and its disillusionment and betrayal.

The theme of the noble grunt is relentlessly hammered home in *Born on the Fourth of July*. Ron Kovic is shown growing up in suburban Long Island, watching a hazily shot, soft-focus Fourth of July parade. Stone establishes him as the icon of American youth: "Ain't he a Fourth of July firecracker in that hat," says his father; "He's my Yankee Doodle Dandy," his mother says. The young Kovic watches wounded World War II veterans walk past and wince at the sound of firecrackers, establishing the theme of the men that wars destroy. Like Taylor in *Platoon,* Kovic exchanges glances with a man who represents his future self. In his autobiography and Stone's film rendition of it, Kovic situates himself as an icon of betrayal, a young man who believed and who was wronged. Two scenes in Vietnam establish Kovic's awakening to the reality of the war. First, his platoon begins shooting at a village and accidentally kills a large number of women and children. As they retreat from this scene under fire, Kovic mistakenly shoots and kills Wilson, a new guy in the platoon, and is told by his commanders to keep this knowledge to himself. Kovic is later wounded and winds up in a gruesome field hospital with a priest offering him the last rites.

The film makes it clear, however, that Kovic's real betrayal comes upon his return to the United States, where he is confined to an appalling veterans hospital that is underfunded because of the drain of money to the war. The film establishes these patients, living in filth and abusively treated by their attendants, as the refuse of the war. When Kovic is finally well enough to go home, his interaction with his family is awkward: his brother is protesting the war, and his friends seem to have forgotten it exists. His transformation from patriotic veteran to antiwar protester comes after he is teargassed and attacked as a bystander at a demonstration on a college campus. The real Ron Kovic was very effective in turning the rhetoric of patriotism around on itself, stating, "I am the living death, the Memorial Day on wheels. I am your Yankee Doodle Dandy, your John Wayne come home, your Fourth of July firecracker exploding in the grave."[30]

The innocent soldier is transformed throughout these films into a cynical, seasoned, yet reflective hero, one who has proven his manhood in battle yet who sees with clarity the folly of the war, who can, in his revelations and bitter new knowledge, stand in for the American public. Yet what is this knowledge? The simple message in Stone's trilogy of Vietnam films is that America learned it could betray its young men.

The cinematic portrayal of the noble grunt is contingent on the establishment of prior innocence. The grunt soldier, who could take it, bears the burden in part because he doesn't know any better, because he believes in the myth of America as the rescuing force. The United States is scripted through these characters as losing its innocence—an innocence apparently regained after having been lost in the Kennedy assassination, an innocence to be mourned again with Watergate, Iran-Contra, and the Oklahoma City bombing. If the grunt soldier is innocent at the war's outset, then the American public can identify through him with a sense of betrayal—we didn't know, we believed. Yet the Vietnam War films provide a context in which battles fought over the war are reenacted within the war itself.

Whose War Is It Anyway?
The War among Us

Self-conscious about the multiple interpretations and highly contested narratives of the war, many Vietnam War films have a recurring theme of Americans fighting not the North Vietnamese Army or the Vietcong but themselves. The films portray the Vietnam War as one characterized by confusion over who the enemy was. The enemy in this war was elusive, invisible, and disguised. The message in many of the Vietnam War films is that the real enemy was America—not simply, as Rambo might put it, that the American public and U.S. government would not let the war be won but rather, as perhaps Oliver Stone would put it, that blind patriotism and anticommunism were the real foes. At the end of *Platoon*, Taylor says:

I think now, looking back, we did not fight the enemy, we fought ourselves—and the enemy was in us. . . . The war is over for me now, but it will always be there—the rest of my days. As I am sure Elias will be—fighting with Barnes for what Rhah called possession of my soul. . . . There are times since I felt like the child born of those two fathers . . . but be that as it may,

those of us who did make it have an obligation to build again, to teach others
what we know and to try with what's left of our lives to find a goodness and
meaning to this life.

"We did not fight the enemy, we fought ourselves"—how quickly that
phrase erases what has just taken place on the screen: a scene in
which the bodies of hundreds of North Vietnamese soldiers are bull-
dozed into the pit of a bomb crater after Taylor, the newborn warrior,
has survived a devastating ambush by killing innumerable Vietnamese. Although these Vietnamese are anonymous, most of the American characters of *Platoon,* characters viewers have come to know and
empathize with, are also dead by its ending. Yet what is this film
really about? The battle for a young man's soul.

The central war in *Platoon* is the war between good and evil, between Elias and Barnes, within the platoon itself; Vietnam is merely
the setting. The most significant killings in the film come at the hands
not of the Vietnamese but of the Americans. Barnes calculatedly
shoots Elias while on patrol, then lies to the other men, saying the
NVA killed him. As they evacuate the area under heavy fire, they
see from the helicopter a wounded Elias running with superhuman
strength away from a large group of Vietnamese. Later in the film,
Taylor avenges Elias's death by killing Barnes in the film's climatic
battle scene. Hence, the deaths that count in the film and through
which the narrative is propelled are those of Americans killing each
other.

Like *Platoon, Casualties of War* hinges on an internecine feud,
in this case between Meserve (played by Sean Penn), a brutal and
unscrupulous soldier who has been on one too many patrols, and
Eriksson, a religious and moral character. The story of an Army private's attempts to bring to light the abduction, rape, and murder of a
young Vietnamese girl, the film is based on an actual account originally published in the *New Yorker.* Several attempts to make the film
in 1970 failed, and it wasn't until after *Platoon* that the script was
revived. The central feud of the film is Eriksson's struggle to expose
Meserve for the rape and murder of an innocent Vietnamese girl,
whom he kidnapped from a village and took along on a patrol "to
have some fun." Eriksson is ostracized and almost killed for not

participating in the rape, then is discouraged by Army officials from pressing charges. The farce of holding a court-martial in the face of a brutal war underscores the film's message. Despite the moving portrayal of the young girl, Mao, and her suffering, she is secondary in importance; in fact, her words are never translated. The film's real focus is the rift in morality among the Americans and their own victimization; they, in particular Meserve, a much-decorated soldier who is finally court-martialed, are the film's casualties of war, rather than the Vietnamese.

Films such as *Platoon* and *Casualties of War* present the war of the indecisive American psyche, the country that could not agree on a narrative under which to fight, the war of the grunt, struggling for survival, versus the antiwar protesters at home—that is, the war produced by the American public's collective guilt over having allowed the war to happen and then mistreating or ignoring the veterans on their return. Just as the veterans' anger over their mistreatment has been mollified to a certain extent by the Vietnam Veterans Memorial, the metaphoric depiction in films such as *Platoon* and *Casualties of War* of the division produced by the war in American society are offered as a cathartic absolution of guilt.

Fragging, or the killing within units of incompetent or potentially dangerous officers, increased as the war went on, with 200 confirmed incidents in 1970 alone.[31] The figure of the incompetent, upper-middle-class commander who could not understand the war at the level of the grunt soldier proliferates in Vietnam War films. In *Platoon* it is the indecisive Lieutenant Wolfe, who cannot command Elias and Barnes and who looks as if he has just stepped into the scene from prep school. Many veterans testify to the fact that incompetent officers were often fragged as a matter of survival—they were considered too dangerous to the grunts. However, in films these officers operate as emblems of the mismanagement of the war in general, as stand-ins for a military establishment that did not understand the horror of daily existence in the war and whose perception of the war as a business cost many lives. These incompetent officers also represent the absent fathers of Vietnam—the sense among the grunts that there was no leadership. The depiction of Americans fighting themselves in these films, the "enemy in us," is clearly an expression of the "real" loss depicted in Vietnam War films—the loss of innocence of the American male and, through him, America's loss of innocence.

Fathers, Sons, Men, and Machines

The war among ourselves is not only the war among American men in Vietnam and between soldiers and antiwar protesters; it is also a struggle between fathers and sons. The American male's loss of innocence in Vietnam War films represents the loss of American masculinity, technological superiority, and global power. Reinscriptions of masculinity and technology go hand in hand in Vietnam War films. A desire to reinscribe the status of high technology is evidenced in two parallel narratives: the fetishizing of technology in the actual film productions, and the depiction of the American soldier as a guerrilla and natural warrior.

To varying degrees, the Vietnam War films have reiterated in their production values the technological spectacle of combat. In *Apocalypse Now, Platoon, Full Metal Jacket, Casualties of War,* and, inevitably, the Rambo series, battle scenes are beautifully and thrillingly staged, the technology of cinema (constituting an arsenal in itself) merging with the technology of war. Filmmaker Jean-Luc Godard once noted that the trouble with antiwar films is that war is always exhilarating on the screen. The film camera's inherent tendency to fetishize its subject matter is compounded in the Vietnam War films by the spectacular nature of war. The "glamorization" of the war, as David James puts it, has been in full force in Hollywood.[32]

But Hollywood is not alone in glorifying combat and its weaponry. Many critical commentaries about the war still display a boyish love of its machinery. Herr writes: "It was incredible, those little ships [Loache helicopters] were the most beautiful things flying in Vietnam (you had to stop once in a while and admire the machinery), they just hung there above those bunkers like wasps outside a nest. 'That's sex,' the captain said. 'That's pure sex.' "[33] This fetishizing of war machines is laden with masculine narratives of control and mastery. In a controversial and well-known essay "Why Men Love War," veteran William Broyles writes:

War *is* beautiful. There is something about a firefight at night, something about the mechanical elegance of an M-60 machine gun. They are everything they should be, perfect examples of their form. . . . Many men loved napalm, loved its silent power, the way it could make tree lines or houses explode as if by spontaneous combustion. . . . I preferred white phosphorous, which exploded with fulsome elegance, wreathing its target in intense and billowing white smoke, throwing out glowing red comets trailing brilliant white plumes. I loved it more—not less—because of its function: to destroy, to kill. The seduction of war is in its offering intense beauty—divorced from all civilized values, but beauty still.[34]

In his eloquent description of the hackneyed story of men and war, Broyles describes not only the spectacle of destructive force but also its special significance for men: "at some terrible level the closest thing to what childbirth is for women: the initiation into the power of life and death." In Vietnam War representations, this spectacle symbolizes the recuperation of manhood; weaponry serves as a stand-in for the American male. This is weaponry as light, heat, sound, the "fulsome elegance" of Broyles's description, divorced from its target and its destruction. This is weaponry to watch; as Herr, whose job as a correspondent was to "watch," wrote, "you had to stop once in a while and admire the machinery." Here, war and cinema merge, both spectacle and spectatorship.

Though the depiction of war as spectacle is central in many of the "realist" Vietnam War films, their reenactment of warfare reveals an ambivalence about technology. In their restagings, the American soldier is seen as a guerrilla fighter. In the screenplay for *Platoon,* Elias is not just any warrior; he is a "natural" warrior, tracking the enemy alone in the bush:

. . . Elias stands silently, listens to the forest. In the distance the firefight can hardly be heard. His helmet gone, his hair hanging free, he is at his best now—alone. He hears it. Somebody running through the jungle, about 100 yards, boots on leaves, coming towards him.

He begins to move lateral to the sound. His steps unheard, better at this than the enemy. . . .

Two more enemy lie dead in the jungle. A rustle of movement, then a CRY—chilling, jubilant, a war cry.

A pair of feet moving lightly over the jungle. A glimpse of Elias. In his full glory. Roaming the jungle, born to it.[35]

Elias is scripted here to represent not an ordinary soldier but one who embodies the potential of war—one who could have won the war and won it the right way, as a guerrilla fighter. He loves fighting the war; it is "natural" for him. Hence Elias, in appropriating the tactics of the Vietnamese, represents a recuperation of American masculinity and technology. He is depicted as beyond technology, part of nature. At the moment before Elias is shot by Barnes, Stone's script reads:

In that moment, Elias understands. Quick as a deer, he makes his move, trying to plunge back into the bush.

Barnes fires. Once, twice, three times—the blast rocking the jungle.

Elias jerking backwards into the bush, mortally wounded. Bird cries. A crime against nature.[36]

Elias, "quick as a deer," the ultimate warrior, is killed, and it is not fratricide but "a crime against nature."

Similarly, Rambo is a natural fighter, with the skills to beat the enemy at their own game; he ends up fighting in the jungle for forgotten POWs with only his trusty knife in hand. Both Rambo and Elias (as Rambo's realist counterpart), the natural warriors, are depicted as Native Americans. Rambo is established in *First Blood* as part Indian and sports stereotypical markers of Native American ethnicity: a bow and arrow, a headband.[37] Similarly, Stone writes in the script of *Platoon* of the real-life Elias:

Dashingly handsome, with thick black hair, a flashing white smile, and Apache blood, Elias was everything we were later going to recognize in Jim Morrison and Joplin and Hendrix, he *was* a rock star but played it out as a soldier; real danger turned him on . . . it broke my heart when I heard Elias died on some hill in the Ashau when one of our grenades went off and killed him. It was unlike Elias; he was too smart to get wasted like that, yet how symbolic of this frustrating war—many of our best troops killed by our own side in accidents. There was even the whispered thought that Elias had been done in by one of our lifers.[38]

Elias could not be killed by the Vietnamese, he had to be killed by one of his own; he was too great a warrior to die in an ordinary fashion. That these two figures, who have operated to redeem the figure of the American soldier, are both implied to be Native

Americans is significant. The heritage of the Native American is shamelessly appropriated to shore up the (white) American soldier's reputation as a skilled and courageous fighter. Moreover, the invocation of the Native American as guerrilla fighter usurps the role played by the Vietnamese, whose guerrilla war tactics ultimately demoralized and defeated the United States. The representation of Americans as guerrillas reiterates an image of Vietnam as a place without technology, a place both primitive and deceptive.

In *Platoon,* the warrior is the essential figure in the reestablishment of manhood, the figure through whom the innocent protagonist learns to be a man. Stone writes: "I would act as Ishmael, the observer, caught between those two giant forces. At first a watcher. Then *forced* to act—to take responsibility and a moral stand. And in the process grow to a manhood I'd never dreamed I'd have to grow to. . . . To move from this East Coast social product to a more visceral manhood, where I finally felt the war not in my head, but in my gut and my soul."[39]

The repeated failure of technology in *Born on the Fourth of July* contrasts with *Platoon.* In *Born on the Fourth of July,* the combat scenes are shot in a murky red haze that evokes the difficulty of seeing in combat, the confusion over where to look, the invisibility of the enemy, and the ease of firing and killing accidentally.

Born on the Fourth of July tells the story of the failure of technology in Vietnam precisely because the film focuses on the veteran body after the war. *Born on the Fourth of July*'s central story begins when Kovic leaves Vietnam and finds himself in a squalid vets' hospital. There, medical technology is defective, out of date, and as dangerous as war machinery. It cannot help Kovic to walk again, nor can medical professionals seem to muster any sympathy ("Will I ever be able to have children?" "No, but we have a very good psychologist here"). Kovic's wounded leg is being drained by a machine so that it will not have to be amputated; when the machine stops working, the young doctor tells him that there have been cutbacks at the hospital because of the war. Here, the high technology of the war is replaced by its refuse.

Like the Vietnam Veterans Memorial, *Born on the Fourth of July* privileges the narrative of the returning Vietnam veteran over the narrative of the war itself. Kovic's story is about the pain and suffering he experienced after the war and his feeling of the betrayal he felt by his compatriots. In his physical paralysis, his impotence, and his rage, Kovic is a powerful icon for all veterans. The film is a graphic depiction of the wounded body, drained by urine bags and enemas, confined to a wheelchair, an object of pity. It is an extended, mournful wail for lost youth and health, for a boy rendered impotent while still a virgin, who is helpless when thrown from his wheelchair. Kovic's body is the body that is not visible in *Platoon* and *Full Metal Jacket,* the body that is shipped out of the scene in a helicopter.

Thus, *Born on the Fourth of July* depicts the loss of innocence and masculinity of the Vietnam veteran and, by extension, the American male in the post–Vietnam War era. That its protagonist is portrayed by Tom Cruise, established as a symbol of masculinity in such movies as *Top Gun,* makes its rendition of the loss of masculinity all the more poignant. In the film, Kovic, long after being wounded, fervently holds onto his belief that the war is a just cause in an attempt to justify his suffering. Yet as he realizes that the veterans are not accepted back in the United States, witnesses antiwar protests on television news, and finally, is beaten up by riot police while watching a campus protest—in short, as he sees that he is treated as the *enemy*—he becomes convinced the war is wrong.

Though Kovic feels mounting anger at the government, the person he blames most for his predicament is his mother. Kovic's father is portrayed as a sympathetic, nurturing man. When Kovic comes home drunk, his father carries him to bed. But his mother cannot face what is happening, and Kovic turns his rage on her. He feels betrayed by her anticommunist and Catholic fervor. In the penultimate scene of the film, a drunken Kovic screams at her about his impotence, grabbing at his crotch and repeatedly yelling "penis" until she is hysterical ("Don't say penis in this house!"). The film establishes that it is because of her fear of sexuality that her son will never realize his own sexuality. She is depicted as the castrating woman, unable to acknowledge the existence of male sexuality and its wounded presence in her son; she is the one he blames for his "dead legs." The implied impotence of all American males, symbolized by Kovic, is presented in the film as the Vietnam War's greatest tragedy.

In this, the film speaks to the genre's larger agenda. As Susan Jeffords notes in her book, *The Remasculinization of America: Gender and the Vietnam War:* "Vietnam representation is only topically 'about' the war in Vietnam or America's military strength or political policymaking. Its true subject is the masculine response to changes in gender relations in recent decades, its real battle that of the masculine to dominate and overpower its 'enemy'—the feminine."[40]

The necessity of repressing the feminine in order to fight the war is most visible in the boot camp scenes in *Full Metal Jacket.* Here the feminine is represented in the figure of Private Leonard Lawrence, dubbed "Gomer Pyle" by the abusive drill sergeant. Pyle, who is feminized by both his real name ("Lawrence what, of Arabia?" mocks the sergeant) and his nickname, is a fat boy who is hopelessly unsuited for boot camp, cannot stop smiling at the abuse, has a crush on Private Joker, and hides doughnuts in his footlocker. When Sergeant Hartman punishes the entire group of recruits for Pyle's mistakes, they turn on Pyle in rage, beating him at night, hating him for what he represents about themselves. After this incident, Pyle goes insane, becomes a crack marksman, and finally blows his brains out after killing the sergeant in the latrine. Pyle is the emblem of the unmasculine, soft and without discipline, whose femininity is a threat to the purpose of the Marine Corps. He must be either trained into a killing machine or discarded. Ultimately, the transformation kills him. Of all the Vietnam War films, *Full Metal Jacket* is the only one that examines the brutal, misogynistic, and racist training of American soldiers before they go to war and the premise that they must excise the feminine within themselves into order to survive.

Jeffords's extensive study reveals the complexities of the rehabilitation of masculinity in Vietnam War literature and film. She argues that gender is the primary narrative of Vietnam War representation, remasculinity its primary aim, that gender "is what Vietnam narrative is 'about.' "[41] Reinscribing masculinity may indeed be a foundation of Vietnam War films, but it is through the question of race that the war is represented as having a redeeming effect.

A Question for the "Real World":
Reinventing Race

Docudramas and cinematic histories function to provide therapeutic relief for collective guilt. Most of the Hollywood Vietnam War films are intended to critique the war by depicting its tragedy and futility, yet none constructs a direct political critique. Although these films condemn the war and attempt to make audiences complicit in it, their concentration on the grunt soldiers—who are, as Aufderheide notes, as far from policymaking as the audience, yet burdened with the same guilt—prevents a larger critique of the political reasons for the war. The popularity of these films, with rare exception, resides in their ability to provide absolution and a sense of redemption. One of the ways they do so is by depicting the Vietnam War as a site where race relations were transcended—where, at a time of racial turmoil at home, men of all colors saw each other as equals and treated each other as brothers. This, according to these films, is something good produced by the experience of Americans in the war.

Many veterans have talked about their changing views of race during the war. However, black veterans also came home from the war to find their neighborhoods in Newark, Washington, D.C., Detroit, Los Angeles, and other cities erupting in riots. The world of race in Vietnam was very different from the "real" world, and in Vietnam combat duty was very different from the "rear." Veteran Miguel Lemus states: "As for the races bit, we had to learn to get along because in time of action there was no color. In action everybody works together as a team; that's what got us back. In the rear that's a different story . . . mainly every group in the rear stayed with their own group—raza to the raza—mayate to the mayate—gabacho to the gabacho."[42]

Many of the reflections of veterans of color make it clear that they do not share perceptions that racial harmony prevailed in the Vietnam War. In 1973, Wallace Terry wrote: "Despite the military's contention that life for blacks is better in service than out, fewer than three black GIs in 10 said they get along better with whites in Vietnam than they did back home. And nearly 65 percent of them expect the racial strife in Vietnam to grow. In the past three years, mistrust and hostility between black and white American troops have increased to a dangerous extent. There have been beatings, killings, racial slurs from both sides and cross burnings."[43]

As the war wound further into confusion, racial tensions increased. Casualty figures for both blacks and Hispanics were unusually high, suggesting that they were more often assigned to combat patrols and other dangerous assignments. Terry notes that black veterans felt they were not awarded coveted rear assignments, medals, and promotions on an equal basis with whites. One of every five Hispanics was killed in action, and one of every two served in a combat unit; corresponding percentages for whites were substantially lower.[44] Many black and Hispanic soldiers saw race as central to the hypocrisy of the war:

In addition to condemning their treatment by white officers, many black soldiers criticized the war itself as racist. From their first combat training, which taught them to dehumanize their foes by calling them "gooks," to press releases that explained high enemy casualty rates in terms that stated that the Vietnamese valued human life less than Americans did, black soldiers found American racism replicating itself abroad. . . . Moreover, in many cases black soldiers identified with the Vietnamese as "brown brothers."[45]

Nevertheless, Vietnam War films have tended to support the myth that racial differences were erased in Southeast Asia. All the Vietnam War films have black and Hispanic characters, although none of them play major roles. In *Platoon* two black characters actually operate as a subtext to Taylor's relationship to his "good" and "bad" fathers, Elias and Barnes. King (played by Keith David) is kind and takes Taylor under his wing, teasing him for being a "crusader" by enlisting in the war ("gotta be rich in the first place to think like that"). Yet the film cannot award to King the authority it gives to Elias. Clyde Taylor writes: "King is actually more of a father-figure to [Chris] than Elias; but deprived of the moral authority that neither the film nor its primary audience will grant him, his characterization tips toward the familiar role of the black male mammy to innocent youth."[46] Like a mammy, King looks after Taylor and acts as his initiator into the dope-smoking world of the "heads," asking nothing in return.

At the opposite end of the racial stereotype is Junior (played by

Reggie Johnson), a cowardly GI who is established early in the film as a negative character when he sleeps on his watch on patrol and blames Taylor when a new guy gets killed. Junior, who attempts to get out of the last ambush by injuring himself yet dresses in the codes of black nationalism, thus operates as a kind of feminization of the angry black male.

The discourse of race, in particular its tangled relationship to gender, is most directly revealed in Vietnam War films in their depiction of the Vietnamese.[47] There are no male Vietnamese protagonists in these films. The majority of the Vietnamese depicted in Vietnam War films are suspicious and incomprehensible, their words untranslated. The real enemies of the Americans, the skilled and resourceful men and women of the Vietcong and the North Vietnamese Army, are thus erased, and the Americans are depicted as fighting themselves through the bodies of anonymous Vietnamese. The Vietnamese are the backdrops of these films, an unseen presence that does not advance the cinematic narrative.

The absence of the male Vietnamese protagonist allows Vietnam to be represented in these films by women. In *Full Metal Jacket,* *Casualties of War,* and *Heaven and Earth,* women are emblems of the victimized Vietnam, not the victorious Vietnam but a feminized, passive, violated country. In all three films, women represent the country of Vietnam under the control of American GIs. At the end of *Full Metal Jacket,* the squad surrounds a wounded young woman, a sniper who has killed several of their men. Kubrick's film implies that her gender is further evidence of the absurdity of the war—that so many Americans could be killed by one person, and a woman at that. Private Joker is challenged to prove his manhood by shooting her at point-blank range, which he does, his face contorted in rage. In *Casualties of War,* Mao's torture, rape, and murder by a patrol are a clear indictment of the American conduct in Vietnam. Yet she is an image of helplessness, raped by soldiers who have lost any moral sense. She is innocent, undeserving, and incomprehensible, forced to communicate through gesture and expression. The Vietnam represented by Mao is unable to defend or speak for herself, a victim.

Oliver Stone's third Vietnam War film, *Heaven and Earth,* is the most insistent in its feminized depiction of the country of Vietnam.

It is no accident that Stone chose Le Ly Hayslip's autobiographies, *When Heaven and Earth Changed Places* and *Child of War, Woman of Peace*, as the basis for his film; they promote a reconciliation of the Vietnamese and American veterans. Hayslip (played by Hiep Thi Le) represents, in many ways, the Vietnam that Americans want: forgiving, working for the cause of American veterans, and in love with consumerism and capitalism. Though she is clearly a survivor, *Heaven and Earth* depicts her as passive in the events that shape her journey. She is victimized by all factions of the war—the French, the Americans, the Vietcong, and the North Vietnamese—yet she forgives them all. Furthermore, because she is portrayed not as an active participant in the war as much as someone swept unwillingly into its consequences, she represents Vietnam not as an instigator or participant in the conflict but as the site where the war is fought by others. The image of a straw hat flying over a field of rice paddies, first seen when Americans arrive at her village in helicopters, is repeated often in the film, a nostalgic image of her country's innocent past.

It is not until Ly arrives in the United States with her American husband (played by Tommy Lee Jones) and children that she begins to question his role in the war or the American ideology she has embraced. The two characters come to represent their two countries: the innocent Vietnam, the duplicitous United States. When she finds out that, as a "military adviser," her husband has been supporting the family by selling arms and that he was involved in atrocities in Vietnam, he asks her, "What did you think I've been doing for the last seventeen years? . . . It was a white lie, a good lie." Though fascinated by the overabundance in this country, she is dismayed by its racism and ignorance about the war. She becomes increasingly independent, the image of postwar Vietnamese-Americans—industrious, successful, and hardworking. Yet somehow Stone's film never awards Ly the role of protagonist, the motivator of the narrative, nor any form of agency. Through her, the country of Vietnam is represented as falling into history rather than shaping it. This representation is due precisely to the dominance of the story of the Vietnam veteran in Vietnam War representation.

Rewriting the Veteran:
Retelling the War Through Its Aftermath

Like the Vietnam Veterans Memorial, Vietnam War films have produced narratives in which the Vietnam veteran is the war's primary
victim. The "innocence" mourned in these films is the innocence of
hundreds of thousands of men who were sent to war and were betrayed by the rest of the country, who lost their youth and their lives.
In films such as *Heaven and Earth, Born on the Fourth of July,* and
Casualties of War, the veteran is the central figure for whom the war
is mourned. *Heaven and Earth* provides the most compelling example of the struggle over whose story the war will tell. Though the film
ostensibly tells the story of Ly's life journey, it is heavily overshadowed by the story of her husband, Steve, who is, not incidentally,
played by a Hollywood star. It is Steve's suffering from the war, his
guilt and his pain, that ultimately take precedence in the film. He is
increasingly abusive, yet her role is to comfort and understand him.

It is Ly's Buddhism that allows her to absolve Steve of his war
crimes, a Buddhism consciously employed in the film to represent
the Vietnamese people's capacity for forgiveness. Ly is convinced,
despite her lack of agency in the events of war, that she was a soldier
in a past life and that she must pay for those experiences in this life.
In other words, she believes she is as guilty as her husband for the
atrocities of war. A Buddhist priest tells her that if she doesn't give
her abusive husband (who has kidnapped her children) a chance, she
will increase her own "soul debt." Perversely, Buddhism is used in
the film to make Ly feel guilt for things she never did and to place
compassion for her husband, who eventually commits suicide, before
her own safety. The central purpose of the film's telling of history
thus emerges: to present an image of Vietnam forgiving the United
States. That *Heaven and Earth* was the least successful of Stone's
films can be attributed not only to its attempt to tell the story of the
war as something other than a male rite of passage but also to the
awkwardness and, ultimately, the halfheartedness with which Stone
tells Hayslip's tale.

Many Vietnam War films achieve catharsis by offering forgiveness
to the American veteran for the war. At the end of *Casualties of War,*

Eriksson awakens from a nightmare to see a young Vietnamese girl, uncannily similar to Mao, sitting across from him on a subway car, and she says to him, "You had a bad dream, didn't you? It's over now, I think." The message is plain: the war is over, it was a bad dream, you are forgiven.

In many of these films, absolution is offered not just to the Vietnam veteran but also to the American public in general. Audiences identify with the innocent grunt soldier who is wounded and betrayed but finds some redemption from the war. (There are some exceptions to this theme; *Full Metal Jacket,* for example, ends not with redemption but with a cynical image of men returning from battle singing the "Mickey Mouse Show" theme song—infantile, absurd, and insane.) The viewers, too, are angry, plagued by guilt at what our country did in Vietnam and seemingly helpless to make it right. Much of the sense of absolution is conveyed by depicting the veteran as a figure of truth, a person within whom the tragedy and pain of the war will be translated into knowledge and wisdom. As Taylor says at the end of *Platoon,* "Those of us who did make it have an obligation to build again, to teach to others what we know and to try with what's left of our lives to find a goodness and meaning to this life." The veteran can, the film implies, give a particular meaning to life because of his experience. Elias is the martyr, and Taylor is his spiritual son, bearing witness; Ron Kovic is both martyr and witness. This experience of having been close to death and survived is imbued with purpose, something for which nonveterans long. As Henry Allen writes, "In their way, I think, they wanted to be veterans, too."

The Vietnam veteran has often been portrayed as a "special" kind of veteran, one for whom the war's difference from previous wars provided an avenue to knowledge. Robert Jay Lifton has written that society cannot treat casually those who have killed. Although the Vietnam veterans were sanctioned to kill, neither they nor the public sustained that sanction. While the war was still being fought, Lifton wrote:

There is something special about the Vietnam veterans. Everyone who has contact with them seems to agree that they are different from veterans of other wars. A favorite word to describe them is "alienated." Veterans Administration reports stress their sensitivity to issues of authority and autonomy

... As a group, they retain the "gnawing suspicion that 'it was all for nothing.' "[48]

Knowledge is seen to be derived not only from difficult experience but also from betrayal. By learning firsthand of the contrast between the narratives of war told in World War II films and the actual experience of war, between what governments say and what they do, the Vietnam veteran is perceived to have acquired a particular type of wisdom. Peter Marin writes:

What impresses me most about the vets I know is the sensibility that has emerged among them in recent years: a particular kind of moral seriousness which is unusual in America, one which is deepened and defined by the fact that it has emerged from a direct confrontation not only with the capacity of others for violence and brutality but also their own culpability, their sense of their own generosity, this kind of learned concern, which colors their moral sensibility, as if there were still at work in them a moral yearning or innocence that had somehow been deepened, rather than destroyed, by the war.[49]

Marin writes of the potential for the Vietnam veteran to produce a new kind of masculinity, one based on comradeship yet also caring and compassion. He claims that innocence has not been lost but rather transformed into a moral sensibility.

This characterization of the archetypal veteran from whom we can learn, through whom the war will be redeemed in some way, through whom America will acquire knowledge, is employed in Vietnam War representation in ways that clearly restage traditional notions of war and men. Veteran Bruce Weigl writes:

That we are made wiser by our experience in war is a myth created and perpetuated by nonwarriors and aging generals. But if you were not one of the unlucky who had his brains blasted across the jungle, or the highlands, or the delta of Vietnam, then you came away with images whose indelible presence on your soul have gone undetected for many years. Freud said that we do that—repress our past lives—to protect ourselves from the overwhelming power horrible memories can hold over us. I think we do it to protect those around us as well, those who were even less prepared for the images than the boy warriors were in the first place. . . . And we don't come away from war with the truth. I don't believe we recognize the truth anymore. But if you managed to board the flight back into the world after a tour of duty in Vietnam . . . then you did come away with a heightened sense of value. What matters and what doesn't.[50]

Though he rejects the idea of the inherent wisdom of the veteran, Weigl persuasively points to the compelling narrative of the veteran as someone who has seen the worst of the American male and, by extension, of America—its brutality, its lack of concern for human life, its potential for extreme violence—and who plays the role, to a certain extent, of protecting America from itself. The "heightened sense of value" described by Weigl is the ability to see through the myth and the national narratives to the irony and hypocrisy beneath.

The Vietnam War films are haunted by the presence of the Vietnam veteran. The story they tell, through the trope of Vietnam, is the veteran's difficult journey back in the United States. For the most part, they condemn the war while restoring the male veteran to well-worn paradigms of manhood and truth. Produced in the context of mainstream American culture, these films, with rare exception, serve the necessary function of producing narratives of redemption, a means of catharsis, and a way to derive something of value from this history.

The Film as Memorial

The Vietnam War films are forms of memory that function to provide collective rememberings, to construct history, and to subsume within them the experience of the veterans. As docudramas, they move from personal memory into cultural memory and finally into history. They are memorials in a certain sense, telling what is often as singular a narrative as Frederick Hart's statue, occasionally an ambivalent tale more analogous to the wall of the Vietnam Veterans Memorial. A film like *Platoon*, which is considered to have told the "real" story of the war, offers a particular kind of closure and allows viewers to feel they have access to that "site of truth" represented by the veteran.[51] In subsuming and reenacting documentary images, such films eclipse the iconic images of the war. The personal memories of Vietnam veterans are merged with the cultural memories produced by documentary images of the war and then reinscribed in narrative cine-

matic representations that make claims to history. When William
Adams writes that, painfully, "what 'really' happened is now so thoroughly mixed up in my mind with what has been said about what
happened that the pure experience is no longer there," he is referring
to this allegiance of image and memory. "Pure" memory is, of course,
always contaminated by the narrativization, by changing memories,
and by reenactment.

Platoon and other Vietnam War films also form part of the healing
process that was begun with the construction of the Vietnam Veterans Memorial in 1982. The narratives of loss, healing, and redemption that emerge from these films are very similar to the narratives
that have emerged at the memorial. *Platoon* has a cathartic effect on
many veterans. Veteran John Wheeler writes: "The Vietnam Memorial was one gate our country had to pass through. *Platoon* is another;
it is part of the healing process."[52] Veteran Thomas Bird concurs:
"Most [Vietnam War films] have helped Americans remember the
war and acted as a kind of therapy for veterans. . . . The best of the
Vietnam films . . . awaken our memories, forcing us to deal with our
remorse for things we did. But we have not yet had the moral courage
as a nation to face up to what has happened to the Vietnamese from
their perspective."[53]

Just as the Vietnam Veterans Memorial is limited by the underly-
ing nationalism of the Washington Mall, these films are limited by
the nationalism of American cinema. They effectively efface the Vietnamese, even reshape a Vietnamese woman's story as one of an
American veteran's struggle with guilt. However, through them, the
American public is seen finally to be listening to the veterans and
compensating for the years of silence. The guilt absolved here is thus
a guilt for the treatment of the veterans, *not* for the effects of the war
on the Vietnamese. Closure is offered here in the reenactment of the
war to redeem the Vietnam veteran, to provide forgiveness—and to
make way for the next war.

Chapter Four

Spectacles of Memory and Amnesia

Remembering the Persian Gulf War

CNN is live and alive as our humanity is about to die.
A Turkish writer

The way a nation remembers a war and constructs its history is directly related to how that nation further propagates war. Hence, the rewriting of the Vietnam War in contemporary American films directly affected the manufactured "need" for the United States's involvement in the Persian Gulf War.[1]

The insistent and ongoing memorialization of World War II in American popular culture continues to haunt subsequent wars: The Vietnam War has been memorialized as the war with the difficult memory, and the Korean War has simply been forgotten. Vietnam has been the war that popular culture needed to rewrite and restage in order to remember, yet, as the Vietnam Veterans Memorial has demonstrated, memories of the war continue to disrupt simple narratives. The Persian Gulf War, by contrast, is a war about which Americans, even during the war itself, were perceived to have a collective amnesia—supposedly produced by the war's elaborate staging before an international audience. Yet the Persian Gulf War is not simply a war of empty spectacle and amnesia. It is remembered in complex ways through its effect upon the lives of its veterans; their presence tangles with the sanitized public story of the war.

Attempts to give the Persian Gulf War a neat narrative reinscribing master narratives of World War II—in which the United States liberates a desperate and weak country imperiled by a dangerous tyrant—are intended to chart the lineage of war directly from 1945 to 1991 in order to establish the Vietnam War (and its shadow, the Korean War) as aberrations. The Persian Gulf War will not need to be rescripted like the Vietnam War; it was expressly manufactured for the screen and a global audience, complete with a premiere date (January 15, 1991) and a cast of familiar characters (the evil, dark tyrant; the fearless newsman; the infallible weaponry). In one sense, the history of the Persian Gulf War was written before it began; it was, like the reinscriptions of Hollywood cinema, a spectacular orchestration of a new ending for the Vietnam War.

Indeed, the Persian Gulf War was choreographed as the ending of the "Vietnam Syndrome," the national "malaise" that fueled popular sentiment against interventions with American troops in foreign conflicts.[2] The military perceived the renewed image of a sensational, efficient American war machine as a tool with which to eradicate images of the failure of technology in Vietnam. The image of American helicopters landing Marines on the roof of the U.S. embassy in Kuwait City in January 1991 could wipe out the humiliating image of helicopters evacuating people from the roof of the U.S. embassy in Saigon in 1975.[3]

The Vietnam Syndrome was an image of emasculation, a "disease" that prevented the government from displaying strength. Abouali Farmanfarmanian notes that the "travesty of manhood" perpetrated by the Vietnam War was reiterated in the Iran hostage crisis of 1979:

The 1979 hostage drama left America impotent, unable to wield its might. The small, confused, rather desperate attempt at freeing the hostages led to a humiliating catastrophe in the desert near Tabas, Iran. While the U.S. army was looking pitiful in the sand, white American masculinity—since all African American and white women hostages were released by the Iranian captors—was gagged, tied, and put on display for the world to see.[4]

The hostage crisis also signaled the end of the administration of Jimmy Carter (whom Farmanfarmanian terms "forever the antimacho") and the election of the icon of American rugged masculinity, Ronald Reagan, as president.

Although the term "syndrome" applied to Vietnam before the advent of AIDS, it carried with it all the associations of a diseased condition—a "syndrome" as a weakened state, with a vulnerable immune system (read: military defense). The post–Vietnam War agenda of the Persian Gulf War was clear when a gleeful President George Bush declared, "The Vietnam Syndrome is over!" The Gulf War offered certain symbolic kinds of closure in the public arena for the fragmented narratives of the Vietnam War; yet by their very presence the Gulf War veterans, like the Vietnam veterans, have prevented the history of this war from remaining uncontested.

It is almost a cliché at this point to refer to the collective amnesia that surrounds the Persian Gulf War. This amnesia is fueled by the war's lack of a final outcome (Hussein's continued existence), the rescripting in public discourse of the war as a president's neglect of domestic issues (the public was quick to forget his "victory" and elect Bill Clinton in his place), and the spectacle of television images (which told the story not of war but of weaponry) that constituted the war's representation. The Gulf War was so quickly forgotten in public discourse that it needed to be restaged rather than remembered on its second anniversary, as President Bush bombed Iraq yet again, producing identical images of missiles in the night sky.

What was the purpose of this war, and what should its national memory have been? The government never adequately answered the question of how this six-week war, fought in countries that most Americans had never heard of, defended the national interest. Rather, it became clear that the Gulf War served very specific domestic interests of the U.S. military, which sought to test its weaponry and to establish its continued importance in a post–Cold War era.

I would argue that the cultural memory of the Persian Gulf War is particularly contradictory precisely because the military's attempts to regulate its public representation were so stringent. This was no accident but rather a primary legacy of the Vietnam War; one of the lessons the military establishment learned quite well was that its lack of control over media representation of the Vietnam War had had disastrous consequences for its public image. Because representation of the Gulf War was heavily controlled, the cultural memory of this war has been slower to evolve. Yet there are 700,000 veterans of the Gulf War whose stories are increasingly filtering into public discourse and whose struggles with a strange and unidentified disease, Gulf War Syndrome, have been increasingly difficult for the government to ignore. It is through these veterans that the simple narrative of the Gulf War is disrupted and through their bodies that cultural memory of the war is produced.

The Television Image:
The Immediate and the Virtual

The American public "experienced" the Persian Gulf War through the medium of television, and television's images are central to its history. Yet television images have a slippery relationship to the making of history. The essence of the television image is transmission. It is relentlessly in the present, immediate, simultaneous, and continuous. Hence, television is defined by its capacity to monitor (in the form of surveillance cameras) and to be monitored, transmitting its image regardless of whether we continue to watch it. Raymond Williams wrote that television is defined by "flow," its capacity to unify fragmentary elements and to incorporate interruption.[5]

Television is coded, like all electronic technology, as immediate and live. It is about the instant present, in which information is more valuable the more quickly we get it, the more immediate it is.[6] Television allows for an immediate participation in the making of history; it produces "instant history."[7] When television images become "historic" images—the lone student halting a tank at Tiananmen Square, the fall of the Berlin Wall, the bombs exploding at night over the city of Baghdad—they retain some of the cultural meaning of electronic technology, connoting the instant and the ephemeral. Their low-resolution, slightly blurred quality allows them to retain a sense of immediacy, as if they were presenting the unfolding of history rather than its image set in the past.

The Persian Gulf War was the first actual television war of the United States. Though the Vietnam War is often termed the first "living room war," its images were shot almost exclusively on film and hence subject to the delays of the developing process. There was always at least a twenty-four-hour delay before images of the Vietnam

War reached the United States. The Persian Gulf War, by contrast, took place in the era of satellite technology and highly portable video equipment. It was technologically possible for the world to watch the Persian Gulf War as it happened. This is why military censorship was instituted in such a strict fashion—to make sure that it was *not* seen live. Still, claims of the "immediate" and the "live" reigned. Reporters in the Persian Gulf have noted that many of their stories never aired because they were delayed for a day or two by military censors. Any information that was not "immediate" was considered irrelevant by news producers. The illusion of live coverage given by the twenty-four-hour Cable News Network (CNN) worked in consort with military censorship to mark war news useless unless it was instantaneous.

Thus, one of the ironies of Persian Gulf War is that although it could have been copiously and immediately documented, it was instead depicted in sterile coverage that yielded very few images. Most of what the American audience saw were maps, still photographs of reporters, and live images of reporters in Israel. CNN's round-the-clock television coverage of the war offered only the illusion that viewers could see everything. The few images that were produced did not accumulate in cultural memory but rushed past in a succession of replays. Ernest Larsen writes: "This was the first war in history that everyone could turn off at night in order to sleep . . . and then switch on again in the morning to know if the world had yet fallen to pieces. The knowledge that such television produces tends not to accumulate, in part because each new moment literally cancels, without a trace, what we have just seen."[8]

That the Persian Gulf War was fought in the era of satellite technology affected not only the choice of images that were disseminated in the media but also the surveillance and weapons systems of the war itself. The Gulf War was apparently one of the first in which a computer virus was used as a weapon.[9] Electronic and satellite communications rendered the actual site of the war unclear. As McKenzie Wark writes:

Did the Gulf War take place in Kuwait, Baghdad or Washington? Was the site the Middle East or the whole globe? This is a particularly vexing point. If Iraqi commanders order a SCUD missile launch via radio-telephone from Baghdad, the signal may be intercepted by orbiting US satellites. Another satellite detects the launch using infra-red sensors. Information from both will be relayed to the Pentagon, then again to US command HQ in Saudi Arabia and to Patriot missile bases in Saudi Arabia and Israel.[10]

Wark describes the common notion that the expanded "theater" of the Gulf War included electronic space. This "virtual war" of satellite technology was above all a war of communication vectors. This contributed to the illusion that only those watching CNN, like the TV spectators at a sports event, knew what was "really" happening in the war. As reporter Scott Simon has said:

People around the world often had the sensation of being wired into that war. During the first week, the telephone rang in our workroom in Dhahran. "Get down to the bomb shelter," said an editor on the foreign desk who was watching television. "They've just launched a SCUD at you." And a minute later in eastern Saudi Arabia, the air raid sirens sounded. Weeks later, I stood in line with some soldiers waiting to make phone calls back to the United States. "Calling home before the ground war begins?" I asked. And a paratrooper answered, "Calling to find out what's happening in this war. My folks can really see it." . . . Sometimes I have to remind myself that when I say, "I was there—I saw that," I saw that only on television, just like the people watching the war in Kansas or Kenosha.[11]

Simon evokes the pervasive conflation during the Gulf War of the television experience with the "real" story. Yet it is too simple to allow the Gulf War to be historicized as a virtual high-tech war. Though the image of the war on CNN may have made it appear that the television screen was the war's primary location, this illusion effaced the war that took place among human bodies and communities. The capacity to render the Gulf War in retrospect as a virtual war eclipses the fact that it was still a conventional war, fought with conventional weaponry, in which the body of the other was obliterated. Implicit in many of these statements is the concept that the "real" war is that which is recorded by a camera.

Image Icons

In this context of censorship and virtual participation, the few images of the war that did filter through took on tremendous significance in defining its narratives. The two images that have emerged as most iconic of the Persian Gulf War—bombs in the night sky over Baghdad

Figure 13. Night sensor image of Baghdad, Persian Gulf War, 1991. Leslie Wong/ ABC.

and the point-of-view approach of the "smart" bomb to its target— contrast sharply with the iconic images of the Vietnam War.

Baghdad's fiery night sky is an image of both spectacle and the "unseen." Shot by an ABC cameraman with a special "night sight" heat-sensor lens, it is a surreal, otherworldly image that easily evokes the facile appearance of missiles chasing targets in video games (Figure 13). The "beauty" of war is shown here at its most extreme, formally and aesthetically riveting. One pilot said, "I could see the outline of Baghdad lit up like a giant Christmas tree. The entire city was just sparkling."[12] The Vietnam War never produced such images of war as spectacle, the bombs' destructive power sanitized and erased in the darkness. The image of the Baghdad night has commonly been likened to a Fourth of July scene. Indeed, it was reenacted with fireworks at the 1991 Fourth of July celebration in New York, only a month after the huge "welcome home" parade for veterans of the Gulf War, completing the metaphor.

Figure 14. Missile-cam image, Persian Gulf War. © 1991 Cable News Network, Inc. All rights reserved.

The image of the night sky over Baghdad was initially mythologized in the media as depicting Allied Patriot missiles shooting down Iraqi SCUD missiles headed for Israel and Saudi Arabia. However, since the Gulf War, it has been revealed that the video actually depicted the SCUDS coming apart at the end of their flight and falling into pieces onto the Patriots.[13] Yet these qualifying explanations have not changed the meaning of this image as it achieves historic status: It signifies the myth of the war as one of clean technology.

The other image icons of the Gulf War—the electronic "missile-cam" footage taken from aircraft and bombs—also emphasize the predominating narrative of the war as a battle of technology. These images portray targeted buildings as seen through the crosshairs (and then exploding) and point-of-view perspectives of a bomb's approach to a site, flashing off the instant before impact (Figure 14). They carry power not only because they are the first popular images of their kind but also because they provide the viewer with a particular experience of military hardware voyeurism. In these images, the technologies of media and war merge to the point of inseparability. It can be said, however, that these technologies have always been inseparable, as television technology has always been derived from technology developed through military research. As Wark notes, "Most of the technologies now accessible to television, including the portable satellite news-gatherers (SNG), are the civilian progeny of equipment developed for military applications." [14]

These missile-cam images are "secret" images, shown to audiences in the camaraderie of the military briefing room, usually on a small screen, with a military spokesman using a pointer to brief the "American public" on the interpretive codes needed to understand "our" weaponry. This approach allowed Gen. Norman Schwarzkopf and other military officials to employ sports metaphors, as if they were football coaches narrating their team's plays. Despite the presence of several woman reporters, the military briefing room for the press during the Gulf War was a male domain deliberately constructed as secretive and exclusive. The good-humored inside jokes and comradeship of word jockeying in these press conferences made clear the clubby relationship between the press and the military, masking the fact that many questions went unasked and unanswered. The shared secrecy implied in the presentation of these images is also the result of their visual coding as images of surveillance. In black and white and framed with crosshairs, these images of bombs exploding on their targets thus afforded audiences the feeling of having a special kind of sight, a privileged view.

The camera image has a long history in both the propagation of wars and their documentation and memorialization. Since World War I, camera technology has been integral to the battlefield and image surveillance of the enemy, an essential strategic device. As Paul Virilio has written:

Thus, alongside the "war machine," there has always existed an ocular (and later optical and electro-optical) "watching machine" capable of providing soldiers, and particularly commanders, with a visual perspective on the military action under way. From the original watch-tower, through the anchored balloon to the reconnaissance aircraft and remote-sensing satellites, one and the same function has been indefinitely repeated, the eye's function being the function of a weapon.[15]

These two roles of the camera—as a device for constructing cultural memory and history and as a device for waging warfare—were inseparable in the production of images of the Gulf War. Yet what distinguishes the Gulf War surveillance images from previous ones is not only their technological proficiency but, more important, their use as the primary *public* images of the war; indeed, they have become the image icons of the war. As part of a well-orchestrated public relations and censorship campaign, these missile-cam images served to screen out images that were never taken or never shown.[16] Hence, American viewers—and, by extension, the rest of the world, watching CNN—not only were given the illusion that they were welcomed into the military briefing room but also were situated as spectators within the frame of reference of the bomb. The camera's point of view was the bomb's point of view and the viewer's point of view. Watching these images, the viewer can imagine being in the bomber, imagine being the bomb itself, blasting forward and exploding in an orgasmic finale, the spectator and the weapon merged. Ironically, the audience did not seem to be implicated. Rather, the bombs took on agency, absolving viewers as distanced spectators.

Metaphors of sight were prevalent during the Gulf War; struggles over who had access to and control over the power to see dominated the war. At press briefings, Gen. Norman Schwartzkopf talked initially of blinding Saddam Hussein—"We took out his eyes"—by destroying his air force, and American weaponry was consistently referred to as having vision. For instance, the "thermal night sight" employed by American tanks was described as allowing them to fight at night or in bad weather, when "Iraqi tanks were virtually blind." Thus, "smart weapons" meant weapons that could "see." This emphasis on sight included a concern with concealment through the use of stealth bombers and other stealth technology.

The preoccupation with establishing American technology's ability to see can be directly traced to the representations of American technology in the Vietnam War. The "inpenetrable" jungle foliage of Vietnam has been consistently blamed for the inability of American

military technology to win the war (hence the campaign of massive
defoliation by Agent Orange perpetrated by the U.S. in Vietnam).
Not coincidentally, the desert terrain of the Middle East provided
the ideal terrain for sight, enabling the American military to see its
own technology at work. These "smart" weapons (only 70 percent of
which, it was revealed after the war, hit their targets) were awarded
intelligence, sight, and even memory—they were said to "hold the
characteristics of enemy vehicles in their memory."[17]

Dis-Remembering Bodies

The contrast between these images and the iconic images of the Vietnam War—Kim Phuc fleeing naked from napalm, the point-blank
killing of a Vietcong suspect by General Loan, the victims of the My
Lai massacre—is obvious. The image icons of the Gulf War are of
weapons and targets, not of human beings. Military censorship kept
reporters and their cameras where they often had access only to distant images of bombers taking off and weapons in the sky. Images of
the dead, of incinerated bodies on the road to Basra (the scene of
the "turkey shoot" by U.S. planes on retreating Iraqis), were shown
only selectively by the U.S. media. They clearly did not fit into the
script, which cast the weapons as the subjects of the war and the
bodies of American, Allied, Kuwaiti, and Iraqi soldiers and civilians
as extras.

The "bloodless" coverage of the war erased the effects of this
weaponry on the sentient bodies of civilians. The iconic images of
the Vietnam War gained their power by portraying graphically the
damage war inflicts upon the human body—the torn flesh of Kim
Phuc, the piles of dead at My Lai, the graphic images of wounded
American soldiers. Whereas Vietnam War images show terror at the
moment of death, the images of the Gulf War depict spectacle at the
moment of the bomb's impact. Instead of images of man against man,
these are images of weapons against weapons. This is clearly a reaction to the bodies of the Vietnam War, the bodies of the war dead
listed relentlessly on the Vietnam Veterans Memorial, and the problematic bodies of the Vietnam veterans, bodies that have resisted
simple narratives of history.

In the Gulf War, bodies and weapons were reified in the media.

Dead civilians were referred to as "collateral damage" and Iraqi soldiers as "targets" (objects of the "turkey shoot"), whereas weapons
were ascribed the human characteristics of sight and memory. The
media thus adopted without irony the technospeak of the military.
They depicted the destruction caused by American bombs only once,
when an Iraqi bomb shelter was destroyed, killing several hundred
people. This image was shown all over the world, but only in very
limited and sanitized form in the United States, amid assertions that
it had been faked or that Hussein had deliberately placed innocent
civilians at a strategic military site. The general absence of images of
destruction erased from the screen and the American psyche the
spectacle of the war victims' bodies, coded already as the dark bodies
of the other. Even the graphic images of the "highway of death" of
retreating Iraqi forces on the road to Basra concentrated on the man-
gled and burned corpses of cars and trucks rather than the people
who had been killed inside.

Ironically, the desert landscape of the Persian Gulf contributed to
this absence of bodies; the desert is mythologized in American culture as an uninhabited site. The image of the desert landscape as both
postapocalyptic (already inscribed as a site of war) and unpeopled is
reinforced by the fact that most of the desert in the United States is
occupied by the military; the Nevada desert is even the site of nuclear
tests.

Instead of images of human beings at war, the media presented
images of a war of machines: tanks, bombs, helicopters, and planes.
Body counts (a central focus of government and media reports of the
Vietnam War) were replaced by weapon counts. The only bodies that
counted in the coverage of the war were the bodies of reporters and
the single, sanitized body of the American military. The vast majority
of the footage from the Gulf War showed reporters standing before
the camera on the outskirts of combat zones. A significant amount of
the coverage concerned the safety of reporters, some of whom were
evacuated by force from Baghdad so that they couldn't witness the
war, others of whom were photographed wearing gas masks in Tel
Aviv. These reporters were the surrogate bodies under peril, standing
in for the American soldiers and Iraqi people, whose moments of
danger went unrecorded.

Unlike the fragmented body of the American military during the

Vietnam War, the body of the military in the Gulf War was perceived as a whole, moving forward in a single mass. Elaine Scarry writes that the convention of imaging an army as a singular body "assists the disappearance of the human body from accounts of the very event that is the most radically embodying event in which human beings ever participate."[18] Thus, the depiction of the American forces as a singular mass allowed for an effacement of the actual sentient bodies of men and women at risk. Similarly, the bodies of Iraqi soldiers were subsumed into a single unit and obliterated from view by American officials' consistent use of Saddam Hussein as their surrogate. These officials talked of "bombing Saddam," which, Hugh Gusterson notes, "submerged individual Iraqi soldiers into the single unloved figure of Saddam Hussein."[19] Scarry adds that "the disappearance of the injurable bodies of the enemy citizenry has as counterpart, in almost any war, the magnification of the injury that the enemy can inflict."[20] She contends that in the Gulf War, the potential threat of Iraq was exaggerated through "nuclear blackmail"—Bush justified his actions on the contention that Iraq was months away from using nuclear weapons—and through a magnification of the television coverage of Iraq's invasion of Kuwait, coverage orchestrated in its entirety by a public relations firm hired by a small group of wealthy Kuwaitis.[21]

The bodies rendered invisible through this process were clearly marked by race and gender. The Arab body was subsumed into the Orientalist portrayals of Saddam Hussein as the quintessential terrorist, Iraqi forces as fanatic followers, and the Middle East as a place of dark chaos. The disruptive issue of gender was also efficiently effaced. The presence of many women among U.S. forces did not offset a reinscription of the American male soldier's masculinity, lost in the Vietnam War. American masculinity was reinscribed through the hypermasculine weaponry, which stood in for the American soldier and for a president fighting his image as a "wimp."

Largely through the media's preoccupation with the service of significant numbers of American women in the Gulf, sexual equality emerged as a redeeming narrative of the war. However, these women were almost exclusively portrayed as mothers and pictured with photographs of their children. Ironically, in the midst of a significant amount of rhetoric about "family values," the military was issuing orders to women who had just given birth and sending both parents of small children to war—a hypocritical policy that the media largely overlooked. At the same time, the media depiction of women soldiers in the Gulf was filled with ambivalence about the upheaval of traditional gender divisions in war. The preoccupation with their motherhood negated their role as soldiers and placed them in the more traditional role of women in wartime—as mothers who send their sons off to war. If the women were mothers, they could be construed as unthreatening to the gendered military status quo; yet they were also depicted as soldiers fighting symbolically for their children. They were, ironically, both figures of power and traditional icons of womanhood.

Given the hypermasculine narratives surrounding the American participation in the Gulf War, with President Bush and military leaders swaggering before the cameras and the masculine-coded weaponry proclaimed as victorious, the emergence of women soldiers had to be played down in public discourse by traditional images. Bodies, whether marked by race, gender, or the fragility of flesh, were rendered invisible in the spectacular images of the Gulf War. The pleasures of viewing spectacle necessitate the absence of its consequences. The bodies of the Gulf War needed to be dis-remembered in order for the story of technological prowess to be told.

The Image Becomes History: Television and Film Memories

What emerged from the sterile and highly orchestrated images of the Gulf War was a discourse of heroes (in particular weapons as heroes), one that had been conspicuously lacking in the aftermath of the Vietnam War. These men and women supposedly arrived home untraumatized and pristine, their bodies intact. They were greeted by huge "welcome home" parades, including the largest (and most expensive) ticker-tape parade (in the era of computers, ticker tape had to be specifically manufactured) in the history of New York City. They symbolized the new veteran, replacing the older, angrier Vietnam veteran, the reminder of defeat. These parades celebrated not just the end of a six-week war but the end of the legacy of Vietnam—the stain of defeat, the loss of America's standing as a technologically superior world power. All this boyish excitement was a backlash against the intense sorrow expressed at the Vietnam Veterans Memorial, an attempt to change the message: War is not about loss and pain; it is not about dead Americans; it is about smart weapons and fiery night spectacles.

However, the Gulf War cannot be reduced to a rescripting of the Vietnam War. The popular view is that cultural amnesia about the war was produced by its quick, sound-bite media coverage, its apparent lack of long-lasting outcome, the minimal number of American casualties, and the narcissism of American national discourse. Both the amnesia and the memory of the Gulf War are directly connected to the kinds of images it produced. As electronic images, the images of the Gulf War carry with them the problematic relationship of television to history. Television forces a rethinking of memory and history, although it is true that images acquire cultural currency in many different forms—television images are often distributed and historicized as still images, and famous documentary still and film images are often reenacted in docudramas.

Nonetheless, many critics have proclaimed television the end of history and memory. For them, television is the marker of postmodern excess, of time with no meaning. Stephen Heath writes: "Exhausting time into moments, its 'now-thisness,' television produces forgetfulness, not memory, flow, not history.[22] That the image icons of the Gulf War are forgettable is relatively uncontested, yet this lack of cultural currency comes not simply from their status as instant television images. They are forgettable in their empty spectacle. Michael Rogin writes that "spectacle is the cultural form of amnesiac representation, for spectacular displays are superficial and sensately intensified, short-lived and repeatable."[23] Spectacle is about forgetting.

Yet I would argue that the essence of history on television is repetition, reenactment, and docudrama. Like the docudramas of the Vietnam War, television reenactments offer particular kinds of catharsis that in their mix of memory and fantasy produce forms of remembrance.[24] George Gerbner argues that the heavily choreographed coverage of the Gulf War made it already a docudrama:

Instead of full and accurate reports and documentaries, network "docudramas" shot in sync sound on location and in Hollywood studios took audiences to the Persian Gulf War movie. Realistic shots of training, tanks maneuvering in the sand, simulated trench warfare, attacks on the enemy lurking in the darkness, scripted scenes of camp life and the "home front," patrols on a mission firing into the darkness, a full sequence of mission control launching a Patriot and scoring a "hit," and even "hostages" being beaten alternated with promos of *Die Hard 2* and *Terminator 2*.[25]

Hence, in its docudrama form, its catchy title ("Desert Storm"), and its reiteration of war- and action-film clichés, the Gulf War appeared already to be highly scripted narrative interspersed with "real life" episodes.

Hollywood has produced one significant film about the Gulf War, one which both reiterates and departs from the codes of Vietnam War films and which was written by Patrick Duncan of *84 Charlie MoPic*. *Courage Under Fire* (1966) begins with the expected images of the Baghdad night sky and missile-cam shots, but it also portrays intense ground combat. It tells the story of an increasingly complex military in which conflict over gender roles, friendly fire, post-traumatic stress disorder, and Gulf War Syndrome are foregrounded over simple codes of war. However, as in *Platoon*, the film's primary narrative is the conflict between American soldiers (in this case, the ultimately fatal response of a helicopter crew to its female captain, Karen Walden, played by Meg Ryan), with the Iraqis presented as anonymous bodies, mere props for war games and internecine conflicts. Like the media coverage, *Courage Under Fire* demonstrates ambivalence about women in combat, establishing sexual equality as a redeeming Gulf War narrative while portraying Walden as a dedicated mother who has to leave a child behind. While it is ultimately a pro-military film, through its central character (played by Denzel Washington), who attempts to find the truth of the incident and to discover a hero, the film also presents an image of the Gulf War as troubling and ambiguous, with long-lasting consequences.

Television and the Nation

The Gulf War was watched, by CNN's estimate, by a total of one billion people in 108 nations.[26] It was heralded as an event that established the international scope of the television viewing audience and put CNN on the global map. However, the television coverage of the Gulf War was also instrumental in the development of the concept of a unified national audience. It was through presumption of a collective viewing experience that the war created a sense of national participation. Despite the popular notion that television makes viewers passive and isolated, it can provide the impression of communality, one that was heightened during the Gulf War with the global reach of CNN's "live" coverage—the whole world, along with George Bush and Saddam Hussein, watching the same channel.

The shared pleasures of television spectatorship during the Gulf War were derived not only from this sense of national and global techno-community (with the U.S. and the Soviet Union joined on the same side in this post–Cold War war) but also through the highly structured process of identification between spectator and weapon. Television's voyeuristic qualities were brought to an extreme—not only were we seeing without being seen, we were seeing the destructive act itself, the moment of impact. Robert Stam writes: "During the Gulf War, television spectatorship became deeply imbricated with personal and national narcissism. . . . Americans were distracted from the humdrum realities of a declining economy, from the collapsing bank system, from racial tension and discrimination, by the dubious pleasures of a spectacular war."[27] This tension of immediacy, sadism, and a slight tinge of complicity was thus integral to the pleasures of spectatorship. We saw, we were "there," yet the technology kept us (and the cameras that extended our sight) at a safe distance.

The war coverage worked to skew the experience of nationality. After the war was over, CNN was recast as the entity that "fought" the war. W.J.T. Mitchell notes that the CNN video documentary of the war is dedicated not to the soldiers but "to the brave men and women of CNN" and that Maj. Gen. Perry Smith, CNN's war consultant, titled his book *How CNN Fought the War.*[28] CNN is thus refigured as the government, with its reporters standing in for the troops in an attempt to claim veteran status (reminiscent of the claims by directors and actors of Vietnam War films to have experienced the war itself).

CNN coverage did not, apparently, help citizens formulate informed opinions about the war. Michael Morgan, Justin Lewis, and Sut Jhally found that Americans supported the war despite a stunning ignorance about many of the basic facts that led to its outbreak—for instance, the shift in the U.S. position on Iraq's invasion of Kuwait, or the fact that Kuwait was not a democracy before the invasion (hence, the war was not in reality a "fight for democracy").[29] In addition, the study found that the more television Americans watched, the less they knew.

That American viewers participated in an imagined national audience during the Gulf War and emerged with stories of fiction and fantasy is, of course, nothing new. The public knowledge of the facts of the Vietnam War is also thin. However, in the case of the Gulf War, the public was incited to "experience" the war as Americans in a highly structured, narrowly defined scenario that allowed little room for the complexities of American public opinion. Consent was manufactured quickly and remained firmly intact as media myth (protests against the war received appallingly little coverage), allowing little room for nuance or resistance.

Nationalizing the Yellow Ribbon

The Gulf War would appear, then, to have a monolithic historical narrative that significantly overshadows any production of cultural memory to counter it. The media and military worked in concert to circumscribe the cultural memory of the war and to dictate its historicization. Yet they cannot control the cultural memory of a war in which there were 700,000 returning veterans. Even in the face of well-orchestrated government attempts to control this war, to prevent it from resembling any moment of the Vietnam War, the American public produced its own memories of the Gulf War.

The rituals of burying the dead, even of receiving the casualties in the United States, were kept secret by the military. At Dover Air Force Base, where the dead arrived, the military prohibited photographers and reporters, marking a significant change of policy. John Farrell notes, "In the last decade, Dover has become something of a totem for Americans, a place where the nation traveled, via television, to mourn its lost."[30] The crew of the Challenger, the Marines who died in Lebanon, and the dead from U.S. invasions into Panama and Grenada were all ritually mourned at Dover. The military's restriction of the press from Dover during the Gulf War was an obvious

attempt to avoid connotations with the body bags returning from the
Vietnam War.

Although this traditional arena was closed off, many Americans
participated in rituals of remembering those at war. The most obvious
among these was the yellow ribbon. Stories about the origin of the
yellow ribbon as a symbol of remembrance vary. On one hand, it is
attributed to a 1973 Tony Orlando song, "Tie a Yellow Ribbon 'Round
the Old Oak Tree," about an ex-convict returning home from prison
who asks his wife to tie a yellow ribbon on the tree if she still loves
him (the song ends with his seeing a "hundred yellow ribbons"). Tell-
ingly, this song is often misrepresented as being about a Vietnam
veteran. The origin of the ribbons is also traced to the Civil War,
when wives and loved ones of soldiers wore yellow ribbons, a custom
linked, in turn, to the 1949 John Wayne film *She Wore a Yellow
Ribbon*.[31]

However, the most important origin story of the yellow ribbon is
its emergence during the Iran hostage crisis of 1979. From 1979 to
1981, Penne Laingen tied a yellow ribbon around a tree in her front
yard for her husband, who was being held hostage at the U.S. embassy in Teheran. According to popular accounts, Laingen sparked a
trend in which the families and hometowns of the hostages displayed
yellow ribbons to signal their hopes for the hostages' safe release.
Since then, the ribbons have cropped up in other situations, including the disappearance of children in Atlanta in the early 1980s.

In each of these cases, the yellow ribbon has come to symbolize a
means of remembering someone who is away, possibly in danger.
Originally, a yellow ribbon referred to a specific person. This purpose
distinguishes them from the proliferation of ribbons of different colors that emerged in the early 1990s: red ribbons for AIDS awareness,
pink ribbons for the fight against breast cancer, purple ribbons
against urban violence, and so on. Whereas these ribbons symbolize
political stands, yellow ribbons initially conveyed a personal message
intended to be shared in a community and by the nation. In the
Gulf War, the yellow ribbons were worn by family members, war
supporters, and antiwar protesters, the latter in an attempt to convey
support for the troops while opposing U.S. policy. Gulf War protest-

ers sought not to repeat what is now considered a mistake of the Vietnam War protesters: failure to separate the warrior from the warmongers.

Yet because of its history, the yellow ribbon also connotes feminization. Laura Marks argues that the yellow ribbons refer "specifically to women as sexually faithful stay-at-homes whose constancy is crucial to the morale of individual soldiers, and hence of the military as a whole. Because of the persistent myth that returning Vietnam veterans' lives were destroyed by the country's hostile welcome home, the admonition now comes laden with guilt."[32]

When, during the Gulf War, the yellow ribbons were exhibited as a symbol by people with diverse stands on the war, their meaning began to shift, and they easily became appropriated as a national symbol. They came to symbolize not simply personal concern for an individual far away but a national display of patriotism. Like the phrase "support our troops," which was employed with different intent by both pro- and antiwar factions, the yellow ribbon acquired several meanings. A tension emerged between personalized yellow ribbons offered solely as talismans for the safety of a loved one at war and the mass-produced yellow ribbons employed amid spectacles such as the jingoistic Super Bowl halftime ceremony in January 1991. The yellow ribbon was transformed from a personal expression into an avowal of faith in the imagined national community, a means by which consent was created, and a symbol of America's renewed confidence in its role as a world power.

The yellow ribbons were endlessly promoted on television, which ultimately functioned as a central means by which they evolved from individualized statements into a national symbol. However, despite being coopted by the nationalist narratives created in the television theater of the war, the yellow ribbons were still a means of personal expression, of measuring the cost of the war in human terms. Between an individual's crafting of a yellow ribbon and the yellow ribboning of a nation, the war's meaning shifts between cultural memory and national myth.

Cultural Memory and Gulf War Syndrome

The national yellow ribboning and the huge welcome home for the Gulf War veterans prompted some to ask, "What about the Vietnam veterans?" and "Why don't people with AIDS get yellow ribbons?"[33] The public response to the Gulf War veterans was a painful reminder to both Vietnam veterans and people with AIDS of their invisibility in American culture. However, the visibility of the Gulf War veterans was short-lived. The military worked in concert with the media to present the Gulf War as a single, tightly scripted narrative. Yet the presence of veterans does not allow for such a simple historicization. The veterans of the Gulf War were supposed to exorcise the specter of the Vietnam veterans. They fought in a short war in which they were well protected and well armed; they enjoyed immense support at home and were given a huge welcome home parade. Hence, they were awarded all the things the Vietnam veterans had been denied. They were not supposed to have problems, as the Vietnam veterans had; they were supposed to go back to being productive citizens and to fade from public consciousness.

Yet since 1992 large numbers of Gulf War veterans have been turning up at hospitals run by the Department of Veterans Affairs with a broad array of unexplained symptoms—fatigue, headaches, rashes, aching joints, memory loss—which they attribute to their time spent in the Gulf. At first physicians diagnosed these symptoms as psychological problems, variations on post-traumatic stress syndrome. However, after approximately 20,000 of the 700,000 troops who served in the Gulf had sought medical treatment for a variety of ailments, the term "Gulf War Syndrome" was coined. There is some speculation that the syndrome may be contagious, perhaps caused by a virus, because family members of veterans have also been affected. Studies show that among affected veterans, 78 percent of their spouses are affected, and 25 percent of their children born since the war suffer from chronic respiratory problems. An abnormally high percentage of the children of Gulf War veterans have severe birth defects.[34] Gulf War Syndrome has been the subject of several inconclusive government studies and is the focus of an intense debate about whether and how veterans should be compensated.

In American culture, a syndrome has come to represent a set of symptoms (a condition, not a disease) that connotes susceptibility. For instance, Acquired Immune Deficiency Syndrome (AIDS) weakens the functioning of healthy immune systems so that the body is unable to resist infection effectively. The name "Gulf War Syndrome" thus implies a transformed physical condition, a weakened body. It is deeply ironic that a war commonly perceived to have wiped out the "Vietnam Syndrome" has produced an unexplained syndrome of its own. The Vietnam Syndrome is defined as a mentality of overprotection, a weakness of resolve and a fear of repeating a national mistake. Gulf War Syndrome is emblematic of a bodily response—the unexplained symptoms that follow a war experience. This syndrome has recalled for Gulf War veterans the effects of Agent Orange and the battles fought by Vietnam veterans to be compensated for their exposure to this chemical agent, which has caused fatal cancer in many veterans and birth defects in some of their children.

Cultural memory of the Gulf War is thus asserted through the bodies of its veterans and their family members. These memories are working against the historicization of the Gulf War as a high-tech virtual war in which bodies, American or other, did not exist. The damaged bodies of the veterans threaten to expose secretive government agendas. Rumors have been rampant since the emergence of Gulf War Syndrome that U.S. troops were subject to chemical attack, which the government chose not to inform them about, and that the anti-chemical drugs they were given were untested and highly toxic. These damaged bodies also attest to the fact that this was not a clean war of "surgical strikes" but one in which a huge area was subject to environmental destruction, with extensive oil and chemical fires and water pollution. Recent research also has shown that the U.S. military's efforts to "protect" the troops may have backfired; in combination, the insecticide sprayed on troops and the drugs they took to prevent nerve damage in chemical attack are toxic to the nervous system.[35]

The persistence of Gulf War Syndrome attests to the trauma of the postwar experience. The Gulf War veterans did not suffer through year-long tours of duty, as the Vietnam veterans did. Although they were greeted as returning war heroes, they were also the subjects of public debate about how much hardship and danger they actually experienced, particularly in comparison to the Vietnam veterans. Robert Jay Lifton writes, "Since our side seemed to be doing almost all the fighting, a number of Americans began to wonder whether 'war'—which suggests a struggle between two armed forces—was the right term for what was occurring."[36] These soldiers were not supposed to experience postwar trauma, yet Gulf War Syndrome appears to be exactly that. How much of this trauma is attributable to the veterans' realization of the discrepancy between the experience of war and its representation, their visceral understanding of war's incommensurability with everyday life? There are many potential medical reasons for Gulf War Syndrome, but the government's difficulty in defining its causes cannot be separated from what its existence implies—that these veterans will not erase the presence of the Vietnam veterans as troubling reminders of the costs of war.

It is unclear how the U.S. government will eventually explain Gulf War Syndrome and whether it will compensate veterans who suffer from it. Yet it is evident that the bodies of the Gulf War veterans, which like those of the Vietnam veterans are bodies of survivors, will continue to tangle with the official history that the war was a clean exercise. In a sense, the American veterans thus offer a reminder of the Arab soldiers and civilians who were killed or injured in the war, whose bodies remain invisible to the American public. It is testament to the complexity of American national discourse that even this war, with its policed public representation, has a contested meaning and emerging cultural memory. Gulf War Syndrome is the cultural memory of the Gulf War, the memory that war has deeply troubling and long-lasting consequences, that it is neither instant nor virtual.

Chapter Five

AIDS and the Politics of Representation

The AIDS epidemic represents a profound sense of upheaval in medical progress, national community, and cultural politics. As an event that disrupts certain previously held "truths," it is described by many cultural critics as postmodern. Postmodernity has been defined as a condition of antimemory, a reworking and refolding of events in an endless cycle that produces no memory and no history. Yet the AIDS epidemic has produced an extraordinary discourse on memory and the problems of remembering and forgetting. In the debates over how AIDS is represented in popular culture, the media, and art, in the remembering that takes place through the AIDS Memorial Quilt, and in the depictions of the immune system and HIV in popular science, memory—in all its urgency and fragility, its images and testimonies—is a constant refrain.

AIDS has primarily affected specific populations in American society, certain "categories" of Americans whose relationship to the mainstream is tenuous and fraught with conflicting agendas of inclusion and exclusion. Gay men, inner-city blacks and Latinos, and people with hemophilia, the populations hit hardest by the epidemic, constitute challenges to the idea of a homogenous American public.[1] AIDS emerged early and devastatingly in urban gay communities, which predominantly comprise middle-class professionals. From the beginning, AIDS was associated in this country with practices regarded as deviant (homosexuality, drug use, sexual promiscuity). Yet because it affected at least one community that has a sophisticated understanding of the media and marketing, the representation of AIDS has been hotly contested in a variety of public arenas—alternative media, art museums, and public protests. Indeed, the cultural politics of AIDS have been like those of no other disease. AIDS has spawned what Paula Treichler has termed "an epidemic of signification,"[2] a proliferation of cultural meanings that parallels the medical epidemic. Furthermore, this "epidemic of signification," in which AIDS has been labeled everything from a CIA plot to a disease introduced by aliens or "God's punishment for our weaknesses," has spawned a significant amount of cultural, political, and linguistic analysis.

AIDS has emerged as a public phenomenon and a public-health crisis at a particular historical moment of emerging identity politics. Social groups, individually and in coalition, are claiming political identities derived from specific shared characteristics—gender, race, sexuality, ethnicity. Because AIDS has primarily affected disenfranchised groups, now defined by identity categories, debates about its representation have overlapped debates, both popular and academic, about political correctness and the usefulness of identity politics. The emergence of AIDS in the historical moment of the 1980s places it within the legacy of the cultural upheaval of the 1960s and 1970s. Those social movements formed the basis for the identity politics of the 1980s and 1990s and fostered public policies such as affirmative action that have come under attack in the 1980s and 1990s. AIDS began killing many young gay men at a moment in history when the visibility of the gay and lesbian community was at its height. It started killing many intravenous-drug users at a time when black and Latino communities were struggling to confront the explosion of drug use in inner-city neighborhoods and when the legacy of the civil rights and Chicano movements had produced active criticism of racist public policies and media representations. The emergence of AIDS was simultaneous with the rise of a politically powerful religious right determined to scale back public policies begun in the 1960s and wielding a rhetoric of morality, shame, and narrowly defined "family values." The AIDS epidemic began after the "sexual revolution," at a time when increased discussion of sexuality and publicly funded sex education were already under attack. It has also been the catalyst for a large body of art indebted to the avant-garde trends of the late 1960s and coinciding with the religious right's culture war on what it perceives to be "deviant" art.

The emergence of AIDS as a "full-blown" medical and cultural phenomenon thus speaks volumes about this moment in American history. It has produced a public discourse of hysteria and blame and a simultaneous counterdiscourse of criticism and defiance. AIDS has been extensively examined both in academic circles and through the highly visible and vocal presence of activists. The complexity of AIDS as a biomedical condition, one that is refiguring medical practice and research protocols, is thus replicated in the disease's cultural representation. Questions of how AIDS should be discussed and how the person with AIDS should be named and represented have paralleled questions of medicine and public policy, such as how experimental drugs should be tested, how research funding can best be allocated, and how people should be educated about prevention.

Because of these particularities, the AIDS epidemic has produced an array of cultural objects through grassroots efforts, cottage industries, and big business. These include the NAMES Project's AIDS Memorial Quilt, a significant number of books, and innumerable fundraising buttons, pins, posters, T-shirts, red ribbons, and slogans. Popular science writings and photographs have produced public images of HIV and AIDS as cultural entities, with "personalities" and specific characteristics. All of these are elements in the production of cultural memory of the AIDS epidemic. In Chapter 6 I examine the AIDS Quilt and its role in cultural memory, and in Chapter 7 I discuss the representation of AIDS and HIV in medicine and popular science. In this chapter I frame the politics of AIDS representation, in particular its effect upon how individuals respond to the epidemic or become marked by it in their lives and deaths. Though AIDS is a global pandemic, in the United States it is represented primarily as a national phenomenon, one often perceived to have infected the nation as a whole. In this chapter, I would like to tease apart the meanings of America's reckoning with AIDS.

Figures of Contamination

In the early 1980s in the United States, the person with AIDS was represented as a figure of disease whose meanings bore the legacy of centuries of disease representation. Throughout history, infected people have often been depicted as vessels containing a disease, as extensions of it. For instance, the person infected with tuberculosis was seen in the nineteenth century as a human incarnation of the disease itself, embodying both its tragic and its romantic characteristics. Similarly, the person with AIDS is seen to become AIDS, irrevocably altered by its presence.

The representation of AIDS can thus be charted through the history of representation of infectious and sexually transmitted diseases such as the plague, tuberculosis, leprosy, and syphilis as well as the history of images of the insane, the "perverse," and the homosexual as pathological figures. Historians have noted that tuberculosis was perceived as a disease that affected gifted, emotional, and spiritual individuals, a romantic affliction that heightened one's sense of creativity and tragedy. In contrast, because of its association with sexual contact, syphilis carried with it the stigma of moral deviancy. Sander Gilman has written that the syphilitic was marked from the beginning as a figure of sexual excess.[3] Yet syphilitic dementia, too, was romanticized as an aid to artistic genius. Susan Sontag notes that the protagonist of *Docter Faustus* voluntarily contracts syphilis as part of a bargain with the devil and that it provides him with twenty-four years of creative genius. She writes, "This romanticizing of the dementia characteristic of neurosyphilis was the forerunner of the much more persistent fantasy in this century about mental illness as a source of artistic creativity or spiritual originality."[4]

Like syphilis, AIDS carries the stigma of moral deviance, yet it also bears the image of a plague, a scourge upon an entire community. This emphasis on AIDS's contagiousness overstates its infectious potential. AIDS is not communicable through water, air, or insects, as are the plague and tuberculosis; it can be transmitted only through specific and intimate contact with bodily fluids such as blood and semen. Early fears that the disease could be spread through casual contact produced public hysteria in the mid-1980s and facilitated the imaging of AIDS as a twentieth-century plague. Although most people now know that AIDS cannot be easily transmitted, this "plague" image has stuck, in part because of the fact that many young people are dying in this epidemic. Consequently, AIDS carries the legacy of meanings attached both to infectious diseases, such as the plague and tuberculosis, and to sexually transmitted diseases, such as syphilis.

With the development of antibiotics that could cure syphilis, Sander Gilman argues, the image of the morally deviant person was temporarily without a corresponding disease:

[T]he "taming" of syphilis and other related sexually transmitted diseases with the introduction of antibiotics in the 1940s left our culture with a series of images of the mortally infected and infecting patient suffering a morally repugnant disease but without a sufficiently powerful disease with which to associate these images. During the 1970s there was an attempt to connect these images with genital herpes, but even though it is a sexually transmitted disease, its symptomology was too trivial to warrant this association over the long run. AIDS was the perfect disease for such associations, even if it was not a typical sexually transmitted disease.[5]

These associations with contamination and moral deviancy, compounded by terror of a plague, gave rise to tremendous fears in the 1980s, prompting discussions of quarantine in the Senate and the exclusion of children with AIDS from public schools.

Katherine Park has written that the politics of blame that developed with AIDS in American society must be situated within the tradition of European Christian culture. Park argues that the "idea of a moral plague" originated with leprosy.[6] In the early Middle Ages the concept of disease as divine punishment bore little currency, but by the eleventh and twelfth centuries leprosy was increasingly associated with sexual vice, and lepers were eventually quarantined in colonies. Park attributes this shift not only to the tendency of the Christian tradition to sexualize evil but also to what R. I. Moore calls "the formation of a persecuting society," which persecuted, among others, Jews, lepers, heretics, and homosexuals.[7] In this kind of society, disease cannot be naturalized; it must be assigned a cause, attributed to specific social subgroups, and linked to immorality.

Park's formulation raises interesting questions about the politics of blame. What aspects of late twentieth-century American culture, for instance, mark it as a "persecuting society" steeped in the European Christian tradition? How did the circumstances of the transmission of AIDS make it the "perfect" disease for a politics of blame? Ironically, leprosy is now known to be significantly less transmissible than initially thought; like AIDS, it was mythologized to be highly infectious, in part because of the visible and shocking physical deformation it can cause.

The figure with AIDS, like the syphilitic and the leper, represents the capacity to infect the *morals* of the greater population. In the United States, this image is irrevocably tied to the fact that gay men constituted the first visible group of people dying of AIDS. Though studies now reveal that large numbers of intravenous-drug users contracted AIDS-related pneumonia in the early 1980s, these statistics caused little alarm. Not only did IV-drug users fail to constitute a demographic category, but their deaths were not considered unusual.[8] However, when otherwise healthy, middle-class gay men began displaying symptoms of strange "opportunistic" diseases, medical professionals were inclined to identify a new disease "syndrome." That AIDS was first called GRID (Gay-Related Immune Deficiency) underscores its initial and powerful association with gay men and their sexual habits and attitudes, in particular the embrace by some of promiscuity as sexual freedom. Thus, the person contaminated with AIDS was from the beginning considered a figure of sexual deviancy and threat. Even more than the leper or the syphilitic, the person with AIDS was perceived to be socially irresponsible and hedonistic, who sacrificed life and health for perverse pleasure with strangers. It did not matter that AIDS had infected people of diverse sexual persuasions, lifestyles, and ages, that many individuals had been infected before AIDS and its means of transmission were identified, or that the gay community was the first to organize AIDS health care and education programs. Each person with AIDS was marked by association with the figure of the narcissistic and reckless gay man.

For the American public at large, the response to the AIDS epidemic shifted in 1985 from a fear of the infectious gay plague to a panic over heterosexual sex. This shift was precipitated in part by the announcement that one of America's icons of middle-class masculinity, Rock Hudson, was dying of AIDS. Despite his recalcitrant public acknowledgment of the disease, Hudson became the means through which straight, white, middle-class America saw themselves vulnerable to AIDS.

As a 1950s icon of clean sexuality and virility, Hudson was an unlikely catalyst in the American public's reaction to homosexuality before the 1970s.[9] Hudson's closeted sexuality symbolized America's denial of homosexuality in its midst. His disclosure of his illness forced into public view a deeply conflicted image of the person with AIDS—the embodiment of American manhood now contaminated, wasting away. That such an icon could be revealed to be both gay and sick with AIDS exacerbated the crisis of American masculinity, already in upheaval in the aftermath of the Vietnam War. Frank Rich asked:

Does Hudson's skill at playing a heterosexual mean that he was a brilliant actor, or was this just the way he really was, without acting at all? I suspect that most Americans believed that Hudson, who seemed so natural on screen, was playing himself, which means that in the summer of 1985 we had to accept the fact that many of our fundamental, conventional images of heterosexuality were instilled in us (and not for the first time) by a homosexual.[10]

Hudson was perceived as perpetrating a betrayal (most obviously manifested by considerable public interest in whether the women who had played romantic leads opposite Hudson felt at risk or betrayed) and a fraud upon the American public, to which he had represented good, safe (heterosexual) manhood. In death he became perceived as the person who contaminated American sexuality and blurred the boundary between gay and straight, a boundary that is both transgressed and policed in the context of the epidemic.

Although the disclosure of Hudson's disease made the person with AIDS seem familiar (and thereby instigated a panic about AIDS among heterosexuals), his complex public image did not reduce the correlation of AIDS with sexual deviancy. Indeed, it may have acted to shift the association of the epidemic with gay (deviant) sexuality to simply deviant sexuality and the threat of the bisexual man. In 1985 the public threat was that deadly consequences of sex would "spread" to the "general population." Many people with AIDS have publicly noted their shock when in July 1985 *Life* magazine published a cover that read, "Now No One Is Safe from AIDS," as if those already infected were outside the general public.[11] This "no one" served to mark those already struggling with AIDS as not "anyone," but it also created an awareness of AIDS as a condition not neatly restricted to specific categories of people.

Media representations of the person with AIDS as a source of contamination and sexual deviancy proliferated in the mid- to late 1980s, primarily in the form of starkly lit photographs portraying signs of the disease: lesions, wasting limbs, loss of hair. These images must be seen in the context of a history of the documentation of disease and deviancy. Since its invention in the early nineteenth century, photography has been deployed by social institutions as a means of cataloguing, documenting, and labeling medical pathologies. In nineteenth-century Europe, hospitals routinely set up photographic laboratories to create visual records of disease, physical deformity, and mental illness. Many historians of photography, citing Michel Foucault's argument that power in modern societies is enacted through institutionalization and normalization rather than through repression, have noted the role that photography played in instituting medical norms, creating categories of deviance (such as homosexuality), and aiding in the social policing of the state. Roberta McGrath argues that photography aided in the construction of medical pathologies precisely because it does not allow the patient to speak:

The doctor, armed with the photograph, provided the lay counterpart to the miracle in a society where the ministering of souls had been replaced by the ministering of bodies. The patient, within this matrix, was allotted to the role of audio-visual aid. They became "the books out of which the medical student must read at bedside" or "a portable painting which must be forever observed." Increasingly the patient became a symptom of her/his disease.[12]

Photographs, including x-ray images, became tools in the representation of the patient as a vessel of disease—indeed, as simply the terrain on which the disease was manifested; they tended to dehumanize the patient. This tradition of medical photography affected the representation of people with AIDS, in that photographs of patients automatically tend to reduce the subject to a symptom of the disease. Thus, even "well-intended" images of people marked by disease can serve to reinforce fear of contamination.

Douglas Crimp has written at length about the politics of documentary photographs of people with AIDS. He argues that critically lauded documentary photographs by Nicholas Nixon and Rosalind Solomon—in which people with AIDS are seen alone, deteriorating over a period of time until death—reinforce traditional notions of photographic realism. Some critics suggested that the subjects eventually became so exhausted by disease that they lost their self-consciousness and allowed the camera to register their "true" selves. Crimp states that these images are imbued with contradictions; although they imply a "consensual" relationship between the photographer and the subject, these photographs convey not growing trust but rather the subject's increased abandonment of self.[13] Hence, rather than gaining a sense of the subject's humanity, spectators witness the subject's loss of identity, his or her surrender to the camera's gaze. For Crimp, these are "phobic" images that reinforce the labeling of the person with AIDS (PWA) as contaminating:

[T]here is a deeper explanation for portrayals of PWAs, and especially gay male PWAs, as desperately ill, as either grotesquely disfigured or as having wasted to fleshless, ethereal bodies. These are not images that are intended to overcome our fear of disease and death, as is sometimes claimed. Nor are they meant only to reinforce the status of the PWA as victim or pariah, as we often charge. Rather, they are, precisely, *phobic* images, images of the terror at imagining the person with AIDS as still sexual.[14]

The fear of people with AIDS or HIV is precisely that they are not always visibly diseased, that contaminating figures can circulate among the "healthy" population without detection. Documentary photographs of the disfigured, drained bodies of those in the final stages of disease thus offer reassurance that the person with AIDS is detectable, not invisible or among "us."

One of the first protests dealing specifically with the politics of the visual representation of AIDS took place at Nicholas Nixon's exhibition of black-and-white photographs at the Museum of Modern Art

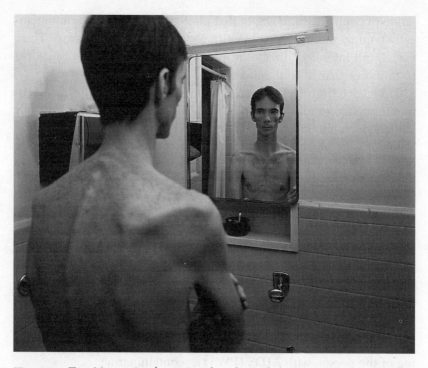

Figure 15. Tom Moran, October 1987. Photo by Nicholas Nixon. Courtesy Zabriskie Gallery.

in 1988 (see Figure 15). A group of protesters from ACT UP (AIDS Coalition to Unleash Power) handed out flyers protesting the photographic exhibition as a misguided attempt to give the disease a "face." Their critique served notice that public representations of AIDS would no longer go unmarked or unanalyzed. Their flyer read, in part:

No More Pictures without Consent: We believe the representation of people with AIDS affects not only how viewers will perceive PWAs outside the museum, but, ultimately, crucial issues of AIDS funding, legislation, and education. In portraying PWAs as people to be pitied or feared, as people alone and lonely, we believe that this show perpetuates general misconceptions about AIDS without addressing the realities of those of us living every day with this crisis as PWAs and people who love PWAs. . . . The PWA is a human being whose health has deteriorated not simply due to a virus, but due to government inaction, the inaccessibility of affordable health care, and institutionalized neglect in the forms of heterosexism, racism, and sexism. We demand the visibility of PWAs who are vibrant, angry, loving, sexy, beautiful, acting up and fighting back. Stop Looking at Us; Start Listening to Us.[15]

On one hand, this flyer expresses a sophisticated analysis of the effects of visual representations upon public opinion, health care, and government policy, as well as a critique of the concept of "natural" disease. On the other hand, it displays an almost naive engagement with the question of what constitute "good" and "bad" images. The demand for exclusively positive images of people with AIDS in itself constitutes a problematic assertion. What does it mean to require the "positive" in the context of an epidemic in which the reality is that people are dying, often quite painfully? Though ACT UP members offer a complex reading of the power of documentary images, their attempt to replace these images can also be read as a desire to police AIDS representation. Simon Watney writes:

It is understandable that AIDS activists are outraged by the relentless fatalism and negativity of most images of people living with AIDS, but we should not be tempted simply to duplicate the disavowal of the mass media with our own forms of denial. For it would be profoundly misleading to imagine that totally "positive" images are ultimately more truthful or representative of AIDS than the most morbid excesses of photojournalism and documentaries.[16]

Watney argues that the desire to balance media representations of AIDS with positive images plays on the illusion that a "single universal 'truth' " of AIDS is attainable. Hence, the AIDS epidemic poses essential problems regarding the concept of documentary truth and faithful representation. Indeed, it demonstrates that the representation of AIDS can never simply be subject to the codes of documentary truth precisely because the epidemic is so immediate and highly politicized. Jan Grover notes that Nixon's and Solomon's work "tells us nothing about the historic battles surrounding AIDS and its representation."[17] Yet, one could ask, is this the role of the documentary photograph, and isn't an untimely death always political? In the politics of AIDS representation, the documentary can no longer remain unmarked.

The Figure with AIDS:
Divided Communities

In the U.S. media, the person with AIDS has been identified as a gay man or, occasionally, a drug addict. The diverse range of people affected by AIDS and involved in activism and support has been reduced in the media to this narrow profile, just as medical models of AIDS have relied, inaccurately, on a single patient profile. The reality is that AIDS has had different effects on gay and inner-city communities. The epidemic has spurred the formation of coalitions of previously unconnected communities, yet the issue of "ownership" of the epidemic has increased tensions between what were already divided communities. These debates over ownership have been fueled by conflicts between the gay community and inner-city communities about responsibility for and control of the politics and maintenance of the epidemic.

The construction of an AIDS community in the United States has taken place in a particular context of volunteerism, primarily on the part of gay men and lesbian and straight women. Gay men and lesbians often see AIDS activism and support work as necessary for the survival of their communities; white, middle-class heterosexual women have been involved in AIDS volunteering in part because of women's traditional involvement in health care and often because of their individual relationships with gay men. Cindy Patton notes that large numbers of such women became involved in AIDS volunteering in 1985–1986, at the height of the widespread hysteria about contracting AIDS through casual contact. She writes:

Heterosexual white women also volunteered in large numbers, but not because they were depicted as at risk of HIV from their boyfriends or husbands, but because they are the traditional volunteer reservoir. . . . This influx of women was taken as a sign that the white middle-class was educated about AIDS and had overcome its homophobia. But heterosexual white men were almost never volunteers unless they had a close relative with AIDS.[18]

The changing definition of the gay community from one of sexual pleasure to one of healing and caring created an opportunity for straight white women to accept that community in new ways.

The participation of straight white women in AIDS support has been little noted, as if their involvement is considered only natural. Indeed, a shift has taken place in the relationship between the heterosexual female population and the gay community, which has increasingly made noticeable the lack of participation by heterosexual men. The participation of many older women in the AIDS movement also marks a unique and very new coalition.

Yet the AIDS crisis has served less as a catalyst to bridge-building than as an example of the profound divisions of race and privilege that exist in this country. Ownership of the epidemic is one not of partnership but of finger-pointing. Black organizations accuse white organizations, for instance, of wanting to "own" the epidemic by refusing to surrender their status as experts, whereas white organizations have accused the black and Latino communities, in particular the black church, of refusing to "own" it.[19] These kinds of accusations reveal how these communities are perceived to have no overlap—all gays are coded as white and middle-class, all blacks and Latinos as potential drug users.

If AIDS had been confined to poor inner-city black and Latino neighborhoods, it would not necessarily have been "discovered" and defined for years, given those communities' limited ability to push for government action. The opportunistic infections that occur in those exposed to HIV through sharing IV-drug needles tend to be different from those of individuals exposed via sexual activity—many gay men developed the otherwise rare Kaposi's sarcoma, whereas many drug users contracted pneumonia and were often dead by the time epidemiologists tried to contact them.[20] Hence, the profile of AIDS as a gay male disease eclipsed the epidemic in the inner cities for years.[21] The medical emphasis on a single patient profile has widened the divisions between the communities affected by AIDS. In black and Latino communities, AIDS is yet another problem in a broader context of inadequate government services, appallingly inadequate health care, and systematic economic struggle. Cindy Patton writes that in these communities,

instead of being articulated as a wholly new issue into which enormous group resources must be shifted—which was the approach in the gay communities (though not without great concern that AIDS was sidetracking other gay civil rights efforts)—AIDS, though viewed as important, was seen as a phenomenon already understandable through the existing analysis of government neglect, of poverty and of lack of access to health care and education.[22]

The response in black communities to AIDS is also intimately tied to the scientific hypothesis that AIDS originated in Africa,[23] one that has angered blacks and spurred the construction of countertheories—for example, that AIDS is the result of a government conspiracy to wipe out the black race.[24] The debates about the black community's resistance to "owning" AIDS often include accusations that it is more homophobic than other ethnic communities. Such accusations are highly suspect. bell hooks notes that "black communities may be perceived as more homophobic than other communities because there is a tendency for individuals in black communities to verbally express in an outspoken way anti-gay sentiments."[25] In addition, Harlon Dalton writes that because of racism, homosexuality in the black community is inevitably linked to the emasculation of the black male produced by Jim Crow and slavery and thus carries a different kind of cultural baggage. Dalton notes that there are several reasons for the black community's response to AIDS:

The first is that many African-Americans are reluctant to acknowledge our association with AIDS so long as the larger society seems bent on blaming us as a race for its origin and initial spread. Second, the deep-seated suspicion and mistrust many of us feel whenever whites express sudden interest in our well-being hampers our progress in dealing with AIDS. Third, the pathology of our own homophobia hobbles us. Fourth, the uniquely problematic relationship we as a community have to the phenomenon of drug abuse complicates our dealing with AIDS. And fifth, many in the black community have difficulty transcending the deep resentment we feel at being dictated to once again.[26]

Thus, battles over the ownership of AIDS are deeply rooted in the history of racism and economic discrimination in this society. Though AIDS is often described as a disease that affects the marginalized in American society, these divisions make it clear that the gay community and communities of color do not share similar experiences of marginalization.

A consequence of these profound differences has been a dramatic range of emotional responses to AIDS. The rage of inner-city communities of color does not necessarily take the style of demonstrations by groups such as ACT UP, which includes civil disobedience at government buildings. The anger that fuels ACT UP and other AIDS activist groups, which have been extremely effective in changing policy and improving treatments, is one derived from entitlement—the idea that the system should be working better for people with AIDS, that people have a right to proper health care and available treatments. This assumption of entitlement is not necessarily shared in inner-city communities, where the system is not perceived as working to one's benefit.

AIDS representation has, in the tradition of disease representation, marked those who have the disease with a particular identity, erasing the profound differences among them. The media's continued linkage of the person with AIDS to the negative stereotype of the reckless gay man masks not only the gay community's AIDS care and education but also the complexity of the epidemic's effect on communities of color. The question of who is deployed to represent the person with AIDS is thus a highly charged issue.

Disclaiming the Victim

The politics of AIDS representation has centered on the issue of who speaks for people with AIDS, and activists have consistently wrestled for control of the debate. This battle has intersected with identity politics, the central tenets of which are proclaiming one's identity and declaring that identity as crucial to one's ability to speak. These discourses have centered on two issues: naming and victimhood.

Naming in the context of AIDS has been associated with a certain amount of risk. Issues of anonymity and stigma were particularly pronounced in the first years of the epidemic, when most people with AIDS chose to keep their illness a secret. In the midst of debates about anonymous testing for HIV, with conservatives demanding that people with AIDS be traced, catalogued, and quarantined and with insurance companies excluding people with AIDS from medical coverage, naming was an act of both defiance and affirmation. In this context, naming oneself as a person with AIDS, or naming a loved one as a person with AIDS, constituted both a stand against discriminatory policies and an assertion of one's identity. Naming might mean loss of insurance, employment, and/or family and friends. Thus, the naming of the dead in the AIDS Memorial Quilt, which has often taken place amid conflict, can still be a highly politicized act of remembering. In the AIDS Quilt, naming is often equivalent to coming out, because representation in the quilt still carries the association of being gay; this connotation resulted, particularly in the first years of the quilt, in many unnamed and partially named panels.

The discourse of self-naming was also a crucial element of debates in the late 1980s and early 1990s about the culture of "victimology." Identity politics—in which specific groups define themselves in terms of race, gender, sexuality, or some other characteristic, to acquire a political voice and others counter with accusations of reverse discrimination—has romanticized the concept of marginalization. Activists are often accused of embracing victimhood for political gain. For example, the popular media have represented feminists as advocating the notion that women are constantly victimized by men and patriarchy, a misrepresentation that exaggerates a small portion of the spectrum of feminist thought. The concept of victimhood can also be seen among middle-class white men, who in the 1990s increasingly claim to be victimized by policies favoring women and minorities, particularly in college admissions and the workplace. The volatile debates in the art world about "victim art" serve as yet another example.[27]

Thus, at the time when the AIDS epidemic emerged in the United States, the idea of "victimhood" was already hotly contested. Very early on, AIDS activists and organizations campaigned against the use of the phrase "AIDS victim." In 1983 a committee at the second International Conference on AIDS issued a statement condemning the use of the term "victim" and endorsing "people with AIDS (PWAs)." In the late 1980s, the NAMES Project issued a flyer that read, in part:

The term "victim" dehumanizes people with AIDS by emphasizing their deaths rather than their strength in living with AIDS. Many people feel that the term "victim" invites a statistical approach to AIDS, and denies the individuality of each person who has lived—and died—with AIDS. More than that, the use of "victim" creates the false impression that People With AIDS are distinct from everyone else. In a very real sense, we are all living with AIDS.

Jan Grover has argued that "AIDS victim" promotes a disabling fear of and pity for the person with AIDS, as well as a fatalism that allows for the blaming of the victim.[28]

Indeed, the term "victim" has become for all practical purposes inoperable. It is no longer possible to think of a context in which one could deploy the term for someone who is not dead—for instance, as a victim of crime, of rape, of the system. In the context of the politics of blame, "victim" can no longer mean someone who is merely unlucky but rather stigmatizes the subject as complicit in his or her victimization. A victim, someone who is rendered powerless by circumstance, cannot speak. Hence, the word itself has shifted meaning, acquiring the signification of blame and disempowerment at a time when cultural politics emphasizes the potential empowerment of all. Similarly, the attempt to change the focus from AIDS "risk groups," a common concept in medicine, to "risk behaviors" is intended to counter the perception of the epidemic as limited to and pervasive within specific social groups.

AIDS activists and cultural critics have argued that it is possible to educate the media and the general public about the effects of language and to replace negative terms with more positive ones. The term "AIDS virus" was criticized, for example, because it implied that testing positive for HIV was equivalent to having AIDS—an erroneous assumption, particularly in light of research questioning the singular role of HIV in causing AIDS.[29] The term "person with AIDS" (or, occasionally, "person living with AIDS") carries with it an array of meanings: the ability to name oneself, the notion of a person existing "with" a disease rather than as a victim of it, and the emphasis on living rather than dying.

This emphasis on living is highly politicized precisely because, unlike cancer, AIDS remains a disease of which one is never considered cured. Though people with HIV and AIDS are living increasingly longer and symptom-free lives, contemporary AIDS medicine primarily emphasizes disease management. Thus, to proclaim oneself "living" is also to counter the image of all people with AIDS as soon to be dead. In addition, the notion of someone "living with AIDS" implies a kind of coexistence or cohabitation, countering the historical concept of the patient as a vessel of the disease, someone transformed into a hybrid of person and illness.

To counter the image of people with AIDS as passive and victimized, ACT UP and other groups have promoted public images of a defiant, angry, and active population. Through the use of slogans such as "Act Up, Fight Back, Act Up, Fight AIDS," volatile and newscatching public demonstrations, and its very powerful logo (an upside-down pink triangle stating "Silence = Death"), ACT UP, especially at its peak in the late 1980s, has converted sophisticated cultural analysis into public spectacle.[30] ACT UP has been singularly successful in raising public awareness of AIDS: its demonstrations at the Federal Drug Administration headquarters prompted the government to change its policies on drug trials, and its posters about issues of racism, AIDS and women, and safe sex have effectively heightened public consciousness. Plastered on billboards, stuck on buses and subways, and spray-painted on sidewalks, AIDS activist art has become ubiquitous in New York and other cities. ACT UP's counter-representations of the epidemic and its affected groups have offset the image of people with AIDS as passively diseased.

The work produced by ACT UP can be seen as an example of the upheaval of certain cultural categories in late-twentieth-century American culture. ACT UP graphics are produced collectively and anonymously, borrow freely from advertising images and well-known artists' stylistic signatures, and are intended to confront and engage an array of audiences at different levels. Although ACT UP's work has been shown in museums and published in books, its primary exhibition space is the street; it is intended as a form of guerrilla art, catching people by surprise (an objective that its increased presence has worked against). Hence, AIDS activist art by groups such as ACT UP, Gran Fury, Testing the Limits, and others can be seen as fundamentally altering the dimensions of the public sphere and redefining the role of art as an enterprise of individual authorship, connoisseurship, and market value. Much of this material is thus not about aesthetics or artistic vision but about a message of urgency. Douglas Crimp and Adam Rolston write:

AIDS activist art is grounded in the accumulated knowledge and political analysis of the AIDS crisis produced collectively by the entire movement. The graphics not only reflect that knowledge, but actively contribute to its articulation as well. . . . They function as an organizing tool, by conveying, in compressed form, information and political positions to others affected by the epidemic, to onlookers at demonstrations, and to the dominant media. But their primary audience is the movement itself. AIDS activist graphics enunciate AIDS politics to and for all of us in the movement.[31]

The function of AIDS activist art is thus to articulate publicly the messages of a loosely organized, diverse movement, to define the movement to itself. It works on a daily basis to counter images of people with AIDS as victims and to produce an image in the larger American culture of AIDS activists (coded as gay activists) as confrontational, angry, and loud.

The Romanticization of AIDS

For the majority of people who have been affected by the AIDS epidemic in the United States, feelings of loss, pain, and grief have often been offset by a recognition of the remarkable courage and sense of purpose displayed by so many people who are living with HIV and AIDS and facing death. It is possible to speak without sentimentality of the palpable spiritual growth that many people have undergone upon finding out they were infected with HIV or had AIDS. For many, this discovery prompts a total change of career, lifestyle, and values, a deeper engagement with philosophical questions of life's purpose and finitude, and a deeper appreciation of their relationships to others. For many people who have worked as volunteers and AIDS care providers, or who have supported friends and/or family members with the disease, the experience has been transformative, sometimes radicalizing people who were previously politically indifferent and often providing them with a profoundly altered sense of life's meaning.

Though it is important to recognize that many different kinds of people have been genuinely touched by the courage of those who have faced AIDS, it is also crucial to note that class and proximity to the heart of the epidemic have affected discourses of spiritual growth. In many inner-city black and Latino communities, AIDS is just another element of hardship, despair, economic deprivation, and lack of access to proper health care. In such contexts, there are limited time and resources to engage with concepts of spiritual growth. Similarly, for many gay men, the relentless loss of so many friends and lovers and the expense and complications of medical treatments have prompted cynicism rather than the satisfaction of finding life's purpose and facing death with dignity.

However, there is plenty of evidence (including the AIDS Quilt) that this epidemic has profoundly touched and altered people's lives, both directly and indirectly. The cultural meanings of AIDS are so complex, and its representation still so rapidly in flux, that it has become an epidemic of romanticization as well as of stigma. In its omnipresence and in the relentlessness of its cultural analysis, AIDS has in some sense been normalized, by which I mean that it no longer is a crisis or emergency situation but rather is part of the everyday. This normalization constitutes both a fatalism about the relentlessness of the epidemic and a romanticism about being touched by it. Both responses have enabled what is now referred to as the "second wave" of the epidemic.

In 1992 AIDS educators in the gay community admitted that, after initial successes, they appeared not to have reached the new generation of gay men, large numbers of whom were practicing unsafe sex.[32] At one level, this failure forced a rethinking of educational models based on the simple notion that if you informed people about how to prevent infection and save their lives, they would change their behavior. AIDS educators have struggled to update this model, which has also proved ineffective in educating youth who feel they are invulnerable. Walt Odets, a therapist working with many gay men, has written that AIDS education failed because its message was too rigid, the rules of safe sex simply impossible for most gay men to follow:

The rigidity of that message has contributed to a widely held sense that contracting HIV is inevitable—"not if but when," as one of my patients put it. As a consequence, many gay men engage impulsively or unthinkingly in risky behavior, behavior that really *could* be avoided, at least most of the time, even over a lifetime. When HIV infection seems inevitable, many men derive comfort from contracting it now, thus eliminating anxiety about *when*.[33]

In retrospect, it seems that AIDS educators did not anticipate the effects of a long-term epidemic on the gay community. So much emphasis was placed on finding a cure in the first decade of the epidemic that the issue of how the community could survive over time was avoided. Odets writes:

Gay male communities, especially those in urban centers, have become accustomed to a form of life completely unimaginable ten years ago: a 50 percent overall infection rate, 10 to 40 percent infection rates among segments of the young gay community, and 70 percent among older groups. In San Francisco, 30 percent of twenty-year-olds will be infected with or dead of AIDS by age thirty; the majority will become HIV-infected at some point during their lifetime.[34]

As a consequence of these high rates of infection in relatively contained urban communities, a culture of positivity has emerged. This shift from the emerging epidemic in the 1980s to the reality of AIDS in the 1990s has produced an outlook predicated on premature death, that is both fatalistic and romantic about the prospect of dying young, and that is based on a heightened awareness of the process of living. Michael Warner writes:

In the eyes of the straight world, gay still means AIDS; to come out is to come into the epidemic. More to the point, our own lives are bound up with positive friends and lovers to such a degree that many gay men are unwilling to say openly that they are negative. It sounds like an affront, a betrayal of the men with whom we identify, and in comparison with whom our troubles may seem trivial. From treatment activism to magazines like *Poz* and *Diseased Pariah News*, and the works of artists like Bill T. Jones and David Wojnarowicz, positive men have developed a culture of articulacy about mortality and the expectations of "normal life." When negative men identify with positive men, they are not just operating out of survivor guilt. They are staking their interests with that culture and taking as their own its priorities, its mordant humor, its heightened tempo, its long view of the world.[35]

The culture of positivity can be seen as a specific phenomenon of well-defined gay communities, in which AIDS is omnipresent in every aspect of cultural life. It has been a primary component in fueling AIDS volunteerism. Indeed, a desire for positivity can be seen as a desire to belong in the gay community, to feel truly at its center. "I thought if I was HIV-positive I'd be so much gayer," one man told the *New York Times*. "People are looking for the red badge of courage, and you get that when you convert."[36]

The equation of gay men with AIDS and HIV and the representation of positivity as inevitably leading to AIDS have also had the effect of negating the presence of gay men who are HIV-negative. David Roman has written that the political concept that "we are all HIV-positive," though effective for providing a united front, erases the experience of the epidemic for gay men who are *not* positive. He writes:

As a public stance of communal identification and solidarity, the HIV-negative's political insistence that "we are all HIV-positive" intervenes in the potential divisions between HIV-negatives and HIV-positives and puts pressure on HIV-negatives to get involved in AIDS activism "as if your life depended on it." But the phrase also plays into the majoritarian hysteria of associative contagion, on the one hand, and the conflation of HIV with gay men on the other.[37]

Roman argues that the representation of HIV-negative gay men in public culture and the arts depicts them as both boring and depressing, their lives hardly worth living.

Much of this romanticization of positivity is understandable; people with HIV and AIDS need to go on living, and to do so they need some source of optimism. Unfortunately, it sets a difficult standard, a requirement for sainthood and spiritual enlightenment, among individuals who may simply want to be sick and angry. Daniel Harris contends that the "happy-go-lucky, can-do attitudes" of popular psychology have produced a context in which a feel-good patina is laid on a tragic situation. He writes that the collision of AIDS with the self-help movement has produced

a dissonance perhaps best expressed in the testimonials of gay men with AIDS who deny the imminence of their death and even claim that the disease is, as one Bay Area patient put it in an interview in the *San Francisco Examiner*, "the most wonderful thing that ever happened in my life." . . .

The modern therapeutic paradigms from which AIDS profiteers derive their methods thus fail spectacularly to acknowledge tragedy and refuse to admit that anything could evade the resourcefulness of the human will.[38]

Though Harris's critique is harsh, it reveals the difficulty of balancing an acknowledgment of the epidemic's devastation with a sense of hope and community.

A sense of belonging is related to intimacy; ironically, in the 1990s, this means that exposure to infection has also shifted meaning. What was once considered reckless and selfish behavior is recoded as heroic, an expression of true love. For many people, gay or straight, unsafe sex is a means of expressing profound intimacy and trust, a gift one gives to someone else.[39] When such intimacy is deemed the truest expression of love, AIDS education can do little to change behaviors. This dilemma may require a complete rethinking of the concept of rationality. Annick Prieur writes that many researchers don't understand what it means to have one's sex life labeled dangerous and can only think of unsafe sex as a negative option in a model of rational choice. She states, "But the world is not that simple; unsafe sex is also rational behaviour—but a wider understanding of rationality is needed: including longing and love and motives for action."[40]

It is also important to acknowledge the historical correlation between danger and sex. For women throughout most of history, the lack of effective birth control and the health risks of pregnancy rendered sex a dangerous activity. Other, often fatal sexually transmitted diseases tinged sexual activity with risk and danger. Thus, the practice of unsafe sex in the gay community is not unique but rather is typical of the relationship of human sexuality to risk.[41]

Ironically, the "second wave" of the epidemic indicates that despite the stigma attached to AIDS in the United States as a whole, within the specific subculture of the gay community AIDS has acquired the romanticism previously associated with tuberculosis. Like those diseases, AIDS has come to be associated with a heightened artistic awareness, a tragic yet romantic early death, a sense of purpose. It may be that this was inevitable in a community devastated so quickly, a community composed of a large number of artists, many of whom have since produced significant works about AIDS. However, AIDS activism, in its confrontational and unsentimental stance, has attempted to counter any romanticization of the epidemic. As Douglas Crimp has written, "We don't need a cultural renaissance; we need cultural practices actively participating in the struggle against AIDS. We don't need to transcend the epidemic; we need to end it."[42]

As the AIDS epidemic has entered its second decade, it has gone through several different cycles of meaning derived from cultural attitudes and medical advancements. The epidemic is increasingly perceived to be tenacious, inevitable, a fact of life, a part of the everyday. Although this perception may serve to reduce the stigma of AIDS, it also takes the urgency out of prevention efforts. The reality of AIDS in the gay community is one of constant mourning, what has been referred to as a kind of medieval context, in which death is commonplace and people are expected to die young. Exhaustion at struggling against AIDS on a daily basis has often prompted people to avoid the process of mourning. The question is continually posed: what does it mean to survive an epidemic?

AIDS as Kitsch

Understanding the cultural meanings of AIDS and the politics of its representation means returning again and again to its initial trajectory in the U.S. population. Because the AIDS epidemic emerged at a particular moment of cultural politics in the 1980s, the language of the epidemic carries a baggage of morality about social and sexual behavior. In addition, the complex commercial aspects of the epidemic, the marketing of disease, can be attributed to AIDS's having deeply affected a population already knowledgeable about marketing and business. The cultural memory of AIDS is being produced through a plethora of objects sold to help AIDS organizations survive, to educate the general public, and to "give the epidemic a human face." These T-shirts, buttons, books, red ribbons, and numerous other items have also been referred to as "AIDS kitsch."

This commercialization can be attributed not only to the marketing skills and resources of the gay community but also to the problems of government funding. The moralistic debates about AIDS have rendered funding and education highly politicized issues. AIDS organizations have had to tap into the commodity culture, targeting industries such as entertainment and fashion, to promote AIDS fundraising as chic. In addition, AIDS is big business in the pharmaceutical industry, and magazines such as *Poz,* a glossy publication filled with ads for AIDS drugs and self-help products aimed primarily at a gay clientele, recognize that people with HIV and AIDS represent a marketing target.

The retailing of AIDS has culminated in Under One Roof, a store operated by volunteers and housed in the NAMES Project's building in San Francisco's Castro district. Patrons can choose from a vast array of AIDS merchandise: T-shirts that read "We're Cookin' up Love for People With AIDS" and "Keep the Love Alive," tote bags designed by well-known artist Keith Haring, buttons, paperweights, "Cuddle Wit" teddy bears, books, posters, postcards, and so forth. Proceeds go to more than seventy AIDS-relief organizations. Under One Roof and the retailing it promotes demonstrate the connection between fundraising and the commercialization of disease.

For many people working in AIDS organizations, the merchandising of the epidemic and the potential sentimentality it can promote represent a small tradeoff for the money these efforts raise and the potential educational message they provide. A Keith Haring AIDS tote bag may be commonplace in the middle of San Francisco, but in a small Midwestern city it could be an opener to a discussion of AIDS. Wayne Salazar, director of Visual Aid, the agency that founded Under One Roof, responds to accusations that the store promotes AIDS kitsch by arguing that the priority is raising money. He states:

Are sentimentality and nostalgia invalid human responses in these postmodern times? If so, then why not subject stores specializing in antique dolls and model railroads to the same critique? At least Under One Roof's sales lead to a greater public good. And is what we do so different from Girl Scouts selling cookies or churches holding bake sales? Is AIDS so sacrosanct that we should be held to a different standard?[43]

Most AIDS workers make a variation of this argument: if these products raise the money to provide support services for people with AIDS, who cares why people are buying them? Yet AIDS merchandising inevitably creates AIDS representation. In July 1994 Daniel Harris wrote a scathing attack on "AIDS kitsch" in *Harper's,* prompting an angry debate. Harris argued that the sentimentalizing of AIDS through AIDS merchandise, the mainstream press (notably *People* magazine), and the "new age" industries surrounding the epidemic has produced very particular stereotypes:

Almost from the inception of the epidemic, AIDS propagandists have found themselves in a peculiar moral bind. One the one hand, they attempt to elicit compassion by portraying victims of the disease as seraphic innocents. . . . At the same time, the epidemic's salesmen must avoid portraying HIV-positive people as bedridden invalids unable to fight for their own interests. Those who die are often embalmed in their obituaries in heroic clichés: "foot soldiers in the war against AIDS" who die after "beautiful battles" and "long and courageous struggles," exhibiting "tenacious spirit" and a "brave refusal to surrender." The representation of the AIDS victim thus oscillates between two extremes of stylization: the childish image of the guiltless martyr clutching his teddy bear and warming "his tiny blue fingers," and the "empowered" image of the stouthearted hero whose gutsy brinkmanship in the face of death is held up as a model of unshakable resolve and pitiless optimism—a punitively high standard of behavior, it should be noted, for people suffering from a deadly disease.[44]

The imaging of people with AIDS as heroic places a burden on those who do not seek a higher meaning in their disease. Moreover, AIDS merchandise walks a fine line between evoking sympathy for those who have the disease and infantilizing them by turning them into the equivalent of children. As such, it sometimes works in opposition to the defiant message of AIDS activism. Like the quilt, however, AIDS merchandise is intended in large part for customers outside the AIDS-affected community, among whom the Hallmark-style technique of engaging the emotions may be most effective.

Although the merchandising of the epidemic by nonprofit organizations can be defended as an effective means of raising necessary funds for primary care, commercial businesses that have used AIDS to sell products are a completely different matter. In the world of postmodern advertising, in which ads masquerade as anti-ads (often not even showing the product), marketing professionals have discovered that the demonstration of a social conscience is an effective means to sell a product. A company can codify itself as socially aware and its product as hip by aligning it with a particular social cause. The consumer can supposedly acquire or demonstrate empathy for that cause through the purchase of the product. Thus, Reebok advertises its running shoes as embodying feminism and female self-empowerment, and Chevron presents itself as the environment's protector with its "People Do" campaign. Similarly, companies such as Esprit clothing, Kenneth Cole shoes, and the Body Shop invoke the message of AIDS (Esprit by profiling young women who do AIDS volunteer work; Cole with an image of baby shoes and text that reads, "This year, because of AIDS, thousands of Americans won't live long enough to fit these shoes"; and the Body Shop by producing AIDS education materials) to convey their social concern. Often such companies donate part of their profits to AIDS organizations. At the same time, they complicate the meanings of AIDS representation in public media.[45]

The corporation most conspicuous in its use of AIDS in advertising is Benetton. In one of the most notorious ad campaigns of the 1980s and 1990s, it uses charged documentary images of violence, disaster, and controversy to sell clothing. The Benetton campaign is successful in large part because the controversies it prompts have generated a huge amount of publicity, giving the company, as intended, a kind of radical chic image (an extraordinary feat given the very ordinary clothing Benetton sells). One of Benetton's most famous ads (which ran, like the others, with no caption or explanation, just the Benetton logo) was an image of AIDS patient David Kirby as he lay on his deathbed surrounded by his family (Figure 16). Though Kirby, with his long beard, looks like an icon of Jesus Christ, his image is also unmistakably marked with signifiers of AIDS: his emaciation and apparent youth.

The Kirby image can be seen as falling within Crimp's definition of "phobic" images of people with AIDS as passive victims. At the same time, however, it can be read as countering images of AIDS patients as alone and without community: Kirby's family and their grief form the primary focus of the photograph.[46] However, one can no longer register this photograph as a documentary image. It is irrevocably changed through its status as an advertisement, the product

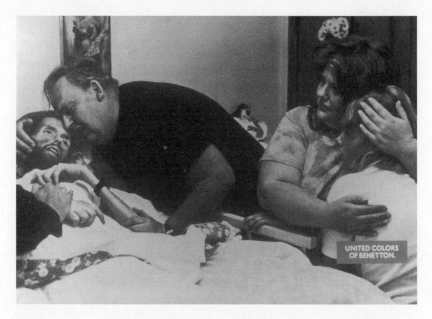

Figure 16. Benetton advertisement: image of David Kirby. Concept: O. Toscani. Spring/Summer 1992. Photo by Theresa Frare. United Colors of Benetton.

of which is remarkably absent. Luciano Benetton argues that the images in Benneton's ads are self-explanatory and need no captions (this argument is particularly specious in Benetton's use of images of disaster, such as an image of Albanian refugees crowded onto and hanging from the decks of a ship, an image that demands contextual explanation).[47] Does AIDS have meaning in the context of contemporary advertising, or is it merely a floating signifier of human tragedy?

Because the fashion industry has been directly affected by the AIDS epidemic, with the deaths of several well-known designers and many others working in the industry, it has raised significant funds for AIDS service organizations. The best-known symbol of the AIDS epidemic, which emerged in part through the fashion industry, is the red ribbon. In 1991 a group called Visual AIDS began making the ribbons—simple pieces of red fabric twisted into a loop and pinned to a shirt or lapel—to raise awareness of AIDS through celebrity events. The ribbons were distributed to presenters of arts awards, such as the Tonys, the Grammys, the Emmys, and the Oscars. In a short time, what had been a novelty item worn by an occasional celebrity became the center of a national industry. Soon red ribbons were turning up not only at AIDS events and arts events but also on the street and at the mall, and designer red-ribbon glitter pins began to flood the market. In 1993 the U.S. Postal Service even issued a red-ribbon stamp promoting AIDS awareness.[48] In terms of ubiquitousness and popularity, the red ribbon was an instant success.

What, precisely, the red ribbon means has been less clear. In the most general sense, it initially was intended to mean "awareness of AIDS" and to render the epidemic visible. By urging high-profile celebrities to wear the ribbons on national television, Visual AIDS wanted to help destigmatize the epidemic. Over time the ribbons came to signify everything from "I am aware of AIDS" and "I care about people with AIDS" to "Let's not forget the problems of AIDS while we are here celebrating" or "I wear this to remember my friends who are sick or have died of AIDS." Their initial message— "I am aware of AIDS"—was eclipsed by the early 1990s, because after almost a decade of AIDS education and media attention, claiming awareness of AIDS meant very little.

As quickly as it entered the public arena, however, the red ribbon was accused of offering an empty message about AIDS. The ribbon, it was charged, allowed people to appear to be doing something for AIDS when in reality they were doing nothing; it allowed celebrities who had never met a person with AIDS or written a check supporting AIDS causes to garner a kind of AIDS cachet. It was not a harmless symbol, critics said, but one that let people off the hook. ACT UP and other activists said the ribbons, like the AIDS Quilt, had no anger. In 1993 ACT UP produced posters that read, "You Can't Lick a Stamp If You're Dead!" referring to the red ribbon stamp (Figure 17), and "We Have Turned Our Anger Into a Piece of Quilt and Red Ribbons."

The debate about the red ribbons, like many debates about the quilt, is fundamentally about the mainstreaming of AIDS discourse and representation. On one hand, the red ribbon is a tool designed to get mainstream America to respond to the epidemic; on the other hand, that response, especially if it begins and ends with the activity

Figure 17. ACT UP poster and stickers. ACT UP Los Angeles.

of wearing a ribbon, can have a normalizing effect, diluting what many people consider the power of AIDS activism—the defiant and angry voice demanding action. This conflict is central to the issue of Americanizing the AIDS epidemic. If the American public becomes convinced that AIDS is a national problem and not limited to specific social groups, and if AIDS is refigured outside of a politics of blame, its meaning will dramatically shift.

Certainly there is evidence that AIDS is becoming less controversial. When the AIDS Quilt is displayed in Washington, D.C., it no longer carries its original meaning: confronting the nation with the AIDS dead it has ignored. Rather, the quilt is embraced by the "nation." When everyone is wearing a red ribbon, statements about AIDS become so diverse as to be incoherent. Indeed, like the yellow ribbons of the Persian Gulf War, the red ribbon has increasingly become a national symbol. Although the wearing of red ribbons has tapered off, they are still a primary image in AIDS merchandise.

The red ribbon of the AIDS epidemic and the yellow ribbon of the Persian Gulf War have spawned an array of other ribbon symbols, including pink ribbons for awareness of breast cancer, blue ribbons to remember those killed in the Oklahoma City bombings in 1995, and white ribbons for various local causes. Indeed, the wearing of a colored ribbon has come to symbolize mainstream participation in a social cause. Given the very passive form of participation involved, however, ribbon-wearing could also be seen as a negation of political action or its reduction to a simple, unengaged act. Although these ribbons are often personalized in their appearance and their intended message, their proliferation and nationalization indicate the fragility of this kind of public discourse. The political messages intended by individuals when they engage with cultural symbols are easily accommodated into American national and commodity culture.

Cultural Memory of AIDS

The production of cultural memory of the AIDS epidemic can thus be seen to take place through memorials, art, commodity culture, activism, popular culture, and alternative media. In its particular historical moment and its ongoing and relentless growth, the AIDS epidemic has generated a unique kind of cultural memory production. The politics of remembering AIDS can never be detached from the fact that the epidemic is still killing people.

The immediacy of the AIDS epidemic produces a different kind of relationship between cultural memory and the concept of healing. What can it possibly mean to heal in the middle of an epidemic? This is, indeed, the problem faced by those seeking to find the "good" in the epidemic. On one hand, the concept of healing foregrounds survival and a sense of redemption; on the other hand, it connotes a kind of closure that is impossible when the epidemic continues.

Cultural memory in the context of AIDS is not about achieving closure but about keeping any sense of closure at bay. The meanings of AIDS and HIV and their relationship to national discourse are so continually in flux that any sense of closure—with the implication that the story of AIDS can be known, told, and understood—is unrealistic. In addition, AIDS activists and service organizations depend upon a sense of urgency to raise funds and to survive. Indeed, as interest in AIDS fades in its second decade, the message of much AIDS activism is, "Don't forget, the epidemic is not over." A rejection of closure is also a preservation of hope, because to keep moving forward in an epidemic that produces extreme burnout one must believe that the story of AIDS is not yet written—that the epidemic will be contained, that a cure will be found, and that it will be historicized as a devastating *moment* in late-twentieth-century America.

Nevertheless, the vast array of AIDS-related cultural products facilitates the movement of personal memories into cultural memory. The cultural memory of AIDS is one of rapid accumulation, conflicting messages, and blurred boundaries between cultural arenas. It is both commodified and radical, both marginalized and mainstream. When a red-ribbon mug, a quilt panel, or a work of art about AIDS conveys the message "don't forget," it has a particular meaning in the present as a call to action. Thus, the production of cultural memory around AIDS is always directly linked, though to varying degrees, to the capacity to mobilize support, be it emotional or financial, for the AIDS community. That the cultural memory of AIDS has been produced across seemingly fluid boundaries of activism, kitsch, folk art, and high culture indicates the postmodern aspects of the phenomenon.

Mainstream American popular culture has taken on the topic of AIDS in a highly tentative manner. A small number of films and television movies have been produced since the mid-1980s, each greeted by a round of critical analysis from AIDS counterdiscourse. Although the similar lack of representation of the Vietnam War in its initial aftermath may indicate that a lag naturally occurs before the popular-culture industry addresses difficult history, the rapid, almost simultaneous reenactment of contemporary crises by television and Hollywood would seem to indicate otherwise. The Vietnam War and the AIDS epidemic have posed problems of representation because they refused the codes of simple narrativity: The trauma of the Vietnam War could not be told through the codes of World War II movies, and the complex politics of AIDS would not conform to the disease-of-the-week formula of television. Hollywood's inability to address AIDS as a primary issue in the 1980s and 1990s powerfully demonstrates the homophobia that exists in an industry in which, as Rock Hudson's life bears witness, celebrities cannot come out of the closet without tarnishing their image.

The two films that indicate the entertainment industry's coming to terms with the reality of AIDS are *Philadelphia* (Jonathan Demme, 1992), for which Tom Hanks won the Academy Award as best actor, and *And the Band Played on: Politics, People, and the AIDS Epidemic* (Roger Spottiswoode, 1993), an HBO film adaptation of Randy Shilts's best-selling book about the history of the epidemic until 1985. Each film was judged in the context of a dearth of popular representation of AIDS. *Philadelphia,* as the first serious Hollywood film by a well-known director to take on AIDS, was particularly burdened. Indeed, although the film was accused of being so tentative about gay life that it bordered on the homophobic (Hanks and his lover, played by Antonio Banderas, have one very brief and much-discussed kiss, and audiences learn little about their community of friends), it is actually more about homophobia than about AIDS. The portrayal by a well-known and highly popular Hollywood actor of someone who is gay and has AIDS (in a film that was deliberately marketed in mainstream America as a courtroom drama), who is subject to discrimination (he is fired from his job as a lawyer in a prestigious law firm) and whose decline and death are presented tragically in the film, was a radical step in mainstream AIDS representation. Indeed, the film, through Hanks's performance, allowed audiences to feel that they had experienced what it is like to be gay in the United States. In addition, through the character of Hanks's reluctant lawyer, played by Denzel Washington, the film exposes the complexities of homophobia. This discourse was paralleled in the media discussion of the film, in which there was considerable attention paid to the actors' feelings about playing gay men and dealing with the topic of AIDS, most likely in order to reassure audiences that they were still heterosexual.

Philadelphia presents the disruptive narrative of AIDS within several cinematic conventions, translating it into familiar and tangible clichés: the little guy fights the system and wins, and two men, of different races and sexualities, work through their mutual suspicions to come to respect each other. In order to fit these conventions, the film needs to avoid any sense of the complexity of the epidemic (Hanks has no difficulties with access to health care; his family is loving and supportive; and though he has lost his job he appears still to have adequate means of support). Yet in having a major Hollywood actor—Denzel Washington—express homophobia and attempt to deal with it, the film pushes popular AIDS representation into new cultural territory.

And the Band Played on tells the story of AIDS as a science detective drama. The film follows Shilts's dramatic charting of the confusion, scientific avarice, and social conflict evident during the first years of the epidemic. It reiterates many of the book's problematic assertions—beginning, inevitably, with a scene of diseased Africa and focusing on Shilts's problematic character of "Patient Zero," the promiscuous gay man on whom scientists wanted to blame the initial spread of AIDS and who personified the contaminating figure with AIDS. The film finds conventions in the AIDS story by centering on the heroic government scientist (Don Francis, played by Matthew Modine) who, despite scanty government funding and conflicting scientific egos, manages to keep fighting to understand the disease. Because the book, which is written in such a cinematic style that it reads like a movie script, was too "controversial" for Hollywood, the film was made eight years after its publication—making it already dated.

Though inevitably subject to criticism that it plays loose with the history of the scientific research, *And the Band Played on* manages to convey complexity of the emergence of the epidemic. Scenes are interspersed with news footage and shots of medical research facilities (the Centers for Disease Control, the National Institutes of Health) and the gay community, and the drama of certain battles, such as the one between the CDC and the blood companies over the industry's initial refusal to believe AIDS was transmitted through blood, is well played. However, in its attempt to tell the story of the scientific community with a good-guys-bad-guys dichotomy (Don Francis of the CDC versus Robert Gallo of the NIH, as played by Alan Alda), the film ignores the importance of early health practitioners in the gay community and the educational work done by the Gay Men's Health Clinic. Alternative science, it would seem, produces the wrong kind of heroes for television.

Although the AIDS epidemic can be packaged in the conventions of contemporary mainstream narratives, it presents a more difficult problem to conventions of storytelling than does the Vietnam War. Vietnam War representation has moved through trends of realism and pure fantasy, but it has almost consistently employed war-movie conventions in its reinscription of manhood and technology. AIDS representation presents more of a rupture precisely because there are no mainstream conventions for the depiction of homosexuality and because the cinematic tradition of portraying disease is one of victimization. Gay male sexuality, which remains a focus of the epidemic, is potentially a much more disruptive narrative than the emasculation of the American soldier or the loss of a war because of the profound threat still posed by homosexuality to concepts of American masculinity.

For these reasons, the AIDS epidemic will not be historicized and rescripted as the Vietnam War has been, to smooth over its rupture. Although the few films and television movies that have emerged may come to represent AIDS to the general public, cultural memory of AIDS is also being actively produced outside of the mainstream—in independent film and video, theater, dance, and art. Just as the emergence of AIDS coincided with a particular moment in the art world, when guerrilla art was being accommodated into the gallery scene and when the religious right was targeting art as a subversive (government-funded) activity, it also coincided with a burgeoning of alternative media, from public-access television to video art to home video cameras.

The emergence of independent video in the late 1960s, which was prompted by the availability of the first portable and consumer-affordable video cameras, coincided with a rhetoric of technological optimism and the "global village." Give the ordinary citizen a video camera and make everyone a producer, it was commonly announced, and the power of the media will tumble in a communications revolution. By the late 1970s, much of this optimism had faded, as cable television proved to be a relatively closed venue and public access was limited by deregulation. With the proliferation of home video cameras in the 1990s, the wielding of a video camera can hardly be considered a political act. However, AIDS proved to be the "ideal" kind of cultural crisis for alternative media: Educational tapes can easily be produced and distributed for free; activists can record demonstrations and distribute copies of them; and video has been used effectively as a tool of self-empowerment for people with AIDS. A huge amount of work in independent video and film spans the categories of AIDS education, documentary, self-help, experimental, and activism.[49] This work is distributed through AIDS organizations and independent distributors to an array of venues, including universities, alternative art spaces, and museums. In addition, throughout the United States there are many public-access television programs about AIDS. The voices of these works are varied, all attempting through various strategies to counter media images of people with AIDS and to work against the image of the figure of contamination.

The explosion of AIDS in the arts beginning in the late 1980s, with Tony Kushner's play *Angels in America* (1993), artwork by David Wojnarowicz and others, art collectives such as Group Material and General Idea, choreography by Bill T. Jones, exhibitions on AIDS and art, and performance works by Karen Finley and others, also quickly produced a backlash. Though in the art world this was manifested in charges of "victim art," in the larger cultural arena it became the staging area for a culture war on the function of art in contemporary society and the role of government funding in supporting art that speaks critically from the margins.

In the early 1990s, the religious right and conservative members of Congress such as Senator Jesse Helms targeted specific works that dealt with AIDS and homosexuality. Photographs by Robert Mapplethorpe of gay male sexuality, images by David Wojnarowicz, Marlon Riggs's video portrayal of black gay men and AIDS, *Tongues Untied* (1989), and other works were used in right-wing literature by such conservative organizations as Donald Wildmon's American Family Association to argue against government funding of the National Endowment for the Arts.

The art about AIDS indicates changing intersections of cultural arenas. AIDS art combines genres of performance, confession, autobiography, and various art media. It transfers easily between the gallery and the street and in doing so helps to redefine each. The conservative focus on art as an indicator of social ills has politicized works originally intended to focus on other aspects of sexuality or disease. This cultural production of AIDS has thus dramatically altered the debate about art and politics and forms a central aspect of the cultural memory of AIDS.

The Americanization of AIDS

The AIDS epidemic is an event through which the deep fissures of American culture have been marked and the gaps in the cultural fabric have been exposed. Indeed, the cultural memory of AIDS is being produced through a clash of meanings. Like the Vietnam War, the AIDS epidemic has prompted the production of shared memory through its traumatic effect on American culture.

As AIDS becomes increasingly "normalized" in American culture, its meaning as a national epidemic shifts. When the AIDS Quilt goes to Washington, D.C., for instance, it testifies that America accepts AIDS just as it resists AIDS. Increasingly, the epidemic exposes the notion of a singular national culture as a fallacy. Yet the ongoing public discourse about AIDS—in particular in the arenas of government, where AIDS funding is debated—in many ways resists acknowledging AIDS as an "American" epidemic. If those who have AIDS or HIV can be defined as marginal and outside the mainstream, then the funding of the services that fight the epidemic can be seen as outside the national interest. The battles of AIDS representation have been precisely about access to the mainstream national culture, be it the culture of commodity exchange or the nation as represented by its institutions of funding. In the AIDS epidemic, the marginal and the mainstream, the commercial and the homemade, the sentimental and the cynical all converge in producing meaning. The complexity of this tangled set of meanings keeps closure at bay; simple narratives cannot take hold.

Chapter Six

Conversations with the Dead

Bearing Witness in the AIDS Memorial Quilt

Events of tragic consequences demand memorials, yet the complexity and urgency of the AIDS epidemic have placed unique demands on the process of memory. Though it has produced many forms of cultural memory, the epidemic's largest and most national memorial is the NAMES Project AIDS Memorial Quilt.

The AIDS Quilt, like the AIDS epidemic, evokes immensity. It consists of an ever-growing number of three-by-six-foot panels, each of which memorializes an individual who died from AIDS (see Figure 18). The quilt has been exhibited throughout the world and includes more than 40,000 panels from twenty-nine countries, yet it represents a mere fraction of those who have died from AIDS.[1] Over 5 million people have viewed the quilt. In its epic size, it attempts to create a visual image of the enormous proportions of the AIDS epidemic, its potential to kill millions of people worldwide.

AIDS Quilt panels are created by friends, lovers, and families of the dead and by concerned strangers. Panels incorporate diverse materials: cloth, leather, photographs, stuffed animals, clothing, wedding rings, credit cards, dolls, flags, champagne glasses, condoms, cowboy boots, feather boas, human hair, old quilts, and cremation ashes, among other things. Panels are consistent, however, in their desire to name the individual and to present artifacts of their lives: pictures, memorabilia, symbols, colors, messages.[2]

Parts of the quilt have toured the country several times, and

Figure 18. NAMES Project AIDS Memorial Quilt, with 20,064 panels on display in 1992. Photo by Mark Theissen. NAMES Project Foundation.

sections are constantly on display at any given time. Thus, every showing of the quilt is unique, with different panels presented in different configurations. The quilt has been shown in its entirety on the Mall in Washington, D.C., four times—in 1987, 1988, 1989, and 1992, when it consisted of over 20,000 panels. It returns in 1996 with an estimated 45,000.

Both the AIDS Memorial Quilt and the Vietnam Veterans Memorial stand as, and invite, testimonials of and to specific individuals, and both attempt to create a community of shared loss. Both have been packaged and popularized in the media. The AIDS Memorial Quilt, however, radically distinguishes itself from the Vietnam Veterans Memorial and from most public memorials through its phenomenology and authorship: the tactile, foldable quality of the cloth, the uniqueness of each panel, and the variation that speaks of the different hands that crafted it. The quilt has created a particular kind of community in which loss and memory are actively shared, even among the highly fractured and divided groups—the gay population,

black and Latino inner-city populations—that are dealing \
AIDS epidemic. It has facilitated and inspired the production
tural memory, the sharing of personal memories to establish a collectivity; it has also brought the politics of identity, gender, race, and
sexuality to the surface and spurred debate over contested notions of
morality and responsibility. The quilt's therapeutic role often conflicts
with what many see as its political role in the debate over AIDS
funding. In addition, the quilt exposes the rift in gay politics between
speaking defiantly from the margins of society and demanding inclusion within the mainstream. In this chapter, I examine how the AIDS
Quilt functions as a memorial constructed in the midst of a war of
rhetoric, identity, the politics of disease, and the struggle for life.

Origin Stories

Like the Vietnam Veterans Memorial, the AIDS Memorial Quilt has
an origin story, one with elements of spontaneity and innocence
about the impact of the project to come. Fittingly, the origin story of
the AIDS Quilt is set in the Castro, the gay district in San Francisco
that serves as an icon for gay communities throughout the United
States. The siting of the quilt's origin in San Francisco is significant
because of the devastating loss from AIDS in that community.[3] The
story begins at a candlelight march in memory of an earlier crisis in
San Francisco, one that preceded the AIDS crisis: the assassinations
of Mayor George Moscone and Supervisor Harvey Milk, an openly
gay politician:

The idea for the Project originated the night of November 27, 1985, when
San Francisco activist Cleve Jones joined several thousand others in the
annual candlelight march commemorating the murders of Mayor George
Moscone and Harvey Milk, San Francisco's first gay supervisor. As the
mourners passed by, they covered the walls of San Francisco's old Federal
Building with placards bearing the names of people who had died of AIDS.
"It was such a startling image," remembers Cleve. "The wind and rain tore
some of the cardboard names loose, but people stood there for hours reading names. I knew then that we needed a monument, a memorial."[4]

The patchwork effect of the placards reminded Jones of a quilt, and
a year later, using spray paint, he made the first panel—for his best

friend, Marvin Feldman, who had died in October 1986. In May 1987, Jones and Michael Smith began organizing the NAMES Project, the organization that raises funds for and maintains the quilt. In October of that year, when the quilt was first displayed in Washington, D.C., it consisted of 1,920 panels.

Jones originally envisioned the AIDS Quilt as a message that would call upon the conscience of the nation. He expected it to produce a huge impact: "I truly believed that when we went to Washington in 1987, it would be like Jericho, that what we had built was so beautiful, so exquisite. I thought, they are going to see the evidence of our labor and they will be moved."[5] Jones conceived the quilt on two levels: a national memorial of epic proportions and a grassroots memorial produced by "quilting bees in little communities with all different kinds of people coming together." The tension between these two levels—the quilt as a massive project versus the quilt as a product of intimate, local communities—is a major part of its complex effect.

Naming the Dead

All memorials participate in the act of naming, from the engraving of individual headstones to the pointed non-naming of the Tomb of the Unknown Soldier. By naming the dead, the quilt produces a collective body count (Figure 19). At Quilt displays, this takes the form of a roll call of the names of the dead, in which community and civic leaders, lovers, family members, friends, and AIDS volunteers read the names out loud, each marking those who were close to them.

Naming has particular significance in the context of the AIDS epidemic. Communities affected by AIDS have struggled with battles over language, metaphor, and representation. In the context of the quilt, naming is often seen as equivalent to coming out, in particular for the families of gay men; a fear of or refusal to name in the quilt often reflects families' fear of acquiring by association the stigma of homosexuality. Panels cannot be altered by anyone but their makers once they have arrived at the NAMES Project and been catalogued. Hence, battles over naming in the quilt take place at the time of panelmaking, often as conflicts between families and lovers. These

Figure 19. Twelve-by-twelve-foot section of the AIDS Memorial Quilt. Photo by David Alosi and Ron Vak. NAMES Project Foundation.

conflicts all seem to imply homophobia—the fear that inclusion in the quilt will reveal a gay identity (whether true or not) to the world. One panel reads:

—I have decorated this banner to honor my brother. Our parents did not want his name used publicly. The omission of his name represents the fear of oppression that AIDS victims and their families feel.

Many disputes over naming have been resolved by the NAMES Project; however, in the first years of the quilt approximately 10 percent of the names were fully or partially withheld. Since the early 1990s, most names have been given in full, testifying, according to NAMES

Project director Anthony Turney, to the increasing destigmatization of AIDS, a process in which the AIDS Quilt has played a primary role.[6]

The AIDS Quilt does not present the singular, uniform cataloguing of names that the Vietnam Veterans Memorial does. The NAMES Project does not restrict the number of panels that can be made for a specific individual; some are honored in several panels made by different people. No relationship between the panelmaker and the panel subject is privileged over another: Panels are made by strangers, families, lovers, friends, and distant admirers. Some people with AIDS even have made their own panels before they died. The process of panelmaking can produce a community of concern, in which strangers reflect on the lives of others and lovers and families meet for the first time.

At the Vietnam Veterans Memorial, people leave personal artifacts in order to individualize the names inscribed uniformly on the wall. In the AIDS Quilt, by contrast, the names are already personalized and distinct. Whereas the Vietnam Veterans Memorial emphasizes lives lost, the AIDS Memorial Quilt emphasizes lives lived. NAMES Project staff member Scott Lago said, "It is a celebration of a person's life. Not a comment on death. Hell, we know he's dead. But she was a scream when she was alive!"[7]

Each panel responds to the question: How can this person be remembered? What elements will conjure up their presence? Individuals are often symbolized in a literal way by their images and artifacts of their lives, their favorite activities or places: a baby's blanket for an infant, a leather jacket for a biker, a pair of scissors for a hairdresser, a blue scrub tunic for a doctor. Often they are commemorated in letters addressed to them (one panel is a large fabric letter, addressed to "Mark Richard, A Better Place").

The quilt panels reflect a diversity of relationships, roles, and audiences. Some speak to the audience in a tone of admonishment, others in direct political anger:

—They gave me a medal for killing two men, and a discharge for loving one—Sgt. Leonard Matlovich.

One of Roger Lyons's panels quotes his testimony before a congressional panel about AIDS:

—I came here to ask that this nation with all its resources and compassion not let my epitaph read "He died of red tape."

Some panels are pointedly dedicated to "those who died alone," "those in prison," "the forgotten," and others not specifically named in the quilt. The quilt thus serves as a sounding board for issues about AIDS; some panelmakers use it to speak to specific audiences, both those who already understand and those who need to be taught.

Some panelmakers use irreverence as a means to celebrate the lives or sense of humor of those they are commemorating, reflecting a desire to make the dead laugh:

—Stardate 10–9–87: Beam me up Scotty.

—Is This Art? No! It's Fred Abrams!

The most noticeable aspect of many panels is their function as testimony, stating quite simply: This person was here. Many panels tell biographies to provide a witnessing to the details of a life that may be known only by a few:

—David R. from Alaska, loved flowers and wanted to open a flower shop but he managed a bank instead (you know how life can be) well he was positive (?HIV?) and full of love, then his health slipped and he met a blond. They robbed the bank of $60,000 and went to LA, the blond lost all the money in Las Vegas, David visited Hawaii, where he was very happy, then his health got worse, he went to NYC, was in tremendous pain, the first two nights he attempted suicide with pills but failed, then succeeded with a plastic bag. 1987.

This witnessing of a life and a death is presented as both biography and admonition: He lived and loved, he was foolish, but he killed himself because of great pain. This disease causes pain and desperation.

Many voices speak in the different panels and even within a single panel, sliding from testimony about the subject to testimony about the relationship between panelmaker and subject to testimony solely about the panelmaker. In fact, many of the quilt panels speak more of the maker than of the subject:

—Ricky—You probably don't remember me. We went to high school together, and you played the organ at my Southern Baptist church. We should

have talked but I guess we were afraid. I still am sometimes . . . Silly, huh?
Watch over me.

—Randy Clarke—My Boy.

Some panels ask for forgiveness and are tinged with overtones of
regret and guilt:

—I couldn't accept the love you offered. I know better now.

—You meant so much to me, I wish I had told you.

—I didn't get a chance to say goodbye.

Through the simple act of testifying or confessing to these feelings
of regret, the speaker achieves a kind of cleansing of guilt. Panelmakers assign meaning to the AIDS deaths through the redemptive transformations those deaths caused.

Significantly, most of these panels are unsigned. Hence, they are
not about authorship or individual production. Those that speak to
the dead need no identification, and for others signing may seem
simply inappropriate. Panels made by families are often signed with
a relationship: Mom, Dad, your brother. The objects in quilt panels
are less cryptic than many of the articles that have been left at the
Vietnam wall, perhaps because their purpose is often intended to be
pedagogical as much as memorial.

Thus, these panels represent a multiplicity of testimonies and
tones, some irreverent, many sad, some regretful. All reflect with
irony on life's finitude. In a panel for James Meade, a scrawl of text
is written around the quilted image of a man lying under a quilt next
to a window:

—Dawn at the window—Birds singing—The cats crying to be fed—Linger-
ing dreams—The light in the tree limbs—Shaving—Putting on a bath-
robe—The smell of the coffee—Ironing a shirt—Picking out a tie—Waking
up Harry—Feeding the cats—The warmth of the toaster—Oatmeal with
raisins—Cleaning the sink—Making the bed—Packing a lunch—Remembering a song—Riding the bus—The weight of a pocketwatch—Telling a
joke—Listening to Mozart—Coworkers complaining and laughing—The
breeze in the grass . . . Bringing flowers to Harry—Chow-mein and fortune
cookies—Brushing the cats—Fourhanded Mozart—Folding the wash—
Watching an old movie on TV—The moon and the fog—Drowsing in the

armchair—The kimono hanging on the wall—The cleanness of clean sheets—Fingernail clippings—Reading in bed—Evening prayer—Stars and sleeping—Dreaming.

This is a middle-class life disrupted. The evocation of the daily life of this gay couple takes on a kind of compelling ordinariness, and small details become charged with loss.

Quilting and Folk Art

Quilts combine old use—tatters—with new use. All parts of them are pregnated with memory. They are always records of accomplishment, solo and mutual, and promises of continuity.

Jeff Weinstein, "A Map of Preventable Death," *Village Voice,* October 1988

Technically, the AIDS Quilt comprises not only quilting but also appliqué, spray paint, embroidery, and other crafts. It is not quilted with a backing or used, as are most quilts, as a blanket to provide warmth. Yet the connotations of warmth and comfort associated with traditional quilts are central to its commemorative role. Visitors touch and stroke the AIDS Quilt. A quilt also connotes nostalgia, family heritage, folk art, Americana, and women's collective work. Jones has said: "I said to myself we need a memorial. Then when the word *quilt* went into my brain, what I remembered was my grandmother tucking me in with this quilt that was made by my great-great-grandmother and has been repaired by various grandmothers and great aunts over the years. I immediately had a very comforting, warm memory and that was the key."[8]

Quilting has multicultural roots in Africa, Europe, India, China, and other places throughout the world.[9] Though Jones and the NAMES Project staff emphasize the international status of the quilt and its place in many traditions of folk art, Jones's description reflects his own midwestern background. His language is steeped in Americana: "I think of it as a strong durable fabric that is made by collaborations of prairie women who have marched with their Conestoga wagons across the plains; it is something that is given as a gift, passed down through generations, that speaks of family loyalty." This image is particularly important when the quilt is shown at the Washington Mall, where it represents an attempt to incorporate those symbolically cast out of America—homosexuals, drug users, the poor—back into the nation. This evocation of American tradition is not without its critics. Daniel Harris has written, "It evokes nostalgia for a simpler, more innocent time, a pastoral world of buggies and butter churns—an America that never existed."[10]

· Indeed, the quilt's relationship to nostalgia is contradictory. The quilt implies a sense of personal and familial continuity, moving through the years from generation to generation. Yet the AIDS epidemic has struck primarily young men, young women, and children, disrupting the life cycle. Many parents have buried their children, many young children have been orphaned, and the sense of generations and "families" within the gay community has been devastated. In addition, many young men have returned to their families from the urban centers where they lived in order to be cared for and die at home, a reversal of the expected movement of children outward from home.[11] Letters to the NAMES Project testify to this unexpected interruption in the life cycle:

—We lost our son. It is hard to believe that one in the prime of life is physically gone from us. Is it not supposed to be the older who depart from the living first? . . . We really didn't begin to know him until he came home in his manhood to spend his waning months with us. . . . He was a teacher, probably our best.

—We were supposed to grow old together.

The family quilt connotes continuity; AIDS creates disruption and broken lineage. In its evocation of the past, a quilt promises a future to which it will be handed down. Moreover, many quilts evoke the presence of previous generations by incorporating scraps of clothing literally worn out by family members. Hence, fabric changes its status in a quilt: A functional article of clothing becomes an element in a design. In keeping with this tradition, many panels in the AIDS Quilt include articles of clothing. But unlike the scraps used in a traditional quilt, these are not clothes that were worn out or outgrown. They are vacated, poignantly empty, echoing the body that once filled them.

Traditionally, quilting has been the handiwork of women. It has been a means by which women, who were excluded from recorded history, created forms of cultural memory. In the United States, quilts were made by women for warmth, friendship, and political expression. The AIDS Quilt draws on several traditions of quilting, including the crazy quilt, the friendship quilt, the fire quilt, and the memory quilt. Like a friendship quilt, the AIDS Quilt incorporates signature panels from quilt displays; like a fire quilt, which was made from scraps for emergencies, it conveys comfort in the context of urgency.[12]

Cleve Jones consciously borrowed from a historical connection between cloth and mourning. In Greek mythology, the fates were said to spin the "thread of life," which was measured and cut to determine the length of a life. In the Jewish tradition, mourners wear a torn piece of cloth to symbolize the torn fabric of life, and during the plague in Europe churches hung banners with the names of the victims.[13] In the westward migration of Euro-Americans, a quilt often stood in for a coffin when someone died on the treeless Great Plains.

As folk art, the AIDS Quilt straddles the realms of art and craft. Produced collectively by thousands of mostly unskilled people, the quilt bears a tenuous relationship to the discourse of art. It has only rarely been shown in art venues such as museums, more commonly being seen in civic centers, churches, schools, and community centers. It has not been subjected to the aesthetic debates of, for instance, the Vietnam Veterans Memorial precisely because it is not being produced by one artist and is perceived as a craft as opposed to a work of art. Hence, although certain panels are aesthetically more ambitious than others, the quilt affords equal status to all panels regardless of elaboration, style, or uniqueness. Many refer to its "democratizing" effect and its "relentless understatement."[14] Some commentators have reflected, seemingly with relief, on the lack of pretension in most panels: "There is extraordinary artistry here, and also a carnival of tackiness. Perhaps that is the most moving and at the same time most politically suggestive thing about the quilt: the lived tackiness, the refusal of so many thousands of quilters to solemnize their losses under the aesthetics of mourning."[15] The AIDS Quilt, in fact, appears to be a kind of reaction to a traditional "aesthetics of mourning." In their bright colors, playfulness, and humor, many of the panels seem to reject the notion of a somber meditation on death.

In the interviews he has given about the quilt, Jones has cited several artistic influences on his original idea, including Maya Lin's memorial, Judy Chicago's *Dinner Party,* and Christo's *Running Fence.* [16] In these projects, the artists dictated their vision to a large number of workers and collaborators. Chicago's project, completed in 1978, is a "feminist last supper," a table setting of hand-crafted ceramic plates and needlework honoring historical women. [17] Christo's *Running Fence,* an immense nylon curtain that wound through the northern California coast, was, like all of his projects, executed by a huge group of people. Unlike the quilt, however, both of these projects have authorship attributed to an individual artist. Jones's relationship to the quilt is considerably different than, for instance, Maya Lin's relationship to the Vietnam Veterans Memorial or Christo's to *Running Fence,* because he has no aesthetic control over the quilt. However, at least initially he saw himself as the quilt's author and as "the only person who knew how it would look" when it was to be first exhibited on the Washington Mall, the "space it was originally designed for."

The Quilt as a War Memorial

What happens when a "war" is memorialized while it is still being fought? The AIDS Quilt takes its place in the tradition of war memorials; but it does so in a radical way. This war is not being fought against a foreign state; in fact, the quilt initially sought to bring recognition of the AIDS epidemic as an American crisis (in response to the notion that AIDS originated in Africa). The quilt depicts many enemies, of which, ironically, the virus is represented as the least and the U.S. government as the most culpable.

AIDS activists have employed many war metaphors in their rhetoric, often comparing their movement to the protests against the Vietnam War. In proclaiming, "AIDS is our Vietnam," these activists equate the U.S. government's AIDS policies of the 1980s and 1990s with its Vietnam War policies of the 1960s and 1970s. The Vietnam War is often represented as a gauge of the country's pain; reiteration at the Vietnam Veterans Memorial of the names of the 58,196 men and women who died establishes a standard of collective grief. Thus, in 1992, when the number of AIDS dead in the U.S. surpassed the 120,000 mark, many AIDS activists noted that twice as many Americans had died from AIDS as in the Vietnam War.

For many, the deaths of thousands of young men equates the AIDS epidemic with a war. One NAMES Project flyer bearing an image of needle and thread states, "Not All Battles Are Fought with a Sword." AIDS activist Vito Russo once said, "You know a lot of people who have lost all their friends, and that's an experience that I don't think a lot of [young] people have in their lifetime except during war." [18]

Like the Vietnam memorial, for which the veterans stipulated an "apolitical" design, the quilt is an overtly political work that has been declared nonpolitical by its creator. Jones has stated:

The Quilt quietly does advocate a certain stance in the fight against AIDS. We are not a political organization—we don't take stands on any of the political issues that surround the AIDS epidemic. But the quilt very eloquently says, "You're to love each other, you're to care for each other, these were real people whose lives were valued and whose memories are cherished." The political message is that human life is sacred.[19]

Yet the quilt, with its messages of loss, anger, and tribute, belies Jones's definition. In fact, Jones would appear to want it both ways: the quilt as a political tool that does not threaten or exclude through its politics. The quilt's educational purpose is clearly political. It is meant to change the average American's—and the average American *politician's*—relationship to AIDS. When displayed in Washington, the quilt has functioned at least initially to call the government to task. Says Jones, "It is very much an accusation, bringing evidence of the disaster to the doorstep of the people responsible for it. We have never depoliticized it to that extent. We want to move them to act." Thus, the quilt accuses more strongly than the Vietnam Veterans Memorial precisely because it is not as easily subsumed into the nationalist discourse of the Washington Mall.

Traditionally, war memorials are not built until the war is over; yet the quilt grows along with the epidemic. Declarations of the quilt's size are deeply ironic—on one hand, they evoke an astonishment and pride at the collective output of grief, rage, and creativity; on the other hand, they serve as a painful reminder of how many have died. The quilt's immediacy derives from its intended purpose as an educational tool: to raise consciousness about AIDS in order to increase government funding, develop adequate treatment methods, and find a cure for AIDS—to stop the dying. Each display of the quilt raises money for local AIDS organizations that provide direct services and primary care for people with AIDS. Thus, the AIDS Quilt intends to end the "war" it memorializes. As such, the debate it produces is very different from that raised by the Vietnam Veterans Memorial: it is a debate not only about how to remember the dead but about how to effectively end the dying.

Locating the Dead:
The Presence of Bodies

The AIDS Quilt provides evidence of the human loss of the AIDS epidemic. Jones says: "When I thought of the quilt I was thinking in terms of evidence. It was in a conversation on Castro Street with my friend Joseph, who is now dead, when the story came out that there were one thousand dead in San Francisco in 1985. I said to Joseph, 'If this were a meadow and there were one thousand corpses lying out here and people could see it, they would have to respond on some level.' "

Each panel corresponds approximately to the size of a body or a coffin; thus, the quilt laid out on the mall in Washington evokes for many an image of war dead strewn across a now quiet battlefield. To many panelmakers and viewers of the quilt, it remains the sole location of the dead. There, the dead are spoken to; there, the dead are perceived to hear and respond. Visitors to quilt displays write messages on signature panels, permitting them to maintain an active relationship with the dead. The quilt evokes conversations with the dead.

—Hey . . . Wait a minute . . . Where did you go? We're not done talking yet. Can you hear me? I really miss you, Jon Stangland.

—Is that you, Clyde?

—Marvin, your grandson has your smiles. We miss you.

—Call collect.

Families and friends often come to the quilt bearing flowers and talismans as one would at a cemetery. Thus, the quilt operates as a surrogate for the bodies of the AIDS dead, placing it within the tradition in this country of memorializing the dead in the absence of their bodies, in which the naming of the individual serves to establish their location. Where are the bodies of the AIDS dead? According to Jones, the majority of gay men who have died of AIDS have been cremated, their ashes scattered. They leave no headstone or physical trace. The AIDS Quilt is the sole testament to their names and their existence. Several panels actually have cremation ashes sewn into pockets. One of the first panels made in Japan was created by an artist with AIDS, who painted calligraphy using red paint mixed with his own blood, literally fixing his body and the virus within the quilt.

The location of bodies symbolically (and literally) within the quilt evokes the larger discourse of bodies in the context of AIDS. One of its distinguishing features is the aging effect of the opportunistic infections that ultimately cause death. These diseases, such as Kaposi's sarcoma, pneumocystis pneumonia, and cytomegalovirus, waste away once strong and healthy bodies to skeletal frames, making those in the advanced stages of AIDS appear to be decades older than they are. In the beginning of the epidemic, when the transmission mechanisms of the virus were not yet known, these were bodies isolated from human touch. One panel in the AIDS Quilt reads: "Steven, hug me." Panelmaker Vicki Hudson explains:

Steven had AIDS when I met him in 1981. We were all frightened about his sickness. He had been deserted by his lover and family. He was a very lonely man. . . . Once, he and I were dancing and when a slow song began to play, he begged for me to hold him and dance with him. To hug him. He was drenched in sweat, and he saw the fear in my face at coming into such close contact with him. It's 1987 now and I know that holding an AIDS victim is not going to give me the virus.[20]

These bodies of people with AIDS, coded as frightening, untouchable, and contaminating, are transformed through the quilt into fabric and cloth, embraceable and tactile forms that evoke warmth and attraction. Many of the dead are remembered at their healthiest, represented by images of youthfulness and vigor, or as children.[21] Panels of figures defined by empty clothing conjure the shape and space of the absent body, uncontaminated and devoid of disease. Thus, the quilt represents a restoration of these bodies to their pre-AIDS status, and reinscribes them as touchable, healthy, and dignified.

The Mourning Process:
For the Dead or the Living?

The quilt foregrounds the needs of the panelmakers. It is a means for lovers, friends, and families to grieve publicly, to share their loss, and to partake in a ritual of paying tribute to the dead.

Creating a panel is a cathartic means of expressing grief and loss. That the act requires considerable effort, time, and work contributes to this catharsis. Letters sent to the NAMES Project testify to the extended and elaborate process involved in making many of the panels. Other letters reveal that the time spent making a panel is itself a memorial, a contemplation of the departed. For this reason, many panelmakers find it difficult to finish, and some make duplicate panels in order to keep one. One individual wrote to the NAMES Project: "I'm glad the panel took so long to make because many people saw me working on it, and I got a chance to talk to them. We talked about Esperando. . . . We talked about AIDS. . . . We talked about friends who died because of the AIDS virus. . . . We talked about love and compassion. . . . And that is important."

The creation of an object in the face of death is an act of connection. Elaine Scarry writes, "The making of an artifact is a social act, for the object (whether an art work or instead an object of everyday use) is intended as something that will both enter into and itself elicit human responsiveness."[22] All objects carry the implication of human contact; the quilt, in its materiality, conveys the message of human connection and community to counteract the isolation and loneliness of AIDS.

Panelmaking is both cathartic and painful, an intense confrontation with grief that will help the panelmaker to heal. Thus, the AIDS

Quilt raises the question of the purpose of mourning. For whom do we mourn when we mourn? The foregrounding of the needs of the living and the creation of a community through the quilt point to mourning not simply as a process of remembering the dead and marking the meaning and value of their lives but also as an attempt to create something out of that loss. The discourse around the quilt is focused on the "good" that can come out of the epidemic—the human resources that were discovered, the strength people found within themselves and within others in the face of tragedy. We mourn not only for the dead but for ourselves.

The outpouring of sentiment toward the AIDS Quilt resembles the embrace of the Vietnam Veterans Memorial as an expression of loss and grief that previously had not been sanctioned. Like the memorial, the quilt mollifies the incommunicability of the experience of loss and isolation, of families who kept silent for fear of the AIDS stigma, of the immense sorrow of losing all of one's friends, and of the prospect of one's own death.

The quilt also enacts specific rituals for grieving. Displays of the quilt, all of which are overseen and organized by the NAMES Project, are systematically set up to allow viewers to take a journey of grief through the quilt. Unlike the journey past the walls of the Vietnam Veterans Memorial, the journey through the quilt is an ever changing one. No display is ever the same; no starting or end point exists.

Each display is a highly structured event. The opening rituals of folding and unfolding the panels, reading the names, signing signature panels, and walking through the display are tightly orchestrated, almost theatrical (see Figure 20). Every display is monitored by local volunteers, each holding a box of tissues, who are instructed when to comfort visitors, when to leave them alone, when and when not to offer them tissues, and never to touch anyone without their permission. This protocol encourages the expression of loss and sorrow—crying is considered the most appropriate response and is properly attended to (with the tissues)—and facilitates both personal and collective grief.[23]

For those living with AIDS, however, a visit to the quilt is not an

Figure 20. Volunteers unfolding the AIDS Quilt, Washington, D.C., 1992. Photo by Mark Theissen. NAMES Project Foundation.

occasion for remembering as much for facing death and seeing past it. The late Vito Russo used to say at rallies, "I am here today because I don't want a quilt with my name on it to be in front of the White House next year"; there are now several panels that bear his name. Thus, for many people with AIDS, the image of the quilt is one of relentless death.[24]

A quilt display can be seen as defining the range of emotions that constitute mourning, including sadness, regret, fear, and pride. However, the quilt's relationship to anger, and the relationship of mourning to anger, has been contested within the AIDS movement. In the activist gay community, there are factions that see mourning and memorializing as opposed to organizing and protesting. Hence, the quilt is sometimes read as taking attention away from the anger of living; one activist wonders, "Why is grief getting all the press, and not the living and the fighting back?"[25]

At issue here is the relationship of collective mourning to anger.

In "Mourning and Melancholia," Sigmund Freud defined mourning as a solitary experience:

Profound mourning, the reaction to the loss of someone who is loved, contains the same painful frame of mind, the same loss of interest in the outside world . . . and the same turning away from any activity that is not connected with thoughts of [the dead]. It is easy to see that this inhibition and circumscription in the ego is the expression of an exclusive devotion to mourning, which leaves nothing over for other purposes or other interests.[26]

Freud's definition leaves no room for the role of collective mourning. Yet for many people living daily with the AIDS crisis, there is no time to indulge in individual grief or to mourn properly the passing of each individual. Many gay men living amidst the epidemic say they no longer attend memorial services because they have been to so many that the memorials have lost their meaning. For many, anger has replaced grief. Is anger a form of mourning? Although Jones foresaw the display of the quilt in Washington as a bringing of evidence before the nation, he defined it as a statement primarily of loss and hope rather than of anger:

The quilt has been used to try and appeal to a high authority. We don't use anger. Anger is released at the quilt, it is expressed in the quilt, but we don't cut people off. And this has been the greatest source of conflict between me and my colleagues in the movement is that they want the quilt to be angrier—let's take it up and use it to surround Bush's summer house. . . . But I think in some quarters anger and the expression thereof are highly overrated. I know when I feel that rage in my stomach and my chest, I am losing T-cells.

For many AIDS activists, mourning is transformed into action through collectivity. Douglas Crimp has written, "For many of us, mourning becomes militancy."[27] Thus, the act of protest has, for many, replaced rituals of mourning. However, for others, mourning in the face of AIDS takes different forms: For those in inner-city communities, mourning may more often be tinged with the rage of despair rather than the anger of a middle-class sense of entitlement; for many families, mourning is a processing of feelings of shame and guilt. In the quilt, mourning is both angry and hopeful but above all something that must be shared.

Women's Work and Men's Grief:
The Gender Politics of the Quilt

Like the Vietnam Veterans Memorial, the AIDS Quilt is the site of contested notions of femininity and masculinity. Much of the quilt's power is derived from its evocation of the tradition of women's collective handiwork. In addition, like the Vietnam Veterans Memorial, it is the site of the construction of notions of manhood, albeit very different ones; it shares the metaphoric language of war as well as of the aftermath of the Vietnam War. Cindy Patton notes: "The generation of men first hit by AIDS was roughly that of Vietnam veterans (there were of course many Vietnam veterans among the early diagnosed cases of AIDS); thus both AIDS and the war are cast as masculine experiences in highly eroticized male-only zones."[28]

Because AIDS was initially seen as a disease of men, many doctors misdiagnosed women and children and failed to warn them about the risk of acquiring the virus.[29] The Centers for Disease Control (CDC) did not change its definition of AIDS to include women's symptomatology until 1986. As a result, many women were misinformed. Women with AIDS have consistently died sooner than men. Although AIDS groups have increasingly attempted to focus on the concerns of women with AIDS, the association of AIDS with gay men, and the consequent emphasis on prevention and treatment among gay men, is still prevalent.

The gender politics of AIDS in the United States thus began with the erasure of women at risk; the gay man operated as a substitute for the female subject. Says Paula Treichler, "There is no need for female representation in the AIDS saga because gay men are already substituting for them as the Contaminated Other."[30] Yet because of gay men's marginal status in the general society, AIDS is not read as a male or masculine disease. Michael Kimmel and Martin Levine write:

No other disease that was not biologically sex-linked (like hemophilia) has ever been so associated with one gender. And yet virtually no one talks about AIDS as a men's disease. . . . In our society, the capacity for high-risk behavior is a prominent measure of masculinity. . . . To men, you see, "safe sex" is an oxymoron: That which is sexy is not safe; that which is safe is not sexy. Sex is about danger, risk, excitement; safety is about comfort, softness, security. . . . [Men with AIDS] are not "perverts" or "deviants" who have strayed from the norms of masculinity. They are, if anything, over-conformists to destructive norms of male behavior.[31]

The coding of AIDS as a gay male disease in the United States has given it an ambiguous and shifting gender status, both male and not male.

In its appropriation of a women's craft, the AIDS Quilt represents a further complication of gender status. Although the quilt's demographics are gradually changing, the majority of the panels in the quilt are memorials to gay men. This means that at a display of the AIDS Quilt the expression of men loving men is not condemned but taken for granted, and celebrated. Men embrace each other, speak of male love, and fathers mourn the loss of their sons, creating a new kind of masculine relationship to the public display of emotion and sorrow. Stoic responses to grief have no place at an AIDS Quilt display.

Often the voices that speak to male love in the quilt are direct, compassionate, and erotic. One well-known panel consists of the image of a silhouetted figure standing against a wall. Around the edges of the figure, drawn by David Kemmeries of his Native American lover, Jac Wall, when Wall was barely able to stand, a handwritten text reads:

—Jac Wall is my lover. Jac Wall had AIDS. Jac Wall died. I love Jac Wall. Jac Wall is a good guy. Jac Wall made me a better person. Jac Wall could beat me in wrestling. Jac Wall loves me. Jac Wall is thoughtful. Jac Wall is great in bed. Jac Wall is intelligent. I love Jac Wall. Jac Wall is with me. Jac Wall turns me on. I miss Jac Wall. Jac Wall is faithful. Jac Wall is a natural Indian. Jac Wall is young at heart. Jac Wall looks good naked. I love Jac Wall. I will be with you soon.

Kemmeries states, "From a distance you can see that it's a person, but you have to get up close to read what he's really about."[32] Here the verb tense reflects the presence of the dead and the complex process of letting go. Jac Wall still is. Though Kemmeries does not sign this panel, his presence marks this text, testifying to the viewers, speaking finally directly to Jac.

The declaration of gay male love is mixed with the unspeakable disruption of what were supposed to be narratives of pleasure and liberation:

—This is the way I felt about Paul in the beginning (April '81)—What is it I like about Paul? His devastating smile, for one thing. Also, his smooth, tight body. Beyond all that, he is intelligent (which somehow surprises me) and supremely confident (which excites and perhaps intimidates me.) At 30, he is a marvel. I think I'm in love. . . . And this is how I felt at the end (March 1987): This is a man I once loved above all others, remember. This is a man I once would gladly have spent my life with. Now he is dead, and I never counted on this. Mike, August '87.

The powerful presence in the quilt of gay male love reveals the marked absence of the voices of heterosexual men. Though fathers make appearances as shadowy figures, they often appear on the sidelines, writing messages that say their wives brought them in order to change their minds about their gay sons, or signing on after their wife has made a panel.[33] Remarkably few panels have been made by straight men as fathers, brothers, or friends. Moreover, involvement in AIDS service organizations has been almost exclusively the work of gay men and of women, both lesbian and straight (although scientific research has been dominated by men). This disproportionate level of women's participation can be attributed to their traditional involvement in health movements and to male homophobia. In the case of the quilt, however, this dynamic is further complicated by associations with quilting and sewing.

The comforting softness of fabric is a primary element in the quilt's gender politics. Some commentators have noted the quilt's "sheer sentiment," whereas others have seen it as "almost embarrassing in its vulnerability."[34] For some activists it is too soft, too passive, too much about loss and not enough about anger. Here, the malleability of the cloth is interpreted, or one could say misinterpreted, as vulnerability.

Yet there is nothing inherently vulnerable about cloth; in fact, the history of flags and political banners attests to cloth's tradition as a powerful symbolic tool. This association of cloth with vulnerability would seem, rather, to be a gendered reading of quilting as women's work. Jones has stated:

I was very conscious that quilting is a women's craft. I remember thinking in the early days before I knew it was going to work that, if nothing else, there are enough angry men with sewing machines out there to put together something for the National March on Washington for Lesbian and Gay Rights. The first panels were made entirely by gay men for gay men, but even that is not exactly true. There have been women involved from the very beginning—lesbian and straight women.[35]

Jones conceived the quilt project specifically in terms of women's work to offset stereotypes of masculinity: "We picked a feminine art to try and get people to look beyond this aggressive male sexuality component." The connotations of the quilt as nurturing, comforting, and protective are thus aligned with the gay community's taking care of its sick and responding with compassion to the dying. Yet this move to appropriate women's work conveys shifting meanings. The domesticating qualities of the quilt are read as both nurturing and potentially sanitizing.

Descriptions of the quilt as passive sound suspiciously like criticisms of the design of the Vietnam Veterans Memorial. Like it, the quilt has an antiphallic intent. In most exhibits the quilt is laid out on the floor, with some sections hung on the walls. Like the memorial, the quilt has a relationship to the ground; visitors interact with it mostly by looking down at it, kneeling by it, and touching it. It does not impose its presence as a solid piece of sculpture but lies flat, much as the Vietnam Veterans Memorial is set within the earth.

Yet the massive size of the AIDS Quilt counters the notion of passivity and softness. Indeed, the most publicized image of the quilt is an image of spectacle, tens of thousands of panels spread out on the Mall in Washington, D.C. This is an image not of intimacy or yielding space but of impressive size and stature. As one writer notes, "The quilt weighs tons. . . . It has the capacity to crush."[36] In its antiphallic and antiaggressive presence, the quilt is not a "feminine" or passive form but an object whose massive size conflicts with its "tuck-me-in" qualities.

Though disdain of quilting has limited the numbers of straight men working on the AIDS Quilt, quilting has acted as a bridge for many women. Stories of the women involved in the quilt, in particular mothers, infuse the letters and panels at the NAMES Project. Many young, white, middle-class, straight women have become involved, as have many older, more conservative women, and there are increasing numbers of panels for women who have died of AIDS. Frequently, these panelmakers are women who have been politicized by the death of their children or husbands. They write of their pain and loss and of finding a new community among their dead son's or husband's gay friends. One woman, a suburban housewife whose husband died from AIDS while denying his bisexuality, states: "I went to strangers—people I thought that I'd never rub shoulders with—for support. . . . I had a driving need to stay with people with AIDS and people who are gay. The men in my support group helped me get acquainted with a side of John I didn't know—the giving, caring side of the gay personality. I'm lucky there are men who have been willing to open themselves to me." [37]

For women such as this, the quilt form itself has acted as a radicalizing force. Many of the quilting bees throughout the country are staffed by women, whose self-perception as quilters is integral to their involvement. These women, who had had no previous contact with AIDS or the gay community, were exactly the type of people Jones had in mind when he conceived the project, which he often describes as one he wants his grandmother to feel she can participate in.

Like the Vietnam Veterans Memorial, the AIDS Quilt disrupts and reconstitutes standard definitions of masculinity and femininity. It is neither a masculine nor a feminine object; rather, it is the site of a refiguring of men's relationship to grief and loss and of women's relationship to memory and masculinity. The quilt makes a statement about how men should grieve, often couched explicitly in terms of what gay men can teach straight men. Whereas the Vietnam War has been represented as the site where American masculinity was lost, the gay movement is a much more radical threat to traditional concepts of heterosexual manhood. Through both of these memorials, new paradigms for a masculine relationship to grief are emerging.

Belonging and Ownership

At the core of debates about the quilt is the question: To whom does the quilt "belong"? Debates about how "gay" the quilt is, and its relationship to the gay community, have taken place in the gay press.

Though inclusion in the quilt still carries the marker of being gay, increasing numbers of women, children, and heterosexual men are represented in a kind of lag effect as the demographics of the epidemic continue to change.

The AIDS Quilt carries particular meaning in the gay community's redefinition of itself. It symbolizes a shift in the gay community's image from one of pleasure to one of caring. This shift has been constructed by both mainstream media and some members of the gay community. In the mainstream media, characterizations of this shift imply that responsibility is incompatible with pleasure-seeking; in the gay press, discussions of "rehabilitation" emphasize that caring and community are aspects of the gay community that were simply invisible to mainstream culture prior to the epidemic. One resident of the Castro states:

During the seventies the gay movement here created an almost totalitarian society in the name of promoting sexual freedom. It evolved without any conscious decision, but there was so much peer pressure to conform that it allowed no self-criticism or self-examination. . . . But AIDS forced a reexamination in the way that few issues do. What we're seeing now is a revolution. We're seeing a reevaluation of life and relationships and what being gay is all about.[38]

In this new image, which is not without its cynical observers ("It's just like the fifties again: people getting married for all the wrong reasons"),[39] the quilt is a marker of the "good" that has come out of the AIDS epidemic: the love and caring generated to comfort those who were dying and those who are suffering loss. An editorial in a gay newspaper, the *San Francisco Sentinel*, states:

The quilt will also help in the long, long struggle for gay emancipation. Whether it is scientifically true or not, AIDS is viewed as a gay disease. The staggering number of lives which the project memorializes will be viewed by America as gay lives. Former priest John McNeill recently observed that while Stonewall brought gay sex out of the closet, the AIDS crisis has brought gay love out of the closet. Indeed, only a heart truly sclerotic from bigotry could look at those panels and not sense the love of their makers.[40]

However, in 1988, Cleve Jones announced that "we are not a gay organization." Jones said that to call the NAMES Project "gay" would be a disservice to the increasing numbers of heterosexual people with

AIDS. Critics countered that the quilt—"born" in, nurtured, and supported by the gay community—was being removed from that community by an organization that was forgetting its roots in the Castro. The NAMES Project was accused of "de-gaying" the quilt, a term that has been used to describe a tactical change in the representation of the epidemic. In discussing the "litany of de-gayed organizations," Robin Hardy wrote in the *Village Voice:* "The most notorious is the NAMES Project—the quilt memorial—which has siphoned hundreds of thousands of dollars out of gay pockets, but omits the word 'gay' in its literature and puts a photograph of a mother and children on the cover of its commemorative booklet."[41]

On one hand, some people see the quilt as too gay, coding all named within it as gay; on the other hand, the NAMES Project is said to be not gay enough. This conflict is the result of the NAMES Project's outreach efforts. Jones states: "We very deliberately adopted a symbol and a vocabulary that would not be threatening to nongay people. We have resisted being labeled as a gay organization. . . . I really believe that if you look at the responses that have sprung up because of the epidemic, ours is really the most inclusive. We mobilize heterosexuals; we mobilize the families that have been afflicted." In his vision of the potential audiences of the quilt, Jones speaks specifically of reaching the unconverted and conceptualizing the quilt as a tool to educate nongay people. He continues:

Over the last five or ten years, I and everyone in my position has found themselves saying something like "it's not just a gay disease." I feel diminished every time I say that, because I don't want to minimize what has happened to me and my world. . . . I have lived in this neighborhood for almost twenty years, and I cannot begin to even count how many people I know that have died; every week there are more people. But I also believe that when the final history of this is written, that HIV will be seen as a disease of poverty and ignorance that destroyed the developing world. It will be remembered as the disease that depopulated one third of Africa, and the disease that wiped out a generation of Brazilians, and that what happened to hemophiliacs and homosexuals in the industrialized world will be seen as really a fluke of nature and society.

Questions of ownership of the AIDS epidemic have been at the core of the epidemic. The initial battle over the United States's refusal to own the epidemic, its insistence that Africa was the source, has now been replaced by a debate over the perceived ownership by the gay community and a perceived refusal by black and Latino communities to own the epidemic. The two-tiered aspects of the AIDS-affected community have become increasingly clear, and the NAMES Project is often implicated in that schism. With ad copy like, "The Laughter. The Love. The Life. In the midst of crisis comes something beautiful, something magical, something that guarantees our friends will always be . . . more than names," it seems apparent that much of the rhetoric is geared specifically at middle-class communities, gay and straight, rather than at inner-city Latino, black, and other poor communities affected by AIDS. The rhetoric of healing and redemption may, in fact, be one of privilege. Is the AIDS Quilt the product of only one part of the community of AIDS in the United States—that is, the people that have the time and resources for "spiritual growth" and mourning?

The quilt has helped both to foster new communities and to reiterate the significant divisions in American society, which have only been exacerbated by the epidemic. The quilt has produced numerous stories about the coming together of strangers: strangers working together to put on a quilt display; people making panels for someone they didn't know; lovers and families working together; mothers and wives finding a community with gay men. For all of the stories, of which there are many, of alienation, rejection, and discrimination that are revealed through the panels of the quilt, there are innumerable stories of the construction of an AIDS-affected community unified in loss. The community-building that takes place around the quilt extends to quilt displays, where people have met and discovered that they had made separate panels for the same person. The complex web of a person's life thus continues to weave after death.

The stories told in the letters sent to the NAMES Project often testify to new alliances within traditional families:

My mom wanted to know if I had ever made a panel for Dennis. I explained that I had tried but it just brought back all of the pain and loss. . . . I returned home last December for Christmas. After dinner we unwrapped our packages. Opening my last gift, I found the most beautiful panel that my family had made for Dennis. My mom, sisters, aunt and grandfather worked together on the quilt. . . . I feel that the NAMES Project provided them a way to let me know they shared my loss. I thank you for giving them a way to let me know they care.

These stories belie the stereotype of gay men as inevitably estranged from their families.[42] In addition, popular accounts of the epidemic rarely consider the kinds of extended "families" that are constructed within the gay community and outside of nuclear family structures. Letters sent to the NAMES Project describe how strangers have chosen to make panels for people who died of AIDS:

—I did not know David Thompson or his lover. I had no photograph to part with or any fond memories of his experiences. We were strangers. But when he died I felt a loneliness that scared me beyond belief. On October 23, 1986, I came upon his death notice in the paper. It read "On Sunday evening, October 12, my lover and best friend David R. Thompson, died of AIDS. It was a wonderful ten years. I will miss him very much." This letter is to David's lover in the hopes that he will realize that his love for David reached out and touched my heart so tenderly.[43]

—We want you to know how much we gained as a family from working on this quilt. Through our work and discussion we have come to love Rodney. Although we know virtually nothing about him, we have all come to think of him after with a very special fondness. I assure you that in thought and prayer, Rodney will remain a part of our family for years to come.

These panels address the question of what it means to remember any life cut short, of how one can be touched by the death of a stranger. They are often produced in local quilting bees, where volunteer panelmakers have only the barest of details: dates of birth and death, occupations, sometimes the knowledge that someone was a drug addict. For these panelmakers, all AIDS deaths are tragic, untimely, unjustified, and lonely.

Yet with all these stories of community-building and redemption, and while the demographics of the quilt are changing as it becomes increasingly diverse, it still remains a project that is primarily white and middle-class. If the quilt is a compelling means to confront and diffuse homophobia, it has only begun to be used as tool to bridge issues of race and class. Difficult divisions exist between the gay community and inner-city black and Latino communities in all facets of the epidemic. Though outreach to communities of color has increased, the quilt is still seen as a white, gay project. Do the quilt's origins in the Castro cause these communities to reject it?

Questions of privilege are directly related to the very nature of the AIDS Quilt. Most organizations that are struggling to deal with AIDS in inner-city black and Latino communities do not have the energy or resources for quilting. Is it a privilege to be able to mourn in the middle of an epidemic? Initially, the quilt only went to those communities that raised the money to sponsor it. Since 1992, the NAMES Project has used some of the funds raised in selling merchandise to display the quilt in high schools and communities that could not otherwise afford it.[44]

Concerns with the quilt's purpose as it continues to grow prompted what Turney calls "an attitudinal shift" in the early 1990s to redefine the quilt's educational role, emphasizing its potential role in communities of color. Turney states: "Our attitude used to be that those who wanted to have the quilt needed to prove to us that we should let this thing go. That has changed dramatically. In a sense, we are knocking on the door and saying 'take this thing.' It is part of seeing the quilt as something to be used; there is no value in having it neatly folded on shelves. . . . People want their memory to be energized."

Cleve Jones conceived the quilt as a project that would "mobilize heterosexuals," bridge the gap between the gay and straight communities, and involve families. In conceiving it as a project in which his grandmother could participate, evoking his own family history, Jones in fact created a very American image of quilting. Yet the quilt means different things in different communities. The quilt represents something quite different to the gay and lesbian community versus heterosexuals, whites versus communities of color. The tensions between these communities about the quilt are in fact central to its meaning.

The Marketing of the Quilt

The AIDS Memorial Quilt has become extraordinarily popular and, despite the debates in the gay community, has generated surprisingly little controversy in the mainstream media. The quilt was featured on the television show *Nightline* in 1988; it was the subject of a storyline in the comic strip *Doonesbury* and has been featured in an episode of the soap opera *All My Children*. The documentary film *Common Threads: Stories From the Quilt* (1989) has been shown widely on public television and won an Academy Award. In 1989 the quilt was nominated for the Nobel Peace Prize.

Hostility against the quilt has been rare. In a Miami display in 1990, a panel was vandalized and two teddy bears cut out;[45] the quilt has also been called a "v.d. blanket" and a "fag scam." At quilt displays, homophobic messages are sometimes written on signature panels; other messages usually respond with anger and dismissal. In general, the quilt is extremely effective in plugging into Middle America—reaching and perhaps transforming those who think the AIDS dead (with the exception of certain "innocent" victims) deserved their fate.[46]

However, there is a tension between the quilt's role in education and outreach and its role as a catharsis for panelmakers. Moreover, its function as a fundraising tool has generated controversy, particularly in the gay press, where some critics have alleged that mass marketing of the quilt betrays the intentions of the panelmakers and the community that has supported it and renders it "political." As the NAMES Project has grown from a grassroots volunteer group to a professional nonprofit organization with thirty employees and an annual budget of $2.5 million, its marketing of the quilt has been perceived by some as a violation of grief.

The marketing of the quilt is, in fact, part of what keeps it funded. Thirty percent of the NAMES Project budget comes from the sale of quilt merchandise, such as T-shirts, videos, *Common Threads*, the coffee-table book *The Quilt*, buttons, and posters. Turney notes:

Merchandising for us has always been and remains (and I see no sentiment to change it) a rather narrowly defined phenomenon. Certainly the vehicles are the usual ones—T-shirts, books, and buttons—but the icons are always very narrow. The reality is that when you are attempting to do programs like the High School Quilt Program, that don't generate a nickel in revenues in themselves, you have to find a way of subsidizing them. Frankly, if that means us selling T-shirts, we will do it.

The commodification of the quilt and the press kits and public relations material generated by the NAMES Project have raised money but also have been subject to debate. Some critics have joked about "the quilt the book, the quilt the movie." Steve Abbott has written:

Panels from the Quilt appeared in the display windows of Neiman Marcus and, later, were used to decorate a mass for the pope's visit. This went beyond—indeed, exploited and manipulated—the private intentions of at least some who were actually making the Quilt. In short, the Quilt no longer belonged to those who were making it—it had become a commodity to be used and controlled by the officers of a bureaucratic institution. Once the Quilt was "embraced" by the media, its "meaning" went beyond even the NAMES Project's control.[47]

The quilt is bright, colorful, easy to understand, and moving, a perfect human interest story on the evening news or in the local paper. Displays of the AIDS Quilt usually generate articles in the local press about AIDS and its effect within the community. However, the quilt's popularity raises the question: does it allow people to grieve for the dead yet ignore those living with AIDS? The NAMES Project tries to dispel such criticism by publicizing, for instance, a survey in which 71 percent of respondents said that "the experience of viewing the quilt inspired them to take positive action in their lives in response to AIDS." Despite the quilt's ability to raise money, the perception remains that it could be draining funds from other AIDS organizations.

Suspicions about the quilt's universal appeal are raised mostly by gay critics, who have good reason to wonder at the ease with which it can move previously homophobic people to cry over the AIDS dead. One writes, "There should be a warning sticker on it: 'Don't feel that by crying over this, you've really done something for AIDS.' "[48] This criticism implies that the quilt sanitizes the AIDS crisis and offers viewers the illusion of participation and concern. One critic states, "What we *don't need* is what the Quilt seems most efficient at raising: pity, guilt, sorrow, and tears."[49] Abbott goes further:

On one hand, the quilt's message is positive. It personalizes the plights of PWAs; it builds support for AIDS care and fundraising; it helps break down previous stereotypes of oppressed communities or subcultures; and it has become a bridge between communities. On the other hand, one reason the quilt was so readily embraced by the media is because it can also be read as a memorial to a dying subculture (i.e., "We didn't like you fags and junkies when you were wild, sexy, kinky and having fun. We didn't like you when you were angry, marching and demanding rights. But now that you're dying and have joined 'nicely' like 'a family in a sewing circle,' we'll accept you").[50]

The NAMES Project has no rules excluding the use of any material in a quilt panel, so sanitization is at the discretion of the panelmaker. Yet the quilt form, its role as an outreach tool to nongays, and the form of a memorial in general are potentially restricting influences. Concerns over sanitization are expressed exclusively by the gay community. Richard Mohr writes:

Because the panels are not essentially tributes, in the sense of honors paid to the dead, their stories—the dead's—need not have been sanitized, as so many obviously have been. Lies of omission abound. A panel for an acquaintance of mine reported that he helped found a gay organization and that he liked Broadway musicals. That is true enough, but what he loved was to eat shit and get beaten up. No mention was made of these activities. His narrators, out of squeamishness, lost his center of gravity. Aside from scattered trinkets of leathermen, sex is bleached right out of The Quilt, although sex was what was most distinctive of so many of the dead.[51]

Mohr's contention raises the question: How does one narratively memorialize a person, and does the phenomenology of the quilt make that process more or less inclusive? Certainly it is contestable that sex was what was most distinctive about most of the dead—a statement that assumes that everyone represented in the quilt was a gay man who would have claimed sexuality as his most distinctive characteristic. Would the dead have wanted to be remembered that way? Furthermore, there are panels that are genuinely unsentimental: a panel for Roy Cohn, a notoriously homophobic and unscrupulous lawyer, reads, "Bully. Coward. Victim." Other panels display black leather (a panel to Mark Metcalf, the heaviest in the quilt, is composed entirely of leather), sequined dresses worn by transvestites, and a shroud with ID tags for a corpse; at least one contains a needle for injecting drugs.

The Quilt and the Nation

Issues of the quilt's potential to sanitize or sentimentalize are integral to debates about the quilt's relationship to the nation and its message when it is displayed on the Mall in Washington, D.C. Criticism of the marketing of the quilt can be read as concern that it is being removed from the realm of cultural memory—where personal memories are consciously shared in an attempt to create a collective memory—and turned into not only a public relations device but also a memorial or monument with nationalist, historical meaning. The implied patriotism and connotations of family heritage implicit in the quilt form threaten to rescript those memorialized in the AIDS Quilt into a narrative of Americana in a country that has systematically marked them as outsiders.

The popular image of the quilt spread out on the Washington Mall is an image of spectacle, operating in tension with the intimacy for which most quilt panels are designed. However, the quilt was conceived both as a site of personal grief and as a project that would make visible the numbers of dead; hence, its enormous size is integral to its message. Large displays of the quilt have a very different kind of effect from smaller displays. Whereas an individual panel carries a particular power by speaking to the dead and the viewer, that same panel carries the weight of the collective message of a community or communities—of a "nation"—when it is part of a large display of the entire quilt on the Washington Mall.

It has been noted that the quilt's "removability" is essential to its meaning in the gay community. Henry Abelove writes: "The project, like [the gay community], has no ongoing places of its own on American soil, no necessary connection anywhere to any major American institution. Nothing located or fixed could serve well as a memorial to our losses."[52] It could also be argued that the quilt's removability is essential to its relationship to the nation, a symbol that, on one hand, can travel to its center but, on the other hand, does not rest there and comes from somewhere else.

Spread out on the Washington Mall, a traditional American handicraft in its most symbolic place, the quilt demands that the nation take notice. A 1989 ad for the quilt presented the sewing needle as "the most important tool in the building of a national monument." This type of rhetoric was a tactic to get the American public to pay attention, but it was also initially a way of defusing the notion that AIDS invaded the United States from foreign territory. Jones has said: "In the first brochure we wrote, we deliberately used the word 'American' in every paragraph. We wanted to apply a uniquely American concept to this disease that everyone wanted to see as foreign."[53]

The AIDS epidemic brings forward the tensions of the "imagined community" of the nation. The hyperindividualization of each panel can be contrasted with the generic identity of the body in the Tomb of the Unknown Soldier, pointing to the impossibility of a singular imagined community. Yet it is much too simple to say that the quilt is oppositional to the nation. The tradition of nationalism in which Jones wanted to situate the quilt is not the nationalist context of stone monuments on the Mall but rather the context of the Mall as a site of protest, a place to "call attention to the nation's conscience" and make "an accusation, bringing the evidence of the disaster to the doorstep of the people responsible for it." Turney calls the quilt a "national guilt trip." However, each time the quilt returns to Washington, its status as an oppositional symbol wanes. In the mid-1990s it can no longer be perceived as a protest to the nation; it has come rather to symbolize national grief. The image of the quilt laid out in Washington can also mean, Peter Hawkins writes, "America has AIDS."[54] One of the quilt's fundamental paradoxes, then, is that by claiming inclusion in the nation for those who have died of AIDS, it also tends to negate their difference.[55]

Has the popularity of the quilt backfired? The quilt may indeed be appropriated into public discourse as a symbol of America's dealing with AIDS. Like the healing represented by the Vietnam Veterans Memorial, the healing represented by the AIDS Quilt is very different when it is attributed to a nation rather than to an individual. The quilt can be a powerful tool in absolving guilt, easing regret, and facilitating redemption for those who make quilt panels. When this absolution of guilt is applied to a nation, it can act as false redemption.

Yet Jones originally saw the quilt as a subversive tool, one that would appear nonthreatening but impart a radical message. The accusatory aspects of the quilt work in tension with its sentimentality. By marking deleted names, anonymous tributes, and gay male love, the quilt refuses to a certain extent to sanitize the epidemic. Though displays are emotional events filled with expressions of sorrow and pain, they are also charged with a fervent air of the determination to live, making it difficult to conceive the quilt as a tribute to a "dying subculture." Because the quilt remains, in Jones's words, "a very powerful symbol of the love and solidarity of the gay and lesbian community," its message will always carry the accusation of homophobia. The AIDS Quilt, like the Vietnam Veterans Memorial, shifts between national and counternational narratives.

The Archive and the Construction of a History

Those working on the AIDS Memorial Quilt began with a vision of the day when the quilt would be finished, when adequate treatments and cures would be found and the dying would stop. They were inspired by the image of a finished quilt, stored for posterity in a museum or archive. Yet the AIDS epidemic shows no signs of ending, and the concept of an ever-expanding memorial poses questions.[56]

The NAMES Project is a self-conscious effort to intervene in history. Letters addressed to the organization show that panelmakers share this sense of the quilt as history. All explicitly bear witness:

—One of his fears was that he would be soon forgotten after his death. I assured him that would not be the case. I am grateful for the opportunity to present this quilt panel as a permanent memorial to F., and one which will help keep his memory alive.

One panel contains a letter written by the panel subject before he died:

—By the time this letter is read to you, I will have gone on to my new life. . . . In the future, when you look at the history books that will be written about AIDS, you will find that one of the highlights of the book will be a chapter on one of the good results of the disease—that is—humanity became more compassionate. From that compassion the world became a better place. And you, my friends, will be the history makers.

Historically, however, quilts are not easily preserved as archival objects of history, and preservation of the AIDS quilt is difficult and costly. For this reason, in 1994 the NAMES Project began the Archive Project, which involves photographing every quilt panel and creating a CD-ROM of the quilt. This record is intended as a management and archive tool, a fundraising mechanism (panelmakers are offered a photograph of their panel or a CD-ROM including it in exchange for a contribution), and an educational resource that can reach a wider audience than the panels themselves. Though it may resolve certain issues of preservation and management, the Archive Project also raises issues of phenomenology and meaning. Can looking at a quilt panel on a computer screen have the same meaning as seeing it and touching it? How important are its physical qualities to experiencing the quilt?

The Archive Project addresses the issue of preservation to a certain degree, but the question of the quilt's future role is always present. Will it and the epidemic ever end? What if the quilt continues to grow—how will it be housed? What if it becomes a burden? The issue of what role the quilt should play in a long-term epidemic, as it approaches its tenth anniversary, is one that, Turney notes, "is constantly asked and constantly side-stepped." He adds, "Human beings love to bring things into being, but they are not so good at identifying the appropriate time to shut things down. The NAMES Project could be an organization to eventually address that issue. Then you would have to ask the question, what are you going to do with this thing?" In the early 1990s, as the quilt continued to grow and the NAMES Project became less centralized, the organization shifted its emphasis to the quilt's potential to promote HIV prevention. This shift in emphasis, from mourning to direct outreach, also came in response to the debates about the quilt's purpose—one originally conceived amid hopes for a short-term epidemic. As the epidemic drags on, the quilt's meaning and purpose change.

The AIDS Quilt is both a new kind of war memorial and a memorial to a "new" kind of epidemic. It constructs a collective, cultural memory that is fractured, multifarious, and diverse. It is a central site of healing in the context of the AIDS epidemic, reaffirming a dignity for many who died of opportunistic diseases that reduced them to a weakened, humiliating state. The quilt has catalyzed a rich discourse about what it means to live, to remember a life, and to pay tribute to the dead. Its message is that memory has purpose. As a site of cultural memory, the quilt creates a community united by sorrow and anger, yet always in tension with itself. It raises fundamental and difficult questions about the conflict between the therapeutic and the political. It is asked, in a certain sense, to represent AIDS and thereby becomes the subject of struggle around who is visible and invisible in the AIDS crisis in the United States and worldwide.

The AIDS epidemic could not have been memorialized in a traditional way because it is not over and because it encompasses highly contested notions of what constitutes normality, moral behavior, and responsibility. Part of its power lies in how it retrieves this discourse of morality and responsibility and turns it back on itself: To be moral, say the quilt panels, is to state a name in the face of discrimination; to be responsible, they say, is to care for the dying. Yet the success of the quilt is a bitter one. As NAMES Project staff person Scott Lago, who died in July 1991, once said, "This is a very successful project, but it's only resting on a pyramid of bones."

Chapter Seven

Bodies of Commemoration

The Immune System and HIV

Cultural memory of AIDS is produced not only through art, popular culture, activism, commodities, and the AIDS Quilt but also through the representation of the effects of AIDS and HIV upon living bodies. Just as the politics of AIDS reflects its emergence at a particular moment in American cultural politics, the biomedical explanations of AIDS are specific to its emergence at a particular moment in the development of immunological science. The meanings assigned to AIDS and HIV in the realm of popular science contribute to cultural memory and politics, because this virus and disease have created a public discussion about scientific concepts of how the body, in particular the immune system, functions.

Like a memorial, a quilt, or an image, the human body is a vehicle for remembrance—through its surface (the memory that exists in physical scars, for instance), its muscular and skeletal structure (the memory of how to walk, the effects of a physical injury), its genetic tissue (the marking of one's lineage and genetic propensities), and its immune system (the memory of the body's encounters with disease). Bodies are often perceived to speak without words: The bodies of Vietnam veterans speak of guilt, forgiveness, and accusation in their very presence; the bodies of people with AIDS speak of suffering, anger, resilience, protest. Bodies are social texts whose meanings change in different contexts; there are distinctions between the gendered and racially marked body of cultural identity, the social body regulated by government institutions, and the biomedical body.

I have been discussing bodies in this book primarily in terms of how survivors' bodies offer testimony and evidence, contain forms of memory, and question history. In this chapter, I would like to focus on a different kind of body that plays a role in the contemporary discourse of memory in the United States. The biomedical body is a historically and culturally specific phenomenon, a body defined by twentieth-century science. It is defined as comprising specific systems, such as the nervous and circulatory systems, and is subject to specific medical formulations of disease and cure, cause and effect. It can be distinguished from, for instance, the body defined by Chinese, homeopathic, Ayurvedic, and other non-Western approaches to medicine, all of which visualize the body using different metaphors. The biomedical body is defined by the sciences of immunology, endocrinology, and neurology, among others. Scientists and physicians perceive it as operating according to a set of medical logics and accessible to visual mapping.

The immune system is a defining aspect of the biomedical body, one considered to establish the uniqueness of the individual. The immune system is described in science as a depository of bodily memory, the system that remembers what has traveled through the body. As such, I would argue, it can be thought of as a kind of memorial. In the context of the AIDS epidemic, the immune system has become a highly contested political field in which notions of self, other, memory, conflict, war, and the nation are at issue. It is an increasingly visible cultural icon, one that signifies both the triumph and the crisis of modern medicine's formulation of the biomedical body.

In this chapter, I analyze popular images and metaphors of the immune system and HIV within the context of cultural memory. Many of our ideas about biomedical bodies come to us via the media, specifically the popular science articles, photographs, and graphics of mass-circulation magazines such as *Time, Newsweek,* and *National Geographic.* I focus on popular discourse, rather than scientific texts or textbooks, because I am interested in how these stories and images enter into the realm of cultural memory and affect people's perceptions and understandings of their own bodies. It can be said that notions of biomedical bodies are directly tied to perceptions of

Americanness; popular models of our biomedical bodies employ the language of nationalism and represent bodily boundaries through metaphors of national borders. In this chapter I will examine how memory is perceived to function in biomedical bodies and how mass culture represents the human immune system.

The Immune System: Remembering the Self

It was only in the 1960s that the idea of an immune *system* came into being.[1] In the same way that memory is often perceived to be crucial to self-identity, the immune system is now commonly seen as essential to a concept of the self. Indeed, popular science often describes its primary function as distinguishing between self and nonself. The media characterize the immune system as a battleground and a communications system, as both an abstract entity that transcends the body and, ironically, as the means by which the body defines its borders.

The role of metaphor in scientific writing is significant and has direct consequences on how people envision their own bodies. Metaphors are not value-neutral mechanisms; they are a means of conceiving the inconceivable and unrepresentable, and they carry with them burdens of association. Metaphors occupy an essential place in scientific description. For instance, Nancy Leys Stepan writes that in nineteenth-century scientific discourse on human difference, analogies between women and nonwhite races brought together a system of implications—each group was implicated in the negative characteristics of the other. Stepan states that "the metaphors function as the science itself—that without them, the science did not exist. In short, metaphors and analogies can be constituent elements of science."[2]

Similarly, it can be argued, the metaphors of the immune system are essential to its scientific definition, and these metaphors reveal a deep fear of difference. Popular medical discourse defines the immune system as a regulating force that identifies the "foreign" within the body; it is thus a primary agent distinguishing between self and nonself. Studies have shown that the immune system is uniquely susceptible to emotional states and is strengthened by a sense of well-being. The effects of self-esteem, hope, social support, and faith in boosting the immune system have been increasingly researched in science and written about in popular books about cancer and AIDS.[3] Indeed, concepts of the immune system as a self-regulating system emerged in the 1960s in part because the idea of a system of balance fit into political, ecological, and alternative medical trends at the time. Cindy Patton writes:

The bacteriological body had been static before and after the assault by germs; the endocrinological body ran hot and cold, oily and dry, not coincidentally (in the first anxious post-war years when endocrinology briefly had its heyday) mapping the gendered tropes of emotionality. The immunological body was more gracefully fluid and fragile, like a dancer in a delicately balanced environment in which it was placed almost without boundaries.[4]

Thus, the concept of the immune system is a product of the times in which it was conceived, when the idea of the body as a thinking system that protects and regulates itself, a system of natural beauty, made sense. Although, as Patton notes, this view sometimes produces an image of an unboundaried immune system environment, it more often suggests a system that is rigidly bounded.

The immune system has a standard narrative. It consists in large part of millions of white blood cells, known as lymphocytes, which have many different functions. There are two different types of lymphocytes: T-cells, which are produced in the thymus gland, and B-cells, which are produced in the bone marrow and which generate antibodies. Lymphocytes interact with cells called phagocytes, or "scavenger" cells, which include macrophages.[5] Macrophages play a key role in the immune system. They constantly circulate within the body and evaluate the cells with which they come into contact. Mary Catherine Bateson and Richard Goldsby write: "Cells interact by touch, you might even say embrace. Both immune cells and invading cells circulate in search of the appropriate significant other to bond to—and, like some human beings in such a search, they respond primarily to externals, recognizing outward clues that identify their target."[6]

The macrophages will identify and engulf a bacterium, virus, or parasite (an antigen) they recognize as "foreign." This difference is displayed on the surface of the macrophage in the form of digested protein fragments. The macrophage must then find a specific helper T-cell among the millions of varieties of such cells in the body. Whereas macrophages discriminate only between self and nonself, T-cells are designed to bind to specific antigens. When the macrophage finds the appropriate T-cell, it displays its newly acquired difference, and the T-cell locks into the receptors of the macrophage. Once this happens, genetically identical T-cells are produced, and antibodies neutralize the antigens. At the same time, T-cells and B-cells generate memory cells.

Notions of the familiar and the foreign dictate the story of the immune system. For instance, the T-cells do not recognize the antigen as "foreign" until it has been consumed by a macrophage. In the immune system story, it is not the "foreign" that is recognized but rather the newly acquired foreignness of a familiar cell.

All encounters with the "foreign" are recorded and retained in memory cells. When the immune system encounters an antigen for the second time, it "recognizes" it and immediately responds to prevent infection. In this story, the immune system's goals are twofold; to destroy the "foreign" element and to create a memory. The immune system is thus steeped in notions of recognition; it is thought to look at an "invader" and to say, "I know you. I have seen you before."

The Immune System and HIV: Warfare and Terrorism

The rigid bodily boundaries of the immune system model are directly related to a depiction of the external world as inherently hostile. There is no room for ambiguity or transgression; a cell is either harmless or dangerous. Foreignness is portrayed as threatening to the viability and wholeness of the body. Sometimes it is even equated with ethnicity: "It can be as difficult for our immune system to detect foreignness as it would be for a Caucasian to pick out a particular Chinese interloper at a crowded ceremony in Peking's main square."[7] A *Time* magazine article describes the hostile environment surrounding the human body:

It's a jungle out there, teeming with hordes of unseen enemies. Bacteria, viruses, fungi and parasites fill the air. They cluster on every surface, from the restaurant table to the living-room sofa. They abound in lakes and in pools, flourish in the soil and disport themselves among the flora and fauna. This menagerie of microscopic organisms, most of them potentially harmful or even lethal, has a favorite target: the human body. . . . Humans are under constant siege by these voracious adversaries. Germs of every description strive tirelessly to invade the comfortably warm and bountiful body.[8]

This is a Cold War story of the world as a dangerous place. In this life-threatening environment, the vulnerable human body relies heavily on its powerful system of defense. Most popular descriptions of the immune system mix metaphors of war with the language of communications and management science. Media accounts describe the immune system as a military organization, with networks of communications that transmit messages and decipher codes—a high-tech war machine:

—Besieged by a vast army of invisible enemies, the human body enlists a remarkably complex corps of internal bodyguards to battle the invaders. They can cleanse the lungs of foreign particles, rid the bloodstream of infectious microorganisms, and weed tissue of renegade cancer cells.[9]

—A response team will include commandos that will guide a force of variously armed personnel into the battle zone and then urge them to attack. . . . Now, as you can imagine, the battle will be brief or protracted, violent or otherwise, depending on the speed with which the intruder is recognised . . . as well as the weaponry he has for resistance and the forces the plant can effectively marshal. One thing is certain; in this highly sophisticated plant bristling with valuable and sensitive equipment, unnecessary force is to be avoided. No use shooting the intruder in the computer room and at the same time permanently damaging the computer.[10]

—Suddenly the site of injury, previously so peaceful, is transformed into a battlefield on which the body's armed forces, hurling themselves repeatedly at the encroaching microorganisms, crush and annihilate them. No one is pardoned, no prisoners taken—although fragments of the invading bacteria, viruses, rickettsias, parasites, and fungal microorganisms are conveyed to the lymph nodes for the rapid training of the defense system's true bloodhounds, the "killer" cells.[11]

The military metaphors for the immune system follow a tradition of biological description in place since the nineteenth century. These metaphors are so pervasive that it has become difficult to imagine the body any other way. These metaphors thus directly affect the ways in which people, including those with AIDS, view their own bodies, and they impose a vocabulary of competence and blame on physiological processes. The images of bodies at war reinforce xenophobic notions of foreignness as inherently threatening and of the foreign as diseased. A macrophage that displays a threatening foreignness on its surface can thus be equated with a person with AIDS, whose "contaminated" state is identified and rejected. Military metaphors reinforce hostility toward the bodies of others and place blame squarely upon the individual: If your immune system army doesn't defend itself properly, then there must be something wrong not only with your self-identity but also with your ability to manage your defense forces.[12]

Increasingly, the dominant metaphors of the immune system involve communication—transmission of and interference with immune responses.[13] However, these metaphors and military metaphors are liberally mixed, with little rationale. Quite often, this results in the image of a factory with a high-tech electronic security system:

Should a would-be saboteur enter the establishment in the early hours of the morning, our spotters would recognise the likelihood that the saboteur is an intruder and move in closer for a better look using a closed-circuit TV camera that locks on to the suspect and freezes a closeup image of his face on one half of a monitor screen. A computer then runs through all of the physical characteristics of the plant's legitimate employees on the other half of the screen, so that with incredible accuracy the physical features of the foreigner and members of the legitimate family are compared.[14]

Here, metaphors of high-tech surveillance technology, computerized databases, and security systems evoke not only industrial narratives of protecting trade secrets and capital but also Cold War narratives of totalitarian surveillance and control. In the context of AIDS politics, with its debates over the definition of the family, the concept of a "legitimate" family unit seems doubly ironic.

Popular texts often describe the immune system in terms of a police state, where cells are asked to display their "proof of identity" and intruders or spies (those who do not speak the same language) are targeted for annihilation.[15] In the nation-state metaphor, the immune system keeps vast files, as the CIA does, to ferret out antigens: "The intruders' descriptions are stored in the vast criminal records of the immune system. When a substance matching one of the stored descriptions makes a new appearance, the memory cells see to the swift manufacture of antibodies to combat it."[16] Implications of innocence and guilt, weighty with meaning in the context of the moral debates around AIDS, pervade these mixed-metaphor descriptions. The body is seen as an innocent and moral social structure whose internal mechanisms of law and order prevent intruders (all marked as criminals) from passing undetected.

In accordance with these mixed metaphors of the immune system as war machine, communications network, and nation-state, popular science casts the human immunodeficiency virus (HIV) as a special kind of "foreign agent," either a spy or a terrorist. HIV is portrayed as a stealthy enemy whose main strategy involves an undetected approach. The virus's ability to "hide out" (or to "smolder") in the body for extended periods of dormancy (in which a person is considered HIV-positive but not to have AIDS) evokes military strategies of concealment. Quite often writers compare HIV's behavior to the ancient battle techniques of Greek myth: "Like Greeks hidden inside the Trojan horse, the AIDS virus enters the body concealed inside a helper T-cell from an infected host."[17] Hardly useful in high-tech warfare, the Trojan horse is replaced by the radar-evading Stealth bomber: "The great mystery has always been why the body cannot knock HIV out completely. One possibility is that the body has trouble 'seeing' all of the virus. Like a Stealth fighter plane, HIV may have hidden parts that do not show up on the immune system's radar screen. As a result the body may not manufacture all the different antibodies that could attack the virus."[18]

HIV's ability to avoid recognition as foreign by the immune system is a primary focus of AIDS research. In the metaphoric language used to describe the virus, this ability to hide firmly suggests intentionality. It is implied that HIV hides in order to survive, that it follows plans of action to avoid detection. Popular discourse depicts the virus as strategic and cunning, an outlaw who has transgressed cell boundaries in disguise and is causing breakdown.[19] Articles consistently refer to the virus as "not innocent" and "devious,"[20] which, by extension, imply that it is evil and criminal; it breaks not only the law of the immune system but also the law of viruses in its ability to deflect recognition. We thus have the image of the immune system as a nation under siege and HIV as a Cold War spy, terrorist, or guerrilla fighter. Writes Treichler: "Clearly, 007 is a spy's spy, capable of any deception: evading the 'fluid patrol officers' is child's play. Indeed, it is so shifting and uncertain we might even acknowledge our own historical moment more specifically by giving the AIDS virus a postmodern identity: a terrorist's terrorist, an Abu Nidal of viruses."[21]

Thus the virus is given identity as Arab and other. Another account describes the virus as activating "suicide programs," evoking images of terrorist suicide bombers.[22] The HIV spy is engaged in a disinformation campaign, a barrage of propaganda. Popular discourse depicts this activity as a reprogramming of the immune system, thus conjuring images of industrial and technological sabotage: "A virus invades the cell's computer, which is locked up in its nucleus, and changes its program. As a virus inserts the program into the computer, it instructs the cell to use its own raw materials, normally present for the production of something useful, to put these materials to work to produce more virus."[23] Some of these accounts ascribe to the virus a certain bossiness and authoritarianism, an ability to issue commands and take over. The virus is the instigator of production, handing down the instructions and reproducing itself into clones that "fan out" like troops to nearby domains. Metaphors of mass production and military organization are thus combined with information metaphors to produce the image of a virulent strain of capitalism.

The metaphor of warfare between the nation-state of the immune system and the invading virus is also imbued with gender stereotypes. Emily Martin notes that the cells of the immune system are assigned different gender roles in the domestic sphere of the body. The phagocytes are depicted as "housekeepers," constantly scouring and cleaning the body. They engulf antigens in a process of "invagination." The T-cells, by contrast, are described in heroic imagery. Called "commanders-in-chief,"[24] they have specialized functions, are organized into armies, and "kill by penetrating or injecting."[25] It is also noted that T-cells are selectively produced, with most of them dying in the thymus gland, where their "training" takes place. According to one scientist, it may be that "the thymus is selecting only the best T-cells, those with the sharpest powers of recognition,"[26] thus implying an elite group. Popular science texts describe macrophages as "devouring" and consuming the foreign elements, T-cells as "killing" them. In a well-known 1986 *National Geographic* article, the hierarchy of these cells is made explicit in the cartoon graphics: Macrophages are depicted by an M with teeth, T-cells by a T with a gun (see Figure 21).[27] In these accounts, the immune system comprises "male" cells that have technological weapons and "female" cells that can do battle only with their bodies.

One would think that in this context HIV would be figured as a hypermasculine outlaw. Yet perhaps because of the virus's identification with gay men its gender identity is ambiguous. One researcher referred to HIV as a "wimpy virus" because it is not highly contagious.[28] The virus can be conceived both as a masculine enemy, destroying and essentially emasculating the male T-cells (former heroes of the immune system), and as a devious foe who uses not force but elaborate strategies of disguise and concealment.[29]

Once evoked, metaphors of warfare, production, and terrorism allow little room for alternative conceptions of the immune system.[30] The domesticating use of language in warfare has been noted by both Carol Cohn and Elaine Scarry. Cohn has written about the use of innocuous terms to describe aspects of nuclear weaponry (to "pat the missile," "silos," and "Christmas tree farms");[31] Scarry has noted how strategies of torture employ domestic objects—a door, a chair, a bathtub—to cause violent pain.[32] In the case of the immune system, popular science presents the inverse—metaphors of war are used to depict warfare in the most intimate and "domestic" context, our own bodies. Depictions of the body as surrounded by hostile adversaries produce a very particular image of the biomedical body—under siege, paranoid, and vulnerable.

Landscapes and Bodily Frontiers: Visual Images of the Immune System

How we imagine and give form to the immune system is directly related to how medical illustrations and photographs in the media

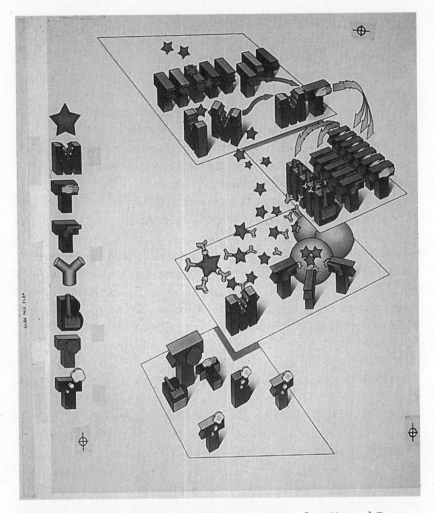

Figure 21. "Cell Wars." Illustration of the immune system from *National Geographic*, June 1986, by Dale D. Glasgow. Macrophages are represented by Ms, T-cells by Ts, B-cells by Bs, viruses by stars, and antibodies by Ys. © National Geographic Society.

represent it. The issue of representability haunts the immune system because it is difficult to render visible activities taking place at a microscopic level within the body. Popular magazines such as *National Geographic* and *Time* have addressed this dilemma by creating characters of the many cells that constitute the immune system's mechanisms and resorting to cartoonlike graphics. The cell fascinates us because it is so fundamental yet invisible to the naked eye. Illustrations of the immune system usually depict cells with letters ("T" for T-cells, for instance) or as spherical shapes with pronglike attachments. The immune system thus begins to look like a set of children's toys with interlocking parts—an innocuous game, decidedly not part of one's body.

The immune system is so synonymous with self that it is difficult to give it form or image. Yet the desire to visualize it, and HIV, is powerful. Metaphors of sight permeate descriptions of the immune system; it must recognize intruders, must "see" them in order to understand them. Popular accounts describe HIV as hiding in cells, concealing itself from sight, and disguising itself to avoid detection. Indeed, HIV is deemed special primarily because of its ability to hide from view, to become inextricably part of the person with AIDS:

The structure of the AIDS virus is almost perfect. The virus lives and replicates within human cells, a perfect place to escape from the body's defenses. Most viruses do this, which is why they are so effective. The virus that causes AIDS, however, performs an even neater trick: it becomes part of the genetic material of the cell. Hiding within this innermost sanctum of our bodies, the virus adopts the ultimate camouflage—it becomes part of the person it infects.[33]

Implicit in these metaphors of sight is the notion that seeing the virus will reveal its truths, that imaging the immune system will reveal how it functions. This concept draws on the legacy of nineteenth-century positivist science in its assumption that visual recognition establishes empirical fact, that the "real" can be visually defined. Photography is a product of this mode of thought, with its concept that the truth can be verified through the camera lens. In fact, the camera was thought from its inception to be a mechanism capable of seeing beyond the human eye, a device that could see deeper into worlds invisible to human sight. Emile Zola reportedly declared, "We cannot claim to have really seen anything before having photographed it."[34] The photograph is said to "capture" reality; indeed, aerial and space photography and microphotography literally can convey images of inner and outer space that the human eye cannot register.

The concept of photographic truth is directly related to its mechanical nature. Because it is produced by a camera, the photograph can be seen as stripped of intentionality. Yet modern discourse attributes to the photograph not only a neutral, empirical capacity but also magical qualities of expression and imagination.[35] The power of the photograph thus derives from its dual meaning; it not only tells the truth but also, supposedly, speaks beyond it. The photograph's ability to record memory and preserve images of the dead contributes to its meaning as a spiritual object. It represents the unattainable yet is infused with the desire to hold the unattainable in one's hands. As Susan Sontag writes:

A photograph is both a pseudo-presence and token of absence. Like a wood fire in a room, photographs—especially those of people, of distant landscapes and faraway cities, of the vanished past—are incitements to reverie. The sense of the unattainable that can be evoked by photographs feeds directly into the erotic feelings of those for whom desirability is enhanced by distance. The lover's photograph hidden in a married woman's wallet, the poster photograph of a rock star tacked up over an adolescent's bed, the campaign-button image of a politician's face pinned on a voter's coat, the snapshots of a cabdriver's children clipped to the visor—all such talismanic uses of photographs express a feeling both sentimental and implicitly magical: they are attempts to contact or lay claim to another reality.[36]

This dual sense of imaging the unattainable and laying claim to reality is central to the effect of scientific photographs. Photography's alliance with science can be traced to its origins. Scientists saw in photography's ability to enlarge or reduce images the opportunity to open up a whole new realm to the human eye, to reveal, as it was often called, the "unsuspected world."[37] Aerial images taken from balloons were among some of the earliest photographs, and microphotography was practiced as early as the 1880s. Scientific drawings of the human body were eventually replaced by photographs. Hence, the photograph also became an integral element in what Michel Foucault has called "biopower"—the modern state's regulation of the body, which coalesced in nineteenth-century Europe, where photography was first invented. Photographs of pathologies and diseased bodies were amassed at hospitals, which set up their own photographic studios at the same time that state institutions were beginning to photograph the criminal and the insane. Photography's role in science was thus directly related to its use as a mechanism of surveillance and social control.

The camera was thus perceived as an objective tool that produced images of reality, a passive device that merely recorded what was there. Such conceptions worked in tension with the concurrent representations of the camera as an active, even aggressive and invasive tool and of the photographer as a heroic figure. Photography offered a means to penetrate darkness and illuminate previously hidden places, microphotography a way to reveal scientific truths. The microscope had been an integral part of science since the seventeenth century; with the addition of photography, microscopic images could be widely disseminated. The earliest microphotographs ("microscope-daguerreotypes") were taken by Alfred Donné and Leon Foucault and published in an anatomical atlas in 1845. Donné wrote at the time: "Before drawing conclusions from our observations, we shall let Nature reproduce herself; we shall fix her upon a daguerreotype plate with all her details and infinite nuances. . . . We are determined to support each new observational fact on a rigorous representation safe from any illusion or preconceived ideas."[38] Here, a traditional concept of a feminized nature is "fixed" by the photographic process so that "she" will reveal "her" secrets.[39]

Contemporary imaging systems have moved far beyond photography to produce magnetic and infrared images, sonograms, high-resolution X-rays, and computer enhanced images.[40] These devices for representing the body's interior have greatly refined diagnostic practice and thus are presented as life-saving mechanisms. One scientist told *National Geographic* that because of the use of computers in medical imaging, "In medicine, as in our society, we have embarked on a scientific revolution unlike any other in man's history."[41]

Within this context, the images of the immune system produced by Lennart Nilsson, a photographer well-known for his representations of the human body's interior, are significant. Nilsson's photographs of the immune system have been published widely in scientific journals, science textbooks, advertisements for medical products, and television programs about AIDS. They have been heavily featured in *Life* and *National Geographic* and in his coffee-table book

The Body Victorious, a portrait of the immune system.[42] Nilsson's photographs are the primary images of the immune system, specifically of its interaction with viruses such as HIV; as such, they are central in explaining how imaging of the body's interior has affected our concepts of our bodies.

Nilsson is perhaps most famous for his photographs of the human fetus, which have played a powerful role in the volatile abortion debate. These images situate the unborn fetus in a landscape of space, erasing the body of the mother and providing the foundation on which arguments for fetal autonomy are made (ironically, these images of fetuses "in space" were actually sent into space on the unmanned spacecraft Voyager I and II in the form of sound signals).[43] In popular accounts, Nilsson is lionized as a heroic figure, a dedicated scientist/artist, a master technician, and a pioneer (he has also photographed DNA molecules) who has looked inside the body and seen its truths. *Life* magazine has described Nilsson as having special access to "invisible worlds":

Lennart Nilsson hears the question again and again, at interviews, awards ceremonies, dinner parties, "hundreds, maybe thousands of times," and he can recognize its subtext. When does life begin? the people ask him. You must know. You have captured sperm and egg on film, peered into women's uteruses, spent endless hours in operating rooms as tubal pregnancies were being removed, much as great artists before you haunted morgues while preparing to paint their sinewy saints.[44]

In these accounts, Nilsson is described in the heroic paradigm of the physician on call, rushing to photograph in the middle of the night. However, noticeably absent in these stories of Nilsson's photographic adventures is any description of the state of the bodies that he is photographing (although the analogy to the morgue in the above quote is telling). His famous images of fetuses, with a few rare exceptions, all were taken after the fetus had been removed from the mother's body. Similarly, almost all of the samples used in his microphotographs were taken from autopsies and biopsies, no longer active, viable only in a controlled environment.[45] Nilsson's microphotography is done in the context of the laboratory.[46]

Yet his images of the immune system do not reflect the sterile setting in which they were produced. Rather, these are images of horizonless landscapes, some colorized to evoke depth, fantastic depictions of the "real." They uphold the reputation of photography as a miraculous science, one possessing the ability to capture the unattainable. These images appear to exist in space, weightless and free-floating. The bodies in Nilsson's photographs are not set in their actual context: incision, dissection, and excision with medical instruments.

Nilsson is not only photographing the body's interior and the immune system but scripting a narrative about it. *National Geographic* describes how Nilsson and his collaborator, Dr. Jan Lindberg, photographed an immune system story:

> For instance, in the battle scene involving macrophages and bacteria, Nilsson and Lindberg took cells and put them in a special nutrient solution to keep them alive. Then they treated the specimens at intervals, removing one sample, then another, from the culture, and coating each with a fixative solution called glutaraldehyde. Like a snapshot, this process "freezes" each specimen at an instant in time. By preserving several samples over several hours, Nilsson and Lindberg established a sequence for the story, just as a moviemaker would string together scenes to form a plot. . . . There Nilsson sits for hours, days, and months, trying one specimen after another until the elements of a story emerge.[47]

Hence, these images of the immune system "at work" are not passively recorded by the camera but heavily orchestrated and compiled to tell a very specific narrative of triumph and defeat.

In one Nilsson image, two red cancer cells, each a spherical mass of fibers, loom out of a textured surface and hold between them a smaller, yellow T-cell. The cancer cells are haloed with light, which gives them a three-dimensional quality. Set against a dark green background, the cancer cells take on an animated quality, as if they were huge creatures rising threateningly out of the earth. Another image, published in *Time* magazine, shows a large black-and-white cell spread out on a flat surface, extending an arm to a yellow, capsulelike bacteria (see Figure 22). Set against a bright orange background, this cell evokes the wavy surface of the ocean, rising off the surface to extend toward the bacteria. The caption to this image tells a dramatic narrative: "Going in for the kill: ever vigilant, a patrolling macrophage

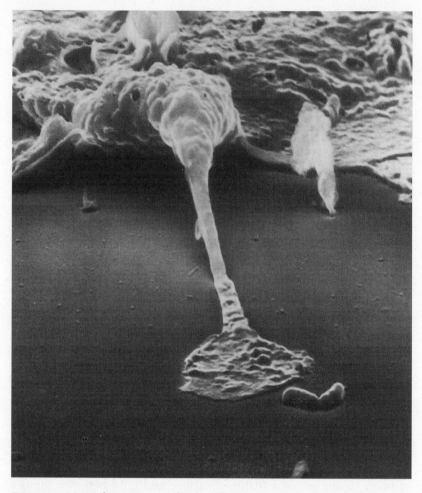

Figure 22. Macrophage "going in for the kill." Micrograph by Lennart Nilsson.
© Boehringer Ingelheim International Gmbh.

sends out a cellular extension known as a pseudopod to engulf and
destroy a bacterial cell before alerting more defenders."[48] In this
light, the orange surface of the image takes on a fiery, dramatic quality, and the extended arm of the macrophage is transformed from an
appendage into a weapon. Other images create landscapes of the
body's tissues. A wound, magnified forty times, appears as a desert
landscape of brown, red, and sandy hues with layers of sediment;

the surface of the tongue and the fibers of the digestive tract are transformed into lunar landscapes of hills, crevices, and cliffs.

All of these electron microscope images are originally gray or blue and then tinted, a fact rarely mentioned. According to *National Geographic,* colorization is "done as an aid to readers, to help distinguish the various parts of cells and tissues."[49] Yet the blues, yellows, and reds are presented in these photographs as natural colors, emphasizing the difference between the body and "foreign" antigens. In one photograph (Figure 23), for instance, a brown T-cell is perforated and covered with tiny particles that represent HIV, colored in a bright blue that gives them an otherworldly quality.

What are the effects of visualizing the interior of the body as a landscape? Historically, landscape painting and photography have evoked a transcendence, the horizon promising liberty and opportunity.[50] The history of microscopy has been about representing the body as an interior and flat landscape.[51] Photographs of the immune system place these traditions in a new image context. They present unearthly landscapes and in a sense resemble photographs taken from outer space. As Donna Haraway has noted, space photographs seem to imply that some*one* was there, when in fact they were taken by a spacecraft (some*thing*).[52] Popular science renders the landscape of space as passive, simply there, photographed by an unmanned, objective recording device. As Haraway notes, in the context of *National Geographic,* the inner space of the body is equated with outer space:

It is photography that convinces the viewer of the fraternal relation of inner and outer space. But curiously, in outer space, we see spacemen fitted into explorer craft or floating about as individuated cosmic foetuses, while in the supposedly earthly space of our own interiors, we see non-humanoid strangers who are supposed to be the means by which our bodies sustain our integrity and individuality, indeed our humanity in the face of a world of others.[53]

Whereas the imaging of space makes it seem more accessible and more human, the imaging of the human immune system as a kind of space landscape distances us from our bodies. When bodily interiors are rendered as landscapes, they lose their fluidity and take on a

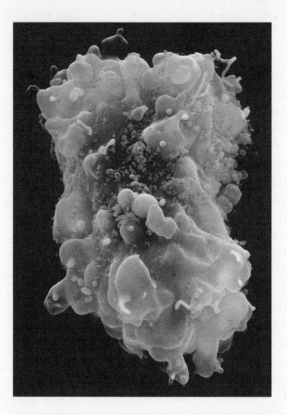

Figure 23. T-cell "under attack" from HIV. Micrograph by Lennart Nilsson. © Boehringer Ingelheim International Gmbh.

static quality; images of the immune system are stationary, stabilized, frozen in time, simultaneously alive and otherworldly, active and passive.

In these images the immune system becomes, like all landscapes, a frontier site for exploration and conquest.[54] This connotation fits perfectly with depictions of immunology as a science that is moving forward into unique and unexplored terrain. Peter Jaret in *National Geographic* portrays immunology as staking out the unexplored terrain of a newly discovered world: " 'We probably know as little about the immune system now,' said researcher Edward Bradley of the Cetus Corporation, 'as Columbus knew about the Americas after his first voyage.' Into what territories will the new frontiers of immunology lead us? Almost certainly deep into the nucleus of the human cell, where lie the elegant DNA spirals that make one cell a macrophage, another a T-cell."[55] This landscape is "just there," waiting to be conquered. This is the standard narrative about science penetrating to the depths of the human cell, where hierarchy is already inscribed (what separates the T-cells from the macrophages, the leaders from the masses, the men from the boys?).[56]

In the "frontiers of immunology," the images of the immune system also refer back to the early descriptions of photography as a medium that can see beyond the human eye and show us what we cannot see. Like aerial and space photographs, they are taken from vantage points inaccessible to human eyesight. And, like the space photographs, they are not taken by a "man with a camera" but by a high-tech machine (with Nilsson figured as a scientist instead of an artist/photographer). The microscopic photographs of the human body survey and enlarge the most minute details of the inner landscape, rendering the tiny huge and monstrous. These images are perceived to be devoid of intentionality, to be "natural" image depictions.

Yet these images also provide a kind of visual pleasure. Landscapes have been valued through Western history not only for their evocation of adventure, travel, and conquest but also for their representation of the sublime. Here, nature is passive yet exhilarating, beautiful, noble, and infinitely complex. Similarly, *The Body Victorious* presents the body as an aestheticized, colorized landscape, a site of wonder. These photographs do not depict the violence (surgery, dissection, etc.) wreaked upon that body; rather, they present a bloodless, multicolored, and fascinating terrain. The change of scale of these microphotographs allows the images to become aesthetic objects, compelling depictions of many different landscapes.

In *Flexible Bodies,* an innovative anthropological study of the meanings of the immune system, Emily Martin interviewed many people, both in and outside the medical community, about their images of and feelings about their immune systems. When presented with images by Nilsson and others of cells interacting, most participants responded with awe yet felt ambivalent about the relationship of the images to their own bodies. One told Martin: "It's actually hard for me to picture these things in my body. . . . I mean they're so microscopic, you know what I mean? That when you magnify it by a certain amount, it's scary."[57] Martin notes that although many people expressed wonder at the photographs as artifacts of scientific knowledge, they still exercised their imaginations in speculating on what the images resembled. She notes that the primary aspect of these images is their lack of context: "The depictions in micrographs are so decontextualized that they could be anything at all, from jellyfish in the ocean deep, to star wars in outer space."[58]

The microscopic images of the immune system depict a universal, unmarked body, one stripped of gender, race, sexuality, or age—precisely the kinds of differences that have marked bodies in the AIDS epidemic. They let us inside the body as if we have not wrenched past its borders.[59] These images operate without an anchoring context, profoundly distanced from touch, smell, sight, and other everyday bodily functions.

Into this "sacrosanct" and distanced landscape comes HIV, which popular graphics and microphotographs depict as visual chaos. HIV is most commonly pictured in stylized scientific illustrations that render it as a spherical shape with a pronged exterior and coils (of RNA) in its center, a cartoonish symbol that often resembles a nuclear bomb. In these images the virus looks huge and lethal, as if it would explode if dropped on one of its prongs, which tend to resemble detonators. The coils in the center of the image have prompted some critics to describe it as a "grenade" that would explode if the coil were pulled.[60]

Images of HIV as explosive parallel descriptions of the virus as a menacing terrorist, with obvious and direct consequences on people living with HIV and AIDS. Science still cannot offer a coherent narrative of what HIV is and how it functions, but in popular media its image is clear—it is huge, it is monstrous, and it can be seen. The most well-known microscopic photographs of HIV depict formless black-and-white entities. In a 1987 article in *Scientific American*, the lead photo depicts a cell that appears to be disintegrating into small, chaotic shapes. The caption explains that a "degenerating T4 cell gives rise to mass of newly made particles of the virus that causes AIDS."[61] The exact location of the virus itself in this picture is not entirely clear; the image of this dark tree shape appears to have no center or coherence. A 1985 *Time* magazine cover featured an amorphous image of HIV under the headline, "AIDS: The Growing Threat, What's Being Done" (Figure 24).[62] In smaller print, the reader is informed that this image is the "virus, magnified 135,000

Figure 24. Cover of *Time* magazine, August 12, 1985. © 1985 Time, Inc. Reprinted by permission.

times, destroying T-cell." The magnification alone makes the virus appear to be rising up to engulf everything in its path. On an inside photo spread, the image of this "deadly culprit" is laid out so that it appears to be engulfing images of an "AIDS family" on the left and an AIDS patient in the hospital on the right. In almost all of these photos, the magnified virus takes on a larger-than-life quality.

Nilsson's images of HIV, which have been called "enigmatically beautiful yet frightening," use colorization to isolate the virus aesthetically and graphically. HIV, clustering on and destroying a cell, shows up in an alien blue. Magnified 250,000 times, HIV is rendered both monstrous and foreign. Seen in Nilsson's coffee-table book, with its descriptions of a body at war with threatening foreign elements, or in articles about the deviousness of HIV, the photographs of the immune system and HIV are already constructed as depicting sites of conflict. In rendering the body as a landscape, these images create universal bodies to illustrate an epidemic that affects individual bodies very specifically marked as different.

Given the politics of representing people with AIDS, images of the immune system fall within an already uneasy context. They cannot remain simply images of science, disconnected somehow from the cultural politics of AIDS. Hence, more so than any other scientific images, they raise the fundamental question of their effect upon the diseased, rather than simply their importance to the scientist. Can we recognize ourselves in the lunar landscapes of microphotography? Should we attempt to do so? Is there any way these images can be seen as empowering beyond the visual pleasure they provide? They offer a challenge to the skills of negotiation for people living with AIDS, for whom visualization of bodily interiors is often essential.

The Immune System as a Site of Memory

Popular science defines the immune system as a depository of bodily memory. In this story, the immune system's goals are twofold: to destroy the "foreign" element and to create a memory of the body's encounter with it. Indeed, the immune system can be read as a memorial, a technology that retains records of the body's activities and what has traveled through it.

Concepts of the immune system are steeped in metaphors of recognition. Memory cells are long-living and may circulate within the body for years, enabling it to respond quickly to familiar foreign elements. This memory is even thought to precede any encounters with other elements, given the fact that we are born with immune systems in place. One author notes: "If we are born with a healthy immune system, it knows even at the moment of birth how to discover and neutralise foreign substances."[63]

The body is constantly regenerating itself and replacing cells; hence, to maintain the continuity provided by biological memory, new cells must acquire information from other cells. Some scientists regard immunological memory as "a kind of learning, whereby the body learns to anticipate likely dangers which can increase the speed and intensity of response."[64] Hence, the body is seen to become wiser and better defended as it acquires immunities.

Popular medical discourse describes this record of learned encounters with antigens as a kind of database. The database metaphor implies a potentially vast record that is instantly available to the immune system. Not surprisingly, popular characterizations of the immune system as a battlefield or security system regard this "database" as a set of "criminal records," with antigens matched with metaphorical mug shots.

The image of immune system memory in these models is similar to a traditional concept of history, in which the body keeps an "official" record in a database. Ironically, none of these accounts addresses the role that vaccination plays in this record-keeping process, in part because it undermines the metaphor of a carefully compiled archive of history. Vaccines can be seen as representing "fake" memories that allow the body to produce antibodies to viruses stronger than those it has actually encountered. Like the fake memories provided to the replicants of *Blade Runner* through photographs, or the "fake" histories that nations often write for themselves, vaccines conjure for the immune system events that never took place. One could call vaccines a kind of mediated memory production, not unlike the kinds of memories we acquire through popular media images—memories of events we never experienced. Thus, the immune system both remembers and forgets, both produces and represses memories.

Contemporary scientific theories of the immune system postulate a body that is significantly less bounded than the model used in popular accounts. These theories have noted how the immune system appears not only to "remember" antigens it has encountered before but also to contain a record of potential "foreign" substances. Martin notes that scientists perceive the immune system as an "anticipatory system," with trillions of different types of antibodies, many designed to match specific potential "invaders." She remarks, "One of my immunology lecturers was fond of stressing the immense variety of antibodies by saying that we even have antibodies specific to antigens that would be found only on Mars!"[65]

If the immune system already has within it antibodies for all potential antigens, then it does more than recognize elements that have already traveled through the body. Indeed, this means that "foreign" elements are not foreign at all but are already recognized within the immune system. Some scientists, such as Danish immunologist Niels Jerne, have defined the immune system as being in a dynamic state of recognition and response within itself. This model not only contradicts the popular image of the immune system as a well-defended fortress besieged by foreign invaders but also has consequences for popular images of viruses such as HIV—not foreign invaders and terrorists but familiar elements already recognized within us.

HIV: A Foreign Agent of Forgetting

According to popular science discourse, when an agent such as HIV disrupts the immune system, it precipitates a crisis of both memory and self. Popular medical discourse describes viruses as parasitic creatures that need to occupy host bodies in order to survive and propagate. They are entities that thrive on difference and appropriation, that trouble notions of boundaries and definitions of self. All viruses carry with them implications of contamination. Yet it can be said that a virus has no meaning without a cell; it is not a "whole." According to Judith Williamson: "Nothing could be more meaningless than a virus. It has no point, no purpose, no plan; it is part of no scheme, carries no inherent significance. And yet nothing is harder for us to confront than the complete absence of meaning . . . meaninglessness isn't just the opposite of meaning, it is the end of meaning and threatens the fragile structures by which we make sense of the world."[66]

Popular medical discourse accords viruses all kinds of intentionality, depicting them as "agents" who change. One virus researcher says that HIV "has evolved together with the immune system. These viruses know the immune system very well by experience."[67] Thus, the virus is granted wisdom; it mutates because it "learns." It refuses to believe the fake memories of the vaccine. The virus only has "purpose" when in contact with cells; otherwise it is a kind of nonentity. Jaret writes: "A virus is a protein-coated bundle of genes containing instructions for making identical copies of itself. Pure information. Because it lacks the basic machinery for reproduction, a virus is not, strictly speaking, even alive."[68] Contradictions abound here. A virus is not "alive," according to science, yet neither is it dead; it can be killed. It is a "bundle" of genes, an incohesive tangle. It "contains instructions" but apparently did not write them itself. It is "pure information," yet information that acquires meaning only when in contact with cells.

Anthony Fauci of the National Institutes of Health has stated that the AIDS epidemic has advanced scientific understandings of the immune system: "AIDS is the perfect disease for studying the immune system. The virus destroys one of the major cells of the system. So, now nature is doing the experiments. It has just pulled out a major chip, and we're watching everything else go haywire."[69] Scientists may regard AIDS as "perfect" and HIV as a wily opponent, but for people living with HIV and AIDS such concepts can be distressing. In many scientific accounts, HIV is viewed as useful in justifying previous research in immunology. The burst of scientific examination of the immune system in the last twenty years is thus depicted as prescient.

HIV disrupts the conventional narrative of a virus's interaction with the immune system. It does so in part because it is a retrovirus, which means that it reverses the normal flow of genetic information from DNA to RNA. Retroviruses, which have been implicated in certain cancers, use an enzyme called reverse transcriptase to transform a chain of viral RNA into a complementary strand of DNA, which is then integrated into the cell's DNA. In this way retroviruses provoke cell division to, for instance, cause cancer. In the case of HIV, once the virus takes over a cell, it is said to "splice" its complete genetic information into the cell's DNA. Thus, HIV is depicted as completely insinuating itself into the genetic makeup of the "host" cell; it "rewrites" the story of the immune system by substituting its own DNA narrative. The genetic identity of the cell has been altered, as has its memory.

Once ensconced, HIV creates a narrative of chaos and communication systems gone awry:

Next, the immune system finally recognizes HIV as an invader. The B cells make antibodies against the AIDS virus. But those antibodies also end up attacking other immune system cells carrying the CD4 receptor because HIV resembles them. The antibodies prevent helper T-cells from communicating with these other immune cells and short-circuit the immune response. At the same time, the HIV-prompted antibodies trigger the release of a second set of antibodies, anti-antibodies against both the first antibodies and the CD4 receptors on helper T-cells. The result: a handful of HIV causes the immune system to self-destruct.[70]

This is just one of the many narratives about how HIV creates chaos in the immune system. Here, a mere "handful" of HIV causes a complete breakdown of the immune system, which can no longer identify self from other.

Popular medical discourse also portrays HIV as special because, like a cold or flu virus, it changes so constantly that the body must constantly re-recognize it. This mutability is not necessarily attributed to cunning on the part of the virus; one writer describes it as carelessness: "Even within one person, the virus can mutate in a matter of hours. This is partly because the virus is sloppy at reproducing itself and makes inaccurate copies."[71] This description implies that HIV does not have an adequate sense of self and hence does not reproduce itself with precision.

HIV provokes a kind of forgetting within the body, turning the body against itself, changing its definition of self. This is a common image of horror. For example, the creature in the film *Alien* (1979) parasitically gestates undetected in the human body and then emerges from within it, self yet definitely not self. In 1901, German bacteriologist Paul Erlich used the term *"horror autotoxicus"* to describe the body's repulsion to attacking itself (for instance, in autoimmune diseases). This turning upon oneself, the inability to separate self from nonself or friend from enemy, is the horror attributed to HIV.

Susan Sontag has written that "cancer was regarded with irrational revulsion, as a diminution of self . . . as a disease to which the psychically defeated, the inexpressive, the repressed—especially those who have repressed anger or sexual feelings—are particularly prone."[72] These attributes imply that with cancer, the repressed self is seen as turning against itself, attacking from within. By contrast, AIDS is read as the result of an invasion that comes from outside the self but transforms the self. The stigma of AIDS is the direct result of the widespread belief that those who acquired AIDS through sex and drug use knowingly exposed themselves through dangerous or "perverse" lifestyles. Hence, whereas a disease that "invades" the body from the outside would normally be seen to infect innocent people, the popular interpretation of AIDS posits that those who acquired HIV did not responsibly protect themselves.[73]

HIV is seen to enter the immune system's most sacred space and to rescript its genetic memory. HIV is constantly described as entering the "innermost sanctum" of the cell and the "sacrosanct environment" of the body.[74] These terms conjure images of an intrusion of private inner chambers, of bodies violated, of an inside no longer secure. This is not the traditional notion of the patient as a vessel or as an extension of disease, of a body under siege from a foreign agent; it is an image of a body with a new identity. AIDS's definition as a syndrome—not a disease but a condition—underscores this notion that it takes over the self. As the person with AIDS becomes the virus, the virus becomes the person with AIDS; in popular discourse, they are both subject to blame.

AIDS then becomes a metaphor for any kind of breakdown, in particular societal breakdown. It is figured as invading not only individual bodies but the United States as a whole, having the potential to kill "America." The fear that the "plague is within us," as Paula Treichler notes, is underscored both by the virus's negation of the boundaries between self and nonself and by its supposed initiation of a breakdown in the structure of American society—the health care structure, the family, the continuity of generations. One of the most frightening aspects of this representation of the virus is the notion that HIV can propagate forgetting and erase the self from memory.

Cultural Memory
and the Immune System

Although metaphors of war, nation-states, terrorists, and memory crisis pervade popular descriptions of the immune system and AIDS, these metaphors are not necessarily the most accurate descriptions of these biological events. Alternative metaphors of both the immune system and HIV do exist. For instance, Mary Catherine Bateson and Richard Goldsby's model of the body as a miniature, self-regulating ecosystem attempts a balance between images of defense and ones of coexistence:

Each of us is like a planet carrying its own small ecosystem on its surface, separated from the core. We all host a large and dynamic microbial community. Bacteria can be found busily coating our teeth with plaque, lurking in competitive company with other tiny creatures in the lungs, and living by the billions in our guts, many of them performing useful services. At each of these sites, there is a fierce struggle to carve out and hold a resource niche, but as long as the skin holds, most of these battles are intermicrobial, fought outside the body and benign.[75]

Bateson and Goldsby emphasize how the body coexists with bacteria and foreign substances in a regulatory fashion. However, their inability to fully dispense with metaphors of conflict and foreignness (indicated by terms such as "fierce struggle" and the idea of skin holding as a barrier) demonstrates just how powerful those metaphors are.

Other theorists have noted that in the 1930s the pioneering Polish biologist Ludwik Fleck rejected conflict metaphors of the immune system, proposing instead the idea of a "harmonious life unit" in which coexistence with bacteria is essential. In Fleck's model, "An organism can no longer be construed as a self-contained, independent unit with fixed boundaries."[76] For Fleck, the metaphor of invasion was inappropriate, because a completely foreign substance would have no coinciding antibodies. He wrote: "It is very doubtful whether an invasion in the old sense is possible, involving as it does an interference by completely foreign organisms in natural conditions. A completely foreign organism could find no receptors capable of reaction and thus could not generate a biological process. It is therefore better to speak of a complicated revolution with the complex life unit than of an invasion of it."[77] Fleck perceived the relationship of the body to different antigens as one of organic exchange and balance. Similarly, in contemporary theories of antibody diversity and in Niels Jerne's network theory, the immune system is one of recognition within itself, a model that rejects not only the rigid distinction between self and nonself but also the metaphors of invasion and battlegrounds. This is an image of a system that is actively transforming, mirroring, refiguring, that is, according to Donna Haraway, "always in a state of dynamic internal responding."[78]

This model of the immune system requires us to refigure the image of the person with AIDS, who, like the virus, is a part of the nation, familiar and recognized within it. It is essential that the immune system be considered limited and finite, not an all-powerful, high-tech wonder. In envisioning the immune system as a site of memory, learning, and, by extension, healing, we can offer ways to rescript images and narratives of HIV and, in turn, to alter the effects of those images on people with AIDS. The idea of a "crisis of memory" generated by HIV in the immune system can be countered by the active discourse of cultural memory.

Scientific models of the immune system as a means of exchange and response are important for thinking not only about the immune system but AIDS as well. In this context, it is impossible to look at HIV as a foreign agent, particularly in light of recent research that questions the standard narrative that HIV acts alone. This research has shown, among other things, that HIV is not necessarily a recent phenomenon but may have coexisted with human beings for decades.[79] The narrative of AIDS, in which HIV avoids detection and

rapidly duplicates itself, may have power as a story, but its relationship to actual biological processes is increasingly unclear. Recent research on longtime survivors of HIV and AIDS raises the issue of
cofactors and makes it clear that very little is understood about the
progression of HIV into "full-blown" AIDS. All of these factors lessen
the power of the HIV narrative and force a rethinking of the image
of HIV as an agent of forgetting, one that rescripts the genes of a cell
and replaces its memory. HIV is part of our bodily memory; it is
familiar; we recognize it.

People with AIDS represent themselves and their bodies' interiors
through the use of various metaphors, ranging from housekeeping to
coexistence to warfare. For some, images of warfare are necessary to
channel anger at the virus, the U.S. government, and American public. ACT UP invokes images of a war against ignorance, incompetent
government officials, and the virus itself. Yet it is difficult, despite the
characterizations of HIV as a terrorist or villain, to make a virus a
tangible enemy. This is why, for instance, diseases have historically
been assigned moralistic and religious explanations—blaming a virus
is not enough. In addition, as the AIDS Quilt demonstrates, there
are complex debates in the AIDS-affected community over the usefulness of anger for people with AIDS. When Cleve Jones says, "I
know when I feel that rage in my stomach and my chest, I am losing
T-cells," he is clearly stating that the paradigm of rage works counter
to his own visualization of the virus in his body.

For others, however, the metaphors of warfare are useful. Before
he died of AIDS, French writer Emmanuel Dreuilhe wrote a book,
Mortal Embrace, in which he deliberately employed the language of
warfare and drew parallels to the legacy of World War II and his role
as a "resistance fighter":

My personal war began two years ago when I was mobilized by AIDS. All
the pleasures of peacetime and my carefree life were suddenly banished, as
if an orchestra had stopped playing to let the theater manager announce
that war had just been declared, that Pearl Harbor had been bombed. Since
then I have devoted myself exclusively to the war effort, because the futility
of civilian life (my thirty-six years of good health) is absurd when survival
itself has become the main imperative. . . . I'm already a war casualty, disfigured by my wounds, but I must go on fighting, disabled as I am.[80]

Dreuilhe defines his "war" on AIDS in terms of nationalism, World War II, and noticeably traditional models of warfare. Significantly, the Vietnam War, with its confusion of enemy and ally, does not provide him with a model of struggle. He defends his strategy against "conscientious objectors," yet he admits that images of AIDS as a mechanism of war can be disempowering: "In my moments of panic, I see AIDS as a tank pulverizing everything in its path, rolling over all the barricades erected by medicine as if they were made of straw, as indifferent to cries of mercy as it is to the snapping of limbs crushed by its passage. This fleeting apparition hurts me more than all the media hysteria."[81] For many people with AIDS, this kind of metaphor of destruction is profoundly disabling, and the idea of coexistence with the virus is crucial. Many consciously employ images of housekeeping, grooming, and cleansing out the virus to create images of a less adversarial relationship between HIV and their own bodies.

Creative images have used visualization and comedy to make the immune system seem more tangible and HIV less lethal. In 1991 artist Nancy Burson created a poster depicting two micrographs, one of a healthy T-cell, the other of a cell infected with HIV, with the words "Visualize This" (Figure 25). Burson's work departs in significant ways from the rhetoric of AIDS activism, and precisely for this reason some feel it places responsibility for AIDS on people living with it. However, Burson's intent is quite different. She sees the image as a tool for visualization.[82] Her work attempts to engage with the scientific image of HIV, to refigure its cultural meaning. However, images of the virus have been deployed so rarely outside science reportage that her work has been subject to misinterpretation. John Greyson also depicts HIV and the immune system in his film *Zero Patience* (1993), in which the character of Patient Zero looks into a microscope at his blood cells and sees actors dressed in costumes swimming in a pool with inner tubes and flippers. In this absurdly funny scene, HIV is a floating drag queen (played by Michael Callen) who scolds the other viruses that want to claim cofactor status and declares that science has yet to understand her.

Ways of visualizing HIV and making it seem less predatory have also emerged in popular psychology. Certain books counsel people with AIDS to talk to the virus and to visualize their immune systems.

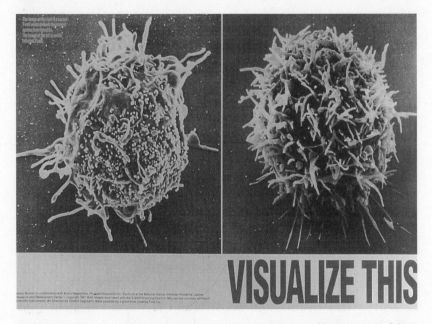

Figure 25. Poster by Nancy Burson showing T-cells. Reprinted by courtesy of the artist.

Like much AIDS merchandise, these techniques have been criticized as no more than a means of denial. One letter written to AIDS reads: "For so long now I've been angry with you for being part of my life. I feel like you have violated my being. The strongest emotion thus far in our relationship has been anger! But now I see you in a different light. . . . I realize now you have become a positive force in my life. . . . But you also led me to the realization that you have no power over me. . . . With love, Paul."[83] Although commentators such as Daniel Harris note that the "empathy industry" misguidedly promotes the idea that people have full control over their lives,[84] one could also argue that little harm is done if people improve their sense of well-being—or even boost their immune systems—by talking to and imaging the virus. As with AIDS merchandise, perhaps its potential efficacy outweighs the problems of representation it poses.

AIDS generates fear not simply of death but of transformation. That is, people fear that those who die of AIDS are no longer the same, that their immune system identities and their selves have been so altered that it is not really they who have died. Although this image is offset by the many stories about people with AIDS who are living life more fully than ever, the fear of AIDS's transformative effect and HIV's so-called insinuation into self-identity is pervasive. I would argue that the prevailing popular notion that AIDS can wipe out the body's memory and erase a person's identity are directly responsible for the desire to create memory and identity from the epidemic— either through the mourning of the dead and celebration of life in the AIDS Quilt or through the declarative marking of identity in AIDS activism.

The metaphors of memory and forgetting used in describing the immune system and AIDS offer us alternative means of envisioning our bodies, in particular the bodies of people with AIDS. This process requires us to foreground the role of survivors in producing cultural memory and to push at the boundaries of history-making. The discourses of memory around both the Vietnam War and AIDS demonstrate that war occupies a central place in what American culture deems worth remembering. The Vietnam War only became an arena for the generation of cultural memories in national contexts when aspects of the lost narratives of national, technological, and masculine superiority could be retrieved. In the AIDS epidemic, the use of the war metaphor was deliberately intended to appropriate the memory discourse of war—to establish that people with AIDS needed to be remembered and honored, that they had been sacrificed in some national cause.

However, the empowering capacity of memory in both these events has come not from the discourse of war but from the discourse of healing. With both the Vietnam Veterans Memorial and the AIDS Quilt, the emphasis on individual loss, pain, and redemption has provided the most fertile ground for the generation of cultural memory. This shift from an overall narrative of war, from an emphasis on the politics of the epidemic, to one foregrounding AIDS's effects on sentient bodies, families, communities, and memories is a means of denaturing the discourse of war. It is crucial that the relationship of memory to war not be left unexamined and that those things deemed worth remembering as a culture extend beyond the discourse of war.

In addition, the role of survivors must be applied to the context of AIDS. The late Bo Huston once wrote:

Of course, I have often enough envisioned myself as part of the AIDS toll. I've seen myself as that victim figure, bedridden and depleted, dying. I have planned out my funeral. Sometimes, though, I have a picture of myself as a survivor, remembering. No longer infected by a virus, then, but bruised and enriched by my experiences of AIDS. Having lived through such struggle, I might just seem grumpy to teenagers who don't know the dreams that wake me up at midnight. But my imagination, my perspective will be layered with bitterness and guilt and fear; with wisdom and humor too, and gratitude. I see my old eyes then: bright and clear, trusting and untrusting, cynical and awed . . . alive.[85]

The survivor is one who remembers.

Ultimately, it is through survivors that cultural memory is rein-scribed, actively produced, and given meaning. In the AIDS epi-demic, the simple concept of survival has had political meaning. It requires a refiguring not only of media stereotypes but also of scien-tific models of AIDS, HIV, and the immune system. It is a challenge to the culture at large, a defiance of the general apathy to death by AIDS. Survivors embody memory, their bodies the texts of memory, their voices its textures. They stand at the juncture of memory and history, tugging by their very presence at the boundaries of each.

Afterword

I end this book by talking about survivors as the embodiment of cultural memory, yet I cannot do this in any simple way. Though survivors may often be the voices of conscience in the process of history-making, the notion of the survivor in the 1990s in the United States cannot remain unexamined. We live in a time when claims to the experience of trauma and to the status of the survivor are highly complex and troubling. For instance, a lucrative popular psychology industry is marketing the idea that we are all survivors of, if not childhood abuse, the equivalent of abuse for which we have no memories. Clearly, the meaning of the term "survivor" has become highly contested.

The survivors of traumatic historical events are powerful cultural figures. They are awarded moral authority, and their experience carries the weight of cultural value. This does not mean that all such survivors are treated as figures of cultural importance. Survivors of historical events are often represented as figures of wisdom in popular culture while ignored in person. This book has investigated the different cultural meanings generated from the experiences of survival. The survival narrative of the Vietnam veteran both retrieves and refigures traditional notions of masculinity and warriorhood. It has, through the limitations of nationalism, operated as a means to erase from cultural view the role of the Vietnamese people as survivors. By contrast, narratives of survivors of AIDS are inevitably written in political terms, as a demand for representation. Both figures frame the historical and cultural moment of the United States in the

1980s and 1990s and build on the legacy of survivors of the Holocaust. Over time, AIDS survivors and Vietnam veterans will change
in relationship to those who are designated survivors of traumas that
follow. Although the messages their presence imparts are varied and
politically unstable, these survivors speak in profound ways of memory's power to reproduce the past through testimony, images, and reenactment.

This book has analyzed the tensions between the narrative of survivors and the concept of the syndrome. It is ironic how the notion
of a syndrome haunts these recent events in American history. The
Vietnam Syndrome, with its image of an emasculated, timid nation,
was replaced by Acquired Immune Deficiency Syndrome, in which
the body is transformed and destroyed by a strategic invader, and
Gulf War Syndrome, an unexplained array of symptoms and genetic
distortions that have produced not heroes but angry and weakened
veterans. The concept of a syndrome is in many ways opposite to that
of the survivor, for a syndrome indicates a transformative process, a
condition that is constitutive rather than temporal, that changes the
individual or the nation into something else. The idea of a syndrome
undermines concepts of agency and resistance—designating survivors of syndromes demands a definition of the term *syndrome* itself.

The Vietnam veteran and the person with AIDS have both become, within specific subcultures, appealing objects of desire whose
suffering is seen as giving them wisdom, an understanding of life's
purpose, and a heightened sense of values. They are objects of both
fear and envy specifically because they are portrayed as having experienced the extremes of human nature and dignity, as having confronted human brutality and fragility, and as having looked death in
the face. The popular romanticization of the Vietnam veteran is
fueled both by public guilt and by an admiring sense that the Vietnam
veteran has confronted both the terror of combat and his own inhu-
manity and capacity for violence. Hence, the veteran can be seen to
speak of the potential for brutality that resides in each of us. The
person with HIV or AIDS, regardless of his or her own experience,
taps into the collective fear of life's finitude, the vulnerability of the
body, and the inevitability of death. The desire for veteran status or
"positivity" is thus a longing for specific meaning and purpose. These

desires are deeply ironic; they also indicate a contemporary tendency to romanticize trauma, a tendency that is troubling in its capacity to both trivialize and sentimentalize the experience of survival.

The Vietnam War and the AIDS epidemic have helped refigure the realms through which cultural meaning is traditionally perceived to emerge. These events have been represented across the boundaries of government, academia, advertising and commodity culture, popular music, film, television, news media, art, activism, and folklore, some of which I have explored here. This broad range of cultural production reveals the changing definitions of high and low, public and private, art and craft, and alternative and mass media in twentieth-century culture. It demonstrates that technologies of memory, from the photograph to the body, generate narratives of remembrance that intersect and build upon each other across cultural arenas.

In the context of contemporary cultural studies, I have explored how cultural memory can form an arena of resistance to dominant forms of national culture. However, resistance is but one form that such memory takes. I hope that this book will be read in concert with works that examine cultural resistance within a framework of power relations. National cultural meaning is consistently and actively under contestation. In fact, it is the contested aspects of these histories and memories that produce their meaning. This is precisely the dynamic that allows those of us who disagree with the values of what we perceive as a national culture still to identify ourselves as constituents of and participants in an American public. It also allows diverse spectators to perceive themselves to be members of a national audience when viewing events of national importance on television.

Cultural meaning does not reside with the text of a particular object, such as the Vietnam Veterans Memorial or the image of the Challenger explosion, so much as it is produced in the act of "consumption," wherein the viewer/citizen engages with its meaning. Hence, the fact that the Vietnam Veterans Memorial and the AIDS Quilt produce many conflicting interpretations does not make them any less effective as memory objects. Similarly, although one might feel that "AIDS kitsch" debases the experience of struggling with AIDS, these objects attest to how the increasingly blurred boundaries of art, commodity culture, and memorials have promoted different kinds of engagement with the concept of an American public.

These contests of meaning take place within the power relations of official institutions and the mass media in relationship to alternative arenas of public culture. The image of the Vietnam War produced in *Platoon,* a mainstream Hollywood film, has much more power to create and influence cultural memory than does the testimony of a veteran who leaves an object at the Vietnam Veterans Memorial. The headline of a *Time* magazine cover that depicts HIV as fomenting chaos in the human body is far more influential than Nancy Burson's poster *Visualize This.* Tom Hanks's gay man dying of AIDS in the film *Philadelphia* has the power to stand for all gay men to an American public that generally does not know people with AIDS. All cultural forms are not equal in their capacity to create meaning. Yet the stories in this book show how complex the interaction of audiences, viewers, spectators, tourists, and citizens with cultural products can be. They provide evidence of the ways in which concepts of a national culture and aspects of a counternational culture coexist.

The cultural products of the Vietnam War and the AIDS epidemic are revealing precisely because they represent events of crisis. Crisis occurs when cultural rules are broken, when the boundaries of cultural arenas become more easily traversed, and when both the structure and the fractures of a culture are most visible. The crisis of masculinity represented by the Vietnam veteran exposes not only the fragility of the 1950s and 1960s model of American manhood but also the centrality of masculinity to national meaning. Science's inability to understand the functioning of HIV not only reveals the disabling aspects of many scientific narratives of disease but also has opened the door for greater participation in defining disease by those who are struggling with illness. The national trauma of having so many young people die has prompted both new communities of concern and a desperate policing of the "traditional American family." Both AIDS and the Vietnam War have shown the tenuousness and rigidity of definitions of national culture.

Although this book embraces the concept of memory as both constitutive and healing, it also intends to provide new ways of thinking about memory and its role in cultural production. My argument for consideration of memory outside of a definition of truth, evidence, and representations of the real has also been an argument for memory as an inventive social practice. We must rethink culture's valorization of memory as the equivalent of experience. If memory is redefined as a social and individual practice that integrates elements of remembrance, fantasy, and invention, then it can shift from the problematic role of standing for the truth to a new role as an active, engaging practice of creating meaning.

Discourses of memory and forgetting are both essential to the construction of national meaning. The "experience" of forgetting, by which I mean a recognition that the shared act of forgetting has taken place, also serves to establish collectivity. The very particular status of the Vietnam veterans as figures of conscience in American culture is contingent upon the understanding that the veterans were initially forgotten and rendered invisible. The urge to remember in the AIDS epidemic recognizes the collective forgetting of those who have died of AIDS. Hence, people are often encouraged to experience themselves as Americans by engaging with technologies of forgetting.

I thus choose to end this book, however ironically, by suggesting that definitions of memory need to place less emphasis on its power to evoke the real and more on its integrated relationship with forgetting. Cultural memory is not in and of itself a healing process. It is unstable and unreliable. Its authenticity is derived not from its revelation of any original experience but from its role in providing continuity to a culture, the stakes in creating values in that culture, and the fundamental materiality by which that culture is defined. By recognizing that memory manifests itself in different and unexpected forms, that it integrates fantasy, invention, and reenactment, that it is a process of engaging with the past rather than a means to call it up, we will come to understand its role in enabling individuals to imbue the past with value in the present.

Notes

Introduction

1. I am aware that the term "America" refers not simply to the United States but to all of the countries of North and South America. Wherever possible I refer to the "United States," but I use the term "America" to refer to the culture of the United States because that term is still quite operative in nationalist culture and I want to invoke its popular meaning. National culture in the United States often employs the concept of "America" to embody particular national icons of freedom, equality, and democracy, all of which are elements in the memory debates of this book.

2. Sigmund Freud, *The Interpretation of Dreams*, trans. James Strachey (New York: Avon Books, [1900] 1965).

3. Maurice Halbwachs, *The Collective Memory*, trans. Francis J. Ditter, Jr. and Vida Yazdi Ditter (New York: Harper & Row, 1980).

4. Pierre Nora, "Between Memory and History: *Les Lieux de memoire*," trans. Mark Roudebush *Representations* (Spring 1989), p. 9.

5. Michel Foucault, *Power/Knowledge*, ed. Colin Gordon, trans. Colin Gordon, Leo Marshall, John Mepham, and Kate Soper (New York: Pantheon, 1980), p. 82.

6. Michel Foucault, "Film and Popular Memory: An Interview with Michel Foucault" (trans. Martin Jordan), *Radical Philosophy* (1975), p. 25. Foucault also used the term "countermemory" to signify memories that work against official discourse.

7. Indeed, there is a preoccupation in science fiction with the idea that human beings are flawed in their capacity to remember. See, for instance, the "Xenogenesis" series by Octavia Butler, in which an alien species called the Oankali come to a postapocalyptic earth in order to crossbreed with humans and maintain a diverse genetic makeup. The Oankali can remember

everything, and they see the humans' limited capacity for memory, as well as their warlike qualities, as a flaw: "Most Humans lose access to old memories as they acquire new ones. They know how to speak, for instance, but they don't recall learning to speak. They keep what experience has taught them—usually—but lose the experience itself. We can retrieve it for them—enable them to recall everything—but for many of them, that would create confusion. They would remember so much that their memories would distract them from the present" (*Adulthood Rites* [New York: Warner Books, 1988], p. 29).

8. Milan Kundera, "Afterword: A Talk with the Author by Philip Roth," in *The Book of Laughter and Forgetting*, trans. Michael Henry Heim (New York: Penguin, 1980), p. 235.

9. Hayden White, "The Value of Narrativity in the Representation of Reality," in *The Content of the Form* (Baltimore: Johns Hopkins Press, 1987), p. 24.

10. Sigmund Freud, "Screen Memories," in *The Standard Edition of the Complete Psychological Works of Sigmund Freud*, Vol. 3, trans. James Strachey (London: Hogarth Press, [1899] 1962), pp. 301–22.

11. In questioning the verifiability of the past, this work probably falls within what has been referred to as the "presentist" approach of memory studies. I would like to question that definition. There has been significant debate on this point through the work of several contemporary sociologists on social or collective memory. Barry Schwartz argues against the "presentist approach" deployed by Halbwachs, among others, that says the representation of the past is constructed by the concerns of the present. According to Schwartz, collective memory is both a "cumulative and an episodic construction of the past," by which he means there are factual elements that remain stationary in the reconstructive narrative ("The Reconstruction of Abraham Lincoln," in David Middleton and Derek Edwards, eds., *Collective Remembering* [Newbury Park, CA: Sage Publications, 1990], p. 104).

Similarly, Michael Schudson argues that "in some respects and under some conditions the past is highly resistant to efforts to make it over" (*Watergate in American Memory* [New York: Basic Books, 1992], p. 206). He continues, "Even though the past is regularly reconstructed, this is done within limits, stopped by the hard edges of resistance the past provides" (p.207). Schudson claims that "these points are ignored by the naive empiricist, who believes that there are hard facts that, accumulated, make up history; they are neglected also by the radical, relativist constructionist, who believes that there is only discourse and no independent world to which discourse is beholden" (p. 218).

These quotes give a sense of this debate in certain arenas of the study of memory, which are summarized by Barbie Zelizer in "Reading the Past against the Grain: The Shape of Memory Studies," *Critical Studies in Mass Communication* (June 1995), pp. 214–39. Much of this work has been hampered by a reductive concept of discourse.

12. Andreas Huyssen, *Twilight Memories* (New York: Routledge, 1995), pp. 2–3.

13. Michel Foucault, "Technologies of the Self," in Luther Martin, Huck Gutman, and Patrick Hutton, eds., *Technologies of the Self* (Amherst: University of Massachusetts Press, 1988), p. 18.

14. For an in-depth discussion of a broad array of approaches in Holocaust memorials, from traditional monuments to anti-monuments, see James Young, *The Texture of Memory* (New Haven: Yale University Press, 1993), and James Young, ed., *The Art of Memory: Holocaust Memorials in History* (New York: Jewish Museum, 1994).

15. Pierre Nora, "Between Memory and History," p. 22. Indeed, the techniques used by orators in the classical art of memory involved locating part of speeches in imaginary objects and places in order to facilitate remembering. For an extended analysis of this topic, see Frances Yates, *The Art of Memory* (Chicago: University of Chicago, 1966), a book that has been influential in defining the importance of ancient rhetorical practices of memory to the present.

16. Roland Barthes, *Camera Lucida*, trans. Richard Howard (New York: Hill and Wang, 1981), p. 93.

17. See Richard Terdiman's discussion of Adorno in *Present Past* (Ithaca: Cornell University Press, 1993), pp. 12–13.

18. Lauren Berlant, *The Anatomy of National Fantasy* (Chicago: University of Chicago Press, 1991), p. 20.

19. In September 1994, gun-control advocates brought 40,000 shoes to symbolize those who had been killed by guns to line the reflecting pool on the Mall in a "Silent March." The shoes, many of which were accompanied by photos and notes, were there to provide physical evidence of the immense toll of gun-related violence (see J. Michael Kennedy, "Symbols of the Slaughter," *Los Angeles Times,* September 7, 1991, p. B1; and Fox Butterfield, " 'Silent March' on Guns Talks Loudly," *New York Times,* September 21, 1994, p. A18). The shoes included both those of people who had been killed by guns and those who wanted to offer support. After the display, the shoes were donated to charity. According to Kennedy, the idea of the shoes was borrowed from the Holocaust Museum, with its display of shoes from the Maidanek concentration camp.

20. John Erni, "Articulating the (Im)possible: Popular Media and the Cultural Politics of 'Curing AIDS,' " *Communication* 13 (1993), p. 40.

21. Friedrich Nietzsche, *On the Genealogy of Morals,* trans. Walter Kaufman and R. J. Hollingdale (New York: Vintage, [1887] 1967), p. 61.

22. Linda Hutcheon, "Beginning to Theorize Postmodernism," *Textual Practice* 1, no.1 (1987), p. 25.

23. Nora, for instance, defines "real memory" as "social and unviolated, exemplified in but also retained as the secret of so-called primitive and archaic societies" ("Between Memory and History," p. 8).

24. Plato stated of writing, "If men learn this, it will implant forgetfulness in their souls: they will cease to exercise memory because they will rely on that which is written, calling things to remembrance no longer from within themselves, but by means of external marks" (R. Hackforth, *Plato's Phaedrus* [Cambridge: Cambridge University Press, 1952], p. 157).

25. I would like to make a distinction between cultural reenactment, which takes the form of docudrama and other representations of the past, and reenactment as it is defined in psychology. In psychological terms, the individual who has been traumatized reenacts the scene of the trauma because he or she is unable to represent it. A well-known case of Pierre Janet's involved a woman who could reenact what she did the night her mother died but was unable to give a narrative, and hence to produce a memory, of what had happened. See Bessel van der Kolk and Onno van der Hart, "The Intrusive Past: The Inflexibility of Memory and the Engraving of Trauma," in Cathy Caruth, ed., *Trauma: Explorations in Memory* (Baltimore: Johns Hopkins, 1995), pp. 158–63.

Chapter One

1. Portrait photographers also found a huge trade in "memento mori," or posthumous photographs. Geoffrey Batchen writes, "Grieving parents could console themselves with a photograph of their departed loved one, an image of the dead *as* dead that somehow worked to sustain the living" ("Ghost Stories: The Beginnings and Ends of Photography," *Art Monthly Australia* [December 1994], p. 4).

2. Roland Barthes, *Camera Lucida,* trans. Richard Howard (New York: Hill and Wang, 1981), p.15.

3. Even the development of digital technologies, which will eventually allow for the creation of photo-real images that are not generated by a camera, will not diminish the role played by photography. Batchen writes, "It should be clear to those familiar with the history of photography that a change in imaging technology will not, in and of itself, cause the disappearance of the photograph and the culture it sustains. For a start, photography

has never been any one technology." He notes that the technologies of camera and film are "the embodiment of the idea of photography or, more accurately, of a persistent economy of photographic desires and concepts. The concepts inscribed within this economy would have to include things like nature, knowledge, representation, time, space, observing subject, and observed object. Thus, if we have to define it, we might say that photography is the desire, whether conscious or not, to orchestrate a particular set of relationships between these various concepts" ("Ghost Stories," p. 7).

4. Kaja Silverman, "Back to the Future," *Camera Obscura* 27 (September 1991), p. 120.

5. Sigmund Freud, "Screen Memories," pp. 289–322.

6. Ibid., p. 322.

7. For an in-depth analysis of Benjamin's use of photographic metaphors to describe history, see Eduardo Cadava, "Words of Light: Theses on the Photography of History," *Diacritics* (Fall/Winter 1992), pp. 84–114.

8. Walter Benjamin, "Theses on the Philosophy of History," in *Illuminations*, trans. Harry Zohn (New York: Schocken Books, 1969), p. 255.

9. As camera technology evolved, the long exposure times of early photography were reduced, until the notion of the "instant" became an integral part of photography's connotations. Time, not synchronized and precisely measured until the late nineteenth century, became atomized. Stephen Kern notes that with this standardization of time in Europe, there was a preoccupation with the question of what constitutes the instant or present: "In the early 1880s Wilhelm Wundt conducted some experiments to determine the duration of the present—that interval of time that can be experienced as an uninterrupted whole. He concluded that its maximum limit was five seconds, and one of his students set it at twelve. Another student found that the shortest interval between separate clicks that the ear could discern was 1/5000 of a second and that the eye could not distinguish sparks less than .044 seconds apart, because it retained an image of an object after it had disappeared" (*The Culture of Time and Space: 1880–1918* [Cambridge: Harvard University Press, 1983], p. 82). Today, our notion of an "instant" is that which can be captured and frozen in time by a still camera.

10. Cadava, "Words of Light," p. 92.

11. The photographs of missing children on milk cartons, shopping bags, and flyers, for example, create an uncanny sense of mortality, making those children seem already dead. Emphatically marking their age frozen in time, these photographs suggest that these children do not look like this now. Contrary to their intended purpose, they invoke feelings of mourning and loss.

12. Benedict Anderson, *Imagined Communities* (London: Verso, 1983), pp. 15–16.

13. Roger Brown and James Kulik, "Flashbulb Memories," in Ulric Neisser, ed., *Memory Observed: Remembering in Natural Contexts* (San Francisco: W. H. Freeman, 1982), p. 24.

14. Ulric Neisser and Nicole Harsch, "Phantom Flashbulbs," in Eugene Winograd and Ulric Neisser, eds., *Affect and Accuracy in Recall* (New York: Cambridge University Press, 1992).

15. Richard Stolley, "The Greatest Home Movie Ever Made," *Esquire* (November 1973), p. 135. Stolley reports that Zapruder returned to his office "incoherent, in a state of shock," according to an employee, and his secretary called the FBI to tell them about the film. Copies were sent to Washington, D.C., and to the Dallas police, but Zapruder was allowed to keep the original. Many news organizations, tipped off by the Dallas police, came to see the film and negotiate with Zapruder, but Stolley found him first and was able to secure the print rights for $50,000. Zapruder was paid a total of $150,000 for all rights. Sensitive to the suggestion that he had profited from Kennedy's death, he donated $25,000 to the family of officer J. D. Tippitt, whom Oswald was thought to have shot and killed while trying to escape (p. 262). The rights to the film have now reverted to the Zapruder family.

16. Robert Hennelly and Jerry Policoff, "JFK: How the Media Assassinated the Real Story," *Village Voice* (March 31, 1992), p. 35.

17. Stolley, "Home Movie," p. 135. Of course, to conspiracy buffs it is evidence of Time/Life's participation in a cover-up.

18. Michael Rogin, "Body and Soul Murder: *JFK*," in Marjorie Garber, Jann Matlock, Rebecca Walkowitz, eds., *Media Spectacles* (New York: Routledge, 1993), p. 9.

19. This level of fantasy is evident in the CD-ROM, *J.F.K. Assassination: A Visual Investigation,* produced by Medio Multimedia. Clearly targeted at amateur conspiracy buffs, the CD-ROM contains the texts of several books on the assassination, the transcripts of the Warren Commission, digitized video of the Zapruder film and three other home movies, 3-D animations of assassination theories, and numerous photographs.

20. Ant Farm got their copy of the film, a Super-8 copy of many generations, from a conspiracy buff, according to whom the film was bootlegged from the lab in which it was originally printed and had been circulating in conspiracy networks for years.

21. A number of theorists have discussed the Challenger explosion as emblematic of the relationship of television to catastrophe. See Mary Ann

Doane, "Information, Crisis, Catastrophe," in Patricia Mellencamp, ed., *The Logics of Television* (Bloomington: Indiana University Press, 1990), pp. 222–40; and Patricia Mellencamp, "TV Time and Catastrophe," in *The Logics of Television,* pp. 240–66.

22. Constance Penley, "Spaced Out: Remembering Christa McAuliffe," *Camera Obscura* 29 (1993), p. 180.

23. David Ellis, "Challenger: The Final Words," *Time* (December 24, 1990), p. 15.

24. Thanks to Eric Fernandes for calling this to my attention.

25. Penley, "Spaced Out," pp. 190–94.

26. Neisser and Harsch, "Phantom Flashbulbs," p. 25.

27. Ibid., p. 30.

28. Ten years later, presidential candidate Patrick Buchanan used the image of the Challenger explosion in a television ad in McAuliffe's home state of New Hampshire. The ostensible reason for drawing on the memory of the explosion was to show Buchanan's role in the moments of crisis of the Reagan administration. However, the ad came under serious attack for its insensitivity to the painful memory of this incident held by the people of New Hampshire. See Michael Kranish, "Ad on Challenger Disaster Creates an Uproar in N.H.," *Boston Globe* (January 11, 1996).

29. Kimberle Crenshaw and Gary Peller, "Reel Time/Real Justice," in Robert Gooding-Williams, ed., *Reading Rodney King/Reading Urban Uprising* (New York: Routledge, 1993), p. 59.

30. Elizabeth Alexander has noted that conservative talk-show host Rush Limbaugh also deployed tools of reenacting the image that paralleled those in the courtroom: "He looped a snippet of the tape over and over and over again until it did look like Rodney King was advancing on the police officers, and no context for the movement was left. There is something compulsive— not to mention dishonest—about Limbaugh and Koon watching over and over again the same piece of film, and using it to consolidate a self-justifying narrative of their own domination" (" 'Can You be BLACK and Look at This?' " in Thelma Golden, ed., *Black Male: Representations of Masculinity in Contemporary American Art* [New York: Whitney Museum of American Art, 1991], p. 108).

31. Seth Mydans, "With Few Witnesses, Videos Are Crucial in Beating Trial," *New York Times,* September 6, 1993, p. 6; and Jessica Crosby, "Truck Driver Says He Doesn't Recall Beating," *Washington Post,* August 26, 1993, p. A4.

32. Sigmund Freud, *The Interpretation of Dreams,* pp. 526–46.

Chapter Two

1. After the memorial was built, a name from an American killed in 1957 was discovered. It was added to the memorial out of order. See Thomas Allen, *Offerings at the Wall* (Atlanta: Turner Publishing, 1995), p. 242.

2. Arthur Danto, "The Vietnam Veterans Memorial," *The Nation* (August 31, 1985), p. 152.

3. Charles Griswold, "The Vietnam Veterans Memorial and the Washington Mall," *Critical Inquiry* 12 (Summer 1986), p. 689.

4. Danto, "The Vietnam Veterans Memorial," p. 153.

5. However, designer Maya Lin was influenced in her design by a memorial by Sir Edwin Lutyens in Thiepval, France, for the dead of the Somme offensive in World War I, which consists of a great arch inscribed with 73,000 names.

6. Tom Wolfe, "Art Disputes War," *Washington Post*, October 13, 1982, p. B4.

7. Kenneth Baker, "Andre in Retrospect," *Art in America* (April 1980), pp. 88–94.

8. See Robert Storr, " 'Tilted Arc': Enemy of the People," in Arlene Raven, ed., *Art in the Public Interest* (Ann Arbor: University of Michigan Press, 1989); and Casey Nelson Blake, "An Atmosphere of Effrontery: Richard Serra, *Tilted Arc,* and the Crisis of Public Art," in Richard Wrightman Fox and T. J. Jackson Lears, eds., *The Power of Culture* (Chicago: University of Chicago Press, 1993), pp. 247–89. Maya Lin admires Serra's work, and her debt to Serra was cited by supporters of *Tilted Arc* in the hearings about the work's potential removal (Blake, "Atmosphere of Effrontery," p. 276).

9. Frederick Hart, "Letter to the Editor," *Art in America* (November 1983), p. 5.

10. Rosalind Krauss, "Sculpture in the Expanded Field," in Hal Foster, ed., *The Anti-Aesthetic* (Port Townsend, WA: Bay Press, 1983), pp. 31–42.

11. Designer Maya Lin calls herself "super site-specific" and did not decide on the final design until she visited the site. However, a traveling version of the wall has toured the country with powerful effect. This effect would seem to be the result of the traveling wall's reference of the site-specific wall, in addition to the power evoked by the inscribed names in whatever location.

12. Jan Scruggs and Joel Swerdlow, *To Heal a Nation* (New York: Harper & Row, 1985), p. 53.

13. Tom Carhart, "Insulting Vietnam Vets," *New York Times*, October 24, 1981.

14. Quoted in Scruggs and Swerdlow, *To Heal a Nation*, p. 100.

15. "Stop That Monument," *National Review,* September 18, 1981, p. 1064.

16. Quoted in Mary McLeod, "The Battle for the Monument," in Helene Lipstadt, ed., *The Experimental Tradition* (New York: Princeton Architectural Press, 1989), p. 125.

17. The other designs in the competition spanned a broad array of approaches. Writes jurist Grady Clay, "The entries included every imaginable form and type of 'memorial,' from a building-sized military helmet to gaunt groups of soldiers looking skyward for a helicopter. There were many variations on the Fallen Comrade theme, and a fascinating variety of memorial glades, walls, mounds, hills, mazes, groves and earthen enclosures, as well as a host of geometric arrangements—open circles, closed circles, broken circles, obelisks—and variegated symbols such as eternal flames, broken columns, a giant pair of combat boots, a massive ceramic-tile American flag, and a permanently maintained dovecote with fluttering doves of peace" (see "Vietnam's Aftermath," *Landscape Architecture* [March 1982], p. 55). Mary McLeod writes that Lin's project accomplished an integration with the landscape and contemplative nature "with a minimum of means, making most of the other entries look overwrought or ostentatious" ("The Battle for the Monument," p. 120).

18. Michael Sorkin, "What Happens When a Woman Designs a War Monument?" *Vogue* (May 1983), p. 122.

19. Quoted in "America Remembers: Vietnam Veterans Memorial," *National Geographic* 167, no. 5 (May 1985), p. 557.

20. "An Interview with Maya Lin," in Reese Williams, ed., *Unwinding the Vietnam War* (Seattle: Real Comet Press, 1987), p. 271.

21. Scruggs and Swerdlow, *To Heal a Nation,* p. 79.

22. Perot's role in this controversy and his tactics in dealing with the VVMF were examined in more detail by the media when he was a presidential candidate in 1992. Perot, who served four years in the Navy in the 1950s and is an advocate for veterans, had actually tried to build a monument in the 1970s but was unsuccessful. He had given an initial $10,000 and then a larger donation of $160,000 to the fund. However, he hated Lin's design. Subsequently, he threatened the fund and was even party to hiring Roy Cohn, a notoriously unscrupulous New York lawyer, to examine the fund's books. The fund was audited by the General Accounting Office, which cleared it in 1984. Jan Scruggs has said, "I found his tactics frightening, but I wasn't going to back down." See John Mintz, "Perot's War," *Washington Post,* July 7, 1992.

Perot is a strong proponent of Hart's statue. In his personal gallery he has a maquette of the statue of three men, in front of which he often poses for photographs. See Michael Kelly, "Where Perot Exhibits a Lifetime of Memories," *New York Times,* June 20, 1992, p. 8.

23. Mary McLeod, "The Battle for the Monument," p. 127.

24. Hart's statue has no official name, but it is informally called "Three Fighting Men," "Three Man Statue," or variations on these names. Duery Felton, Jr., curator of the collection of artifacts left at the memorials, notes that it is ironic that even though Hart chose not to title the statue like most traditional memorials, people feel compelled to name it (telephone interview with author, June 1, 1995).

25. "An Interview with Frederick Hart," in Reese Williams, ed., *Unwinding the Vietnam War* (Seattle: Real Comet Press, 1987), p. 274.

26. Quoted in Rick Horowitz, "Maya Lin's Angry Objections," *Washington Post,* July 7, 1982, p. B1.

27. The Marine Corps War Memorial is heavily dependent on modern-day codes of realism. It is based on a famous, Pulitzer Prize–winning photograph taken by photojournalist Joe Rosenthal and thus is coded as a moment captured from reality. Of the six men in the photograph, three survived the war and posed for sculptor Felix W. de Weldon (for whom Frederick Hart once worked as an assistant). Ironically, the famous Rosenthal photograph depicted not the initial flag-raising but rather the replacement of the small original flag with a larger one. The iconic status of the Iwo Jima Memorial is a direct outcome of its replication of a photographic image. See Marvin Heiferman, "One Nation, Chiseled in Pictures," *The Archive* 25 (1989), p. 10; the National Park Service brochure on the United States Marine Corps War Memorial; and Karal Ann Marling and John Wetenhall, *Iwo Jima* (Cambridge: Harvard University Press, 1991).

According to Marling and Wetenhall, whose book on Iwo Jima is an account of the cultural role played by that image, the men depicted in the photograph (one of whom was Native American) were lauded in the media, although the men who first reached the summit and raised the smaller flag, an act photographed by Lou Lowery, were ignored. Heroism seems to be directly related to its depiction in an iconic image.

28. Quoted in Scruggs and Swerdlow, *To Heal a Nation,* p. 133. Lin has continued to influence the aesthetics of memorials. In 1989 she designed a civil rights memorial for the Southern Poverty Law Center in Montgomery, Alabama, which adds water to the motif of names inscribed on a wall; people touch a chronology of events and the names of those martyred in the civil rights movement as water runs over the inscriptions.

29. Although the Somme memorial that Lin credits with influencing her is inscribed with the names of the dead, many of the names on the arch are quite far away from visitors.

30. Paul Fussell notes that irony constitutes an aid to war memories: "In reading memoirs of the war, one notices the same phenomenon over and over. By applying to the past a paradigm of ironic action, a rememberer is enabled to locate, draw forth, and finally shape into significance an event or a moment which otherwise would merge without meaning into the general undifferentiated stream" (*The Great War and Modern Memory* [New York: Oxford University Press, 1975], p. 30).

31. There were precedents in the antiwar movement for this kind of roll call of names, which is also an integral part of displays of the AIDS Quilt. In November 1969, 45,000 people, each wearing a placard carrying the name of an American killed in the war, marched through Washington, D.C. and each stood one by one before the White House and spoke a name, a process that took forty hours (see James Quay, "Epilogue," in Grace Sevy, ed., *The American Experience in Vietnam* [Norman: University of Oklahoma Press, 1989], pp. 300–302).

32. William Broyles, Jr., "Remembering a War We Want to Forget," *Newsweek* (November 22, 1982), p. 82.

33. Judith Butler, "Review Essay: Spirit in Ashes," *History and Theory* 27, no. 1 (1988), p. 69.

34. See Associated Press, "38 Living Veterans May Be on Memorial," *San Jose Mercury News,* February 15, 1991. The reason for this error appears to be the result of faulty record keeping by the Defense Department and a 1973 fire that destroyed many records. Robert Doubek, a co-founder of the VVMF, decided to include thirty-eight names of casualties for which there were incomplete records because he felt it was better to err by inclusion rather than omission. Cases like this continue to surface.

35. Two early disputes involved a medic who was sent home in a coma and never regained consciousness and a soldier who was killed in a plane crash while returning from leave in Hong Kong. At the time, their exclusion from the memorial was very painful for their families. "I've been absolutely crushed and I'm living my nightmare all over again," said medic Charles McGonigle's mother, Jennie (quoted in "Mothers of 2 Veterans Angry at Vietnam List," *New York Times,* November 18, 1982). Both of these names were later added to the memorial.

36. Peter Ehrenhaus, "Commemorating the Unwon War," *Journal of Communication* 39, no. 1 (Winter 1989), p. 105.

37. It is estimated that more than 9,000 Vietnam veterans have committed suicide since returning from the war (see Peter Meyer and the editors of *Life, The Wall* [New York: St. Martin's Press, 1993], p. 85). According to Duery Felton, approximately 100,000 veterans are thought by the Veterans Administration to have died of war-related causes. While many of them are

memorialized by artifacts left at the wall, they are not listed in any directory. "Another directory is needed," he states, "but how can it be compiled?" (telephone interview with author, June 1, 1995).

38. James Young, "Memory and Monument," in Geoffrey Hartman, ed., *Bitburg in Moral and Political Perspective* (Bloomington: Indiana University Press, 1986), p. 105.

39. The exclusion of the Vietnamese has not, however, precluded their participation as visitors at the memorial. Vietnamese-American Andrew Lam compares the rituals of the memorial to those of Vietnamese shrines. "If there are ghosts in America," he says, "they would comfortably congregate there, for it is the only American place of tragic consequences" ("My Vietnam, My America," *The Nation* [December 10, 1990], p. 725). Many Vietnamese have visited the memorial as a means of forgiving those who fought in the war. Xuan Burns, who was hit by napalm and wounded by U.S. troops, left a letter at the memorial that read, "I want to tell you how sorry I am for what you had to go through for me and my country" (quoted in Karlyn Barker, "At the Wall, Sympathy and Sorrow," *Washington Post,* November 11, 1989).

40. That the veterans perceive the memorial to belong to them was illustrated when President Clinton gave a speech there on Memorial Day in 1993, not long after taking office. In protest of Clinton's status as an evader of the war, some veterans held up signs saying "Never Ever Trust a Draft Dodger," booed, and turned their backs on him when he began to speak (Thomas Friedman, "Clinton, in Vietnam War Tribute, Finds Old Wound Is Slow to Heal," *New York Times,* June 1, 1993). Clearly, despite his status as commander in chief, he was perceived by them not to belong at the memorial.

41. Wayne Slater, "Vet Couldn't Forget . . . Became First Casualty of Vietnam Memorial," *Denver Post,* November 11, 1984.

42. Quoted in Christopher Buckley, "The Wall," *Esquire* (September 1985), pp.61–62.

43. In 1990, a study of Vietnam veterans revealed that 15.2 percent of male Vietnam veterans, or 479,000 of the 3.14 million men who served, currently suffer from post-traumatic stress disorder (Robert Jay Lifton, "Preface to the 1992 Edition," in *Home from the War: Learning From Vietnam Veterans* (Boston: Beacon Press, [1973] 1992), p. ix.

44. Myra MacPherson, "A Different War," in Sevy, ed., *The American Experience in Vietnam,* p. 66.

45. James Fallows, "What Did You Do in the Class War, Daddy?" in A. D. Horne, ed., *The Wounded Generation* (Englewood Cliffs, NJ: Prentice Hall, 1981), pp. 15–29.

46. Similarly, Fallows notes that this class division was integral to a tragic prolongation of the war: "As long as the little gold stars kept going to homes in Chelsea and the backwoods of West Virginia, the mothers of Beverly Hills and Chevy Chase and Great Neck and Belmont were not on the telephones to their congressmen, screaming you killed my boy, they were not writing to the President that his crazy, wrong, evil war had put their boys in prison and ruined their careers. It is clear by now that if the men of Harvard had wanted to do the very most they could to help shorten the war, they should have been drafted or imprisoned en masse" ("What Did You Do in the Class War, Daddy?" p. 20).

47. In their study of American veterans, Richard Severo and Lewis Milford point out that in terms of the government treatment of and public attitude toward veterans, World War II was an exception: "The soldiers of World War II came home as unquestioned heroes after a struggle that the overwhelming majority of Americans saw as just and right against one of history's great villains. Such years had a poignancy and power that quite overshadowed the tepid welcomes given later to the combat veterans of the stalemate that was Korea, whose resolve, patriotism, and very manhood had been unjustly besmirched. . . . The veterans of Vietnam were very much a part of that tradition. They, too, chose to believe that the post–World War II welcome home was the normative thing—not the vilification and false information spread after Korea. In truth, it was the years following World War II that had a stronger claim to being regarded as 'different' " (Richard Severo and Lewis Milford, *The Wages of War* [New York: Simon and Schuster, 1989], p. 420).

48. On the tenth anniversary of the memorial in November 1992, the Friends of the Vietnam Veterans Memorial, an organization that sponsors support services around the memorial, and Electronic Data Systems (EDS), the company founded and sold by Ross Perot, began a program called In Touch. This free electronic service assists people who want to contact others who knew someone named on the wall. Eventually the program will help Vietnam veterans find each other. See Andrew Brownstein, "24 Years Later, Two Finally Are Linked by Loss," *Washington Post,* November 12, 1992.

49. George Swiers, " 'Demented Vets' and Other Myths," in Harrison Salisbury, ed., *Vietnam Reconsidered* (New York: Harper & Row, 1984), p. 198.

50. Peter Marin, "Conclusion," in Salisbury, ed., *Vietnam Reconsidered,* p. 213.

51. Quoted in Susan Wolf, "Women and Vietnam," in Reese Williams, ed., *Unwinding the Vietnam War* (Seattle: Real Comet Press, 1987), p. 245.

52. See Severo and Milford, *The Wages of War,* p. 424; and Karal Ann Marling and John Wetenhall, "The Sexual Politics of Memory: The Vietnam Women's Memorial Project and 'The Wall,' " *Prospects* 14 (1989), p. 358.

53. Quoted in Renny Christopher, "I Never Really Became a Woman Until . . . I Saw the Wall," *Sub/Versions* (1992), p. 7.

54. Quoted in Benjamin Forgery, "Battle Won for War Memorials," *Washington Post,* September 20, 1991.

55. Not surprisingly, Lin is not happy with the addition of the women's statue (see "A Memorial Too Many," *Time* [June 27, 1988], p. 25). The congressional bill for the women's statue, signed in 1989, stipulates that it will be the last addition to the memorial, but according to *The Nation,* there are already other groups, such as Air Force pilots, Navy seamen, and Native Americans, who are demanding their own statues, as well as occasional attempts (including one at the time of the initial debate) to erect a flag at the center of the walls' V (see David Corn and Jefferson Morley, "Beltway Bandits," *The Nation* [June 4, 1988], p. 780). Like many other commentators, these writers have mistakenly assumed that these constituents feel left out of the wall. It would appear, however, that it is Hart's statue that makes them feel excluded.

56. Quoted in Mark Bousian, "Women's Viet Memorial Dedicated," *San Francisco Chronicle,* November 12, 1993.

57. The original design for the women's memorial, by Rodger Brodin, was composed of a single woman standing, cradling a helmet. A model of this statue, "The Nurse," was used for fundraising for the memorial. However, its design was rejected by the Commission of Fine Arts, and a design competition was held in 1990. See Peter Perl, "A Matter of Honor," *Washington Post Magazine* (October 25, 1992), and Marling and Wetenhall, "The Sexual Politics of Memory."

58. Benjamin Forgery, "One Monument Too Many," *Washington Post,* November 6, 1993, p. D7.

59. Laura Palmer, "How to Bandage a War," *New York Times Magazine* (November 7, 1993), p. 40.

60. Quoted in ibid., p. 38.

61. Susan Jeffords, *The Remasculinization of America* (Bloomington: Indiana University Press, 1989), pp. 168–69.

62. Scruggs and Swerdlow, *To Heal a Nation,* p. 93.

63. Ibid., p. 135.

64. Harry Haines, "What Kind of War?" *Critical Studies in Mass Communication* 3, no. 1 (March 1986), p. 10.

65. There is also a "battle" being waged between the vendors who work the highly coveted spots between the memorial and the Lincoln Memorial,

selling T-shirts and other items and offering information about the MIAs. This controversy is the result of competition and disagreements over what kind of merchandise should be sold at the site (see Nolan Walters, "Vendors' War Mars Vietnam Memorial," *San Jose Mercury News,* November 11, 1991, p. 2A).

66. No one is buried on the Washington Mall except James Smithson, who is buried at the Smithsonian (see Charles Griswold, "The Vietnam Veterans Memorial and the Washington Mall," p. 715). The return of bodies from the battlefield is a relatively new historical phenomenon. Many World War I and II American dead are buried in Europe, and it took considerable effort to repatriate the bodies of American dead from Vietnam. There is a long tradition in this country of commemorating the dead in the absence of their bodies, such as those lost at sea. For instance, four memorial headstones at Arlington National Cemetery commemorate casualties from the Persian Gulf War whose bodies were not recoverable.

67. Duncan Spencer, *Facing the Wall* (New York: Macmillan, 1986), p. 51.

68. Michael Herr, *Dispatches* (New York: Avon, 1978), p. 111.

69. Elaine Scarry, *The Body in Pain* (New York: Oxford University Press, 1985), pp. 115–16.

70. Ibid., p. 71.

71. The National Park Service estimates approximately 22 million visitors, the Vietnam Veterans Memorial Fund 30 million.

72. Of these other 150 memorials to the Vietnam veterans, Elizabeth Hess notes, "For the most part it is Frederick Hart, rather than Maya Lin, who has managed to set (conservative) aesthetic and ideological precedents for the cloning of the Vietnam memorial. A strong desire to diminish, rather than engage the radical elements in Lin's design is evident in the majority of these new memorials" ("Vietnam: Memorials of Misfortune," in Reese Williams, ed., *Unwinding the Vietnam War* [Seattle: Real Comet Press, 1987], p. 275). Most of these memorials have conventional realist designs, but several stand out in their innovative approaches to commemoration. One project in Wisconsin includes a hundred-acre memorial park and museum for artifacts and memorabilia, and other projects include memorial trees and time capsules (see Hess, "Memorials of Misfortune," p. 276, and Ben A. Franklin, "143 Vietnam Memorials, Vast and Small, Rising around Nation," *New York Times,* November 9, 1986, p. 26).

In Berkeley, California, the Community Memory Project, a public-access computer network, has set up a computer veterans memorial, the Alameda County Veterans' Memorial (see Judy Ronningen, "Volunteers Create a Computerized War Memorial," *Oakland Tribune,* November 11, 1991, p.

A1; and Barbara Sullivan, "A High-Tech Memorial," *Daily Californian*, November 12, 1991, p. 1). Instigated by musician and activist Country Joe MacDonald, it is essentially a database of information about veterans that people can access by categories such as gender, rank, or individual and to which they can add their remembrances.

The design for the Korean Memorial was rejected twice by the Commission of Fine Arts and finally approved in March 1992 (see Sarah Booth Conroy, "Korean War Memorial Design Fails Again," *Washington Post*, October 25, 1991, and "New Revision for Korean Veterans Memorial," *Washington Post*, March 6, 1992, p. B2). The final design includes a black granite wall with a mural of images of support troops such as medics and nurses. An extension of this wall that represents the Korean peninsula bears the inscription "Freedom Is Not Free." See Todd Purdum, "War in Korea, Fast Receding, Gets a Memorial," *New York Times* (July 28, 1995), pp. A1, A18.

73. Michael Clark, "Remembering Vietnam," *Cultural Critique* 3 (Spring 1986), p. 49.

74. By 1987 Hart had received $85,000 in royalties, much of which had been spent on legal fees suing for copyright infringement (see William Welch, "$85,000 in Royalties for Memorial Sculptor," *Washington Post*, November 11, 1987, D1, D6).

75. Bobbie Ann Mason's novel *In Country* (New York: Harper & Row, 1985), which was made into a film in 1989, is an effective depiction of this fascination by a younger generation for the Vietnam War. The protagonist of the book is a young girl, Sam, whose father died in Vietnam before she was born. She lives with her uncle, who is a veteran. Her attempts to understand the war and somehow to experience it form the central narrative. Fittingly, the book ends with her visiting the memorial with her uncle and grandmother. In a moving scene, they find and touch her father's name, and Sam finds her own name listed for a soldier who was killed: "SAM A HUGHES. It is the first on a line. It is down low enough to touch. She touches her own name. How odd it feels, as though all the names in America have been used to decorate this wall" (p. 245).

76. Evidence of the potential marketing power of the wall can be found in the rather perverse campaigns of two companies, Coors Brewing Company and Service Corporation International (SCI), a funerary and cemetery conglomerate. Both built their own "moving" walls for marketing purposes, against the wishes of the veterans in charge of the traveling memorial. The vets sued Coors, who countersued. Eventually both suits were dropped, and Coors donated the wall to a veterans organization in Texas. Much to these veterans' chagrin, SCI hired Jan Scruggs as an adviser. See Michelle Guido, "A Wall Divided by Commercialism," *San Jose Mercury News*, March 14, 1991.

77. In addition to Scruggs's book, these books are *The Wall: Images and Offerings from the Vietnam Veterans Memorial,* by Sal Lopes; *The Last Firebase: A Guide to the Vietnam Veterans Memorial,* by Lydia Fish; *The Vietnam Veterans Memorial,* by Michael Katakis; *Facing the Wall: Americans at the Vietnam Veterans Memorial,* by Duncan Spencer; *Shrapnel in the Heart: Letters and Remembrances from the Vietnam Veterans Memorial,* by Laura Palmer; *Always to Remember: The Story of the Vietnam Veterans Memorial,* by Brent Ashabranner; *Reflections on the Wall: The Vietnam Veterans Memorial,* by Edward Ezell; *Let Us Remember: The Vietnam Veterans Memorial,* by Louise Graves; *The Wall: A Day at the Veterans Memorial,* edited by Peter Meyer and the editors of *Life;* a children's book, *The Wall,* by Eve Bunting; and *Offerings at the Wall: Artifacts from the Vietnam Veterans Memorial Collection,* by Thomas Allen.

78. The majority of these objects are left at the wall, though occasionally some are left at Hart's statue and the women's statue. The ritual of leaving objects at the memorial began with its construction. The brother of a pilot killed in the war added his Purple Heart to the concrete as it was being poured.

79. This letter, which accompanied a worn photograph of a Vietnamese man and presumably his young daughter, is depicted in Allen, *Offerings at the Wall,* p. 52.

80. The Tomb of the Unknown Soldier would be the most likely location for this kind of ritual, but the presence there of a guard who ritualistically patrols the site most likely discourages leaving any personal artifacts.

81. The archive is at the Museum and Archaeological Regional Storage facility (MARS) in Lanham, Maryland. The collection also contains blueprints of the design, the mold of Hart's statue, documents and the banner from the Vietnam Veterans Memorial Fund, and templates of the name panels.

82. Quoted in Lydia Fish, *The Last Firebase* (Shippensburg, PA: White Mane, 1987), p. 54.

83. Laura Palmer, *Shrapnel in the Heart: Letters and Remembrances from the Vietnam Veterans Memorial* (New York: Vintage, 1988), p. 227.

84. Michel Foucault, *The Archaeology of Knowledge* (New York: Pantheon, 1972), p. 129.

85. From an interview by author with Duery Felton, Jr., in Lanham, Maryland, August 22, 1991.

86. From a telephone interview with author, June 1, 1995.

87. At least one memorial explicitly memorializes participants in both sides of a war. In Okinawa, a memorial unveiled in June 1995 on the fiftieth anniversary of the Battle of Okinawa contains 234,123 names of all who died in the fighting there. The names, including those of all Okinawans who died

in the war, are divided by nationality and will continue to be added as research continues. This is the only memorial to my knowledge that memorializes both the former enemies and the national dead. See Masaie Ishihara, "The Memories of War and the Role of Okinawa in the Promotion of War Peace," paper presented at "The Politics of Remembering the Asia/Pacific War," East-West Center, Honolulu, September 1995.

88. Quoted in Robert Storr, "Chris Burden," *MoMA Members Quarterly* (Fall 1991), p. 5. Storr discusses Burden's work in the exhibition catalogue, *Dislocations* (New York: Museum of Modern Art, 1991), pp. 26–28.

89. Lauren Berlant, "The Theory of Infantile Citizenship," *Public Culture* 5 (1993), p. 395.

90. The limitations of cultural memory in a nationalist context became particularly clear in the appropriations of the Vietnam Veterans Memorial into the antiwar movement of the Persian Gulf War. As testament to the iconic status of the memorial as a statement about the human costs of war, there were several "Desert Storm Memorial Walls" in evidence at antiwar rallies. Here, the inscription of ten to twenty American names seemed ludicrous in light of reports that hundreds of thousands of Iraqis were being killed. Appropriations of the memorial for the Persian Gulf War thus demonstrated both the iconic power of the memorial as well as its limitations.

Chapter Three

1. William Adams, "Still Shooting after All These Years," *Mother Jones* (January 1988), p. 49.

2. Martin Walker, "US Divided over Lessons of History," *Manchester Guardian Weekly* (April 23, 1995), p. 6.

3. Miriam Cooke, "Postmodern Wars," *Journal of Urban and Cultural Studies* 2, no. 1 (1991), p. 29.

4. David James, for instance, notes that the ubiquity of rock-and-roll music in Vietnam War films testifies "that this condition beyond representation exists" ("Rock and Roll in Representations of the Invasion of Vietnam," *Representations* 29 [Winter 1990], p. 85).

5. Herr, *Dispatches*, p. 188.

6. James, "Rock and Roll," p. 87.

7. I do not mean to imply that these were the only films made about the war or that *The Green Berets* was the first. The first American film that was located in Indochina was *Where East Is East* (Tod Browning, 1929). The first that made reference to the civil war in Vietnam was *Saigon* (Leslie Fenton, 1948), with Alan Ladd and Veronica Lake, in which three Air Force veterans end up exposing a money-smuggling plot in Saigon. In *A Yank in Indo-China* (Wallace Grissell, 1952), several Americans are depicted as be-

ing more involved in the war, blowing up a planeload of supplies for the Communists and then being aided by French and Vietnamese forces (a confused plot that surely portends much to come). See Michael Lee Lanning's copious study, *Vietnam at the Movies* (New York: Fawcett Columbine, 1994). The films I have listed here are the most widely seen of those specifically about the war, but there are many other films and many films about veterans—*Billy Jack* (Tom Laughlin, 1971), *Taxi Driver* (Martin Scorsese, 1976), *Rolling Thunder* (John Flynn, 1977)—and other, more masked references to the war, most notably the very popular television series *M*A*S*H*, which was a spinoff from the film (Robert Altman, 1969). Although ostensibly set in a military medical outpost in the Korean War, *M*A*S*H* made unmistakable references to the Vietnam War (which was at its height when the film was released), both in its antiwar and irreverent antimilitary stance and its Asian locale (conflating wars fought on foreign land for the ostensible cause of anticommunism). That the film and the television series could not directly represent the Vietnam War within the constraints of Hollywood and commercial television attests to the problems of representability of this war, in particular during the war and in its immediate aftermath.

8. The 1963 photograph by Malcolme Browne of a Buddhist monk immolating himself in Saigon in protest of the war is also an image that could be considered iconic of the war.

9. Douglas Kahn, "Body Lags," in Nancy Peters, ed., *War after War* (San Francisco: City Lights Books, 1992), p. 44.

10. Robert Hamilton, "Image and Context," in Jeffrey Walsh and James Aulich, eds., *Vietnam Images* (London: Macmillan, 1989), p. 173.

11. Adams tells his account of the taking of this picture: "All of a sudden, out of nowhere, comes General Loan, the national police chief. I was about five feet away from him, and I see him reach for his pistol. I thought he was going to threaten the prisoner. So as quick as he brought his pistol up, I took a picture. But it turned out he shot him. And the speed of my shutter . . . the bullet hadn't left his head yet. It was just coming out the other end. There was no blood until he was on the ground—whoosh. That's when I turned my back and wouldn't take a picture. There's a limit, certain times you don't take pictures" (Eddie Adams, "The Tet Photo," in Al Santoli, ed., *To Bear Any Burden* [New York: E. P. Dutton, 1985], p. 184). The film of the shooting was taken by an NBC crew that was traveling with Adams. The NBC footage was shown on the "Huntley-Brinkley Report" the following day and seen by an audience estimated at 20 million (Robert Hamilton, "Image and Context," pp.173–74). Adams found out later that the man who was shot had earlier killed a police major—who was a friend of Loan's—and his entire family. After the incident and the subsequent publicity, Loan was demoted. He later told Adams, "You know, after that happened, my wife

gave me hell for not taking the film from the photographer. She thinks that all I had to worry about was some photographer's film" (Adams, "The Tet Photo," p. 185).

12. Jorge Lewinski, *The Camera at War* (Secaucus, NJ: Chartwell Books, 1978), p. 211. One of the most well-known antiwar posters was made from Haeberle's image of the bodies strewn on the road, with the words, "Q: And babies? A: And Babies." The text was taken from a Mike Wallace interview with My Lai participant Paul Meadlo (see Lucy Lippard, *A Different War* [Seattle: Real Comet Press, 1990], p. 28). Meadlo's testimony reads as follows: "Q: What did you do? A: I held my M-16 on them. Q: Why? A: Because they might attack. Q: They were children and babies? A: Yes. Q: And they might attack? Children and babies? A: They might've had a fully loaded grenade on them. The mothers might have throwed them at us. Q: Babies? A: Yes . . ."

13. His film is *Kim Phuc* (1984).

14. See Lippard, *A Different War,* pp. 105–109.

15. Herr, *Dispatches,* pp. 209–10.

16. Ron Kovic, *Born on the Fourth of July* (New York: Pocket Books, 1976), p. 54.

17. Thomas Bird, "Man and Boy Confront the Images of War," *New York Times,* May 27, 1990, p. 11.

18. Marine quoted in Herr, *Dispatches,* p. 188.

19. Tim O'Brien, *Going after Cacciato* (New York: Delacorte, 1978).

20. Henry Allen, "Why We Aren't in Vietnam," *Washington Post,* January 25, 1987, p. A25.

21. Steven Spielberg, quoted on the back cover of Oliver Stone and Richard Boyle, *Platoon and Salvador* (New York: Vintage, 1987).

22. Richard Corliss, *"Platoon," Time* (January 26, 1987), p. 56.

23. Albert Auster and Leonard Quart, *How the War Was Remembered* (New York: Praeger, 1988), p. 132.

24. David Halberstam, quoted in Corliss, *"Platoon,"* p. 58.

25. Quoted in Dan Goodgame, "How the War Was Won," *Time* (January 26, 1987), p. 58.

26. Quoted in the documentary film *Hearts of Darkness: A Filmmaker's Apocalypse* (1991).

27. Joan Scott, "Experience," in Judith Butler and Joan Scott, eds., *Feminists Theorize the Political* (New York: Routledge, 1992), pp. 24–25.

28. Quoted in Karen Jaehne, "Company Man," *Film Comment* 25, no. 2 (March/April 1989), p. 15.

29. Pat Aufderheide, "Good Soldiers," in Mark Crispin Miller, ed., *Seeing through Movies* (New York: Pantheon, 1990), p. 84.

30. Ron Kovic, cover of *Born on the Fourth of July*.

31. Stanley Karnow, *Vietnam: A History* (New York: Viking, 1983).

32. James argues that it was in the realm of independent documentary and avant-garde film that attempts were made to deglamorize the war, including avant-garde films such as Carolee Schneemann's *Viet-Flakes* (1965) and documentaries such as *In the Year of the Pig* (1969) by Emile de Antonio, *No Vietnamese Ever Called Me Nigger* (1968) by David Loeb Weiss, and *Hearts and Minds* (1974) by Peter Davis (*To Take the Glamour out of War*, Program Notes, Whitney Museum of American Art, 1990).

33. Herr, *Dispatches*, p. 160.

34. William Broyles, "Why Men Love War," *Esquire* (November 1984), p. 62.

35. Stone, *Platoon and Salvador*, pp. 93–94.

36. Ibid., p. 95.

37. Jeffords, *The Remasculinization of America*, p. 201.

38. Stone, *Platoon and Salvador*, p. 8.

39. Ibid., pp. 9–10.

40. Jeffords, *The Remasculinization of America*, p. 167.

41. Ibid., p. 53.

42. Quoted in Charley Trujillo, *Soldados* (San Jose: Chusma House, 1990), p. 34.

43. Wallace Terry II, "Bringing the War Home," in Clyde Taylor, ed., *Vietnam and Black America* (Garden City, NY: Anchor, 1973), p. 209.

44. Ruben Treviso, "Hispanics and the Vietnam War," in Harrison Salisbury, ed., *Vietnam Reconsidered* (New York: Harper & Row, 1984).

45. Peter Levy, "Blacks and the Vietnam War," in D. Michael Shafer, ed., *The Legacy* (Boston: Beacon Press, 1990), p. 214.

46. Clyde Taylor, "The Colonialist Subtext in *Platoon*," in Linda Dittmar and Gene Michaud, eds., *From Hanoi to Hollywood* (New Brunswick: Rutgers University Press, 1990), p. 171.

47. The only films in which Southeast Asians are distinct characters, although still not the protagonists, are *The Green Berets* (1968); *Good Morning Vietnam* (1987), in which a young VC befriends, and then betrays, an American; and *The Killing Fields* (1984), which is based on the experience of Cambodian photographer Dith Pran in the takeover of Cambodia by the Khmer Rouge and his friendship with American journalist Sydney Schanberg.

48. Lifton, *Home from the War*, pp. 35–36.

49. Peter Marin, "What the Vietnam Veterans Can Teach Us," *The Nation* (November 27, 1982), pp. 558–59.

50. Bruce Weigl, "Stone Incountry," *Cineaste* 15, no. 4 (1987), p. 10.

51. Ironically, at the beginning of the home video version of *Platoon*, former Chrysler Corporation Chairman Lee Iaccoca stands next to a Jeep and decribes the film as a memorial: "This film *Platoon* is a memorial, not to war but to all the men and women who fought in a time and in a place that no one understood, who knew only one thing, they were called and they went. . . . That in the truest sense is the spirit of America. The more we understand it, the more we honor those who kept it alive."

In this complex mix of commercialism, patriotism, and salesmanship, Iaccoca's message is disheartening. If the spirit of America is to go, unquestioningly, when called, then clearly the lessons of the Vietnam War have been ineffective.

52. Quoted in Corliss, "Platoon," p. 57.

53. Bird, "Man and Boy," p. 16.

Chapter Four

1. The chapter epigraph is quoted in Asu Aksoy and Kevin Robins, "Exterminating Angels," in Hamid Mowlana, George Gerbner, and Herbert Schiller, eds., *Triumph of the Image* (Boulder: Westview Press, 1992), p. 206.

2. That the "syndrome" of anti-interventionism is specific to the post–Vietnam War era is contestable, according to Richard Brody and Richard Morin. They argue that Americans have always been anti-interventionist, even during World War II, and that the Persian Gulf War did nothing to change that sentiment ("From Vietnam to Iraq: The Great American Syndrome Myth," *Washington Post,* March 31, 1991, p. B1).

3. See E. J. Dionne, "Kicking the 'Vietnam Syndrome,'" *Washington Post,* March 4, 1991, p. A1.

4. Abouali Farmanfarmanian, "Sexuality in the Gulf War: Did You Measure Up?" *Genders* 13 (Spring 1992), p. 17.

5. Raymond Williams, *Television, Technology, and Cultural Form* (New York: Schocken Books, 1974), pp. 89–94.

6. Television technology and phenomenology are products of an ideology of transmission and immediacy; issues of preservation and archival capacity were simply not a part of the developing television technology of the 1950s and 1960s. Although digital storage will eventually replace videotape, many independent videotapes and television shows have already been lost. Videotapes deteriorate—indeed, no one really knows the shelf life of tape—and older tapes become unplayable when equipment for playing that format becomes obsolete. Ironically, then, the qualities of transmission and speed in television have resulted in a medium that has had to address issues of

preservation at an accelerated rate, although it has only recently begun to do so.

7. George Gerbner, "Persian Gulf War, the Movie," in Mowlana, Gerbner, and Schiller, eds., *Triumph of the Image*, p. 244.

8. Ernest Larsen, "Gulf War TV," *Jump Cut* 36 (1991), p. 8.

9. *U.S. News & World Report* reported in 1992 that U.S. intelligence agents tried to disable an Iraqi air defense network with a computer virus. It was unconfirmed whether the virus was successful ("The Gulf War Flu," *U.S. News & World Report* [January 20, 1992], p. 50).

10. McKenzie Wark, "News Bites," *Meanjin* 50, no. 1 (Autumn 1991), pp. 6–7.

11. Scott Simon, "Weekend Edition," National Public Radio, January 18, 1992.

12. Quoted in Otto Friedrich and the editors of *Time*, eds., *Desert Storm* (Boston: Little, Brown, 1991), pp. 37–38.

13. Journalist Philip Knightly told Simon that "what we were seeing was actually the SCUD missile breaking up of its own volition or under the control of the Iraqi controllers because they realized that if they split the SCUD before the Patriot was able to hone in on it, the Patriot would become confused over which part of the SCUD it should attack. So although it looked like marvelous pyrotechnics in the sky over both Israel and Saudi Arabia, what we were seeing was not what we were told we were seeing" ("Weekend Edition," National Public Radio, January 18, 1992).

14. Wark, "News Bites," p. 15.

15. Paul Virilio, *War and Cinema*, trans. Patrick Camiller (New York: Verso, 1989), p. 3.

16. The censorship of the war worked to prevent images from being taken and specifically to exclude those that violated the narrative being constructed by the government. For instance, the well-known documentary videomaker Jon Alpert, who had been producing segments on Central America and other subjects for NBC's "Today Show" for fifteen years, produced a piece in Iraq with Ramsey Clark about the deaths of civilians and damage caused by bombing. Not only did NBC refuse to run the footage (it was shown on WNET, the New York public television station—where it was framed by hostile commentary—and, ironically, on MTV), but Alpert lost his job as a stringer for NBC as a consequence. NBC is owned by General Electric, which is one of the largest defense contractors in the country (see Danny Schechter, "The Gulf War and the Death of the TV News," *The Independent* [January/February 1992], p. 28).

17. Since the war, it has been revealed that the "smart" weapons were in fact a very small percentage of the bombs dropped on Iraq, about 8.8 per-

cent (see Schechter, "The Gulf War and the Death of the TV News," p. 31). According to Scott Simon, "More than 90 percent of the bombs dropped onto Iraq were huge, blunt, lumbering percussion bombs, fuel air bombs, which burn the air in a man's lungs; or Bouncing Betties, those diabolical basketball-shaped bombs that bounce up to explode at a height that will shatter an average man's spine" ("Weekend Edition," National Public Radio, January 18, 1992).

18. Scarry, *The Body in Pain,* p. 71. The illusion of a single mass did not reduce the confusion about who the enemy was. Of the 148 U.S. casualties from the Gulf War, thirty-five were officially attributed to "friendly fire," or what the military calls "fratricide." Many people die from friendly fire in all wars: 75,000 are estimated to have died from it in World War I. However, the figure for the Gulf War is a relatively high percentage ("Talk of the Nation," National Public Radio, March 4, 1992).

19. Hugh Gusterson, "Nuclear War, the Gulf War, and the Disappearing Body," *Journal of Urban and Cultural Studies* (1991) 2, no. 1, p. 51.

20. Elaine Scarry, "Watching and Authorizing the Gulf War," in Marjorie Garber, Jann Matlock, and Rebecca Walkowitz, eds., *Media Spectacles* (New York: Routledge, 1993), p. 68.

21. See Mark Crispin Miller, *Spectacle: Operation Desert Storm and the Triumph of Illusion* (New York: Simon and Schuster, 1993). According to Miller, in August 1990 the Citizens for a Free Kuwait, with a membership of thirteen people, hired the PR firm of Hill & Knowlton for $5.64 million, which saturated news organizations with television news images, organized Kuwait Student Information Days on college campuses, and distributed a 525-page document on Iraqi abuses to every member of Congress.

22. Stephen Heath, "Representing Television," in Patricia Mellencamp, ed., *The Logics of Television: Essays in Cultural Criticism* (Bloomington: Indiana University Press, 1990), p. 279.

23. Michael Rogin, " 'Make My Day!': Spectacle as Amnesia in Imperial Politics," *Representations* 29 (Winter 1990), p. 106.

24. Until *Courage Under Fire,* the Gulf War was rarely depicted in popular culture. Several action films that were in production during the outbreak of the war changed their plots to include it (see Kathleen Hughes, "Hollywood Rushes Iraq Angles into Plots," *Wall Street Journal,* January 21, 1991, p. B1). ABC broadcast the made-for-television movie *The Heroes of Desert Storm* in fall 1991. A mixture of news footage and reenactment with both actors and actual participants, it begins with the disclaimer that "to achieve realism, no distinction is made among these elements." This is followed by an introduction by President Bush.

25. George Gerbner, "Persian Gulf War, the Movie," p. 254.

26. Mitchell, "From CNN to *JFK*," p. 13.

27. Robert Stam, "Mobilizing Fictions," *Public Culture* (Spring 1992), p. 106.

28. Mitchell, "From CNN to *JFK*," p. 14.

29. Michael Morgan, Justin Lewis, and Sut Jhally, "More Viewing, Less Knowledge," in Hamid Mowlana, George Gerbner, and Herbert Schiller, eds., *Triumph of the Image* (Boulder: Westview Press, 1992), pp. 216–33.

30. John Farrell, "Where We Shroud Our Heroes," *Boston Globe*, February 27, 1991, p. 57.

31. For an extensive discussion of the origin stories of the yellow ribbon, see Lisa Heilbronn, "Yellow Ribbons and Remembrance," *Sociological Inquiry* 64, no. 2 (May 1994), pp. 151–78.

32. Laura U. Marks, "Tie a Yellow Ribbon around Me," *Camera Obscura* 27 (September 1991), p. 55.

33. Quoted in Ann Cvetkovich, "The War against AIDS and War in the Middle East," in Michael Ryan and Avery Gordon, eds., *Body Politics* (Boulder: Westview Press, 1994), p. 38.

34. Marlene Cimons, "Gulf War Syndrome May Be Contagious, Survey Shows," *Los Angeles Times*, October 21, 1994, p. A4; and Kenneth Miller, "The Tiny Victims of Desert Storm," *Life* (November 1995), pp. 46–62.

35. See Philip Hilts, "Gulf War Syndrome: A Clue," *New York Times*, April 21, 1996, p. E2.

36. Lifton, "Preface," *Home from the War*, p. xiii.

Chapter Five

1. Unlike gay men and inner-city populations, people with hemophilia do not identify themselves primarily by race and/or gender. Although those with hemophilia are all male, the hemophiliac community includes their families, wives, lovers, and children, many of whom have also died of AIDS. Because they were infected with AIDS through blood products, they have for the most part been perceived by the general public to be more "innocent" than other victims. However, they have been subjected to the stigma of AIDS contamination, as was evident when communities protested to keep Ryan White out of public school in Kokomo, Indiana, in 1984 and burned the home of the Ray family, which includes several children with hemophilia, in Arcadia, Florida, in 1987.

2. Paula Treichler, "AIDS, Homophobia, and Biomedical Discourse: An Epidemic of Signification," in Douglas Crimp, ed., *AIDS: Cultural Activism/ Cultural Analysis* (Cambridge: MIT Press, 1988), pp. 31–70.

3. Sander Gilman, *Disease and Representation: Images of Illness from Madness to AIDS* (Ithaca: Cornell University Press, 1988), p. 248.

4. Susan Sontag, *AIDS and Its Metaphors* (New York: Farrar, Strauss and Giroux, 1989), p. 23.

5. Gilman, *Disease and Representation,* p. 258.

6. Katherine Park, "Kimberly Bergalis, AIDS, and the Plague Metaphor," in Marjorie Garber, Jann Matlock, and Rebecca Walkowitz, eds., *Media Spectacles* (New York: Routledge, 1993), p. 241.

7. R. I. Moore, *The Formation of a Persecuting Society,* quoted in Park, "Kimberly Bergalis," p. 243.

8. See Randy Shilts, *And the Band Played on* (New York: Penguin, 1987), p. 97; and Richard Goldstein, "AIDS and the Social Contract," in Erica Carter and Simon Watney, eds., *Taking Liberties: AIDS and Cultural Politics* (London: Serpent's Tale, 1989), pp. 81–94.

9. For an analysis of the image of clean sexuality projected by Rock Hudson, see Richard Meyer, "Rock Hudson's Body," in Diana Fuss, ed., *Inside/Out: Lesbian Theories, Gay Theories* (New York: Routledge, 1991), pp. 259–88.

10. Frank Rich, "The Gay Decades," *Esquire* (November 1987), p. 99.

11. Edward Barnes and Anne Hollister, "Now No One Is Safe from AIDS: The New Victims," *Life* (July 1985).

12. Roberta McGrath, "Medical Police," *Ten.8* 14 (1984), p. 15.

13. Douglas Crimp, "Portraits of People with AIDS," in Lawrence Grossberg, Cary Nelson, and Paula Treichler, eds., *Cultural Studies* (New York: Routledge, 1992), p. 118.

14. Crimp, "Portraits of People with AIDS," p. 130.

15. Quoted in ibid., p. 118.

16. Simon Watney, "Representing AIDS," in Tessa Boffin and Sunil Gupta, eds., *Ecstatic Bodies* (London: Rivers Oram Press, 1990), p. 185.

17. Jan Zita Grover, "Visible Lesions: Images of the PWA in America," in James Miller, ed., *Fluid Exchanges* (Toronto: University of Toronto Press, 1992), p. 41.

18. Cindy Patton, *Inventing AIDS* (New York: Routledge, 1990), p. 21.

19. William Deresiewicz, "Against All Odds," in Nancy McKenzie, ed., *The AIDS Reader* (New York: Meridian, 1991), pp. 534–42.

20. Shilts, *And the Band Played on,* p.87.

21. Goldstein, "AIDS and the Social Contract," pp. 81–94.

22. Patton, *Inventing AIDS,* p. 11.

23. The mythic story of the origins of AIDS in Africa has been replicated in several histories of the epidemic, including Randy Shilts's *And the Band Played on.* These histories depict Africa as the tropical, contaminated source of all disease in a hackneyed narrative. Many other books have attempted

to critique this hypothesis—for example, *AIDS, Africa and Racism,* by Richard and Rosalind Chirimuuta, and *Blaming Others,* by Renée Sabatier. In Africa, AIDS is perceived as an invention of the white man (see Treichler, "AIDS and HIV Infection in the Third World," in Barbara Kruger and Phil Mariani, eds., *Remaking History* [Seattle: Bay Press, 1989], p. 46). Laurie Garrett notes that by the mid-1980s the issue of AIDS's origins was so politicized that the World Health Organization insisted, against the views of many scientists, that it had begun simultaneously on three continents. Though it is commonly believed now that HIV has existed at least for several decades and that specific global circumstances in the early 1970s allowed its spread, there is still no consensus on this issue. Garrett writes, "Though it has been the focus of attention of some of the greatest minds in contemporary biomedical science on at least four continents, nobody by 1994 had yet pinpointed a time, place, or key event responsible for the emergence of HIV-1" (*The Coming Plague* [New York: Penguin, 1994], p. 389).

24. See "AIDS 'Plot' against Blacks," *New York Times,* May 12, 1992, p. A22. This editorial, which sparked a number of letters, noted that studies in 1990 and 1992 found that approximately 35 percent of black church members believed that AIDS was a form of genocide of blacks.

25. bell hooks, *Talking Back* (Boston: South End Press, 1989), p. 122.

26. Harlon Dalton, "AIDS in Blackface," in Nancy McKenzie, ed., *The AIDS Reader: Social and Political Ethical Issues* (New York: Meridian, 1991), pp. 127–28.

27. This controversy was most obvious in a 1994 *New Yorker* article by dance critic Arlene Croce about a work by choreographer Bill T. Jones entitled *Still/Here*. Croce sparked outrage by refusing to see the work and review it because she contended, from its pre-publicity, that it was concerned not with art but with dying. She wrote: "If I understand 'Still/Here' . . . it is a kind of messianic traveling medicine show, designed to do some good for sufferers of fatal illnesses, both those in the cast and those thousands more who may be in the audience." She accuses Jones of placing himself beyond criticism because he is working with dying people and declares that "no one goes to 'Still/Here' for the dancing" ("Discussing the Undiscussable," *New Yorker* [December 26, 1994/January 2, 1995], p. 53). That Croce was profoundly mistaken about the work, which is a serious dance theater piece in which the choreography enacts spoken words, is not as important as her contention as a critic that "true" art has nothing to do with death and dying (the list of art works throughout history that deal with this subject is immense) and that the audience cannot engage with these issues without being voyeurs. This is a primary example of how disabling the debate over victimology has become.

28. Jan Zita Grover, "AIDS: Keywords," in Crimp, *AIDS,* p. 29. This

essay by Grover, along with Treichler's "AIDS, Homophobia and Biomedical Discourse," is a crucial text in the cultural criticism of AIDS. Both these analyses of the language deployed in reference to AIDS have influenced larger debates in the media about AIDS representation.

29. Douglas Crimp notes that after AIDS activists spent years trying to get the media to distinguish between HIV and AIDS, it took the public announcement of Magic Johnson in the fall of 1991 to make them do so, precisely because "they finally found it necessary to comply in order to reassure Magic's fans that he was infected with HIV but did not have AIDS" ("Accommodating Magic," in Marjorie Garber, Jann Matlock, and Rebecca Walkowitz, eds., *Media Spectacles* [New York: Routledge, 1993], p. 261).

30. The pink triangle is an inverted reference to the pink triangles homosexuals were forced to wear in Nazi Germany.

31. Douglas Crimp and Adam Rolston, *AIDS Demo Graphics* (Seattle: Bay Press, 1990), pp. 19–20.

32. Walt Odets, "AIDS Education and Harm Reduction for Gay Men: Psychological Approaches for the 21st Century," *AIDS and Public Policy Journal* (Spring 1994), pp. 1–16.

33. Ibid., p. 4.

34. Ibid.

35. Michael Warner, "Unsafe: Why Gay Men Are Having Risky Sex," *Village Voice,* January 31, 1995, p. 35.

36. Quoted in Jane Gross, "Second Wave of AIDS Feared by Officials in San Francisco," *New York Times,* December 11, 1993, p. 8. This association of risk-taking with proving oneself is also evident in the case of young girls in San Antonio, Texas, who have taken part in gang initiations that involve having sex with a gang member who has tested positive for HIV ("Teen Girls Prove They're Tough by Having Sex with HIV Carriers," *San Diego Union-Tribune,* April 27, 1993).

37. David Roman, *Acts of Intervention* (Bloomington: Indiana University Press, forthcoming).

38. Daniel Harris, "Making Kitsch From AIDS," *Harper's* (July 1994), p. 58.

39. This theme was even in evidence in the 1995 Hollywood film *Outbreak.* The film is about a fictitious virus that infiltrates the United States from an infected African monkey and is on the verge of wiping out an entire town, perhaps even the whole country. That the film is about AIDS phobia should go without saying, although it was released, ironically (perhaps, from the production company's point of view, fortuitously), right before the outbreak of Ebola fever in Zaire in the spring of 1995. Though the virus the film depicts is highly infectious and kills people within hours, it bears many

markers of AIDS myth, not only the African-monkey-origin theory but even the skin lesions it produces. Dustin Hoffman plays a scientist who is tracking the virus. As his ex-wife, played by Rene Russo, lies dying, she attempts to touch his cheek, and Hoffman, knowing that it will kill him, takes off his protective gear in order to feel her hand upon his face. True love, the scene appears to say, is risking one's life for intimacy and the expression of love. The message of this scene eerily places it in the context of AIDS in the 1990s, for what it portrays is a romanticization of the act of self-contamination.

40. Quoted in Simon Watney, *Practices of Freedom* (Durham: Duke University Press, 1994), p. 146.

41. Thanks to David Sloane for drawing my attention to this and several other points in this essay.

42. Douglas Crimp, "AIDS: Cultural Analysis/Cultural Activism," in Crimp, *AIDS*, p. 7.

43. Wayne Salazar, "Fighting AIDS with Kitsch," (Letter to the Editor) *Harper's* (October 1994), p. 4.

44. Harris, "Making Kitsch from AIDS," p. 57.

45. Kenneth Cole, for instance, donates 50 percent of the profits from shoes sold on World AIDS Day to AIDS service organizations.

46. Kirby's family felt that it was important for the photograph to be used in the ad precisely because it depicted a family coming together to comfort a person with AIDS (Cheryl Curry, "AIDS Victim's Photo in Ad Tells a Story," *San Jose Mercury News*, May 12, 1992, p. 9A). See also Vicki Goldberg, "Images of Catastrophe as Corporate Ballyhoo," *New York Times*, May 3, 1992.

47. Ingrid Sischy, "Advertising Taboos: Talking with Luciano Benetton and Oliviero Toscani," *Interview* (April 1992), p. 69.

48. Barth Healey, "The Red Ribbon of AIDS Awareness," *New York Times*, November 28, 1993, p. V17.

49. Some of the most important works that have been produced about AIDS in independent video include *Bright Eyes* (Stuart Marshall, 1984), *Danny* (Stashu Kybartus, 1987), *Doctors, Liars, and Women* (ACT UP, 1988), *Tongues Untied* (Marlon Riggs, 1989), *Zero Patience* (John Greyson, 1993), and *Fast Trip, Long Drop* (Greg Bordowitz, 1993). For writing about AIDS videos, see Ann Cvetkovich, "Video, AIDS, and Activism," *Afterimage* (September 1991), pp. 8–11; Alexis Danzig, "Acting UP: Independent Video and the AIDS Crisis," *Afterimage* (May 1989), pp. 5–7; Martha Gever, "Pictures of Sickness: Stuart Marshall's *Bright Eyes*," in Crimp, ed., *AIDS*, pp. 109–26; Brian Goldfarb, "Video Activism and Critical Pedagogy," *Afterimage* (May 1993), pp. 4–8; Alexandra Juhasz, "WAVE in the Media Environ-

ment: Camcorder Activism and the Making of *HIV TV*," *Camera Obscura* 28 (1992), pp. 135–54; *AIDS TV* (Durham: Duke University Press, 1995); Lorraine Kenny, "Testing the Limits: An Interview," *Afterimage* (October 1989), pp. 4–7; and Paula Treichler, "Beyond *Cosmo:* AIDS, Identity, and Inscriptions of Gender," *Camera Obscura* 28 (1992), pp. 21–78.

Chapter Six

1. The NAMES Project now has independent affiliates in twenty-nine countries. In these countries, the quilt is housed centrally, just as the panels of the quilt that are not traveling in the United States are housed in San Francisco. Panels from foreign affiliates are sometimes displayed within the United States, as in the quilt display in Washington, D.C., in October 1992. The vast majority of quilt panels are American.

2. AIDS Quilt panels made in the United States are sent by their makers to the NAMES Project in San Francisco, where they are sewn together in groups of eight according to what region of the country they are from, their pattern and color, and community relevance to form twelve-by-twelve-foot sections. Chapters of the NAMES Project keep twelve twelve-by-twelves and organize displays in their local regions.

3. By 1995, more than 14,000 people had died of AIDS in San Francisco.

4. Cindy Ruskin, *The Quilt* (New York: Pocket Books, 1988), p. 9.

5. From an interview with author in San Francisco, October 22, 1991. "It may be an origin story," Jones told me, "but it's true!" Unless noted otherwise, all quotes from Jones are from this interview. Jones is no longer director of the NAMES Project but still works with the organization as a spokesperson for the quilt.

6. From an interview with author in San Francisco, May 18, 1995. All quotes from Turney are from this interview.

7. Quoted in Joe Brown, "The Quilt," *Washington Post*, October 2, 1988.

8. Quoted in Gary Abrams, "AIDS Quilt Comforting U.S. Grief," *Los Angeles Times*, March 22, 1988.

9. See Patricia Mainardi, *Quilts: The Great American Art* (San Pedro, CA: Miles and Weir, 1978).

10. Harris, "Making Kitsch from AIDS," p. 60.

11. A quilt also evokes a rural context in contrast to the associations of epidemics with cities (see Gilman, *Disease and Representation*). It has been noted that the AIDS Quilt charts, in effect, the migration of gay men to cities throughout the United States, in particular New York, San Francisco, Houston, and Los Angeles (see Lawrence Howe, "The Moving Text," paper delivered at the California American Studies Association, April 1991). Thus,

the rural implication of the quilt form acts to domesticate the image of the disease-ridden urban environment.

12. The women of the Boise Peace Quilt Project carried on the tradition of political quilts. This collective, which was begun in 1981, has made numerous quilts to promote the idea of nonviolence and peace throughout the world, including several collaborative USSR friendship quilts, a Hiroshima quilt, a Sanctuary quilt for political refugees from Central America, and a quilt for Nicaragua. To make the National Peace Quilt in 1984, the women asked fifty children, one from each state, to draw their vision of peace and used their drawings to create the quilt. They then asked every U.S. senator to spend one night sleeping under the quilt and to describe his/her feelings in a Peace Log. This gesture is an extraordinary testament to a belief in the phenomenological capacity of the quilt—that its effect as a comforter can change states of mind. See the brochures of the Boise Peace Quilt Project and the videotape *A Stitch For Time* (1987) by Nigel Noble. Cleve Jones knowingly borrowed from the tradition carried on by the Boise Peace Quilt Project when he conceived the AIDS Quilt.

13. Jonathan Pearlman, "Remembering the Innocent," unpublished paper, 1990.

14. Larry Rinder, "The AIDS Quilt," *Artpaper Minneapolis* (May 1988), p. 9.

15. Elinor Fuchs, "The AIDS Quilt," *The Nation* (October 31, 1988), p. 409.

16. The arpilleras created by Chilean women have also been cited as influences on the AIDS Quilt, and as the quilt expands beyond its initial creation by Jones in the Castro, they are an appropriate analogy. Small embroidered or patchwork wall hangings that depict the daily struggles of these women, the arpilleras were condemnations of the repression under the Chilean military of General Pinochet in which thousands "disappeared." Created anonymously for political purposes, the arpilleras were smuggled out of Chile to call attention to the political oppression there. They share with the AIDS Quilt an immediate political urgency. See Marjorie Agosin, *Scraps of Life: Chilean Arpilleras,* trans. Cola Franzen (Trenton: Red Sea Press, 1987).

17. Judy Chicago, *The Dinner Party* (Garden City, NY: Anchor Press, 1979).

18. Quoted in *Common Threads* (1989), a film by Robert Epstein and Jeffrey Friedman.

19. Quoted in Brown, "The Quilt."

20. Quoted in Ruskin, *The Quilt,* p. 45.

21. I have been struck in both the AIDS Quilt and the Vietnam Veterans Memorial by the number of children's toys that are left for adults. There is

a preponderance of teddy bears left at the memorial, where they seem to connote a childlike innocence and a desire to remember the young soldier as a younger, unsuspecting child. There is also a tradition in the gay community of giving teddy bears to people with AIDS, and many quilt panels incorporate teddy bears.

22. Scarry, *The Body in Pain,* p. 175.

23. Mailings announce quilt displays so that people can request the presence of a certain panel at a display (the fact that panels are sewn together in groups of eight to form twelve-by-twelve-foot sections sometimes causes scheduling conflicts, although panels are grouped as much as possible by location). If all of the panels that are requested cannot fit, some are kept at the "truck stop" and can be brought out and unfolded upon request. An increasing number of displays are smaller and organized by local chapters.

24. There is debate about whether or not the public display of grief is truly therapeutic. While most people involved with the AIDS Quilt believe that it serves a therapeutic function (which many believe is also at odds with its political and fundraising functions), there are those who see that public expression of grief as only partially therapeutic. Russell Friedman, director of the Grief Recovery Institute in Los Angeles, states, "The publicizing of grief doesn't actually help at all. It creates the illusion that 'I'm doing something good,' and while quilts are wonderful, they're not therapeutic. I guess I find a little danger in the public expression of grief . . . it doesn't teach to complete our grief" (quoted in Ellen Uzelac, "The Public Eye of Mourning," *Common Boundary* [November/December 1994], p. 42).

25. Mike Signorile of ACT UP, quoted in Dan Bellm, "And Sew It Goes," *Mother Jones* (January 1989), p. 35.

26. Sigmund Freud, "Mourning and Melancholia," in *The Standard Edition of the Complete Psychological Works of Sigmund Freud, Vol. 14,* trans. James Strachey (London: Hogarth, 1917), p. 244.

27. Douglas Crimp, "Mourning and Militancy," *October* (Winter 1989), p. 9.

28. Patton, *Inventing AIDS,* p. 61.

29. See ACT UP/New York Women and AIDS Book Group, *Women, AIDS & Activism* (Boston: South End Press, 1990); Nancy Stoller Shaw, "Preventing AIDS Among Women," in *The AIDS Reader,* pp. 505–21; Paula Treichler, "AIDS, Gender, and Biomedical Discourse," in Elizabeth Fee and Daniel Fox, eds., *AIDS: Burdens of History* (Berkeley: University of California Press, 1988), pp. 190–266; and Cindy Patton, *Last Served? Gendering the HIV Pandemic* (London: Taylor and Francis, 1994).

30. Treichler, "AIDS, Gender, and Biomedical Discourse," p. 217.

31. Michael Kimmel and Martin Levine, "A Hidden Factor in AIDS," *Los Angeles Times,* June 3, 1990.

32. Quoted in Ruskin, *The Quilt*, p. 53.

33. Compared to those of the mothers, these inscriptions tend to be short on words. For instance, one typical letter at the NAMES Project contains a long section written by a mother, who ends, "A mother holds a child in her arms for a short time, but in her heart forever," and a brief, though moving message from the father: "He was my boy. I loved him and I miss him." Also common are stories told by men whose wives have acted as mediators between them and their gay sons. One man at a quilt display stated, "I haven't spoken to my son since the day he told me he was a homosexual. I told him that in my mind, I no longer had a son, and that if he got sick with AIDS, I didn't want to know about it. My wife forced me to come down here, so I did. I warned her that it wouldn't change my mind any . . . but I want to tell you that I'm going home to phone my son right now and try to talk to him if he'll let me . . . before it's too late" (quoted in Judy Weiser, "Stitched to the Beat of a Heart," *Art Therapy* [November 1989], p. 113). I do not want to imply that all of the parents associated with the AIDS Quilt fit this pattern, simply to indicate that these stories stand out because there are many of them.

34. Rinder, "The AIDS Quilt," p. 9.

35. Quoted in Paul-David Wadler, "Internal Strategies, Community Responses," *Boston Gay Community News,* December 4–10, 1988.

36. Whitney Otto, *How to Make an American Quilt* (New York: Villard Books, 1991), p. 110.

37. Quoted in Ruskin, *The Quilt*, p. 69.

38. Quoted in Frances Fitzgerald, *Cities on a Hill* (New York: Simon and Schuster, 1987), pp. 116–17.

39. Quoted in ibid., p. 115.

40. "Sewing up Memories," *San Francisco Sentinel,* September 18, 1987.

41. Robin Hardy, "Die Harder," *Village Voice,* July 2, 1991, p. 33.

42. Jan Grover points out that the word "family" in the context of AIDS often connotes those who are HIV-negative, when, in fact, "families often contain and accept openly gay and lesbian children—and parents—as well as IV drug users" ("AIDS: Keywords," p. 23). Grover's example is a 1986 congressional bill on AIDS and the family, passed with virtually no opposition, that legalized the creation of designated-donor pools that would allow families to donate blood within the family to prevent transmission of HIV from anonymous donors. The bill thus defines the family as inherently HIV-negative and anyone who is HIV-positive as outside of the realm of the family. In 1992, a National Institutes of Health study found that blood donated by "loved ones" was no safer from infectious agents than the general supply, with the exception of HIV, which appeared in 4.6 donations of 100,000, compared with 10 in 100,000 in the general blood supply (Associ-

ated Press, "Blood of Loved Ones Is No Safer Than General Supply," *New York Times,* November 12, 1992, p. A9).

43. Quoted in Ruskin, *The Quilt,* p. 63.

44. The National High School Quilt Program was established by the NAMES Project in 1994 with the aim of using the quilt as a tool for education and HIV prevention in high schools throughout the country. The NAMES Project provides a high school with one twelve-by-twelve section of the quilt, which is then the focus for HIV prevention programs that are already approved for the school. Studies by the NAMES Project show that 85 to 90 percent of the students feel that having the quilt there makes a difference in how they perceive AIDS, their own risk, and their own understanding of what it means to die of AIDS. Turney states, "What the quilt does is put a human face on the statistics, and most HIV prevention programs are about statistics and threats." In these programs the students are put in charge of caring for the quilt panels so that, according to Turney, they become invested in them while they are there.

45. Associated Press, "AIDS Advocates Report Quilt Vandalized," *New York Times,* September 20, 1990, p. B5.

46. Indeed, the quilt has a fervent and dedicated following and actually has acquired a cult status in some circles. There are people who follow the quilt, traveling from display to display, who are called "threadheads" by the NAMES Project staff.

47. Steve Abbott, "Meaning Adrift," *San Francisco Sentinel,* October 14, 1988.

48. Michael Musto, "La Dolce Musto," *Village Voice,* October 25, 1988.

49. Quoted in Elizabeth Kastor, "Mending a Patchwork of Pain," *Washington Post,* October 8, 1992, p. C9.

50. Abbott, "Meaning Adrift."

51. Richard Mohr, "Text(ile)," in *Gay Ideas* (Boston: Beacon Press, 1992), p.121.

52. Henry Abelove, "The Politics of the 'Gay Plague': AIDS as a U.S. Ideology," in Michael Ryan and Avery Gorden, *Body Politics: Disease, Desire, and the Family* (Boulder: Westview, 1994), p. 7.

53. Quoted in Wadler, "Internal Strategies, Community Responses."

54. Peter Hawkins, "Naming Names," *Critical Inquiry* (Summer 1993), p. 777.

55. In 1988, sections of the AIDS Quilt were acquired by the Smithsonian Institution as part of its Division of Medical Sciences and thus subsumed into the national discourse of that institution, but the "fit" was awkward. Smithsonian curator Ray Kondratas stated: "There is no question whether we should collect part of the quilt. But there is considerable sensitivity about

how it will be perceived and presented to the public. We're a national institution and we have to be very careful about how controversial subjects are
treated" (quoted in Coimbra Sirica, "Smithsonian to Collect some AIDS
Quilt Panels," *San Francisco Chronicle,* October 7, 1988). What is so controversial about memorializing an epidemic, one wants to ask?

56. The quilt also raises the question of the uniqueness of AIDS and the
memorialization of epidemics in general. Arguments about the specialness
of AIDS tend to work both ways. On one hand, AIDS activists and care
professionals argue that AIDS is a special disease that requires priority funding and care; yet at the same time they argue against policies that mark
AIDS as special for discriminatory reasons.

AIDS activism has raised the issue of how research and treatment of
other diseases are funded, and the quilt has pointed up the fact that those
who have died of other diseases have not been collectively memorialized. In
fact, the AIDS Quilt has spawned the creation of many other quilts, including the Children's Quilt Project (for children with HIV), a cancer quilt, a
quilt in Detroit for teenage victims of urban violence, and one for victims
of the Oklahoma City bombing. Prior to this, with the exception of medieval
plague memorials, there have not been other memorials to those who have
died in an epidemic.

Chapter Seven

1. Anne Marie Moulin, "The Immune System: A Key Concept for the
History of Immunology," *History and Philosophy of the Life Sciences* (1989),
pp. 221–36.

2. Nancy Leys Stepan, "Race and Gender: The Role of Analogy in Science," *ISIS* (1986), p. 267.

3. See, for instance, the popular book by Bernie Siegel, *Love, Medicine
and Miracles* (New York: Harper & Row, 1986); and Howard Kaplan, "Social
Psychology of the Immune System: A Conceptual Framework and Review
of Literature," *Social Science and Medicine* (1991), pp. 909–23.

4. Patton, *Inventing AIDS,* p. 59.

5. T-cells are divided into subgroups. These include helper T-cells,
which amplify the initial immune response; cytotoxic or killer T-cells, which
neutralize cells that contain foreign antigens; and suppressor T-cells, which
curtail the immune response when the "event" is over.

6. Mary Catherine Bateson and Richard Goldsby, *Thinking AIDS* (New
York: Addison-Wesley, 1988), p. 30.

7. John Dwyer, *The Body at War* (New York: Mentor/Penguin, 1990), p.
39.

8. Leon Jaroff, "Stop That Germ!" *Time* (May 23, 1988), p. 56.

9. Peter Jaret, "Our Immune System: The Wars within," *National Geographic* (June 1986), p. 702. According to Emily Martin, this essay by Jaret was extremely popular and prompted a number of other publications to run cover stories on the immune system. See Martin, *Flexible Bodies* (Boston: Beacon Press, 1994), pp. 50–51.

10. Dwyer, *The Body at War,* p. 41.

11. Lennart Nilsson with Jan Lindberg, *The Body Victorious* (New York: Delacorte, 1987), p. 20.

12. The idea that one has to manage one's defense forces, or "troops," effectively seems to be ironically (and not merely coincidentally) analogous to the Vietnam War, with its loss of management of the troops.

13. See Donna Haraway, "The Biological Enterprise: Sex, Mind and Profit from Human Engineering to Sociobiology," in *Simians, Cyborgs, and Women* (New York: Routledge, 1991); and Treichler, "AIDS, Homophobia, and Biomedical Discourse," p. 59.

14. Dwyer, *The Body at War,* p. 41.

15. See Emily Martin, "Toward an Anthropology of Immunology: The Body as Nation State," *Medical Anthropology Quarterly* (December 1990), p. 412; and *Flexible Bodies,* Chapter 1.

16. Nilsson and Lindberg, *The Body Victorious,* p. 28.

17. Jaret, "Our Immune System," p. 723.

18. Christine Gorman, "Returning Fire against AIDS," *Time* (June 24, 1991), p. 44.

19. See, for instance, Judith Williamson's analysis in "Every Virus Tells a Story: The Meaning of HIV and AIDS," in Erica Carter and Simon Watney, eds., *Taking Liberties: AIDS and Cultural Politics* (London: Serpent's Tale, 1989), pp. 69–80.

20. Thomas Matthews and Dani Bolognesi, "AIDS Vaccines," in *The Science of AIDS: Readings From Scientific American* (New York: W. H. Freeman, 1988), p. 101.

21. Treichler, "AIDS, Homophobia, and Biomedical Discourse," p. 60.

22. Gina Kolata, "How AIDS Smolders: Immune System Studies Follow the Tracks of H.I.V.," *New York Times,* March 17, 1992, p. B5.

23. Dwyer, *The Body at War,* p. 18.

24. Jaret, "Our Immune System," p. 708.

25. Martin, "Toward an Anthropology of Immunology," p. 416.

26. Quoted in Jaret, "Our Immune System," p. 716.

27. Jaret, "Our Immune System," p. 708.

28. Patton, *Inventing AIDS,* p. 127.

29. In his descriptions of the homophobic language and old-boys'-club

attitude of many heterosexual male scientists, David Black notes that one scientist referred to the phagocytes as "fagocytes," adding that these are cells "whose job is to kill off fags." Black calls this an example of a kind of "social immune system," in which these physicians attempt to distinguish self from nonself—that is, themselves as straight men from gay men (*The Plague Years: A Chronicle of AIDS, Epidemic of Our Times* [New York: Simon and Schuster, 1986], p. 81).

30. Emily Martin notes that people in her study who employed nonmilitary images of the immune system were younger than their baby-boomer counterparts: "In our interviews, all manner of people could produce military images: young people, old people, and especially aging baby boomers, who came of age during the cold war era of the 1940s and 1950s, when imagery of the body as a fortress or a castle was most vibrant. But *all* the examples that struck me as the most elaborated, vivid departures from military imagery came from people in their late teens and early twenties, people coming of age at a time when cold war assumptions are being drastically shaken and a new sensibility about how the body relates to the world may be arising" (*Flexible Bodies*, p. 71).

31. Carol Cohn, "Sex and Death in the Rational World of Defense Intellectuals," *Signs* (1987), pp. 687–718.

32. Scarry, *The Body in Pain*, p. 41.

33. Steve Connor and Sharon Kingman, *The Search for the Virus* (New York: Penguin, 1988), p. 2.

34. Quoted in Georges Didi-Huberman, "Photography—Scientific and Pseudo-scientific," in Jean-Claude Lemagny and André Rouille, eds., *A History of Photography: Social and Cultural Perspectives*, trans. Janet Lloyd (New York: Cambridge University Press, 1987), p. 71.

35. See Allan Sekula, "On the Invention of Photographic Meaning," in Victor Burgin, ed., *Thinking Photography* (London: Macmillan, 1982), p. 108.

36. Susan Sontag, *On Photography* (New York: Delta, 1977), p. 16.

37. Didi-Huberman, "Photography—Scientific and Pseudo-scientific," p. 71.

38. Quoted in ibid., p. 70.

39. Concepts of nature as a female entity that science needed to tame, control, and "penetrate" emerged in the seventeenth century with such thinkers as Francis Bacon, the "father" of modern scientific thought. Feminist critics of science, such as Evelyn Fox Keller, have critiqued these concepts as perpetuating a notion that women represent nature and men represent the sphere of culture. See, for example, Evelyn Fox Keller, *Reflections on Gender and Science* (New Haven: Yale University Press, 1985).

40. Howard Sochurek, "Medicine's New Vision," *National Geographic* (January 1987), pp. 2–41.

41. Quoted in ibid., p. 40.

42. Nilsson's books include *Sweden in Profiles* (1954), *Life in the Sea* (1961), *A Child Is Born* (1966), *Behold Man* (1973), *Nature Magnified* (1984), and *The Body Victorious* (1987). It is interesting to note that in *Behold Man,* published in 1973, the idea of an immune system is significantly underplayed, barely mentioned in fact, whereas it is glorified fourteen years later in *The Body Victorious.*

43. See the catalogue essay by Rune Hassner in *Lennart Nilsson* (Goteborg, Sweden: Hasselblad Center, 1990). For an analysis of the role of images in fostering the idea of fetal autonomy, see Rosalind Petchesky, "Foetal Images: The Power of Visual Culture in the Politics of Reproduction" in Michelle Stanworth, ed., *Reproductive Technologies* (Minneapolis: University of Minnesota Press, 1987); and Carol Stabile, "Shooting the Mother: Fetal Photography and the Politics of Disappearance," *Camera Obscura* 28 (January 1992), pp. 179–205.

44. David Van Biema, "Master of an 'Unbelievable, Invisible World,'" *Life* (August 1990), p. 44.

45. Robert Poole, ed., *The Incredible Machine* (Washington, D.C.: National Geographic Society, 1986), p. 376.

46. With the use of fiberoptics and miniaturized video cameras, Nilsson has also photographed within the living body. The *Nova* television program, "The Miracle of Life" (1982), is a documentary of the reproductive process, and Nilsson took the majority of the images with fiberoptics. References to Nilsson's access to human specimens tend to be very oblique and rather startling, as in this *Life* magazine article: "Nilsson can maintain a human egg cell in a climate-controlled box while photographing it under magnification, then return it unharmed to the fertility clinic from which he borrowed it" (Van Biema, "Master of an 'Unbelievable, Invisible World,'" p. 46). Who, one wants to ask, gave him permission, and does the woman to whom this egg belongs know it has been gone?

47. Poole, *The Incredible Machine,* pp. 376–77.

48. Jaroff, "Stop That Germ!" p. 57.

49. Poole, *The Incredible Machine,* p. 376.

50. See Christopher Knight, "The Persistent Observer," in *25 Years of Space Photography* (Pasadena: Baxter Art Gallery, 1985), p. 11.

51. See for instance, Lisa Cartwright's discussion of the history of X-ray imaging and medical photographs in *Screening the Body* (Minneapolis: University of Minnesota Press, 1995).

52. Donna Haraway, "The Biopolitics of Postmodern Bodies: Constitu-

tions of Self in Immune System Discourse," in *Simians, Cyborgs, and Women*, p. 221.

53. Ibid., p. 222.

54. The 1966 science fiction film *Fantastic Voyage* constructs the interior of the human body as both a space landscape and a site of Cold War conflict. In the film, the Pentagon has devised a technique to miniaturize anything to microscopic proportions, as has the "other side." The problem is that they can make it work for only sixty minutes. The secret to prolonging the process is known by an eminent Russian scientist who was injured by spies when he defected and is now in a coma. The military miniaturizes a surgical team (which includes Raquel Welch as the beautiful assistant to the famous surgeon—and, of course, a traitor who attempts to sabotage the mission) in a nuclear-powered submarine that looks like a space ship. The team is injected into the patient's bloodstream to destroy a blood clot in his brain. Dramas ensue, and at one point Welch is attacked by very aggressive antibodies. In a final scene, the traitor scientist is engulfed, along with the now-deserted sub, by a large white blood cell.

The opening text of the film clearly situates the inner body as a kind of spacescape: "This film will take you where no one has ever been before; no eye witness has actually seen what you are about to see. But in this world of ours where going to the moon will soon be upon us and where the most incredible things are happening all around us, someday, perhaps tomorrow, the fantastic events you are about to see can and will take place." *Fantastic Voyage* was the inspiration for Body Wars, the most popular ride at EPCOT Center at Walt Disney World in Orlando, Florida. In this ride, viewers sit before a screen in a room equipped with a hydraulic flight simulator. They are supposed to imagine that they have been miniaturized and injected into the body of someone who has received a splinter in his finger, and they follow a doctor through the lungs, heart, and brain. Body Wars is in the Wonders of Life pavillion (sponsored by Metropolitan Life), where visitors can also view an animated show called Cranium Command, which depicts "how the brain functions as the communications center for the body" (Walt Disney World press release).

55. Jaret, "Our Immune System," p. 732.

56. This narrative also figures HIV as a kind of persistent tourist, a parasitic traveler. Insofar as the immune system retains a record of what has traveled through the body, HIV can be seen as the traveler who refuses to leave—the colonizer. The debates over the origin of AIDS, consistently implicating Africa as the origin of the disease and suggesting that the virus was transmitted to humans from monkeys, bring into sharp focus problems of colonial and postcolonial narratives. Africa, a colonized continent, is read

as the origin for all viruses and "new" diseases, coded as the tropical site of uncontrollable microorganisms, vulnerable bodies, and transgressions between nature and culture (see Donna Haraway, *Primate Visions* [New York: Routledge, 1989]). In its postcolonial state, Africa is subsequently read as the source of a virus that colonizes in turn the bodies of Americans, a virus derived from primates (to whom, by inference, the Africans are considered to be in closer proximity, a vestige of nineteenth-century racist science). In the narrative of African origin, the bodies of Africans with AIDS are effaced, and the virus is read as recolonizing the West from its contaminated site of postcolonialism.

57. Quoted in Martin, *Flexible Bodies,* p. 173.

58. Martin, *Flexible Bodies,* p. 179.

59. The cover for a *Time* magazine article on the immune system and AIDS (Jaroff, "Stop That Germ!") shows a photo of a man looking down at his chest, which is pulled open to reveal a cartoon scene in which the "white-cell wonder" boxes the "vicious virus." The image is meant to be humorous, but in its combination of photography and cartoon graphics, it has a very unsettling effect. This image presents a transgression of bodily boundaries that the usual cartoon graphics and the microphotographs of the immune system do not acknowledge.

60. See Treichler, "AIDS, Homophobia, and Biomedical Discourse," p. 61; and Jan Grover, "AIDS, Keywords, and Cultural Work," in Lawrence Grossberg, Cary Nelson, and Paula Treichler, eds., *Cultural Studies,* p. 238.

61. Robert Gallo, "The AIDS Virus," *Scientific American* (January 1987), p. 47.

62. Claudia Wallis, "AIDS: A Growing Threat," *Time* (August 12, 1985).

63. Nilsson and Lindberg, *The Body Victorious,* p. 27.

64. Bateson and Goldsby, *Thinking AIDS,* p. 33.

65. Martin, *Flexible Bodies,* p. 36.

66. Williamson, "Every Virus Tells a Story," p. 69.

67. Quoted in "Many Masks of AIDS Virus That Defeat Immune System," *Newsday,* December 12, 1991.

68. Jaret, "Our Immune System," p. 710.

69. Quoted in Jaroff, "Stop That Germ!" p. 57.

70. Joel Davis, *Defending the Body* (New York: Atheneum, 1989), p. 186.

71. Joel Achenbach, "AIDS Conundrum," *Oakland Tribune,* February 5, 1991.

72. Sontag, *AIDS and Its Metaphors,* p. 12.

73. Depictions of HIV also evoke the narratives of postmodern warfare characteristic of the Vietnam War: the unseen and undetected enemy in the form of the Vietcong and "civilians," the disruptive effect of guerrilla warfare

on "conventional" warfare, and the erosion of American masculinity, technological superiority, and national prowess. Just as representations of the Vietnam War define it as "fighting not the enemy but ourselves," the body with AIDS is read both as a body at war with an intruder and a body at war with itself.

74. Connor and Kingman, *The Search for the Virus,* p. 2; and Dwyer, *The Body at War,* p. 39.

75. Bateson and Goldsby, *Thinking AIDS,* p. 27.

76. Ludwik Fleck, *Genesis and Development of a Scientific Fact,* ed. Thaddeus Trenn and Robert Merton, trans. Fred Bradley and Thaddeus Trenn (Chicago: University of Chicago Press, [1935] 1979), p. 60.

77. Fleck, *Genesis and Development of a Scientific Fact,* p. 61.

78. Haraway, "The Biopolitics of Postmodern Bodies," p. 218.

79. For a thorough description of the debates and conflicting stories over the origins of HIV, see Garrett, *The Coming Plague,* pp. 361–89.

80. Emmanuel Dreuilhe, *Mortal Embrace,* trans. Linda Coverdale (New York: Hill and Wang, 1988), pp. 7–8.

81. Ibid., p. 28.

82. See Robert Atkins and Thomas Sokolowski, eds., *From Media to Metaphor: Art about AIDS* (New York: Independent Curators Incorporated, 1992), p. 34.

83. Quoted in Harris, "Making Kitsch from AIDS," p. 58.

84. Harris, "Making Kitsch from AIDS," p. 58.

85. Bo Huston, "After War," in Nancy Peters, ed., *War after War* (San Francisco: City Lights Books, 1992), p. 141.

Bibliography

General

Alexander, Elizabeth. " 'Can You Be BLACK and Look at This?': Reading the Rodney King Video(s)." In *Black Male: Representations of Masculinity in Contemporary American Art*. Edited by Thelma Golden. New York: Whitney Museum of American Art, 1994: 91–110.

Anderson, Benedict. *Imagined Communities*. London: Verso, 1983.

Barthes, Roland. *Camera Lucida: Reflections on Photography*. Translated by Richard Howard. New York: Hill and Wang, 1981.

Batchen, Geoffrey. "Desiring Production Itself: Notes on the Invention of Photography." In *Cartographies: Post-structuralism and the Mapping of Bodies and Spaces*. Edited by Rosalyn Diprose and Robyn Ferrell. North Sydney: Allen & Unwin, 1991: 13–26.

———. "Ghost Stories: The Beginnings and Ends of Photography." *Art Monthly Australia* (December 1994): 4–8.

Benjamin, Walter. *Illuminations*. Translated by Harry Zohn. New York: Schocken Books, 1969.

———. *Reflections*. Translated by Edmund Jephcott. New York: Harcourt Brace Jovanovich, 1978.

———. "Doctrine of the Similar." *New German Critique* 17 (Spring 1979): 65–69.

Berlant, Lauren. *The Anatomy of National Fantasy: Hawthorne, Utopia, and Everyday Life*. Chicago: University of Chicago Press, 1991.

———. "The Theory of Infantile Citizenship." *Public Culture* 5 (1993): 395–410.

Bryan, C.D.B. *The National Geographic Society: 100 Years of Adventure and Discovery*. New York: Harry Abrams, 1987.

Butler, Judith. "Review Essay: Spirit in Ashes." *History and Theory* 27, no. 1 (1988): 60–70.

————. "Endangered/Endangering: Schematic Racism and White Paranoia." In *Reading Rodney King/Reading Urban Uprising.* Edited by Robert Gooding-Williams. New York: Routledge, 1993: 15–22.

Cadava, Eduardo. "Words of Light: Theses on the Photography of History."
Diacritics (Fall/Winter 1992): 84–114.

Cartwright, Lisa. *Screening the Body: Tracing Medicine's Visual Culture.*
Minneapolis: University of Minnesota Press, 1995.

Cavell, Stanley. "The Fact of Television." In *Video Culture: A Critical Investigation.* Edited by John Hanhardt. Rochester: Visual Studies Workshop
and Peregrine Smith Books, 1986: 192–218.

Crenshaw, Kimberle, and Gary Peller. "Reel Time/Real Justice." In *Reading
Rodney King/Reading Urban Uprising.* Edited by Robert Gooding-
Williams. New York: Routledge, 1993: 56–70.

Crosby, Jessica. "Truck Driver Says He Doesn't Recall Beating." *Washington
Post* (August 26, 1993): A4.

Danto, Arthur C. "Moving Pictures." *Quarterly Review of Film Studies* 4,
no.1 (Winter 1979): 1–21.

Didi-Huberman, Georges. "Photography—Scientific and Pseudo-scientific."
In *A History of Photography: Social and Cultural Perspectives.* Edited
by Jean-Claude Lemagny and André Rouille. Translated by Janet Lloyd.
New York: Cambridge University Press, 1987: 71–75.

Doane, Mary Ann. "Information, Crisis, Catastrophe." In *The Logics of Television: Essays in Cultural Criticism.* Edited by Patricia Mellencamp.
Bloomington: Indiana University Press, 1990: 222–40.

Druckery, Timothy. "From Reproduction to Technology: Photography
for the Video Generation." *Afterimage* 17, no. 4 (November 1989): 12–
21.

Ellis, David. "Challenger: The Final Words," *Time* (December 24, 1990):
15.

Foucault, Michel. *The Archaeology of Knowledge and Discourse on Language.* Translated by A. M. Sheridan Smith. New York: Pantheon, 1972.

————. *Power/Knowledge: Selected Interviews and Other Writings 1972–
77.* Edited by Colin Gordon. Translated by Colin Gordon, Leo Marshall,
John Mepham, and Kate Soper. New York: Pantheon, 1980.

Freud, Sigmund. *The Interpretation of Dreams.* Translated by James Strachey. New York: Avon Books, [1900] 1965.

Gilmore, Ruth Wilson. "Terror Austerity Race Gender Excess Theater." In
Reading Rodney King/Reading Urban Uprising. Edited by Robert
Gooding-Williams. New York: Routledge, 1993: 23–37.

Hackforth, R. *Plato's Phaedrus.* New York: Cambridge University Press,
1952.

Haraway, Donna. *Primate Visions: Gender, Race, and Nature in the World of Modern Science.* New York: Routledge, 1989.

——. *Simians, Cyborgs, and Women: The Reinvention of Nature.* New York: Routledge, 1991.

Heath, Stephen. *Questions of Cinema.* Bloomington: Indiana University Press, 1981.

——. "Representing Television." In *The Logics of Television: Essays in Cultural Criticism.* Edited by Patricia Mellencamp. Bloomington: Indiana University Press, 1990: 267–302.

Hennelly, Robert, and Jerry Policoff. "JFK: How the Media Assassinated the Real Story." *Village Voice* (March 31, 1992): 33–39.

hooks, bell. *Talking Back: Thinking Feminist, Thinking Black.* Boston: South End Press, 1989.

Hunt, George. "A Remarkable Photographic Feat." *Life* (April 30, 1965): 3.

Hutcheon, Linda. "Beginning to Theorize Postmodernism." *Textual Practice* 1, no. 1 (1987): 10–33.

Jameson, Fredric. *Postmodernism, Or the Cultural Logic of Late Capitalism.* Durham: Duke University Press, 1991.

Keller, Evelyn Fox. *Reflections on Gender and Science.* New Haven: Yale University Press, 1985.

Kern, Stephen. *The Culture of Time and Space: 1880–1918.* Cambridge: Harvard University Press, 1983.

Knight, Christopher. "The Persistent Observer." In *25 Years of Space Photography.* Pasadena: Baxter Art Gallery, California Institute of Technology, 1985: 8–19.

Kranish, Michael. "Ad on Challenger Disaster Creates an Uproar in N.H." *Boston Globe* (January 11, 1996).

Krauss, Rosalind. "Sculpture in the Expanded Field." In *The Anti-Aesthetic: Essays on Postmodern Culture.* Edited by Hal Foster. Port Townsend, WA: Bay Press, 1983: 31–42.

Lippard, Lucy. "Moving Targets/Moving Out." In *Art in the Public Interest.* Edited by Arlene Raven. Ann Arbor: University of Michigan Press, 1989: 209–28.

Lyman, Peter. "The Politics of Anger: On Silence, Ressentiment, and Political Speech." *Socialist Review* 57 (May/June 1989): 55–74.

Lyotard, Jean-Francois. *The Postmodern Condition: A Report on Knowledge.* Translated by Geoff Bennington and Brian Massumi. Minneapolis: University of Minnesota, 1979.

MacCannell, Dean. *The Tourist: A New Theory of the Leisure Class.* New York: Schocken Books, 1976.

Marder, Elissa. "*Blade Runner's* Moving Still." *Camera Obscura* 27 (September 1991): 89–107.

Martin, Luther, Huck Gutman, and Patrick Hutton, eds. *Technologies of the Self: A Seminar with Michel Foucault.* Amherst: University of Massachusetts Press, 1988.

McGrath, Roberta. "Medical Police." *Ten.8* 14 (1984): 13–18.

Mellencamp, Patricia. "TV Time and Catastrophe, or beyond the Pleasure Principle of Television." In *The Logics of Television: Essays in Cultural Criticism.* Edited by Patricia Mellencamp. Bloomington: Indiana University Press, 1990: 240–66.

———. *Indiscretions: Avant-Garde Film, Video, & Feminism.* Bloomington: Indiana University Press, 1990.

Minh-ha, Trinh T. "Documentary Is/Not a Name." *October* no. 52 (Spring 1990): 77–100.

Mitchell, W. J. T. "From CNN to *JFK:* Paranoia, Melodrama, and American Mass Media in 1991." *Afterimage* (May 1992): 13–17.

Mydans, Seth. "With Few Witnesses, Videos Are Crucial in Beating Trial." *New York Times* (September 6, 1993): 6.

Neale, Steve. *Cinema and Technology: Image, Sound, Colour.* Bloomington: Indiana University Press, 1985.

Nichols, Bill. *Representing Reality: Issues and Concepts in Documentary.* Bloomington: Indiana University Press, 1991.

Nietzsche, Friedrich. *On the Genealogy of Morals.* Translated by Walter Kaufmann and R. J. Hollingdale. New York: Vintage, [1887] 1967.

Nilsson, Lennart. "Drama of Life before Birth." *Life* (April 30, 1965).

———. "The First Days of Creation." *Life* (August 1990).

Nilsson, Lennart, with Mirjam Furuhjelm, Axel Ingelman-Sundberg, and Claes Wirsen. *A Child Is Born.* New York: Dell, 1966.

Nilsson, Lennart, and Jan Lindberg. *Behold Man: A Photographic Journey of Discovery inside the Body.* Boston: Little, Brown, 1973.

Petchesky, Rosalind Pollack. "Foetal Images: The Power of Visual Culture in the Politics of Reproduction." In *Reproductive Technologies: Gender, Motherhood and Medicine.* Edited by Michelle Stanworth. Minneapolis: University of Minnesota Press, 1985: 57–80.

Pomasanoff, Alex. *The Invisible World.* Boston: Houghton Mifflin, 1981.

Rogin, Michael. *Ronald Reagan: The Movie.* Berkeley: University of California Press, 1987.

———. "Body and Soul Murder: *JFK.*" In *Media Spectacles.* Edited by Marjorie Garber, Jann Matlock, and Rebecca Walkowitz. New York: Routledge, 1993: 3–22.

Rosler, Martha. "Image Simulations, Computer Manipulations: Some Considerations." *Afterimage* 17, no. 4 (November 1989): 7–11.

Scarry, Elaine. *The Body in Pain: The Making and Unmaking of the World.* New York: Oxford University Press, 1985.

Scott, Joan. "Experience." In *Feminists Theorize the Political.* Edited by Judith Butler and Joan Scott. New York: Routledge, 1992: 22–40.

Sekula, Allan. "On the Invention of Photographic Meaning." In *Thinking Photography.* Edited by Victor Burgin. London: Macmillan, 1982: 84–109.

———. "The Body and the Archive." *October* 39 (Winter 1986): 3–64.

Sobchack, Vivian. "Inscribing Ethical Space: Ten Propositions on Death, Representation, and Documentary." *Quarterly Review of Film Studies* (Fall 1984): 283–300.

———. *The Address of the Eye: A Phenomenology of Film Experience.* Princeton: Princeton University Press, 1992.

———. "The Scene of the Screen: Envisioning Cinematic and Electronic 'Presence.' " In *Materialities of Communications.* Edited by Hans Ulrich Gumbrecht and Karl Ludwig Pfeiffer. Palo Alto: Stanford University Press, 1992.

Sochurek, Howard. "Medicine's New Vision." *National Geographic* (January 1987): 2–41.

Sontag, Susan. *On Photography.* New York: Delta, 1977.

Spillers, Hortense. "Mama's Baby, Papa's Maybe: An American Grammar Book." *Diacritics* (Summer 1987): 65–81.

Stabile, Carol. "Shooting the Mother: Fetal Photography and the Politics of Disappearance." *Camera Obscura* 28 (January 1992): 179–205.

Stepan, Nancy Leys. "Race and Gender: The Role of Analogy in Science." *ISIS* 77 (1986): 261–77.

Stepan, Nancy Leys, and Sander L. Gilman. "Appropriating the Idioms of Science: The Rejection of Scientific Racism." In *The Bounds of Race: Perspectives on Hegemony and Resistance.* Edited by Dominick LaCapra. Ithaca: Cornell University Press, 1991: 72–103.

Stolley, Richard. "The Greatest Home Movie Ever Made." *Esquire* (November 1973): 133–35, 262–63.

Tagg, John. *The Burden of Representation: Essays on Photographies and Histories.* London: Macmillan, 1988.

Taussig, Michael. *Mimesis and Alterity: A Particular History of the Senses.* New York: Routledge, 1993.

Van Biema, David. "Master of an 'Unbelievable, Invisible World.' " *Life* (August 1990): 44–46.

Vasseleu, Cathryn. "Life Itself." In *Cartographies: Poststructuralism and the Mapping of Bodies and Spaces.* Edited by Rosalyn Diprose and Robyn Ferrell. North Sydney: Allen & Unwin, 1991: 55–64.

Wark, McKenzie. *Virtual Geography.* Bloomington: Indiana University Press, 1994.

White, Hayden. *Metahistory: The Historical Imagination in Nineteenth-Century Europe.* Baltimore: Johns Hopkins University Press, 1973.

———. *Tropics of Discourse: Essays in Cultural Criticism.* Baltimore: Johns Hopkins University Press, 1978.

———. "The Narrativization of Real Events." *Critical Inquiry* 7, no. 4 (Summer 1981): 793–98.

———. *The Content of the Form: Narrative Discourse and Historical Representation.* Baltimore: Johns Hopkins University Press, 1987.

———. "Historiography and Historiophoty." *American Historical Review* 93, no. 5 (December 1988): 1193–99.

Williams, Raymond. *Television: Technology and Cultural Form.* New York: Schocken Books, 1974.

Memory

Adorno, Theodor. "What Does Coming to Terms with the Past Mean?" In *Bitburg in Moral and Political Perspective.* Edited by Geoffrey Hartman. Bloomington: Indiana University Press, 1986: 114–29.

Berger, John. "Ways of Remembering." *Camerawork* 10 (July 1978).

Bergson, Henri. *Matter and Memory.* Translated by Nancy Margaret Paul and W. Scott Palmer. New York: Zone Books [1910] 1988.

Bodnar, John. *Remaking America: Public Memory, Commemoration, and Patriotism in the Twentieth Century.* Princeton: Princeton University Press, 1992.

Bommes, Michael, and Patrick Wright. " 'Charms of Residence': The Public and the Past." In *Making Histories: Studies in History-Writing and Politics.* Edited by Richard Johnson, Gregor McLennan, Bill Schwartz, and David Sutton. London: Hutchinson, 1982: 253–301.

Brown, Roger, and James Kulik. "Flashbulb Memories." In *Memory Observed: Remembering in Natural Contexts.* Edited by Ulric Neisser. San Francisco: W. H. Freeman, 1982: 23–40.

Burke, Peter. "History as Social Memory." In *Memory.* Edited by Thomas Butler. New York: Basil Blackwell, 1989.

Butler, Thomas, ed. *Memory.* New York: Basil Blackwell, 1989.

Caruth, Cathy. "Unclaimed Experience: Trauma and the Possibility of History." *Yale French Studies,* no. 79 (1991): 181–92.

———, ed. *Trauma: Explorations in Memory.* Baltimore: Johns Hopkins University Press, 1995.

Casey, Edward S. "Keeping the Past in Mind." In *Descriptions.* Edited by

Don Ihde and Hugh Silverman. Albany: State University of New York Press, 1985: 36–56.

Clark, Mary T. *Augustine of Hippo: Selected Writings.* Ramsey, NJ: Paulist Press, 1984.

Connerton, Paul. *How Societies Remember.* New York: Cambridge University Press, 1989.

Crary, Jonathan. "Spectacle, Attention, Counter-Memory." *October* 50 (Fall 1989): 97–107.

Deleuze, Gilles. *Bergsonism.* Translated by Hugh Tomlinson and Barbara Habberjam. New York: Zone Books [1966] 1988.

Derrida, Jacques. *Memoires: For Paul de Man.* Translated by Cecile Lindsay, Jonathan Culler, Eduardo Cadava, and Peggy Kamuf. New York: Columbia University Press, 1989.

Eco, Umberto. "Architecture and Memory." *Via* 8 (1986): 88–94.

Fentress, James, and Chris Wickham. *Social Memory.* Oxford, England: Blackwell, 1992.

Flax, Jane. "Re-Membering the Selves: Is the Repressed Gendered?" *Michigan Quarterly Review* 26, no. 1 (Winter 1987): 92–110.

Foote, Kenneth. "To Remember and Forget: Archives, Memory, and Culture." *American Archivist* 53 (Summer 1990): 378–92.

Foucault, Michel. "Film and Popular Memory: An Interview with Michel Foucault." Translated by Martin Jordan. *Radical Philosophy* 11 (1975): 24–29.

Freud, Sigmund. "Screen Memories." In *The Standard Edition of the Complete Psychological Works of Sigmund Freud. Vol. 3.* Translated by James Strachey. London: Hogarth Press, [1899] 1962: 301–22.

———. "Mourning and Melancholia." In *The Standard Edition of the Complete Psychological Works of Sigmund Freud, Vol.14.* Translated by James Strachey. London: Hogarth, 1917: 243–58.

Frisch, Michael. "American History and the Structures of Collective Memory: A Modest Exercise in Empirical Iconography." *The Journal of American History* 75, no. 4 (March 1989): 1130–55.

Fussell, Paul. *The Great War and Modern Memory.* New York: Oxford University Press, 1975.

Halbwachs, Maurice. *The Collective Memory.* Translated by Francis J. Ditter, Jr. and Vida Yazdi Ditter. New York: Harper & Row, 1980.

———. *On Collective Memory.* Translated and edited by Lewis Coser. Chicago: University of Chicago Press, [1952] 1992.

Herlihy, David. "Am I a Camera? Other Reflections on Films and History." *American Historical Review* 93, no. 5 (December 1988): 1186–92.

Hutton, Patrick. "The Art of Memory Reconceived: From Rhetoric to Psychoanalysis." *Journal of the History of Ideas* 48, no. 3 (July–September 1987): 371–92.

———. "Collective Memory and Collective Mentalities: The Halswachs-Aries Connection." *Historical Reflections/Reflexions Historiques* 15, no. 2 (1988): 311–22.

———. *History as an Art of Memory.* Hanover, NH: University of Vermont, 1993.

Huyssen, Andreas. *Twilight Memories: Marking Time in a Culture of Amnesia.* New York: Routledge, 1995.

Jacobus, Mary. "Freud's Mnemonic: Women, Screen Memories, and Feminist Nostalgia." *Michigan Quarterly Review* 26, no. 1 (Winter 1987): 117–39.

Johnson, George. *In the Palaces of Memory: How We Build the Worlds Inside Our Heads.* New York: Vintage Books, 1991.

Johnson, Richard, Gregor McLennan, Bill Schwartz, and David Sutton, eds. *Making Histories: Studies in History-Writing and Politics.* London: Hutchinson, 1982.

Kaes, Anton. *From Hitler to Heimat: The Return of History as Film.* Cambridge: Harvard University Press, 1989.

Kaha, C. W. "Memory as Conversation." *Communication* 11, no. 2 (1989): 115–22.

Kammen, Michael. *Mystic Chords of Memory: The Transformation of Tradition in American Culture.* New York: Alfred Knopf, 1991.

Katriel, Tamar. "Sites of Memory: Discourses of the Past in Israeli Pioneering Settlement Museums." *Quarterly Journal of Speech* 80 (February 1994): 1–20.

Knapp, Steven. "Collective Memory and the Actual Past." *Representations* 26 (Spring 1989): 123–49.

Kruger, Barbara, and Phil Mariani, eds. *Remaking History.* Seattle: Bay Press, 1989.

Kuchler, Susanne, and Walter Melion. *Images of Memory: On Remembering and Representation.* Washington, D.C.: Smithsonian Institution Press, 1991.

Kundera, Milan. *The Book of Laughter and Forgetting.* Translated by Michael Henry Heim. New York: Penguin, 1980.

Lang, Kurt, and Gladys Engel Lang. "Collective Memory and the News." *Communication* 11, no. 2 (1989): 123–39.

Levi, Primo. "The Memory of Offense." In *Bitburg in Moral and Political Perspective.* Edited by Geoffrey Hartman. Bloomington: Indiana University Press, 1986: 130–37.

Lipsitz, George. *Time Passages: Collective Memory and American Popular Culture.* Minneapolis: University of Minnesota Press, 1990.

Liss, Andrea. "Contours of Naming: The Identity Card Project and the Tower of Faces at the United States Holocaust Memorial Museum." *Public* 8 (1993): 108–34.

Locke, Don. *Memory.* London: Macmillan, 1971.

Loftus, Elizabeth, Mahzarin Banaji, Jonathan Schooler, and Rachael Foster. "Who Remembers What? Gender Difference in Memory." *Michigan Quarterly Review* 26, no. 1 (Winter 1987): 64–85.

Lowenthal, David. "The Timeless Past: Some Anglo-American Historical Preconceptions." *The Journal of American History* 75, no. 4 (March 1989): 1263–80.

Luria, A. R. *The Mind of a Mnemonist.* Translated by Lynn Solotaroff. Cambridge: Harvard University Press, 1968.

———. *The Neuropsychology of Memory.* Translated by Basil Haigh. Washington, D.C.: V. H. Winston, 1976.

Maier, Charles S. *The Unmasterable Past: History, Holocaust, and German National Identity.* Cambridge: Harvard University Press, 1988.

Middleton, David, and Derek Edwards, eds. *Collective Remembering.* Newbury Park, CA: Sage, 1990.

Mink, Louis O. "Everyman His or Her Own Annalist." *Critical Inquiry* 7, no. 4 (Summer 1981): 777–83.

———. *Historical Understanding.* Edited by Brian Fay, Eugene O. Golub, and Richard T. Vann. Ithaca: Cornell University Press, 1987.

Morrison, Toni. *Beloved.* New York: Alfred Knopf, 1987.

———. "The Site of Memory." In *Out There: Marginalization and Contemporary Cultures.* Edited by Russell Ferguson, Martha Gever, Trinh T. Minh-ha, and Cornel West. Cambridge: MIT Press, 1990: 299–305.

Neisser, Ulric, ed. *Memory Observed: Remembering in Natural Contexts.* San Francisco: W. H. Freeman, 1982.

Neisser, Ulric, and Nicole Harsch. "Phantom Flashbulbs: False Recollections of Hearing the News About *Challenger.*" In *Affect and Accuracy in Recall: Studies of "Flashbulb" Memories.* Edited by Eugene Winograd and Ulric Neisser. New York: Cambridge University Press, 1992: 9–31.

Neisser, Ulric, and Robyn Fivush, eds. *The Remembering Self: Construction and Accuracy in the Self-Narrative.* New York: Cambridge University Press, 1994.

Nerone, John. "Professional History and Social Memory." *Communication* 11, no. 2, 1989: 89–104.

Nietzsche, Friedrich. *The Use and Abuse of History.* Translated by Adrian Collins. Indianapolis: Bobb-Merrill Educational Publishing, [1874] 1957.

Nora, Pierre. "Between Memory and History: Les Lieux de memoire." *Representations* 26 (Spring 1989): 7–25.

O'Connor, John E. "History in Images/Images in History: Reflections on the

Importance of Film and Television Study for an Understanding of the Past." *American Historical Review* 93, no. 5 (December 1988): 1200–09.

Olander, William, ed. *The Art of Memory/The Loss of History.* New York: New Museum of Contemporary Art, 1985.

Parkin, Alan J. *Memory and Amnesia: An Introduction.* Oxford: Basil Blackwell, 1987.

Penley, Constance. "Spaced Out: Remembering Christa McAuliffe." *Camera Obscura* 29 (1993): 178–213.

Perlman, Michael. *Imaginal Memory and the Place of Hiroshima.* Albany: State University of New York Press, 1988.

Phillips, James. "Distance, Absence, and Nostalgia." In *Descriptions.* Edited by Don Ihde and Hugh Silverman. Albany: State University of New York Press, 1985: 64–75.

Popular Memory Group. "Popular Memory: Theory, Politics, Method." In *Making Histories: Studies in History-Writing and Politics.* Edited by Richard Johnson, Gregor McLennan, Bill Schwartz, and David Sutton. London: Hutchinson, 1982: 205–52.

Proust, Marcel. *Remembrance of Things Past.* Translated by C. K. Scott Moncrieff and Terence Kilmartin. New York: Vintage, [1913–1927] 1982.

Rabinowitz, Paula. "Wreckage Upon Wreckage: History, Documentary and the Ruins of Memory." *History and Theory* (1993): 119–37.

Roediger, Henry L. "Memory Metaphors in Cognitive Psychology." *Memory and Cognition* 8, no. 3, 1980: 231–46.

Rogin, Michael. " 'Make My Day!': Spectacle as Amnesia in Imperial Politics." *Representations* 29 (Winter 1990): 99–123.

Rosenstone, Robert. "History in Images/History in Words: Reflections on the Possibility of Really Putting History onto Film." *American Historical Review* 93, no. 5 (December 1988): 1173–85.

———, ed. *Revisioning History: Film and the Construction of a New Past.* Princeton: Princeton University Press, 1995.

Roth, Michael S. "Remembering Forgetting: Maladies de la Memoire in Nineteenth-Century France." *Representations* 26 (Spring 1989): 49–68.

Santner, Eric. *Stranded Objects: Mourning, Memory, and Film in Postwar Germany.* Ithaca: Cornell University Press, 1990.

Schudson, Michael. "The Present in the Past versus the Past in the Present." *Communication* 11, no. 2 (1989): 105–14.

———. "Ronald Reagan Misremembered." In *Collective Remembering.* Edited by David Middleton and Derek Edwards. Newbury Park, CA: Sage, 1990: 108–19.

———. *Watergate in American History: How We Remember, Forget, and Reconstruct the Past.* New York: Basic Books, 1992.

Schwartz, Barry. "The Social Context of Commemoration: A Study in Collective Memory." *Social Forces* 61, no. 2 (December 1982): 374–402.

———. "The Recovery of Masada: A Study in Collective Memory." *The Sociological Quarterly* 27, no. 2 (1986): 147–64.

———. "The Reconstruction of Abraham Lincoln." In *Collective Remembering*. Edited by David Middleton and Derek Edwards. Newbury Park, CA: Sage, 1990: 81–107.

Silverman, Kaja. "Back to the Future." *Camera Obscura* 27 (September 1991): 109–32.

Sorabji, Richard. *Aristotle on Memory*. Providence: Brown University Press, 1972.

Spence, Jonathan D. *The Memory Palace of Matteo Ricci*. New York: Viking Penguin, 1984.

Taylor, Julie. "Body Memories: Aide-Memoires and Collective Amnesia in the Wake of Argentine Terror." In *Body Politics: Disease, Desire, and the Family*. Edited by Michael Ryan and Avery Gordon. Boulder: Westview, 1994: 192–203.

Terdiman, Richard. "Deconstructing Memory: On Representing the Past and Theorizing Culture in France Since the Revolution." *Diacritics* (Winter 1985): 13–36.

———. *Present Past: Modernity and the Memory Crisis*. Ithaca: Cornell University Press, 1993.

Thelen, David. "Memory and American History." *The Journal of American History* 75, no. 4 (March 1989): 1117–29.

Tonkin, Elizabeth. "Memory Makes Us: We Make Memory." In *Narrating Our Pasts: The Social Construction of Oral History*. Edited by Elizabeth Tonkin. New York: Cambridge University Press, 1992: 97–112.

Toplin, Robert Brent. "The Filmmaker as Historian." *American Historical Review* 93, no. 5 (December 1988): 1210–27.

Tribe, Keith. "History and the Production of Memories." *Screen* 18, no. 4 (Winter 1977–78): 9–22.

Turim, Maureen. *Flashbacks in Film: Memory and History*. New York: Routledge, 1989.

Uzelac, Ellen. "The Public Eye of Mourning." *Common Boundary* (November/December 1994): 39–43.

Van der Kolk, Bessel, and Onno van der Hart. "The Intrusive Past: The Flexibility of Memory and the Engraving of Trauma." In *Trauma: Explorations in Memory*. Edited by Cathy Caruth. Baltimore: Johns Hopkins University Press, 1995: 158–82.

Yates, Frances. *Giordano Bruno and the Hermetic Tradition*. Chicago: University of Chicago Press, 1964.

————. *The Art of Memory.* Chicago: University of Chicago Press, 1966.

Zelizer, Barbie. *Covering the Body: The Kennedy Assassination, the Media, and the Shaping of Collective Memory.* Chicago: University of Chicago Press, 1992.

————. "Reading the Past Against the Grain: The Shape of Memory Studies." *Critical Studies in Mass Communication* 12, no. 2 (June 1995): 214–39.

Memorials

Adams, William. "Remembering Vietnam." *Democracy* 3, no. 2 (Spring 1983): 73–77.

Allen, Thomas. *Offerings at the Wall: Artifacts from the Vietnam Veterans Memorial Collection.* Atlanta: Turner Publishing, 1995.

Aoki, Elizabeth. "Nurse Killed in Vietnam Is Honored." *Washington Post* (June 21, 1989).

Ashabranner, Brent. *Always to Remember: The Story of the Vietnam Veterans Memorial.* New York: G. P. Putnam's Sons, 1988.

Associated Press. "38 Living Veterans May Be on Memorial." *San Jose Mercury News* (February 15, 1991).

Ayres Jr., B. Drummond. "Solemn Roll-Call Floats over Vietnam Memorial." *New York Times* (November 11, 1992): A8.

Baker, Kenneth. "Andre in Retrospect." *Art in America* (April 1980): 88–94.

Barker, Karlyn. "At the Wall, Sympathy and Sorrow." *Washington Post* (November 11, 1989).

Bartimus, Tad. "New Battle Breaks Out at Little Bighorn Site." *San Jose Mercury News* (August 7, 1990): 2A.

Battiata, Mary. "Remembrance on a Train." *Washington Post* (November 10, 1984): A1, A6.

Beardsley, John. "Personal Sensibilities in Public Places." *Artforum* (Summer 1981): 43–45.

Bee, John D. "Eros and Thantos: An Analysis of the Vietnam Memorial." In *Vietnam Images: War and Representation.* Edited by Jeffrey Walsh and James Aulich. London: Macmillan, 1989: 196–204.

Berdahl, Daphne. "Voices at the Wall: Discourses of Self, History and National Identity at the Vietnam Veterans Memorial." *History & Memory* 6, no. 2 (Fall/Winter 1994): 88–118.

Blair, Carole, Marsha S. Jeppeson, and Enrico Pucci, Jr. "Public Memorializing in Postmodernity: The Vietnam Veterans Memorial as Prototype." *Quarterly Journal of Speech* 77, no. 3 (August 1991): 263–88.

Blake, Casey Nelson. "An Atmosphere of Effrontery: Richard Serra, *Tilted Arc,* and the Crisis of Public Art." In *The Power of Culture: Critical*

Essays in American History. Edited by Richard Wightman Fox and T. J. Jackson Lears. Chicago: University of Chicago Press, 1993: 247–89.

Bombeck, Erma. "The Wall of Names, the Call for Peace." *Detroit Free Press* (July 4, 1989).

Bousian, Mark. "Women's Viet Memorial Dedicated." *San Francisco Chronicle* (November 12, 1993): A1, A17.

Braithwaite, Charles. "Cultural Communication among Vietnam Veterans: Ritual, Myth, and Social Drama." In *Cultural Legacies of Vietnam: Uses of the Past in the Present.* Edited by Peter Ehrenhaus and Richard Morris. Norwood, NJ: Ablex Publishing, 1990: 145–70.

Brisbane, Arthur S. "A Cycle of War and Remembrance." *Washington Post* (November 8, 1984): A1, A4.

———. "President Leads Tribute to Vietnam Veterans." *Washington Post* (November 12, 1984): A1, A14.

Brown, Melissa. "Memorials, Not Monuments." *Progressive Architecture* (September 1985): 43–45.

Brownstein, Andrew. "24 Years Later, Two Finally Are Linked by Loss." *Washington Post* (November 12, 1992): A1, A16.

Broyles, William, Jr. "Remembering a War We Want to Forget." *Newsweek* (November 22, 1982): 82–83.

———. "A Ritual for Saying Goodbye." *U.S. News & World Report* (November 10, 1986).

Buckley, Christopher. "The Wall." *Esquire* (September 1985): 61–73.

Bumiller, Elizabeth. "The Memorial, Mirror of Vietnam." *Washington Post* (November 9, 1984).

Bunting, Eve. *The Wall.* New York: Clarion Books, 1990.

Butterfield, Fox. " 'Silent March' on Guns Talks Loudly: 40,000 Pairs of Shoes, and All Empty." *New York Times* (September 21, 1994): A18.

Capasso, Nicholas. "Vietnam Veterans Memorial." In *The Critical Edge: Controversy in Recent American Architecture.* Edited by Tod Marder. Cambridge: MIT Press, 1985: 189–202.

———. "Constructing the Past: Contemporary Commemorative Sculpture." *Sculpture* (November/December 1990): 56–63.

Capps, Lisa. "The Memorial as Symbol and Agent of Healing." In *The Vietnam Reader.* Edited by Walter Capps. New York: Routledge, 1991: 272–89.

Carhart, Tom. "Insulting Vietnam Vets." *New York Times* (October 24, 1981).

Carlson, A. Cheree, and John Hocking. "Strategies of Redemption at the Vietnam Veterans Memorial." *Western Journal of Speech Communication* (Summer 1988) 52: 203–15.

Carlson, Peter. "Back to the Wall." *Washington Post Magazine* (November 6, 1988).

Christopher, Renny. "I Never Really Became a Woman until . . . I Saw the Wall." *Sub/Versions* Working Paper 9, University of California, Santa Cruz, 1992.

Chua-Eoan, Howard G., and Deborah Papier. "Along the Wall, Gifts from the Heart." *People* (June 1, 1992): 109–11.

Clardy, Jim. "Warehouse Is Giant Scrapbook for Mementoes Left at Vietnam Wall." *Washington Times* (May 28, 1990): D1.

Clay, Grady. "Vietnam's Aftermath: Sniping at the Memorial." *Landscape Architecture* (March 1982): 54–56.

Clines, Francis. "Tribute to Vietnam Dead: Words, a Wall." *New York Times* (November 11, 1982): 1.

Coleman, Jonathan. "First She Looks Inward." *Time* (November 6, 1989): 90–94.

Conroy, Sarah Booth. "Korean War Memorial Rejected." *Washington Post* (July 26, 1991).

———. "Korean War Memorial Design Fails Again." *Washington Post* (October 25, 1991): B2.

———. "New Revision for Korean Veterans Memorial." *Washington Post* (March 6, 1992): B2.

Corn, David, and Jefferson Morley. "Beltway Bandits: The War on the Wall." *The Nation* (June 4, 1988): 780.

Danto, Arthur C. "The Vietnam Veterans Memorial." *The Nation* (August 31, 1985): 152–55.

———. "Gettysburg." *Grand Street* (Spring 1987): 98–116.

Doubek, Robert. "The Story of the Vietnam Veterans Memorial." *The Retired Officer* (November 1983): 17–24.

Dowling, Carrie. "Private Visits to Wall Reunite Two Veterans." *Washington Times* (May 28, 1985).

Ehrhart, W. D. "Midnight at the Vietnam Veterans Memorial," *Journal of American Culture* 16, no. 3 (Fall 1993): 109.

Ellis, Caron Schwartz. "So Old Soldiers Don't Fade Away: The Vietnam Veterans Memorial." *Journal of American Culture* 15, no. 2 (Summer 1992): 25–30.

Ellis, David. "They Also Served." *People* (May 31, 1993): 90–91.

Ezell, Edward Clinton. *Reflections on the Wall: The Vietnam Veterans Memorial*. Harrisburg, PA: Stackpole, 1987.

Fish, Lydia. *The Last Firebase: A Guide to the Vietnam Veterans Memorial*. Shippensburg, PA: White Mane, 1987.

Foley, Jack. "Wall Pays Tribute to Indians Killed in Vietnam." *San Jose Mercury News* (May 21, 1992): 4B.

Forgery, Benjamin. "Washington's Monumental Excess." *Washington Post* (June 16, 1990): B1, B9.

―――. "Battle Won for War Memorials: CFA Approves Women's Vietnam, Black Patriots Designs." *Washington Post* (September 20, 1991): B1.

―――. "The Gash That Healed." *Washington Post* (November 7, 1992): G1.

―――. "One Monument Too Many." *Washington Post* (November 6, 1993): D1, D7.

Forster, Kurt W., ed. "Monument/Memory." *Oppositions* 25 (Fall 1982).

Fox, Terrance. "The Vietnam Veterans Memorial: Ideological Implications." In *Vietnam Images: War and Representation*. Edited by Jeffrey Walsh and James Aulich. London: Macmillan, 1989: 211–20.

Franklin, Ben A. "143 Vietnam Memorials, Vast and Small, Rising around Nation." *New York Times* (November 9, 1986): 26.

Friedman, Thomas L. "Clinton, in Vietnam War Tribute, Finds Old Wound Is Slow to Heal." *New York Times* (June 1, 1993): A1, A10.

Gamarekian, Barbara. "Design Sought for New Vietnam Monument." *New York Times* (August 20, 1990): A16.

Gans, Adrienne. "The War and Peace of the Vietnam Memorials." *American Imago* 44, no. 4 (Winter 1987): 315–29.

Glassberg, David. "Monuments and Memories." *American Quarterly* 43, no. 1 (March 1991): 143–56.

Goldberger, Paul. "Vietnam Memorial: Questions of Architecture." *New York Times* (October 7, 1982).

Graves, Louise. *Let Us Remember: The Vietnam Veterans Memorial*. Washington, D.C.: Parks and History Association, 1984.

Griswold, Charles L. "The Vietnam Veterans Memorial and the Washington Mall: Philosophical Thoughts on Political Iconography." *Critical Inquiry* 12 (Summer 1986): 688–719.

Grunwald, Lisa. "Facing the Wall." *Life* (November 1992): 29–36.

Guido, Michelle. "A Wall Divided by Commercialism." *San Jose Mercury News* (March 14, 1991): 1A.

Haines, Harry. "What Kind of War? An Analysis of the Vietnam Veterans Memorial." *Critical Studies in Mass Communication* 3, no. 1 (March 1986): 1–20.

―――. "The Vietnam Veterans Memorial: Authority and Gender Representation in Cultural Representation." In *Vietnam Images: War and Representation*. Edited by Jeffrey Walsh and James Aulich. London: Macmillan, 1989: 205–10.

Hart, Frederick. "Letter to the Editor." *Art in America* (November 1983): 5.

―――. "An Interview with Frederick Hart." In *Unwinding the Vietnam*

War: From War into Peace. Edited by Reese Williams. Seattle: Real Comet Press, 1987: 273–74.

Heiferman, Marvin. "One Nation, Chiseled in Pictures: The Monumental Nature of American Photography." In "Lee Friedlander: American Monuments." *The Archive* 25 (1989).

Hess, Elizabeth. "A Tale of Two Memorials." *Art in America* (April 1983): 121–26.

———. "Vietnam: Memorials of Misfortune." In *Unwinding the Vietnam War: From War into Peace.* Edited by Reese Williams. Seattle: Real Comet Press, 1987: 262–79.

Hoekema, David. "A Wall for Remembering." *Commonweal* (July 15, 1983): 397–99.

Horowitz, Rick. "Maya Lin's Angry Objections." *Washington Post* (July 7, 1982): B1, B6.

Howett, Catherine. "The Vietnam Veterans Memorial: Public Art and Politics." *Landscape* 28, no. 2 (1985): 1–9.

Hubbard, William. "A Meaning for Monuments." *The Public Interest* 74 (Winter 1984): 17–30.

Huyssen, Andreas. "Monument and Memory in a Postmodern Age." *Yale Journal of Criticism* 6, no. 2 (Fall 1993): 249–61.

Ishihara, Masaie. "The Memories of War and the Role of Okinawa in the Promotion of War Peace." Paper presented at "The Politics of Remembering the Asia/Pacific War," East-West Center, Honolulu, September 1995.

Katakis, Michael. *The Vietnam Veterans Memorial.* New York: Crown, 1988.

Kelly, Michael. "Where Perot Exhibits a Lifetime of Memories." *New York Times* (June 20, 1992): 8.

Kennedy, J. Michael. "Symbols of the Slaughter." *Los Angeles Times* (September 7, 1994): B1, B4.

LaFraniere, Sharon, and Priscilla Painton. "Ex-Soldiers Search for Familar Faces." *Washington Post* (November 12, 1984): A1, A14.

Landers, Ann. "Name on 'The Wall' Doesn't Comfort Mother." *Oakland Tribune* (December 10, 1989).

Lang, John. "A Memorial Wall That Healed Our Wounds." *U.S. News & World Report* (November 21, 1983).

Life Magazine. "A Monument to Infamy." (March 1988): 6.

Lin, Maya Ying. "An Interview with Maya Lin." In *Unwinding the Vietnam War: From War into Peace.* Edited by Reese Williams. Seattle: Real Comet Press, 1987: 271–72.

Lindberg, Tod. "Of Arms, Men and Monuments." *Commentary* 78 (October 1984): 51–56.

Linenthal, Edward. *Sacred Ground: Americans and Their Battlefields.* Urbana: University of Illinois Press, 1991.

————. "The Boundaries of Memory: The United States' Holocaust Memorial Museum." *American Quarterly* 46, no. 3 (September 1994): 406–33.

Loose, Cindy. "Tears in the Footsteps of the Fallen." *Washington Post* (September 21, 1994): B1, B5.

Lopes, Saul, ed. *The Wall: Images and Offerings from the Vietnam Veterans Memorial.* New York: Collins Publishers, 1987.

Marling, Karal Ann, and John Wetenhall. "The Sexual Politics of Memory: The Vietnam Women's Memorial Project and 'The Wall.' " *Prospects* 14 (1989): 341–72.

————. *Iwo Jima: Monuments, Memories and the American Hero.* Cambridge: Harvard University Press, 1991.

Mayo, James. *War Memorials as Political Landscape: The American Experience and Beyond.* New York: Praeger, 1988.

McConnell, Frank. "A Name for Loss: Memorials of Vietnam." *Commonweal* (August 9, 1985): 441–42.

McDonnell, Larry. "America's Wailing Wall." *Asbury Park Press* (October 5, 1986).

McIntyre, Mike. "Gifts of Grief." *San Diego Union* (May 14, 1989).

McLeod, Mary. "The Battle for the Monument: The Vietnam Veterans Memorial." In *The Experimental Tradition: Essays on Competitions in Architecture.* Edited by Helene Lipstadt. New York: Princeton Architectural Press, 1989.

Meyer, Peter, and editors of *Life,* eds. *The Wall: A Day at the Vietnam Veterans Memorial.* New York: St. Martin's Press, 1993.

Miller, Judith. "Holocaust Museum: A Troubled Start." *New York Times Magazine* (April 22, 1990): 34–48.

Miner, Betsy, and Andrea Stone. " 'The Wall': Reflection of a War Turns 10." *USA Today* (November 6, 1992): 10A.

Mintz, John. "Perot's War: Viet Vets' 'Tombstone.' " *Washington Post* (July 7, 1992): A1, A6.

Morganthau, Tom. "Honoring Vietnam Veterans—At Last." *Newsweek* (November 22, 1982): 80–86.

Morris, Richard. "The Vietnam Veterans Memorial and the Myth of Superiority." In *Cultural Legacies of Vietnam: Uses of the Past in the Present.* Edited by Peter Ehrenhaus and Richard Morris. Norwood, NJ: Ablex Publishing, 1990: 223–28.

National Geographic. "America Remembers: Vietnam Veterans Memorial." 167, no. 5 (May 1985): 552–73.

National Park Service. *Vietnam Veterans Memorial Official Park Guide.*

National Review. "Stop that Monument." (September 18, 1981): 1064.

Newsweek. "Heroes, Past and Present: A Memorial." (July 6, 1987): 52–61.

New York Times. "Mothers of 2 Veterans Angry at Vietnam List." (November 18, 1982).

―――. "The Black Gash of Shame." (April 14, 1985).

―――. "Mementoes at the Vietnam Memorial." (September 9, 1986).

―――. "Vietnam Memorial Gathers Own Collection of Artifacts." (November 10, 1991).

―――. "Vietnam Dead Hailed on Father's Day." (June 22, 1992): A8.

Norman, Michael. "Voices at the Wall." *New York Times Magazine* (May 27, 1990): 15–16.

O'Connor, John J. "A Vietnam Veteran's Healing Mission." *New York Times* (May 27, 1988): B8.

Palmer, Laura. *Shrapnel in the Heart: Letters and Remembrances from the Vietnam Veterans Memorial.* New York: Vintage, 1988.

―――. "15,000 Pieces of History Give Vietnam Wall 'Soul.' " *Seattle Times* (October 29, 1989).

―――. "How to Bandage a War: The Nurses of Vietnam, Still Wounded." *New York Times Magazine* (November 7, 1993): 36–43, 68, 72–73.

Perl, Peter. "A Matter of Honor." *Washington Post Magazine* (October 25, 1992): 16–31.

Pulley, Brett. "Indian-Tribute Plan Sparks a New Battle at Little Bighorn." *Wall Street Journal* (October 15, 1990): 1.

Purdum, Todd. "War in Korea, Fast Receding, Gets a Memorial." *New York Times* (July 28, 1995): A1, A18.

Quay, James. "Epilogue." In *The American Experience in Vietnam: A Reader.* Edited by Grace Sevy. Norman: University of Oklahoma Press, 1989: 300–302.

―――. "Life Liberty, and the Right to Protest." In *The Vietnam Reader.* Edited by Walter Capps. New York: Routledge, 1991: 205–12.

Ragon, Michel. *The Space of Death: A Study of Funerary Architecture, Decoration, and Urbanism.* Translated by Alan Sheridan. Charlottesville: University Press of Virginia, 1983.

Rathbun, Elizabeth. "A Living Museum." *Federal Times* (November 18, 1985).

Ronningen, Judy. "Volunteers Create a Computerized War Memorial." *Oakland Tribune* (November 11, 1991): A1, A9.

Schmitt, Eric. "Female Vietnam Veterans Welcomed Home." *New York Times* (November 12, 1993): A1, A12.

Scott, Grant. "Meditations in Black: The Vietnam Veterans Memorial." *Journal of American Culture* 13, no. 3 (Fall 1990): 37–40.

Scruggs, Jan. *The Wall That Heals*. McLean, Va.: Vietnam Veterans Memorial Fund, 1992.

Scruggs, Jan, and Joel Swerdlow. *To Heal a Nation: The Vietnam Veterans Memorial*. New York: Harper & Row, 1985.

Simmons, John K. "Pilgrimage to the Wall." In *The Vietnam Reader*. Edited by Walter Capps. New York: Routledge, 1991: 253–58.

Slater, Wayne. "Vet Couldn't Forget . . . Became First Casualty of Vietnam Memorial." *Denver Post* (November 11, 1984): 1A, 4A.

Sniffen, Michael. "Mistake Puts Veterans among Vietnam Dead." *San Jose Mercury News* (February 11, 1991).

Sorkin, Michael. "What Happens When a Woman Designs a War Monument?" *Vogue* (May 1983): 120, 122.

Spencer, Duncan. *Facing the Wall: Americans at the Vietnam Veterans Memorial*. London: Macmillan, 1986.

Storr, Robert. " 'Tilted Arc': Enemy of the People?" In *Art in the Public Interest*. Edited by Arlene Raven. Ann Arbor: University of Michigan Press, 1989: 269–86.

————. "Chris Burden." *MoMA Members Quarterly* (Fall 1991): 5.

Strait, Jerry L., and Sandra Strait. *Vietnam War Memorials: An Illustrated Reference to Veterans Tributes Throughout the United States*. Jefferson, N.C.: McFarland, 1988.

Sullivan, Barbara. "A High-Tech Memorial: Computer Chip Lets Families Honor Fallen Veterans." *Daily Californian* (November 12, 1991): 1.

Talk of the Town. "Notes and Comment." *The New Yorker* (March 27, 1989): 33–34.

Tauber, Peter. "Monument Maker." *New York Times Magazine* (February 24, 1991): 49–55.

Thomas, C. David, ed. *As Seen by Both Sides: American and Vietnamese Artists Look at the War*. Boston: University of Massachusetts Press, 1991.

Time. "The Wall's Mistaken Men." (November 23, 1987): 31.

————. "A Memorial Too Many." (June 27, 1988): 25.

United Press International. "Mothers of 2 Veterans Angry at Vietnam List." *New York Times* (November 18, 1982).

Van Buren, Abigail. "Dear Abby: Memorial for a Forgotten War." *San Francisco Chronicle* (January 2, 1989).

Vasari Diary. "Vietnam Memorial War." *Art News* (January 1983).

Vespa, Mary. "His Dream Was to Heal a Nation with the Vietnam Memorial, But Jan Scruggs' Healing Isn't Over Yet." *People* (May 30, 1988): 85–87.

Von Eckardt, Wolf. "The Vietnam Veterans Memorial in Washington." Unpublished paper, 1986.

Wagner-Pacifici, Robin, and Barry Schwartz. "The Vietnam Veterans Memorial: Commemorating a Difficult Past." *American Journal of Sociology* 97, no.2 (September 1991): 376–420.

Walker, Martin. "US Divided over Lessons of History." *Manchester Guardian Weekly* (April 23, 1995): 6.

Walker, Susan. "The Vietnam Veterans Memorial and MARS Dedicated to Keeping Memories Alive." *Stars and Stripes* (January 15, 1990).

Walters, Nolan. "Vendors' War Mars Vietnam Memorial." *San Jose Mercury News* (November 11, 1991): 2A.

Weingarten, Paul. "The Black Wall." *The Chicago Tribune* (April 21, 1985).

Welch, William. "$85,000 in Royalties for Memorial Sculptor." *Washington Post* (November 11, 1987): D1, D6.

Wheeler, John. "Offerings at the Wall." *Washington Post* (September 13, 1992): C3.

Williams, Lorna. "Tears and Tributes." *Military Lifestyle* 19, no. 10 (November/December 1987).

Wolfe, Tom. "Art Disputes War: The Battle of the Vietnam Memorial." *Washington Post* (October 13, 1982): B1–4.

Wye, Deborah. *Committed to Print: Social and Political Themes in Recent American Art.* New York: Museum of Modern Art, 1988.

Young, James E. "Memory and Monument." In *Bitburg in Moral and Political Perspective.* Edited by Geoffrey Hartman. Bloomington: Indiana University Press, 1986: 103–13.

———. "The Biography of a Memorial Icon: Nathan Rapoport's Warsaw Ghetto Monument." *Representations* 26 (Spring 1989): 69–106.

———. "The Counter-Monument: Memory against Itself in Germany Today." *Critical Inquiry* 18, no. 2 (Winter 1992): 267–96.

———. *The Texture of Memory: Holocaust Memorials and Meaning.* New Haven: Yale University Press, 1993.

———, ed. *The Art of Memory: Holocaust Memorials in History.* New York: Jewish Museum, 1994.

Zinsser, William. " 'I Realized Her Tears Were Becoming Part of the Memorial.' " *Smithsonian* (September 1991): 32–43.

War

Adair, Gilbert. *Hollywood's Vietnam.* New York: Proteus, 1981.

Adams, Eddie. "The Tet Photo." In *To Bear Any Burden.* Edited by Al Santoli. New York: E. P. Dutton, 1985: 182–85.

Adams, William. "Still Shooting after All These Years." *Mother Jones* (January 1988): 47–49.

Aksoy, Asu, and Kevin Robins. "Exterminating Angels: Morality, Violence and Technology in the Gulf War." In *Triumph of the Image: The Media's War in the Persian Gulf—A Global Perspective.* Edited by Hamid Mowlana, George Gerbner, and Herbert Schiller. Boulder: Westview Press, 1992: 202–21.

Allen, Henry. "Why We Aren't in Vietnam: Don't Think You've Been to War Just Because You Saw 'Platoon.' " *Washington Post* (January 25, 1987): A25.

Anderegg, Michael, ed. *Inventing Vietnam: The War in Film and Television.* Philadelphia: Temple University Press, 1991.

Arendt, Hannah. "Home to Roost: A Bicentennial Address." *New York Review of Books* 22, no. 11 (June 26, 1976): 4.

Arlen, Michael J. *Living Room War.* New York: Penguin, 1982.

Aufderheide, Pat. "Oliver Stone as Pulp Artist." *Cineaste* 15, no. 4, 1987: 5.

———. "Good Soldiers." In *Seeing through Movies.* Edited by Mark Crispin Miller. New York: Pantheon, 1990: 81–111.

Auster, Albert, and Leonard Quart. *How the War Was Remembered: Hollywood & Vietnam.* New York: Praeger, 1988.

Barra, Allen. "Welcome to the Jungle: Brian De Palma's Dirty Little War." *Village Voice* (August 22, 1989): 37–44.

Baskir, Lawrence M., and William Strauss. "The Vietnam Generation." In *The Wounded Generation: America after Vietnam.* Edited by A. D. Horne. Englewood Cliffs, NJ: Prentice Hall, 1981.

Bayles, Martha. "The Road to *Rambo III:* Hollywood's Visions of Vietnam." *New Republic* (July 18/25, 1988): 30–35.

Becker, Carol. "Men in Suits." *Journal of Urban and Cultural Studies* 2, no. 1 (1991): 93–98.

Bennet, James. "How the Media Missed the Story." In *The Gulf War Reader: History, Documents, Opinions.* Edited by Micah Sifry and Christopher Cerf. New York: Times Books, 1991: 355–67.

Berg, Rick. "Losing Vietnam: Covering the War in an Age of Technology." *Cultural Critique* 3 (Spring 1986): 92–125.

Berg, Rick, and John Carlos Rowe. "The Vietnam War and American Memory." In *The Vietnam War and American Culture.* Edited by Rick Berg and John Carlos Rowe. New York: Columbia University Press, 1991.

Bird, Thomas. "Man and Boy Confront the Images of War." *New York Times* (May 27, 1990): 11, 16.

Bly, Robert. "The Vietnam War and the Erosion of Male Confidence." In *Unwinding the Vietnam War: From War into Peace.* Edited by Reese Williams. Seattle: Real Comet Press, 1987: 161–75.

Boose, Lynda. "Techno-Muscularity and the 'Boy Eternal': From the Quagmire to the Gulf." In *Gendering War Talk*. Edited by Miriam Cooke and Angela Woollacott. Princeton: Princeton University Press, 1993: 67–106.

Brody, Richard, and Richard Morin. "From Vietnam to Iraq: The Great American Syndrome Myth." *Washington Post* (March 31, 1991): B1.

Brown, David. "Triumphant in the Desert, Stricken at Home." *Washington Post* (July 24, 1994): A1, A18.

Broyles, William, Jr. "Why Men Love War." *Esquire* (November 1984): 55–65.

———. *Brothers in Arms: A Journey from War into Peace*. New York: Alfred Knopf, 1986.

Burns, Ken. "The Painful, Essential Images of War." *New York Times* (January 27, 1991).

Caldarola, Victor. "Time and Television War." *Public Culture* 4, no. 2 (Spring 1992): 127–36.

Caputo, Philip. *A Rumor of War*. New York: Holt, Rinehart and Winston, 1977.

Cawley, Leo. "The War about the War: Vietnam Films and American Myth." In *From Hanoi to Hollywood: The Vietnam War in American Film*. Edited by Linda Dittmar and Gene Michaud. New Brunswick: Rutgers University Press, 1990: 69–80.

Ceplair, Larry. "A B-Movie for Middle Class Liberals." *Cineaste* 15, no. 4 (1987): 6.

Cimons, Marlene. "Gulf War Syndrome May Be Contagious, Survey Shows." *Los Angeles Times* (October 21, 1994): A4.

Clark, Michael. "Vietnam: Representations of Self and War." *Wide Angle* 7, no. 4 (1985): 4–11.

———. "Remembering Vietnam." *Cultural Critique* 3 (Spring 1986): 46–78. (Reprinted in *The Vietnam War and American Culture*. Edited by Rick Berg and John Carlos Rowe. New York: Columbia University Press, 1991.

Clausewitz, Carl von. *On War*. Translated by Col. J. J. Graham. New York: Penguin, [1832] 1968.

Cohn, Carol. "Sex and Death in the Rational World of Defense Intellectuals." *Signs* 12, no. 4 (1987): 687–718.

———. "The Language of the Gulf War." *Center Review* (Center for Psychological Studies in the Nuclear Age) 5, no. 2 (Fall 1991): 1–15.

———. "Wars, Wimps, and Women: Talking Gender and Thinking War." In *Gendering War Talk*. Edited by Miriam Cooke and Angela Woollacott. Princeton: Princeton University Press, 1993: 227–46.

Comber, Michael, and Margaret O'Brien. "Evading the War: The Politics of the Hollywood Vietnam Film." *History: The Journal of the Historical Association* 73 (June 1988): 248–60.

Cooke, Miriam. "Postmodern Wars: Phallomilitary Spectacles in the DTO." *Journal of Urban and Cultural Studies* 2, no. 1 (1991): 27–40.

Corliss, Richard. "*Platoon:* Viet Nam, The Way It Really Was, on Film." *Time* (January 26, 1987): 54–61.

Desser, David. " 'Charlie Don't Surf': Race and Culture in the Vietnam War Films." In *Inventing Vietnam: The War in Film and Television*. Edited by Michael Anderegg. Philadelphia: Temple University Press, 1991: 81–102.

Dionne, Jr., E. J. "Kicking the 'Vietnam Syndrome.' " *Washington Post* (March 4, 1991): A1, A21.

Dittmar, Linda, and Gene Michaud, eds. *From Hanoi to Hollywood: The Vietnam War in American Film*. New Brunswick: Rutgers University Press, 1990.

Doherty, Thomas. "Full Metal Genre: Stanley Kubrick's Vietnam Combat Movie." *Film Quarterly* 42, no. 2 (Winter 1988–89): 24–30.

———. "Witness to War: Oliver Stone, Ron Kovic and *Born on the Fourth of July*." In *Inventing Vietnam: The War in Film and Television*. Edited by Michael Anderegg. Philadelphia: Temple University Press, 1991: 251–68.

Easthope, Anthony. "Realism and Its Subversion: Hollywood and Vietnam." In *Tell Me Lies about Vietnam: Cultural Battles for the Meaning of the War*. Edited by Alf Louvre and Jeffrey Walsh. Philadelphia: Open University Press, 1988: 30–49.

Economist, The. "Nostalgia Tours." (February 18, 1989): 27.

Edelman, Bernard, ed. *Dear America: Letters Home from Vietnam*. New York: W. W. Norton, 1985.

Egendorf, Arthur. *Healing from the War: Trauma and Transformation after Vietnam*. Boston: Houghton Mifflin, 1985.

Ehrenhaus, Peter. "Commemorating the Unwon War: On Not Remembering Vietnam." *Journal of Communication* 39, no. 1 (Winter 1989): 96–107.

———. "On Americans Held Prisoner in Southeast Asia: The P.O.W. Issue as 'Lesson' of Vietnam." In *Cultural Legacies of Vietnam: Uses of the Past in the Present*. Edited by Peter Ehrenhaus and Richard Morris. Norwood, NJ: Ablex Publishing, 1990: 9–26.

Ehrenhaus, Peter, and Richard Morris, eds. *Cultural Legacies of Vietnam: Uses of the Past in the Present*. Norwood, NJ: Ablex Publishing, 1990.

Elshtain, Jean Bethke. *Women and War*. New York: Basic Books, 1987.

Elshtain, Jean Bethke, and Sheila Tobias, eds. *Women, Militarism, and War.* Savage, MD: Rowman & Littlefield, 1990.

Emerson, Gloria. *Winners & Losers: Battles, Retreats, Gains, Losses and Ruins from a Long War.* New York: Random House, 1976.

English, Bella. "When Words Go to War." *Boston Globe* (February 27, 1991): 21.

Enloe, Cynthia. *Does Khaki Become You? The Militarization of Women's Lives.* Boston: Pandora, 1983.

————. *Bananas, Beaches and Bases: Making Feminist Sense of International Politics.* Berkeley: University of California Press, 1989.

————. "Womenandchildren." *Village Voice* (September 25, 1990): 29, 32–33.

Esper, George, and Associated Press. *The Eyewitness History of the Vietnam War 1961–1975.* New York: Ballantine, 1983.

Ewen, Stuart. "The Public Eye: A Report from the Couch." *Artforum* (March 1991): 13–15.

Falk, Richard. "What War?" *The Nation* (February 3, 1992): 112–13.

Fallows, James. "What Did You Do in the Class War, Daddy?" In *The Wounded Generation: America After Vietnam.* Edited by A. D. Horne. Englewood Cliffs: Prentice Hall, 1981: 15–29.

Farmanfarmanian, Abouali. "Sexuality in the Gulf War: Did You Measure Up?" *Genders* 13 (Summer 1992): 1–29.

Farrell, John. "Where We Shroud Our Heroes." *Boston Globe* (February 27, 1991): 57–64.

Fitzgerald, Frances. *Fire in the Lake: The Vietnamese and the Americans in Vietnam.* New York: Vintage, 1972.

————. "Casualties of Cinema: De Palma Runs Amok." *Village Voice* (August 22, 1989): 45.

Fralin, Frances. *The Indelible Image: Photographs of War 1846 to the Present.* New York: Harry Abrams, 1985.

Freedman, Samuel. "The War and the Arts." *New York Times Magazine* (March 31, 1985): 50–57.

Friedrich, Otto, and the editors of *Time,* eds. *Desert Storm: The War in the Persian Gulf.* Boston: Little, Brown, 1991.

Gelb, Leslie. "Iraq, The Movie." *New York Times* (January 20, 1991): 19.

Gerbner, George. "Persian Gulf War, the Movie." In *Triumph of the Image: The Media's War in the Persian Gulf—A Global Perspective.* Edited by Hamid Mowlana, George Gerbner, and Herbert Schiller. Boulder: Westview Press, 1992: 243–65.

Gibson, James. *The Perfect War: Technowar in Vietnam.* Boston: Atlantic Monthly Press, 1986.

————. "American Paramilitary Culture and the Reconstitution of the Vietnam War." In *Vietnam Images: War and Representation*. Edited by Jeffrey Walsh and James Aulich. London: Macmillan, 1989: 10–42.

Goff, Stanley, Robert Sanders, and Clark Smith. *Brothers: Black Soldiers in the Nam*. Novato, CA: Presidio Press, 1982.

Goodgame, Dan. "How the War Was Won." *Time* (January 26, 1987): 58.

Gray, J. Glenn. *The Warriors: Reflections on Men in Battle*. New York: Harper & Row, 1959.

Griffiths, Eric. "The Aesthetics of War." *Times Literary Supplement* (March 1, 1991).

Griffiths, Philip Jones. *Vietnam Inc*. London: Macmillan, 1971.

Gusterson, Hugh. "Nuclear War, the Gulf War, and the Disappearing Body." *Journal of Urban and Cultural Studies* 2, no. 1 (1991): 45–56.

Haines, Harry. " 'They Were Called and They Went': The Political Rehabilitation of the Vietnam Veteran." In *From Hanoi to Hollywood: The Vietnam War in American Film*. Edited by Linda Dittmar and Gene Michaud. New Brunswick: Rutgers University Press, 1990: 81–97.

Halberstam, David. "Television and the Instant Enemy." In *The Gulf War Reader: History, Documents, Opinions*. Edited by Micah Sifry and Christopher Cerf. New York: Times Books, 1991: 385–88.

Hallin, Daniel C. *The "Uncensored War": The Media and Vietnam*. New York: Oxford University Press, 1986.

Hamilton, Robert. "Image and Context: The Production and Reproduction of the Execution of a VC Suspect by Eddie Adams." In *Vietnam Images: War and Representation*. Edited by Jeffrey Walsh and James Aulich. London: Macmillan, 1989: 171–83.

Hammer, Joshua. "Cashing in on Vietnam." *Newsweek* (January 16, 1989): 38–39.

Hayslip, Le Ly. *Child of War, Woman of Peace*. New York: Doubleday, 1993.

Hayslip, Le Ly, and Jay Wurts. *When Heaven and Earth Changed Places*. New York: Penguin, 1989.

Heilbronn, Lisa. "Yellow Ribbons and Remembrance." *Sociological Inquiry* 64, no. 2 (May 1994): 151–78.

Hellmann, John. "The New Journalism and Vietnam: Memory as Structure in Michael Herr's *Dispatches*." *South Atlantic Quarterly* 79, no. 2 (Spring 1980): 141–51.

————. *American Myth and the Legacy of Vietnam*. New York: Columbia University Press, 1986.

Herr, Michael. *Dispatches*. New York: Avon, 1978.

Hilts, Philip. "Gulf War Syndrome: Is It a Real Disease?" *New York Times* (November 23, 1993): C1, C12.

————. "Gulf War Syndrome: A Clue." *New York Times* (April 21, 1996): E2.

Hoagland, Jim. "What a McDonald's Could Do in Hanoi." *Washington Post* (National Weekly Edition) (March 19–25, 1990): 28.

Hoberman, J. "America Dearest." *American Film* 13, no. 7 (May 1988): 39–45.

————. "Vietnam on Five Dollars a Daily." *Premiere* (April 1989): 144–47.

————. "Vietnam: The Remake." In *Remaking History.* Edited by Barbara Kruger and Phil Mariani. Seattle: Bay Press, 1989: 175–96.

————. "Believe It or Not: Girls with Guns." *Artforum* (September 1991): 26–27.

Horne, A. D., ed. *The Wounded Generation: America after Vietnam.* Englewood Cliffs: Prentice Hall, 1981.

Howell-Koehler, Nancy, ed. *Vietnam: The Battle Comes Home.* Dobbs Ferry, NY: Morgan & Morgan, 1984.

Hughes, Kathleen. "Hollywood Rushes Irag Angles into Plots." *Wall Street Journal* (January 21, 1991): B1.

Isaacs, Arnold. "GIs as Murderers: The Fallacy in the Vietnam Movies." *Washington Post* (December 13, 1989): A25.

Jaehne, Karen. "Company Man: Charlie MoPic Shoots to Kill." *Film Comment* 25, no. 2 (March/April 1989): 11–15.

Jakaitis, John M. "Two Versions of an Unfinished War: Dispatches and Going after Cacciato." *Cultural Critique* 3 (Spring 1986): 191–210.

James, David. "Presence of Discourse/Discourse of Presence: Representing Vietnam." *Wide Angle* 7, no. 4 (1985): 41–51.

————. *Allegories of Cinema: American Film in the Sixties.* Princeton: Princeton University Press, 1989.

————. "Documenting the Vietnam War." In *From Hanoi to Hollywood: The Vietnam War in American Film.* Edited by Linda Dittmar and Gene Michaud. New Brunswick: Rutgers University Press, 1990: 239–54.

————. "Rock and Roll in Representations of the Invasion of Vietnam." *Representations* 29 (Winter 1990): 78–98.

————. *To Take the Glamour Out of War: American Film against the War in Vietnam.* Program Notes. New York: Whitney Museum of American Art, 1990.

Jeffords, Susan. "Friendly Civilians: Images of Women and the Feminization of the Audience in Vietnam Films." *Wide Angle* 7, no.4 (1985): 13–22.

————. "The New Vietnam Films: Is the Movie Over?" *Journal of Popular Film and Television* 13, no. 4 (Winter 1986): 186–94.

————. " 'Things Worth Dying For': Gender and the Ideology of Collectivity in Vietnam Representation." *Cultural Critique* (Winter 1987–88): 79–103.

————. "Debriding Vietnam: The Resurrection of the White American Male." *Feminist Studies* 14, no. 3 (Fall 1989): 525–43.

————. *The Remasculinization of America: Gender and the Vietnam War.* Bloomington: Indiana University Press, 1989.

————. *Hard Bodies: Hollywood Masculinity in the Reagan Era.* New Brunswick: Rutgers University Press, 1994.

Kahn, Douglas. "Body Lags." In *War after War: City Lights Review.* Edited by Nancy J. Peters. San Francisco: City Lights Books, 1992: 43–46.

Karnow, Stanley. *Vietnam: A History.* New York: Viking, 1983.

Katzman, Jason. "From Outcast to Cliche: How Film Shaped, Warped and Developed the Image of the Vietnam Veteran, 1967–1990." *Journal of American Culture* 16, no. 1 (Spring 1993): 7–24.

Keller, Evelyn Fox. "From Secrets of Life to Secrets of Death." In *Body/ Politics: Women and the Discourses of Science.* Edited by Mary Jacobus, Evelyn Fox Keller, and Sally Shuttleworth. New York: Routledge, 1990: 177–91.

Kinney, Judy Lee. "The Mythical Method: Fictionalizing the Vietnam War." *Wide Angle* 7, no. 4 (1985): 35–40.

————. "*Gardens of Stone, Platoon,* and *Hamburger Hill:* Ritual and Remembrance." In *Inventing Vietnam: The War in Film and Television.* Edited by Michael Anderegg. Philadelphia: Temple University Press, 1991: 153–65.

Klare, Michael T. *Beyond the "Vietnam Syndrome": U.S. Interventionism in the 1980s.* Washington, D.C.: Institute for Policy Studies, 1981.

Klein, Michael. "Historical Memory, Film, and the Vietnam Era." In *From Hanoi to Hollywood: The Vietnam War in American Film.* Edited by Linda Dittmar and Gene Michaud. New Brunswick: Rutgers University Press, 1990: 19–40.

Kovic, Ron. *Born on the Fourth of July.* New York: Pocket Books, 1976.

Kuberski, Philip Francis. "Genres of Vietnam." *Cultural Critique* 3 (Spring 1986): 168–88.

Lakoff, George. "Metaphor and War: The Metaphor System Used to Justify War in the Gulf." *Journal of Urban and Cultural Studies* 2, no. 1 (1991): 59–72.

Lam, Andrew. "My Vietnam, My America." *The Nation* (December 10, 1990): 724–26.

Lang, Daniel. *Casualties of War.* New York: Pocket, [1969] 1989.

Lanning, Michael Lee. *Vietnam at the Movies.* New York: Fawcett Columbine, 1994.

Larsen, Ernest. "Gulf War TV." *Jump Cut* 36 (1991): 3–10.

Larsen, Lotte. "The Yellow Ribboning of America: A Gulf War Phenomenon." *Journal of American Culture* 17, no. 1 (Spring 1994): 11–22.

Leary, Kevin. "Ribbons Say 'We Support the Troops.'" *San Francisco Chronicle* (February 26, 1991): B3, B5.

Lehman, Peter, ed. "Vietnam and the Media." Special Issue. *Wide Angle* 7, no. 4 (1985).

Lelyveld, Joseph. "The Enduring Legacy." *New York Times Magazine* (March 31, 1985): 29–43.

Levidow, Les, and Kevin Robins, eds. *Cyborg Worlds: The Military Information Society.* London: Free Association, 1989.

Levinson, Nan. "Snazzy Visuals, Hard Facts and Obscured Issues." *Index on Censorship* 20, nos. 4&5 (April/May 1991): 27–29.

Levy, Peter B. "Blacks and the Vietnam War." In *The Legacy: The Vietnam War in the American Imagination.* Edited by D. Michael Shafer. Boston: Beacon Press, 1990: 209–32.

Lewinski, Jorge. *The Camera at War: War Photography from 1848 to the Present Day.* Secaucus, NJ: Chartwell Books, 1978.

Lichty, Lawrence, and Raymond Carroll. "Fragments of War: *Platoon.*" In *American History/American Film: Interpreting the Hollywood Image.* Edited by John E. O'Connor and Martin A. Jackson. New York: Continuum, 1988: 273–87.

Life. "MIA: Are Any Still Alive?" 10, no. 12 (November 1987): 110–24.

Lifton, Robert Jay. *Home from the War: Learning from Vietnam Veterans.* Boston: Beacon Press, [1973] 1992.

Lippard, Lucy. *A Different War: Vietnam in Art.* Seattle: Real Comet Press, 1990.

Louvre, Alf, and Jeffrey Walsh, eds. *Tell Me Lies about Vietnam: Cultural Battles for the Meaning of the War.* Philadelphia: Open University Press, 1988.

Lyons, Paul. "Vietnam: Ambiguous Reconciliation." *Socialist Review* 18 (April/June 1988): 55–71.

MacPherson, Myra. "A Different War." In *The American Experience in Vietnam: A Reader.* Edited by Grace Sevy. Norman: University of Oklahoma Press, 1989: 53–74.

Mann, Judy. "America's Overlooked Veterans." *Washington Post* (January 17, 1992): E3.

Marin, Peter. "What the Vietnam Veterans Can Teach Us." *The Nation* (November 27, 1982): 558–62.

———. "Conclusion." In *Vietnam Reconsidered: Lessons from a War.* Edited by Harrison Salisbury. New York: Harper & Row, 1984: 213.

Marks, Laura U. "Tie a Yellow Ribbon around Me: Masochism, Militarism and the Gulf War on TV." *Camera Obscura* 27 (September 1991): 55–75.

Mason, Bobbie Ann. *In Country.* New York: Harper & Row, 1985.

McKeever, Robert. "American Myths and the Impact of the Vietnam War: Revisionism in Foreign Policy and Popular Cinema in the 1980s." In *Vietnam Images: War and Representation.* Edited by Jeffrey Walsh and James Aulich. London: Macmillan, 1989: 43–56.

Miles, Sara. " 'The Real War': Post-Vietnam Low-Intensity Conflict." In *Unwinding the Vietnam War: From War into Peace.* Edited by Reese Williams. Seattle: Real Comet Press, 1987: 316–39.

Miller, Kenneth. "The Tiny Victims of Desert Storm." *Life* (November 1995): 46–62.

Miller, Mark Crispin. *Spectacle: Operation Desert Storm and the Triumph of Illusion.* New York: Simon and Schuster, 1993.

Mills, Nick, and the editors of Boston Publishing Co. *The Vietnam Experience: Combat Photographer.* Boston: Boston Publishing Co., 1983.

Mitchell, W.J.T. "From CNN to *JFK:* Paranoia, Melodrama, and American Mass Media in 1991." *Afterimage* (May 1992): 13–17.

Mithers, Carol Lynn. "Missing in Action: Women Warriors in Vietnam." *Cultural Critique* 3 (Spring 1986): 79–90. (Reprinted in *The Vietnam War and American Culture.* Edited by Rick Berg and John Carlos Rowe. New York: Columbia University Press, 1991.

Modleski, Tania. "A Father is Being Beaten: Male Feminism and the War Film." *Discourse* 10, no. 2 (Spring/Summer 1988).

Morgan, Michael, Justin Lewis, and Sut Jhally. "More Viewing, Less Knowledge." In *Triumph of the Image: The Media's War in the Persian Gulf— A Global Perspective.* Edited by Hamid Mowlana, George Gerbner, and Herbert Schiller. Boulder: Westview Press, 1992: 216–33.

Morrow, Lance. "A Bloody Rite of Passage." *Time* (April 15, 1985): 20–31.

Myers, Thomas. *Walking Point: American Narratives of Vietnam.* New York: Oxford University Press, 1988.

New York Times. "Patriot System Called a 'Failure.' " (January 9, 1992).

Norman, Michael. *These Good Men.* New York: Pocket, 1989.

O'Brien, Tim. *Going after Cacciato.* New York: Delacorte, 1978.

———. "The Vietnam in Me." *New York Times Magazine* (October 2, 1994): 48–57.

O'Mara, Richard. "In a Gulf of Darkness." *Index on Censorship* 20, nos. 4& 5 (April/May 1991): 30–31.

Page, Tim. *Nam.* New York: Alfred Knopf, 1983.

Paris, Michael. "The American Film Industry and Vietnam." *History Today* 37 (April 1987).

Polner, Murray. *No Victory Parades.* New York: Holt, Rinehart, Winston, 1971.

Porteous, Katrina. "History Lessons: *Platoon.*" In *Vietnam Images: War and*

Representation. Edited by Jeffrey Walsh and James Aulich. London: Macmillan, 1989: 153–59.

Quart, Leonard. "A Step in the Right Direction for Hollywood." *Cineaste* 15, no. 4 (1987): 6.

Quindlen, Anna. "The Back Fence." *New York Times* (January 20, 1991): 19.

Reardon, Betty. *Sexism and the War System.* New York: Teachers College Press, 1985.

Renov, Michael. "Imaging the Other: Representations of Vietnam in '60s Political Documentary." In *From Hanoi to Hollywood: The Vietnam War in American Film.* Edited by Linda Dittmar and Gene Michaud. New Brunswick: Rutgers University Press, 1988: 255–68.

Ronell, Avital. "Support Our Tropes." In *War after War: City Lights Review.* Edited by Nancy J. Peters. San Francisco: City Lights Books, 1992: 47–51.

Rowe, John Carlos. "Eye-Witness: Documentary Styles in the American Representations of Vietnam." *Cultural Critique* 3 (Spring 1986): 126–50. Reprinted in *The Vietnam War and American Culture.* Edited by Rick Berg and John Carlos Rowe. New York: Columbia University Press, 1991.

Safer, Morley. *Flashbacks: On Returning to Vietnam.* New York: Random House, 1990.

Salisbury, Harrison E., ed. *Vietnam Reconsidered: Lessons from a War.* New York: Harper & Row, 1984.

Santoli, Al. *To Bear Any Burden: The Vietnam War and Its Aftermath in the Words of Americans and Southeast Asians.* New York: E. P. Dutton, 1985.

Scarry, Elaine. "Watching and Authorizing the Gulf War." In *Media Spectacles.* Edited by Marjorie Garber, Jann Matlock, and Rebecca Walkowitz. New York: Routledge, 1993: 57–73.

Schanberg, Sydney. "A Muzzle for the Press." In *The Gulf War Reader: History, Documents, Opinions.* Edited by Micah Sifry and Christopher Cerf. New York: Times Books, 1991: 368–75.

Schechter, Danny. "Gulf War Coverage." Z (December 1991): 22–25.

———. "The Gulf War and the Death of the TV News." *The Independent* (January/February 1992): 28–31.

Schell, Jonathan. *The Real War: The Classic Reporting on the Vietnam War.* New York: Pantheon, 1988.

Schickel, Richard. "Danger: Live Moral Issues." *Time* (May 27, 1985): 91.

Schmeisser, Peter. "The Pool and the Pentagon." *Index on Censorship* 20, nos. 4–5 (April/May 1991): 32–34.

Schmitt, Eric. "Racing through the Darkness in Pursuit of Scuds." *New York Times* (February 24, 1991): 17.

Scodari, Christine. "Operation Desert Storm as 'Wargames': Sport, War, and

Media Intertextuality." *Journal of American Culture* 16, no. 1 (Spring 1993): 1–5.

Severo, Richard, and Lewis Milford. *The Wages of War: When America's Soldiers Came Home—From Valley Forge to Vietnam.* New York: Simon and Schuster, 1989.

Sevy, Grace, ed. *The American Experience in Vietnam: A Reader.* Norman: University of Oklahoma Press, 1989.

Shafer, D. Michael, ed. *The Legacy: The Vietnam War in the American Imagination.* Boston: Beacon Press, 1990.

Sharrett, Christopher. "Born on the Fourth of July." *Cineaste* 17, no. 4 (1990): 49–50.

Sheehan, Neil. *A Bright Shining Lie: John Paul Vann and America in Vietnam.* New York: Random House, 1988.

Sifry, Micah, and Christopher Cerf, eds. *The Gulf War Reader: History, Documents, Opinions.* New York: Times Books, 1991.

Sklar, Robert, ed. "*Platoon:* A Critical Symposium." *Cineaste* 15, no. 4 (1987): 4–11.

Smith, Julian. *Looking Away: Hollywood and Vietnam.* New York: Scribner, 1975.

Spark, Alasdair. "Flight Controls: The Social History of the Helicopter as Symbol of Vietnam." In *Vietnam Images: War and Representation.* Edited by Jeffrey Walsh and James Aulich. London: Macmillan, 1989: 86–111.

Springer, Claudia. "Vietnam: A Television History and the Equivocal Nature of Objectivity." *Wide Angle* 7, no. 4 (1985): 53–60.

Squiers, Carol. "Special Effects." *Artforum* (May 1991): 25–27.

Stam, Robert. "Mobilizing Fictions: The Gulf War, the Media, and the Recruitment of the Spectator." *Public Culture* 4, no. 2 (Spring 1992): 101–26.

Stone, Oliver, and Richard Boyle. Platoon *and* Salvador: *The Original Screenplays.* New York: Vintage, 1987.

Studlar, Gaylyn, and David Desser. "Never Having to Say You're Sorry: Rambo's Rewriting of the Vietnam War." In *From Hanoi to Hollywood: The Vietnam War in American Film.* Edited by Linda Dittmar and Gene Michaud. New Brunswick: Rutgers University Press, 1988: 101–12.

Swiers, George. " 'Demented Vets' and Other Myths—The Moral Obligation of Veterans." In *Vietnam Reconsidered: Lessons from a War.* Edited by Harrison Salisbury. New York: Harper & Row, 1984: 196–201.

Taylor, Bruce. "The Vietnam War Movie." In *The Legacy: The Vietnam War in the American Imagination.* Edited by D. Michael Shafer. Boston: Beacon Press, 1990: 186–206.

Taylor, Clyde. "The Colonialist Subtext in *Platoon*." In *From Hanoi to Holly-wood: The Vietnam War in American Film*. Edited by Linda Dittmar and Gene Michaud. New Brunswick: Rutgers University Press, 1990: 171–74.

————, ed. *Vietnam and Black America: An Anthology of Protest and Resistance*. Garden City, NY: Anchor, 1973.

Terry, Wallace, II. "Bringing the War Home." In *Vietnam and Black America: An Anthology of Protest and Resistance*. Edited by Clyde Taylor. Garden City, NY: Anchor, 1973: 200–219.

Theweleit, Klaus. *Male Fantasies. Volume 1: Women Floods Bodies History*. Translated by Stephen Conway. Minneapolis: University of Minnesota Press, 1987.

————. *Male Fantasies. Volume 2: Male Bodies: Psychoanalyzing the White Terror*. Translated by Erica Carter and Chris Turner. Minneapolis: University of Minnesota Press, 1989.

Time. "Special Section: Ten Years Later, Viet Nam Still Stirs Uneasy Memories." (April 15, 1985).

Tollefson, James W. "Indochinese Refuges: A Challenge to America's Memory of Vietnam." In *The Legacy: The Vietnam War in the American Imagination*. Edited by D. Michael Shafer. Boston: Beacon Press, 1990: 262–79.

Treviso, Ruben. "Hispanics and the Vietnam War." In *Vietnam Reconsidered: Lessons from a War*. Edited by Harrison Salisbury. New York: Harper & Row, 1984: 184–86.

Trujillo, Charley, ed. *Soldados: Chicanos in Viet Nam*. San José: Chusma House, 1990.

Tuchman, Barbara. *The March of Folly: From Troy to Vietnam*. New York: Ballantine Books, 1984.

Tuleja, Tad. "Closing the Circle: Yellow Ribbons and the Redemption of the Past." *Journal of American Culture* 17, no. 1 (Spring 1994): 23–30.

U.S. News & World Report. "The Gulf War Flu." (January 20, 1992): 50.

Virilio, Paul. *War and Cinema*. Translated by Patrick Camiller. New York: Verso, 1989.

Virilio, Paul, and Sylvere Lotringer. *Pure War*. Translated by Mark Polizzotti. New York: Semiotext(e), 1984.

Vlastos, Stephen. "America's 'Enemy': The Absent Presence in Revisionist War History." In *The Vietnam War and American Culture*. Edited by Rick Berg and John Carlos Rowe. New York: Columbia University Press, 1991.

Walker, Keith. *A Piece of My Heart: The Stories of 26 Women Who Served in Vietnam*. Novato, CA: Presidio, 1985.

Waller, Douglas, and John Barry. "The Day We Stopped the War." *Newsweek* (January 20, 1992): 16–25.

Walsh, Jeffrey. "First Blood to Rambo: A Textual Analysis." In *Tell Me Lies About Vietnam: Cultural Battles for the Meaning of War.* Edited by Alf Louvre and Jeffrey Walsh. Philadelphia: Open University Press, 1988: 50–61.

Walsh, Jeffrey, and James Aulich, eds. *Vietnam Images: War and Representation.* London: Macmillan, 1989.

Wark, McKenzie. "News Bites: War TV in the Gulf." *Meanjin* 50, no.1 (Autumn 1991): 5–18.

Weigl, Bruce. "Welcome Home." *The Nation* (November 27, 1982): 549.

———. "Stone Incountry: A Platoon of the Mind." *Cineaste* 15, no. 4 (1987): 10.

Weiss, Stephen, Clark Dougan, David Fulghum, Denis Kennedy, and the editors of Boston Publishing Co. *The Vietnam Experience: A War Remembered.* Boston: Boston Publishing, 1986.

Wheeler, John. *Touched with Fire: The Future of the Vietnam Generation.* New York: Franklin Watts, 1984.

Williams, Reese, ed. *Unwinding the Vietnam War: From War into Peace.* Seattle: Real Comet Press, 1987.

Wolf, Susan. "Women and Vietnam: Remembering in the 1980s." In *Unwinding the Vietnam War: From War Into Peace.* Edited by Reese Williams. Seattle: Real Comet Press, 1987: 243–60.

Wood, Robin. *Hollywood from Vietnam to Reagan.* New York: Columbia University Press, 1986.

AIDS and the Immune System

Abelove, Henry. "The Politics of the 'Gay Plague': AIDS as a U.S. Ideology." In *Body Politics: Disease, Desire, and the Family.* Edited by Michael Ryan and Avery Gordon. Boulder: Westview, 1994: 3–17.

Achenbach, Joel. "AIDS Conundrum." *Oakland Tribune* (February 5, 1991).

Ackerman, Jennifer Gorham. "The Healer within." In *The Incredible Machine.* Edited by Robert Poole. Washington, D.C.: National Geographic Society, 1986: 157–219.

ACT UP/New York Women and AIDS Book Group. *Women, AIDS & Activism.* Boston: South End Press, 1990.

Alonso, Ana Maria, and Maria Teresa Koreck. "Silences: 'Hispanics,' AIDS, and Sexual Practices." *Differences* 1, no. 1 (Winter 1989).

Altman, Dennis. "AIDS: The Politicization of an Epidemic." *Socialist Review* 14, no. 6 (November/December 1984): 93–109.

———. *AIDS in the Mind of America.* Garden City, NY: Anchor, 1986.

———. "Legitimation Through Disaster: AIDS and the Gay Movement."

In *AIDS: Burdens of History.* Edited by Elizabeth Fee and Daniel M. Fox. Berkeley: University of California Press, 1988: 316–44.

Arno, Peter. "An Expanded Role for Community-Based Organizations." In *The AIDS Reader: Social Political Ethical Issues.* Edited by Nancy Mc-Kenzie. New York: Meridian, 1991: 497–504.

Associated Press. "AIDS Epidemic Passes Milestone: 200,000 Cases, over 100,000 Dead." *Washington Post* (January 17, 1992): A3.

———. "Blood of Loved Ones Is no Safer Than General Supply, Study Finds." *New York Times* (November 12, 1992): A9.

Atkins, Robert, and Thomas W. Sokolowski, eds. *From Media to Metaphor: Art About AIDS.* New York: Independent Curators Inc., 1991.

Baker, Rob. *The Art of AIDS: From Stigma to Conscience.* New York: Continuum, 1994.

Barnes, Edward, and Anne Hollister. "Now No One Is Safe from AIDS: The New Victims." *Life* (July 1985).

Barrett, Wayne. "Straight Shooters: AIDS Targets Another Lifestyle." *Village Voice* (October 29, 1985).

Bateson, Mary Catherine, and Richard Goldsby. *Thinking AIDS: The Social Response to the Biological Threat.* New York: Addison-Wesley, 1988.

Ben-Levi, Jack. "From Euphoria to Sobriety, from Reverie to Reverence: David Wojnarowicz and the Scenes of AIDS Activism." *Public* 8 (1993): 138–160.

Black, David. *The Plague Years: A Chronicle of AIDS, The Epidemic of Our Times.* New York: Simon and Schuster, 1986.

Boffin, Tessa, and Sunil Gupta, eds. *Ecstatic Bodies: Resisting the AIDS Mythology.* London: Rivers Oram Press, 1990.

Brownlee, Shannon. "Plotting a Fresh Attack in the War on AIDS." *U.S. News & World Report* (December 30, 1991/January 6, 1992): 62.

Callen, Michael. *Surviving AIDS.* New York: Harper-Collins, 1990.

Camus, Albert. *The Plague.* Translated by Stuart Gilbert. New York: Modern Library, 1948.

Carter, Erica, and Simon Watney, eds. *Taking Liberties.* London: Serpent's Tail, 1989.

Chirimuuta, Richard and Rosalind. *AIDS, Africa and Racism.* London: Free Association Books, 1989.

Clum, John. " 'The Time Before the War': AIDS, Memory, and Desire." *American Literature* 62, no. 4 (December 1990): 648–67.

Cohen, Fred. "Friendly Contagion: Harnassing the Subtle Power of Computer Viruses." *The Sciences* (September/October 1991): 22–28.

Connor, Steve, and Sharon Kingman. *The Search for the Virus: The Scientific Discovery of AIDS and the Quest for a Cure.* New York: Penguin, 1988.

Cowley, Geoffrey. "Chronic Fatigue Syndrome: A Modern Medical Mystery." *Newsweek* (November 12, 1990): 62–70.

———. "The Future of AIDS." *Newsweek* (March 22, 1993): 47–52.

Crimp, Douglas. "AIDS: Cultural Analysis/Cultural Activism." In *AIDS: Cultural Analysis/Cultural Activism.* Edited by Douglas Crimp. Cambridge: MIT Press, 1988: 3–16.

———. "How to Have Promiscuity in an Epidemic." In *AIDS: Cultural Analysis/Cultural Activism.* Edited by Douglas Crimp. Cambridge: MIT Press, 1988: 237–71.

———. "Mourning and Militancy." *October* 51 (Winter 1989): 3–18.

———. "Portraits of People with AIDS." In *Cultural Studies.* Edited by Lawrence Grossberg, Cary Nelson, and Paula Treichler. New York: Routledge, 1992: 117–33.

———. "Accommodating Magic." In *Media Spectacles.* Edited by Marjorie Garber, Jann Matlock, and Rebecca Walkowitz. New York: Routledge, 1993: 255–66.

———, ed. *AIDS: Cultural Analysis/Cultural Activism.* Cambridge: MIT Press, 1988: 3–16.

Crimp, Douglas, and Adam Rolston. *AIDS Demo Graphics.* Seattle: Bay Press, 1990.

Croce, Arlene. "Discussing the Undiscussable." *New Yorker* (December 26, 1994/January 2, 1995): 54–60.

Curry, Cheryl. "AIDS Victim's Photo in Ad Tells a Story." *San Jose Mercury News* (May 12, 1992), p. 9A.

Cvetkovich, Ann. "Video, AIDS, and Activism." *Afterimage* (September 1991): 8–11.

———. "The War Against AIDS and War in the Middle East." In *Body Politics: Disease, Desire, and the Family.* Edited by Michael Ryan and Avery Gordon. Boulder: Westview, 1994: 38–44.

Daedalus. Living with AIDS: Part II (Summer 1989).

Dalton, Harlon L. "AIDS in Blackface." In *The AIDS Reader: Social Political Ethical Issues.* Edited by Nancy McKenzie. New York: Meridian, 1991: 122–43.

Danzig, Alexis. "Acting Up: Independent Video and the AIDS Crisis." *Afterimage* (May 1989): 5–7.

Davis, Joel. *Defending the Body: Unraveling the Mysteries of Immunology.* New York: Atheneum, 1989.

Del Zotto, Augusta. "Latinas with AIDS." *This World* (April 9, 1989).

Deresiewicz, William. "Against All Odds: Grass-Roots Minority Groups Fight AIDS." In *The AIDS Reader: Social Political Ethical Issues.* Edited by Nancy McKenzie. New York: Meridian, 1991: 534–42.

Diprose, Rosalyn, and Cathryn Vasseleu. "Animation-AIDS in Science/Fiction." In *The Illusion of Life: Essays on Animation*. Edited by Alan Cholodenko. Sydney: Power Publications, 1991: 145–60.

Dreuilhe, Emmanuel. *Mortal Embrace: Living with AIDS*. Translated by Linda Coverdale. New York: Hill and Wang, 1988.

Duesberg, Peter. "Human Immunodeficiency Virus and Acquired Immunodeficiency Syndrome: Correlation But Not Causation." In *The AIDS Reader: Social Political Ethical Issues*. Edited by Nancy McKenzie. New York: Meridian, 1991: 42–73.

Dwyer, John M. *The Body at War: The Miracle of the Immune System*. New York: Mentor/Penguin, 1990.

Epstein, Steven. "Democratic Science? AIDS Activism and the Contested Construction of Knowledge." *Socialist Review* 21, no. 2 (April/June 1991): 35–64.

Erni, John. "Articulating the (Im)possible: Popular Media and the Cultural Politics of 'Curing AIDS.' " *Communication* 13 (1992): 39–56.

Essex, Max, and Phyllis Kanki. "The Origins of the AIDS Virus." In *The Science of AIDS: Readings from Scientific American*. New York: W. H. Freeman, 1988: 27–38.

Fauvel, John. "AIDS Culture." *Science as Culture* 7 (1989): 43–68.

Fee, Elizabeth. "Sin Versus Science: Venereal Disease in Twentieth-Century Baltimore." In *AIDS: The Burdens of History*. Edited by Elizabeth Fee and Daniel M. Fox. Berkeley: University of California Press, 1988: 121–46.

Fee, Elizabeth, and Daniel M. Fox, eds. *AIDS: The Burdens of History*. Berkeley: University of California Press, 1988.

———, eds. *AIDS: The Making of a Chronic Disease*. Berkeley: University of California Press, 1992.

Feldman, Douglas, ed. *Culture and AIDS*. New York: Praeger, 1990.

Feldman, Jamie. "Gallo, Montagnier, and the Debate Over HIV: A Narrative Analysis." *Camera Obscura* 28 (1992): 101–34.

Fineberg, Harvey. "The Social Dimensions of AIDS." In *The Science of AIDS: Readings from Scientific American*. New York: W. H. Freeman, 1988: 111–22.

Fitzgerald, Frances. *Cities on a Hill*. New York: Simon and Schuster, 1987.

Fleck, Ludwik. *Genesis and Development of a Scientific Fact*. Edited by Thaddeus Trenn and Robert Merton. Translated by Fred Bradley and Thaddeus Trenn. Chicago: University of Chicago Press, [1935] 1979.

Fox, Renee, Linda Aiken, and Carla Messikomer. "The Culture of Caring: AIDS and the Nursing Profession." In *A Disease of Society: Cultural and Institutional Responses to AIDS*. Edited by Dorothy Nelkin, David Willis, and Scott Parris. New York: Cambridge University Press, 1991: 119–49.

Fulwood, Sam III, and Marlene Cimons. "Blacks and AIDS: No Magic Cure." *Los Angeles Times* (December 24, 1991): A1–A11.

Gagnon, Monica. "A Convergence of Stakes: Photography, Feminism, and AIDS." In *Fluid Exchanges: Artists and Critics in the AIDS Crisis*. Edited by James Miller. Toronto: University of Toronto Press, 1992: 53–64.

Gallo, Robert C. "The First Human Retrovirus." *Scientific American* 255, no. 6 (December 1986): 88–98.

———. "The AIDS Virus." *Scientific American* 256, no. 1 (January 1987): 47–56.

Gallo, Robert C., and Luc Montagnier. "AIDS in 1988." In *The Science of AIDS: Readings from Scientific American*. New York: W. H. Freeman, 1988: 1–12

Garrett, Laurie. *The Coming Plague: Newly Emerging Diseases in a World Out of Balance*. New York: Penguin, 1994.

Gever, Martha. "Pictures of Sickness: Stuart Marshall's *Bright Eyes*." In *AIDS: Cultural Analysis/Cultural Activism*. Edited by Douglas Crimp. Cambridge: MIT Press, 1988: 109–26.

Gilman, Sander L. "AIDS and Syphilis: The Iconography of Disease." *October* 43 (Winter 1987): 87–108.

———. *Disease and Representation: Images of Illness from Madness to AIDS*. Ithaca: Cornell University Press, 1988.

Gladwell, Malcolm. "When Is It a 'Special' Disease?" *Washington Post* (June 2, 1991).

Goldberg, Vicki. "Images of Catastrophe as Corporate Ballyhoo." *New York Times* (May 3, 1992).

Goldfarb, Brian. "Video Activism and Critical Pedagogy: Sexuality at the End of the Rainbow Curriculum." *Afterimage* (May 1993): 4–8.

Goldstein, Richard. "AIDS and Race: The Hidden Epidemic." *Village Voice* (March 10, 1987).

———. "AIDS and the Social Contract." In *Taking Liberties: AIDS and Cultural Politics*. Edited by Erica Carter and Simon Watney. London: Serpent's Tail, 1989: 81–94.

Golub, Edward S. *Immunology: A Synthesis*. Sunderland, MA: Sinauer Associates, 1987.

Gore, Rick. "The Awesome Worlds within a Cell." *National Geographic* (September 1976): 355–95.

Gorman, Christine. "Returning Fire against AIDS." *Time* (June 24, 1991): 44.

———. "Are Some People Immune to AIDS?" *Time* (March 22, 1993): 49–51.

Gould, Stephen Jay. "The Terrifying Normalcy of AIDS." In *The AIDS Reader: Social Political Ethical Issues.* Edited by Nancy McKenzie. New York: Meridian, 1991: 100–106.

Green, Jesse. "The Year of the Ribbon." *New York Times* (May 3, 1992): B1.

Grmek, Mirko D. *History of AIDS: Emergence and Origin of a Modern Pandemic.* Translated by Russell Maulitz and Jacalyn Duffin. Princeton: Princeton University Press, 1990.

Gross, Jane. "Second Wave of AIDS Feared by Officials in San Francisco." *New York Times* (December 11, 1993): 1, 8.

Grover, Jan Zita. "AIDS: Keywords." In *AIDS: Cultural Analysis/Cultural Activism.* Edited by Douglas Crimp. Cambridge: MIT Press, 1988: 17–30.

———. "AIDS, Keywords, and Cultural Work." In *Cultural Studies.* Edited by Lawrence Grossberg, Cary Nelson, and Paula Treichler. New York: Routledge, 1992: 227–39.

———. "Visible Lesions: Images of the PWA in America." In *Fluid Exchanges: Artists and Critics in the AIDS Crisis.* Edited by James Miller. Toronto: University of Toronto Press, 1992: 44–51.

Hall, Dennis. "No Laughing Matter: Values, Perception, and the Demise of AIDS Jokes." *Journal of American Culture* 16, no. 2 (Summer 1993): 25–30.

Harris, Daniel. "AIDS and Theory." *Lingua Franca* (June 1991): 16–19.

———. "On Reading the Obituaries in the *Bay Area Reporter.*" In *Fluid Exchanges: Artists and Critics in the AIDS Crisis.* Edited by James Miller. Toronto: University of Toronto Press, 1992: 163–68.

———. "Making Kitsch from AIDS." *Harper's* (July 1994): 55–60.

Haseltine, William, and Flossie Wong-Staal. "The Molecular Biology and the AIDS Virus." In *The Science of AIDS: Readings from Scientific American.* New York: W. H. Freeman, 1988: 13–26.

Hassner, Rune, ed. *Lennart Nilsson.* Goteborg, Sweden: Hasselblad Center, 1990.

Healey, Barth. "The Red Ribbon of AIDS Awareness." *New York Times* (November 28, 1993): V17.

Healy, Chris. "AIDS and the Arts of Conversation." *Public Culture* 7 (1995): 465–72.

Heyward, William, and James Curran. "The Epidemiology of AIDS in the U.S." In *The Science of AIDS: Readings from Scientific American.* New York: W. H. Freeman, 1988: 39–50.

Hilts, Philip. "American Scientist Who Found H.I.V. Is Investigated Anew." *New York Times* (March 2, 1992): A1–A10.

Hochhauser, Mark. "Media Misrepresentation of AIDS: AIDS Is a Noun, Not an Adjective." Unpublished paper, 1990.

Huston, Bo. "After War." In *War After War: City Lights Review*. Edited by Nancy J. Peters. San Francisco: City Lights Books, 1992: 137–42.

Jaret, Peter. "Our Immune System: The Wars within." *National Geographic* (June 1986): 702–35.

Jaroff, Leon. "Stop That Germ!" *Time* (May 23, 1988): 56–64.

Juhasz, Alexandra. "WAVE in the Media Environment: Camcorder Activism and the Making of *HIV TV*." *Camera Obscura* 28 (1992): 135–54.

————. *AIDS TV: Identity, Community and Alternative Video*. Durham: Duke University Press, 1995.

Kaplan, Howard. "Social Psychology of the Immune System: A Conceptual Framework and Review of the Literature." *Social Science & Medicine* 33, no. 8 (1991): 909–23.

Kenny, Lorraine. "Testing the Limits: An Interview." *Afterimage* (October 1989): 4–7.

Kimmel, Michael, and Martin Levine. "A Hidden Factor in AIDS: 'Real' Men's Hypersexuality." *Los Angeles Times* (June 3, 1990).

Kinsella, James. *Covering the Plague: AIDS and the American Media*. New Brunswick: Rutgers University Press, 1989.

Klein, Jan. *Immunology: The Science of Self-Nonself Discrimination*. New York: John Wiley and Sons, 1982.

Kobasa, Suzanne Ouellette. "AIDS Volunteering: Links to Past and Future Prospects." In *A Disease of Society: Cultural and Institutional Responses to AIDS*. Edited by Dorothy Nelkin, David Willis, and Scott Parris. New York: Cambridge University Press, 1991: 172–190.

Kolata, Gina. "How AIDS Smolders: Immune System Studies Follow the Tracks of H.I.V." *New York Times* (March 17, 1992): B5, B8.

Kraft, Scott. "AIDS Devastates Africa." *Oakland Tribune* (March 1, 1992): A1–A12.

Kramer, Larry. *Reports from the Holocaust: The Making of an AIDS Activist*. New York: St. Martin's Press, 1989.

Kubler-Ross, Elisabeth. *AIDS: The Ultimate Challenge*. New York: Collier Books, 1987.

Lazarus, Judith. "The AIDS Ribbons' Tangled Message: Why Some See Red." *Los Angeles Times* (March 24, 1993): F1, F6.

Leibowitch, Jacques. *A Strange Virus of Unknown Origin*. New York: Ballantine, 1985.

Lemonick, Michael. "The Killers All Around." *Time* (September 12, 1994): 62–69.

Levine, Carol. "AIDS and Changing Concepts of Family." In *A Disease of*

Society: Cultural and Institutional Responses to AIDS. Edited by Dorothy Nelkin, David Willis, and Scott Parris. New York: Cambridge University Press, 1991: 45–70.

Lippard, Lucy. "Silence Still = Death." *High Performance* (Fall 1991): 28–31.

———. "Passenger on the Shadows." *Aperture* 137 (Fall 1994): 6–25.

Manalansan, Martin F., IV. "Ethnicity, Sexuality and AIDS: The Case of a Gay Filipino American Man." Paper presented at the American Anthropological Association Annual Meeting, November 1991.

Mann, Jonathan, James Chine, Peter Piot, and Thomas Quinn. "The International Epidemiology of AIDS." In *The Science of AIDS: Readings from Scientific American.* New York: W. H. Freeman, 1988: 51–62.

Markoff, John. "Can Computer Viruses Be Domesticated?" *New York Times* (October 6, 1991).

Marshall, Stuart. "Picturing Deviancy." In *Ecstatic Bodies: Resisting the AIDS Mythology.* Edited by Tessa Boffin and Sunil Gupta. London: Rivers Oram Press, 1990: 19–36.

Martin, Emily. "Toward an Anthropology of Immunology: The Body as Nation State." *Medical Anthropology Quarterly* 4, no. 4 (December 1990): 410–26.

———. "The End of the Body?" *American Ethnologist* 19, no. 1 (February 1992): 121–40.

———. "Histories of the Immune System." *Culture, Medicine & Psychiatry* (1992): 67–76.

———. *Flexible Bodies: Tracking Immunity in American Culture from the Days of Polio to the Age of AIDS.* Boston: Beacon Press, 1994.

Matthews, Thomas, and Dani Bolognesi. "AIDS Vaccines." In *The Science of AIDS: Readings from Scientific American.* New York: W. H. Freeman, 1988: 101–10.

McKenzie, Nancy, ed. *The AIDS Reader: Social Political Ethical Issues.* New York: Meridian, 1991.

McMillan, Liz. "AIDS as Metaphor." *Chronicle of Higher Education* (October 19, 1994): A18–A20.

Meredith, Ann. "Until That Last Breath: Women with AIDS." In *AIDS: The Making of a Chronic Disease.* Edited by Elizabeth Fee and Daniel M. Fox. Berkeley: University of California Press, 1992: 229–44.

Meyer, Richard. "Rock Hudson's Body." In *Inside/Out: Lesbian Theories Gay Theories.* Edited by Diana Fuss. New York: Routledge, 1991: 259–88.

Miller, James, ed. *Fluid Exchanges: Artists and Critics in the AIDS Crisis* Toronto: University of Toronto, 1992.

Mohammed, Juanita. "WAVE in the Media Environment: Camcorder Activism in AIDS Education." *Camera Obscura* 28 (1992): 153–56.

Morse, Stephen S. "AIDS and beyond: Defining the Rules for Viral Traffic." In *AIDS: The Making of a Chronic Disease.* Edited by Elizabeth Fee and Daniel M. Fox. Berkeley: University of California Press, 1992: 23–48.

Moulin, Anne Marie. "The Immune System: A Key Concept for the History of Immunology." *History and Philosophy of the Life Sciences* 11 (1989): 221–36.

Navarre, Max. "Fighting the Victim Label." In *AIDS: Cultural Analysis/ Cultural Activism.* Edited by Douglas Crimp. Cambridge: MIT Press, 1988: 143–46.

Navarre, Mireya. "Agencies Slowed in Effort to Widen Definitions of AIDS." *New York Times* (February 10, 1992): A1–12.

Nelkin, Dorothy, David P. Willis, and Scott V. Parris, eds. *A Disease of Society: Cultural & Institutional Responses to AIDS.* New York: Cambridge University Press, 1991.

Newsday. "Many Masks of AIDS Virus That Defeat Immune System." (December 12, 1991).

New York Times. "The AIDS 'Plot' Against Blacks." (May 12, 1992): A22.

Nilsson, Lennart, with Jan Lindberg. *The Body Victorious.* New York: Delacorte, 1987.

Norman, Colin. "A New Twist in AIDS Patent Fight." *Science* 232 (April 18, 1986): 308–309.

Nussbaum, Bruce. *Good Intentions: How Business and the Medical Establishment Are Corrupting the Fight against AIDS, Alzheimers, Cancer and More.* New York: Penguin, 1990.

Odets, Walt. "AIDS Education and Harm Reduction for Gay Men: Psychological Approaches for the 21st Century." *AIDS and Public Policy Journal* (Spring 1994): 1–16.

Oppenheimer, Gerald M. "In the Eye of the Storm: The Epidemiological Construction of AIDS." In *AIDS: Burdens of History.* Edited by Elizabeth Fee and Daniel M. Fox. Berkeley: University of California Press, 1988: 267–300.

Padgug, Robert A., and Gerald M. Oppenheimer. "Riding the Tiger: AIDS and the Gay Community." In *AIDS: The Making of a Chronic Disease.* Edited by Elizabeth Fee and Daniel M. Fox. Berkeley: University of California Press, 1992: 245–78.

Palca, Joseph. "AIDS: The Evolution of an Infection." *Science* (November 15, 1991): 941.

Park, Katherine. "Kimberly Bergalis, AIDS, and the Plague Metaphor." In

Media Spectacles. Edited by Marjorie Garber, Jann Matlock, and Rebecca Walkowitz. New York: Routledge, 1993: 232–53.

Patton, Brian. "Cell Wars: Military Metaphors and the Crisis of Authority in the AIDS Epidemic." In *Fluid Exchanges: Artists and Critics in the AIDS Crisis*. Edited by James Miller. Toronto: University of Toronto Press, 1992: 272–86.

Patton, Cindy. *Sex and Germs: The Politics of AIDS*. Boston: South End Press, 1985.

———. *Inventing AIDS*. New York: Routledge, 1990.

———. *Last Served? Gendering the HIV Pandemic*. London: Taylor & Francis, 1994.

Playfair, J.H.L. *Immunology at a Glance*. Oxford: Blackwell Scientific Publications, 1979.

Poole, Robert M., ed. *The Incredible Machine*. Washington, D.C.: National Geographic Society, 1986.

Potts, Eve, and Marion Morra. *Understanding Your Immune System*. New York: Avon, 1986.

Redfield, Robert, and Donald Burke. "HIV Infection: The Clinical Picture." In *The Science of AIDS: Readings from Scientific American*. New York: W. H. Freeman, 1988: 63–74.

Rich, Frank. "The Gay Decades." *Esquire* (November 1987): 87–100.

Roman, David. *Acts of Intervention*. Bloomington: Indiana University Press, forthcoming.

Ronell, Avital. "A Note on the Failure of Man's Custodianship: AIDS Update." *Public* 8 (1993): 56–67.

Rosenberg, Charles E. "Disease and Social Order in America: Perceptions and Expectations." In *AIDS: Burdens of History*. Edited by Elizabeth Fee and Daniel M. Fox. Berkeley: University of California Press, 1988: 12–32.

Sabatier, Renée. *Blaming Others: Prejudice, Race and Worldwide AIDS*. Philadelphia: New Society Publishers and the Panos Institute, 1988.

Sadownick, Doug. "ACT UP Makes a Spectacle of AIDS." *High Performance* (Spring 1990): 26–31.

Salazar, Wayne. "Fighting AIDS with Kitsch." (Letter to the Editor) *Harper's* (October 1994): 4–5.

San Diego Union-Tribune. "Teen Girls Prove They're 'Tough' by Having Sex with HIV Carriers." (April 27, 1993).

Schoofs, Mark. "Can You Trust Your Lover? Gay Couples Weigh the Risk of Unprotected Sex." *Village Voice* (January 31, 1995): 37–39.

Seidman, Steven. "Transfiguring Sexual Identity: AIDS and the Contemporary Construction of Homosexuality." *Social Text* (Fall 1988): 187–205.

Shaw, Nancy Stoller. "Preventing AIDS among Women: The Role of Community Organizing." In *The AIDS Reader: Social Political Ethical Issues.* Edited by Nancy McKenzie. New York: Meridian, 1991: 505–21.

Shilts, Randy. *And the Band Played On: Politics, People and the AIDS Epidemic.* New York: Penguin, 1987.

Siegel, Bernie. *Love, Medicine and Miracles.* New York: Harper & Row, 1986.

Smith, Geoffrey. "Historical Perspectives on AIDS: Society, Culture, and STDs." *Queens Quarterly* (Summer 1989): 244–62.

Sontag, Susan. *AIDS and Its Metaphors.* New York: Farrar, Straus and Giroux, 1989.

Treichler, Paula. "AIDS, Homophobia, and Biomedical Discourse: An Epidemic of Signification." In *AIDS: Cultural Analysis/Cultural Activism.* Edited by Douglas Crimp. Cambridge: MIT Press, 1988: 31–70.

———. "AIDS, Gender, and Biomedical Discourse: Current Contests for Meaning." In *AIDS: Burdens of History.* Edited by Elizabeth Fee and Daniel M. Fox. Berkeley: University of California Press, 1988: 190–266.

———. "AIDS and HIV Infection in the Third World: A First World Chronicle." In *Remaking History.* Edited by Barbara Kruger and Phil Mariani. Seattle: Bay Press, 1989: 31–86.

———. "Beyond *Cosmo:* AIDS, Identity, and Inscriptions of Gender." *Camera Obscura* 28 (1992): 21–78.

Todd, John. "A Most Intimate Foe: How the Immune System Can Betray the Body It Defends." *The Sciences* (March/April 1990): 20–27.

von Boehmer, Harald, and Pawel Kisielow. "How the Immune System Learns about Self." *Scientific American* (October 1991): 74–81.

Wallis, Claudia. "Knowing the Face of the Enemy." *Time* (April 30, 1984): 66–67.

———. "AIDS: A Growing Threat." *Time* (August 12, 1985): 40–47.

Warner, Michael. "Unsafe: Why Gay Men Are Having Risky Sex." *Village Voice* (January 31, 1995): 33–36.

Watney, Simon. "The Rhetoric of AIDS." *Screen* 27, no. 1 (January/February 1986): 72–85.

———. *Policing Desire: Pornography, AIDS and the Media.* Minneapolis: University of Minnesota Press, 1989.

———. "Missionary Positions: AIDS, 'Africa,' and Race." *Differences* 1, no. 1 (Winter 1989).

———. "Photography and AIDS." In *The Critical Image: Essays on Contemporary Photography.* Edited by Carol Squiers. Seattle: Bay Press, 1990: 173–92.

———. "Representing AIDS." In *Ecstatic Bodies: Resisting the AIDS My-*

thology. Edited by Tessa Boffin and Sunil Gupta. London: Rivers Oram Press, 1990: 165–92.

———. *Practices of Freedom*. Durham: Duke University Press, 1994.

Weber, Jonathan, and Robin Weiss. "HIV Infection: The Cellular Picture." In *The Science of AIDS: Readings from Scientific American*. New York: W. H. Freeman, 1988: 75–84.

Weeks, Jeffrey. "Post-modern AIDS?" In *Ecstatic Bodies: Resisting the AIDS Mythology*. Edited by Tessa Boffin and Sunil Gupta. London: Rivers Oram Press, 1990: 133–41.

Whitmore, George. *Someone Was Here: Profiles in the AIDS Epidemic*. New York: New American Library, 1988.

Williamson, Judith. "Every Virus Tells a Story: The Meaning of HIV and AIDS." In *Taking Liberties: AIDS and Cultural Politics*. Edited by Erica Carter and Simon Watney. London: Serpent's Tail, 1989: 69–80.

Ziegler, Philip. *The Black Death*. New York: John Daly, 1969.

Zinkernagel, Rolf M., and Hans Hengartner. "Games That Viruses Play." *Nature* 354 (December 12, 1991): 433–34.

AIDS Memorial Quilt and Related Texts

Abbott, Steve. "Meaning Adrift: The NAMES Project Quilt Suggests a Patchwork of Problems and Possibilities." *San Francisco Sentinel* (October 14, 1988).

Abrams, Garry. "AIDS Quilt Comforting U.S. Grief." *Los Angeles Times* (March 22, 1988).

Agosin, Marjorie. *Scraps of Life: Chilean Arpilleras*. Translated by Lola Franzen. Trenton: Red Sea Press, 1987.

Associated Press. "AIDS Advocates Report Quilt Vandalized." *New York Times* (September 20, 1990): B5.

Atkins, Robert. "The Look." *Village Voice* (October 27, 1987).

Baker, Ann. "A Mother's Cry for Help." *PWA Coalition Newsline* 49 (November 1989): 22–23.

Bellm, Dan. "And Sew It Goes." *Mother Jones* (January 1989): 34–35.

Bernstein, Ellen. "AIDS: The Struggle to Sensitize the Jewish Community." *Atlanta Jewish Times* (March 15, 1991).

Bishop, Katherine. "Denying AIDS Its Sting: A Quilt of Life." *New York Times* (October 5, 1987).

Brown, Joe. "The Quilt: A Battle Flag in the War on AIDS." *Washington Post* (October 2, 1988).

Butler, Katy. "Non-Profit Media Campaign: Cleve Jones and the Names Project." *Media Alliance* (October/November 1988): 9.

Carr, C. "Armies of the Dawn: Gay Rites." *Village Voice* (October 20, 1987).

Carvajal, Doreen. "Separate Patches to Mark Exhibit for Latino Victims." *Philadelphia Inquirer* (May 4, 1989).

Chicago, Judy. *The Dinner Party: A Symbol of Our Heritage.* Garden City, NY: Anchor Press, 1979.

Christy, Barbara. "The Greatest Quilt on Earth." *Flying Needle* (November 1988).

Crichton, E. G. "Is the NAMES Quilt Art?" *Out/Look* (Summer 1988): 5–10.

Dixon, Tom. "A Healing of Hearts." *Frontiers* (April 6–20, 1988): 60–63.

Dunlap, David. "Quilt Unfolds Painful Story of AIDS." *New York Times* (June 20, 1988).

Eckles, Erin. "For Many Survivors, the Quilt Is Still Too Strong a Reminder of Their Lost Loved Ones." *Washington Blade* (October 6, 1989).

Ferrero, Pat, Elaine Hedges, and Julie Silber. *Hearts and Hands: The Influence of Women and Quilts on American Society.* San Francisco: Quilt Digest Press, 1987.

Ford, Dave. "The Quilt's Balancing Act." *San Francisco Sentinel* (March 4, 1988).

———. "AIDS Quilt: Stiches in Time." *San Francisco Examiner* (April 3, 1988): E1.

———. "AIDS Quilt: Unease in Midwest." *San Francisco Examiner* (April 27, 1988).

———. "Names Quilt Cliches Take on Greater Meaning." *San Francisco Examiner* (May 11, 1988).

———. "Gay Grief Turns to Anger in Nation's Capital." *San Francisco Sentinel* (October 14, 1988).

Freeman, Mark. "The Quilt Goes to Motown." *Coming Up!* (August 1988): 4–7.

Fuchs, Elinor. "The AIDS Quilt." *The Nation* (October 31, 1988): 408–409.

Gentry, Gerry. "The NAMES Project: A Catharsis of Grief." *The Christian Century* (May 24–31, 1989): 550–51.

Gilliam, Dorothy. "New Efforts to Ease the Fear of AIDS." *Washington Post* (October 8, 1990): B3.

Goldman, Jane. "Women of the Quilt." *Deneuve* 2, no. 1 (January/February 1992): 32–37.

Gordon, Rachel. "Nations Piece Together Plan for AIDS Quilts." *San Francisco Independent* (July 31, 1990): 4.

Graham, Trey. "Making all the Pieces Fit." *Washington Blade* (October 9, 1992): 1, 31–35.

Hardy, Robin. "Die Harder: AIDS Activism Is Abandoning Gay Men." *Village Voice* (July 2, 1991): 33–34.

Hawkins, Peter. "Naming Names: The Art of Memory and the NAMES Project AIDS Quilt." *Critical Inquiry* 19, no. 4 (Summer 1993): 752–79.

Hippler, Mike. "Cleve Jones: The Name Behind the NAMES Project." *Bravo! San Diego* (April 7, 1988).

Hippocrates. "Patchwork Memorial." (January/February 1989).

Hoffman, Pat. "Piecing Together Love." *Fellowship* (September 1988): 11.

Howe, Lawrence. "The Moving Text: The NAMES Project." Paper delivered at the California American Studies Association Conference, San Jose State University, April 1991.

Israels, Dave. "Growing Pains at the NAMES Project." *San Francisco Bay Guardian* (April 13–20, 1988).

Kalmansohn, David. "Remember Their Names." *L.A. Dispatch* (October 26, 1988).

Kastor, Elizabeth. "Mending a Patchwork of Pain." *Washington Post* (October 8, 1992): C1, C9.

Knight, Christopher. "A Stitch in Time." *Art Issues* 2 (1988).

Leon, Eli. *Who'd a Thought It: Improvisation in African-American Quiltmaking.* San Francisco: San Francisco Craft and Folk Art Museum, 1987.

Lewando, Isabel. "Emblematic of Short, Loved Lives." *York County Coast Star* (May 17, 1989).

Lipsett, Linda Otto. *Remember Me: Women and Their Friendship Quilts.* San Francisco: Quilt Digest Press, 1985.

Mainardi, Patricia. *Quilts: The Great American Art.* San Pedro: Miles & Weir, 1978.

Masters, Brooke. "AIDS Quilt Captures Fear behind the Loss." *Washington Post* (October 8, 1989): D3.

Mayer-Gibbons, Gerrie. "The Names Project Sweepstakes." *The Advocate* (August 1, 1989): 22–23.

McCabe, Michael. "Controversy Growing over the AIDS Quilt." *San Francisco Chronicle* (December 3, 1988): A10.

McCalls. "Commemorating a Movement, a Friend." (April 1991): 66.

McDonough, Jim. "The Mediagenic Quilt." Unpublished paper.

———. "More Than a Memorial: The AIDS Quilt as Catalyst." Unpublished paper.

Mohr, Richard D. "Text(ile): Reading the NAMES Project's AIDS Quilt." In *Gay Ideas: Outing and Other Controversies.* Boston: Beacon Press, 1992: 105–28.

Moore, Harold. "A Legacy of Love." *Just Out* (September 1988): 14.

Murray, Tom. "Voices from the Heart." *San Francisco Sentinel* (October 17, 1987).

Muschamp, Herbert. "Labyrinth." *Artforum* (December 1987): 12.

Musto, Michael. "La Dolce Musto." *Village Voice* (October 25, 1988).

Newquist, Jay. "Names Project Helps AIDS Awareness, Raises Funds for Local Services." *Bay Area Reporter* (June 5, 1989): 16–17.

Otto, Whitney. *How to Make an American Quilt.* New York: Villard Books, 1991.

Parris, Fred. "Names Project Quilt Is Powerful Symbol of AIDS Crisis." *The Nan Monitor* 2, no. 2 (Winter 1988): 1–30.

Pearlman, Jonathan. "Remembering the Innocent." Unpublished paper, 1990.

Podolsky, J. D., and Shawn Lewis. "The Killing Quilt." *People* (November 15, 1993).

Porter, Patricia. "AIDS Proclamation Raises Ire in Pismo." *San Luis Obispo Telegram-Tribune* (October 9, 1990): A5.

Rinder, Larry. "The AIDS Quilt." *Artpaper Minneapolis* (May 1988): 9.

Robb, Christina. "A Stitch for Eternity." *Boston Globe Magazine* (June 12, 1988).

Ruskin, Cindy. *The Quilt: Stories from the NAMES Project.* New York: Pocket Books, 1988.

San Francisco Sentinel. "Sewing up Memories." (September 18, 1987).

Showalter, Elaine. "Common Threads." In *Sister's Choice: Tradition and Change in Women's Writing.* Oxford: Clarendon Press, 1991: 145–75.

Sirica, Coimbra M. "Smithsonian to Collect Some AIDS Quilt Panels." *San Francisco Chronicle* (October 7, 1988).

Sischy, Ingrid. "Advertising Taboos: Talking to Luciano Benetton and Oliviero Toscani." *Interview* (April 1992).

Standman, Michael. "An Open Letter to Cleve Jones and the NAMES Project." *Seattle Gay News* (November 18, 1988).

Sternberg, Steve. "The Life and Death of Tom Fox." *Atlanta Journal* (August 20, 1989).

Talk of the Town. *The New Yorker* (October 5, 1987): 31–32.

This Week in Texas. "Cancelled Visa Cards Will Become Part of Quilt." (September 30–October 6, 1988): 39.

Thorsell, William. "Memorial Metaphors." *Globe and Mail* (June 24, 1989).

Trescott, Jacqueline. "In Service to the Quilt." *Washington Post* (October 6, 1989): C1, C6.

Vandervelden, Mark. "The Names Project Quilt Memorializes Thousands." *The Advocate* (November 10, 1987).

Van Ness, Cynthia. "Artists Respond to AIDS." *Empty Closet* (April 1989): 12–13, 15.

Wadler, Paul-David. "Internal Strategies, Community Responses." *Boston Gay Community News* (December 4–10, 1988).

Walker, Alice. "Everyday Use." In *Norton Anthology of Literature by Women.* Edited by Sandra M. Gilbert and Susan Guber. New York: Norton, 1985.

Washington Post. "The Many Faces of AIDS." (October 9, 1992): A1, A19–21.

Wasterman, Kathy Ann. "Stories of Love, Sorrow Blanket Ellipse." *Washington Post* (October 7, 1989): B3.

Weinstein, Jeff. "A Map of Preventable Death." *Village Voice* (October 18, 1988): 26–27.

———. "Names Carried into the Future: An AIDS Quilt Unfolds." In *Art in the Public Interest.* Edited by Arlene Raven. Ann Arbor: University of Michigan Press, 1989.

Weiser, Judy. "Stitched to the Beat of a Heart, to Comfort Terrors of the Dark." *Art Therapy* (November 1989): 113–14.

———. "A Quilt to Comfort the Terrors of the Dark." *Gallerie* (1990): 16–18.

White, Allen. "Ann Landers Attacked for Not Responding to Anti-Quilt Letter." *Bay Area Reporter* (May 25, 1989): 13.

———. "Bush Snubs Names Quilt." *Bay Area Reporter* (October 12, 1989).

Wlazelek, Ann. "Family, Friend Dispute Man's AIDS Quilt Tribute." *The Morning Call* (1991): A1, A9.

Index

Abbott, Steve, 213
Abelove, Henry, 215
Acquired Immune Deficiency Syndrome. *See* AIDS
ACT UP, 154–55, 159, 162–63, 173–74 fig. 17, 250
Adams, Eddie, 90–93, 100, 279n11
Adams, William, 86, 89, 121
Adorno, Theodor, 11
Advertising: and AIDS, 170–73; as cultural memory, 10, 257
Agent Orange, 63, 73, 132, 143
AIDS, 10, 12, 80, 145–47, 197; activism and, 154–55, 159–62, 168, 176, 180, 194–96, 201, 204, 251, 259, 295n56; and Africa, 158, 286n23, 299n56; and America, 14, 175, 181–82, 215–17, 248, 258; art of, 162–63, 165, 175, 179–81; commodity culture of, 12, 168–76; cultural memory of, 9, 175–83, 220, 255–59; cure for, 14, 161–62, 165, 176; divisions over, 156–59, 165; drug use and, 150, 157; education, 164–65, 167, 171, 180, 218; family and, 208–10, 293n42; gender politics of, 156–57, 202, 204–6; and generations, 15, 192, 248; healing in, 16; hemophilia and, 145, 285n11; identity politics and, 146, 160–61, 185; as kitsch, 168–70, 176, 257; naming in, 271n31; origins of, 158, 286n23; racial politics of, 157–59, 287n24; and religious right, 15, 181; representation in popular culture, 177–79; romanticization of, 163–68; as postmodern, 16–17; stigma of, 285n11; as syndrome, 124, 143, 247, 256; videotapes of, 180–81, 289n49; and Vietnam War, 14–16, 257–59; volunteerism and, 156–57, 163, 166, 186. *See also*

AIDS, people with; AIDS Memorial Quilt; HIV
AIDS, International Conference on, 160
AIDS, people with (PWAs), 142, 148–55, 161, 178, 226; photographs of, 242, 289n46; romanticization of, 16, 163–71, 256, 288nn36,39; stigma of, 159–61, 164, 186–87, 197–98, 252–53; as survivors, 5, 12, 161, 255–56. *See also* Patient Zero
AIDS Memorial Quilt, 3, 6, 10, 147, 164, 170, 176, 220, 250, 257; as American, 13, 191–93, 215–17; archive of, 217–18; bodies in, 192, 197; conversations in, 187–91, 196–97; as cultural memory, 145, 183, 185, 215, 218–19; displays of, 199–200; as educational tool, 195; families and, 192, 204, 210; as folk art, 191–93; gender politics of, 202–6; images in, 11, 61, 20, 198; individuals interacting with, 10, 196–200; international aspects of, 183, 197, 290n1; location of, 10, 215, 290nn2,11; naming in, 160, 186–90; number of visitors to, 183; maintenance of, 218; makers of, 183; marketing of, 211–13; as outreach tool, 208–11, 218, 294n44; as political tool, 201, 292n. 24, 194, 196, 212–14; size, 183, 205, 290n2; vandalization of, 212; as war memorial, 194–96, 218; in Washington, D.C., 13, 14, 175, 181, 184 fig. 18, 186, 195–96, 200–201 fig. 20, 205, 215–16. *See also* Names Project
AIDS virus. *See* HIV.
Alexander, Elizabeth, 267n30
Alien, 247
Allen, Henry, 96
Alpert, Jon, 283n16
American Family Association, 181

351

Compositor: Maple-Vail Book Mfg. Group, Inc.
Text: 11/13.5 Caledonia
Display: Caledonia
Printer and Binder: Maple-Vail Book Mfg. Group, Inc